Threads

DONNA NEWLANDS

Copyright © 2020 Donna Newlands

ISBN: 978-1-925952-83-4
Published by Vivid Publishing
A division of Fontaine Publishing Group
P.O. Box 948, Fremantle
Western Australia 6959
www.vividpublishing.com.au

 A catalogue record for this book is available from the National Library of Australia

All rights reserved. No part of this publication may be reproduced, stored in a retrieval system or transmitted in any form or by any means, electronic, mechanical, photocopying, recording or otherwise, without the prior written permission of the copyright holder.

For my Mum & Dad, my fallen heroes, and my good friend Judy who lost her fight with Cancer in 2019. My world is a little less shiny without your walking here.

ACKNOWLEGEMENTS

Thank you to my daughter, Jacqueline Newlands and my niece, Rachelle Hooke, for the first read-through and feedback.

A posthumous thank you to Judy Brasier, who passed away before she could finish her read-through.

Thank you to The Expert Editor team for the edit.

Thank you to Fontaine Publishing Group for getting my book prepped, printed and out there and everything in between.

Finally, thank you to my family, my living heroes, for the love and support you continuously show me. My world is a better place because you walk here.

1

Animal Husbandry

Phoebe

My eyes water, my nose streams, and my throat is scratchy and swollen, making swallowing nigh on impossible; I don't have time to succumb to a flu virus. My skin prickles and goose bumps swarm all over; I'm feverish…I feel like death warmed up. An annoying tickle makes me sneeze mere seconds before I can get the tissue to cover my mouth, "Achoooooweee!"

James Stevenson, my manager and close friend, looks up from whatever he is reading, and his mouth pulls into a stupid grin. He thinks my sneezes are quirky and cute. He stands and looks pointedly at me then he walks up to my desk.

"You look absolutely terrible, Phoebe! Go home and take a fist full of cold and flu tablets, then go to bed."

The fact that I look as horrendous on the outside as I feel on the inside adds insult to injury and my irritability kicks up a notch. "I can't. I'm allergic to codeine. Look Jay, I've only got to get through another three hours, I'm just going to stick it out." The last bit sounds whiny, but I feel too ill to care.

He's not happy with my answer. I'm not sure if it's my tone or the words but he is having none of it and his response brooks no argument.

"The hell you are. I don't want your flu and I can assure you nobody else in the office wants it either. Apart from that, you look really,

really ill. Seriously, go home and go to bed, and don't bother coming in tomorrow. Just stay home until you're feeling better."

I can't keep the edge from my voice as I spit back at him, "Oh that's nice, that is! Here I am thinking you are worried about *my* state of health but it's actually *your* health you're concerned about! Fine! I'll go home."

"Good girl; take care of yourself."

His reply is a little patronising, but I let it slide. Resigning myself to the inevitable, I briskly clear my desk and turn off the PC; I no longer give a crap about anything except laying my head on a pillow and sinking into oblivion. My nose drips incessantly, and I want to stuff a tissue up each nostril to stem the flow. I fetch my bag and coat and make my way out of the building and into the car park. I don't even say goodbye to anyone as I walk out, the effort is more than I can muster.

Outside, I see that a watery sun has made a wan attempt to shed light but even as underwhelming as that is, the sunlight still makes my eyeballs throb and ache in their sockets. My head pounds and my swollen throat is getting more painful by the minute; I'm longing for my bed. At least I can manage a few hours of sleep before the kids return from school…and maybe John can cook dinner tonight for a change. I turn the key in the ignition and as the car splutters to life, an explosive sneeze tears from me without warning, spraying fine mist everywhere, followed directly by an expletive. I hiss a breath through my teeth and wait for the searing pain in my throat to ease.

The traffic is light and by some miracle, I manage to make it all the way without encountering any red lights. I can't be bothered backing the car into the garage, so I park at the kerb out front, lock it and make my way to the house. I see that the security door is unlocked, and this confounds me as I'm sure I locked it before I left for work this morning.

It is only early April; how can I be getting the flu in April? Where is the mild autumn we were promised? The Bureau of Meteorology is full of guesstimating idiots; I could do a better job of predicting our weather using an Ouija board and a shot glass full of vodka. Add to that, Mother Nature is a bipolar bitch and she is off her medication.

I slide my key into the front door and as it swings inwards in a wide arc, I am immediately conscious of noises inside the house. All the blood drains from my face and floods my extremities. Trying to control my breathing, my pulse races and the roar of my own blood thrums in my ears. All senses are on high alert as I stand on the threshold, debating the fight or flight response warring within me; the thought of disturbing a burglar makes me want to run for the hills… if I could just assemble my thoughts and gather the energy. Within seconds, I establish that the sounds are coming from my bedroom and my breath catches in my swollen throat. There is more than one voice and I wonder about the group of violent thieves currently in the news that are terrorising our neighbourhoods in packs, breaking into houses and stealing the occupant's belongings in broad daylight whilst they are out. The noises grow louder and finally I tune into the sounds.

Oh, dear God! They are sounds of unrestrained lust. Son of a bitch! White hot anger replaces the fear that had me teetering on the doorstep and when I detect John's voice – the familiarity of it laced with arousal - my heart thuds harder, rocking me in place and sending adrenaline coursing through me. Damn it! My husband is having sex in *our* bed! How fucking *dare*, he! What an arsehole. An indignant rage rips through me like lightning and propels me into action and I storm to the bedroom. With the adrenaline hit fuelling my anger I shove the door wide open. Fuming, my face is a mask of rage; the earlier physical and mental response to illness is lost in the ire. Then the rage transforms into open mouthed shock and horror as I see John in a compromising position with another man. What the hell? My brain cannot process what my eyes are seeing, and I stand there, stupefied for a moment, unsure if I'm interpreting the scene correctly. Finally, my mouth stops opening and closing like a fish drowning in oxygen and I find my voice. I manage to stutter his name and it sounds anguished to my ears.

"J-john?"

John and his 'friend' (a loose description for the bear-like beast taking part in the union on my bed) both stop gyrating suddenly and look at me in alarm, frozen in their outlandish coupling from which I cannot avert my eyes. All three of us are staring at each other in shocked silence. I watch in disgust the deflation of the other man's appendage, which John is holding in his hand as he embraces him from behind. I'm horrified into speechlessness, so I turn and run from the room. I just keep running out of the door, grabbing my keys and handbag as I flee the house and the stranger I've been married to for almost twenty-one years. I dive into the car and shakily put the key in the ignition. My fingers fumble in my haste and it feels like minutes have ticked by as my panic consumes me. Finally, I start the car and speed away before John can disentangle himself and follow me.

I drive on autopilot, not really conscious of where I'm heading. My phone lights up on the seat beside me and I reach over and 'decline' John's call. It takes ten minutes of mindless driving before the images of John with that other man flash through my mind and I'm forced to pull over to the side of the road, exit hurriedly and throw up what little I have in my stomach. I'm hunched over like a dog taking a shit on the nature strip, retching into the gutter. Tears are streaming down my face, which feels hot and numb. My arms and legs begin to shake, and I look for all intents and purposes to be having a fit beside my car. It dawns on me that this is the shock kicking in.

Questions start flooding my mind. What should I do? Where should I go? I don't know how to handle this... what about the kids? My brain derails and I find myself asking why he couldn't have been in bed with another woman? Wait, what am I thinking? I could *not* handle infidelity with a woman either, I would be just as hurt and confused. Except it was a man... why is John screwing a man? I don't know how to feel. I don't know what to make of it. Anger ignites inside me again and I wonder why he couldn't just keep his fucking dick in his pants? If he's going through a mid-life crisis, why couldn't he just buy a Porsche like everyone else?

Mechanically, I stand up and swipe at a disgusting tendril of drool clinging to my mouth, then climb back into the car, belt up and continue to drive away from the mess that is behind me. My phone lights up again as John continuously calls even after I hang up on him repeatedly. I presume he is in damage control and is trying to reach me to explain, as if what I saw could be explained away. I turn my phone off completely and focus on getting far away. I don't want to talk to him and I don't want to hear him explain this shit to me. I need time to process it all. I find myself in Chelsea's driveway.

Chelsea, my closest friend, is warm and caring and she will know what to do. At the very least she will sit with me and let me pour it all out. As expected, she is home; she is almost always home at this time of day. Chelsea has Tourette's syndrome and works five nights a week stocking shelves at a supermarket; a far cry from the marine biology career that her education certifies she is qualified for. She has finally found a job she can perform, even with her condition, as she can feel the tic series coming and prepare for it.

I rap my knuckles firmly on the hard wooden door and it swings open before I even manage the third knock. Chelsea beams at me; she is pleasantly surprised to see me in the middle of the day and has no idea that all my stars have been stolen.

"Hello beautiful. To what do I owe this divine pleasure?"

Chelsea takes a look at my face and immediately, her demeanour changes from joy to concern. "What's up, hon? Pheebs, you okay?"

I sob and dive into her arms like a lost child. Chelsea hugs me hard while I try to gain a little composure. Then I hear her grunt and feel her tics start up and I know she is powerless to hold them off for long, so I pull away and duck to avoid a couple of swift punches to the back and the possible dislodgement of my spleen. Even in the midst of my own crisis I feel sorry for her. I stand back and wait. Her tics start with the usual low ape-like grunts deep in her chest, followed with two quick beatings with her fist to her chest, another ape-like grunt, her eyes twitch and her leg shoots out and across her body. This is all wrapped up with a "whoooooossshhh", which is repeated two to three times, depending on her stress levels.

I wait it out with a patience I don't feel. When she's done, I ask if I can come in for a cup of coffee and a chat. Chelsea is already making her way to the kitchen to put the kettle on. I wait until she places the steaming mug of instant coffee in front of me before I speak, trying to articulate my thoughts into words. It pours out of me, but Chelsea has no idea how big my revelation is and keeps interrupting. I stifle my annoyance.

"I came home early today. James sent me home sick with this… head cold or flu or whatever it is that I have."

"Do you want something to take for it? I've got paracetamol or ibuprofen if that helps".

I am the epitome of patience as I pause and look at her, then continue "I will in a minute, I just want to wait a bit."

Chelsea finally gets the hint, "Sure, sorry hon, continue."

"Well, I opened the front door and I could hear noises inside. I absolutely freaked out, thinking someone had broken in or something. Anyway, it wasn't long before it became apparent that the noises were… um…well…sex noises. So, thinking John was having sex with another woman in our bed, I went bursting through the door, ready to cave both of their heads in with my umbrella."

Chelsea forgets herself and says, "Jesus, who was it?"

I continue to be patient, training for sainthood "Oh it was John all right, but he was…um…" I let the sentence die as Chelsea's tics start up again. I quietly sip my coffee and wait. After the last spontaneous spasm ends, like we haven't just waited through the tic series with only the ticking of the clock on the wall competing for my attention, Chelsea gasps, "Oh God, did you spring him masturbating?"

I'm perplexed. Really, Chelsea? Like that's what has me over here freaking out? "No, he was having sex with another man"

Chelsea sits up like a meerkat in her seat; her eyes large and incredulous, "He was *what*? Holy shit! Are you *serious*? Oh honey, what did you do? How did you react? Did he see that you saw?"

I stare at her because she is babbling. After a pause, she tries to articulate her babble, "Sorry, I'm a little shocked."

"That makes two of us! Even though I flung the door open, they didn't hear me because they were so engrossed in what they were doing. I was so shocked at first that I just stared at them while they were jerking around on the bed, then I said his name and that's when they both looked up and saw me"

Chelsea's hands fly to her mouth in horror. "What did John say?"

"He didn't say anything, or if he did, I didn't hear it. I just ran the hell out of there. I don't know what to do. I don't know what to think! He tried to call me, but I declined his call and then turned my phone off. I just can't face him. I really don't know what to do."

Chelsea's morbid curiosity makes her seem cold, but I know she is shocked, and her brain is just popping out stupid questions, "So, what were they doing? Was it like, you know, in the arse or what?"

I want to laugh but think I might not be able to stop, and I don't want to sound like I've become completely unhinged so I get offended instead and answer her in a bitchy tone. "How the hell should I know? It's not like I ran around to the side of the bed to checkout their screwing style. I was stunned…stupefied."

Chelsea is embarrassed and mumbles, "Sorry, I can't believe I just asked that"

I let out my breath. I feel ill and exhausted, "It's all right, Chels, we're both a bit shocked. I really don't know. I don't *want* to know. What I *do* know is that the bloke he was screwing was John's bitch, if you get my drift"

"Oh my God, how can you go home now? Jesus Pheebs…"

I shake my head at her. This thought is simultaneously running through my own head, "I know! What about Seth and Mercedes? I don't know if he's just discovered he's gay, if he's bisexual, if he has always been this way or if he's experimenting…maybe it's me not ticking all the boxes? I just don't know. There are so many questions, but I don't know where to start and I'm not sure I want to hear the answers to them all".

Chelsea's phone rings on the kitchen wall, startling us both. She gets up and looks at the caller ID on the screen and gasps, "Shit, its John. Do I say you're not here?"

The blood drains from my face; I'm not ready to talk to him so I hiss at her, "I'm *definitely* not here if he asks. You don't know anything. Play dumb"

Chelsea's face morphs into a bored expression, like she's going for an Oscar. She picks up the phone and calmly starts speaking. "Hi John. Ah, no she's not. It's the middle of the day; she'd be at work, wouldn't she?"

Chelsea smiles and nods at me, proud of her skilled response. The smile slides from her face and a scowl replaces it. I wonder what John has said. I don't have to wait long.

"Well if you know she's here, why are you ringing and asking stupid questions? Why are you driving past my house like a bloody creep? Go home…"

I whip my head around to peer out of the living room windows. I can't see him; he must be parked a little way up the street. What the hell is he doing? I want him to leave me alone.

Chelsea gives a huge sigh, like she's exhausted, then looks over at me and rolls her eyes. She raises one hand and makes puppet-talking gestures with her hand at the phone. In the silence of her apartment, I can hear his voice all tinny coming out of the receiver. John pleads with Chelsea until her tics start up again.

She grunts like an ape then panic-bellows into the phone, "John, oh bloody fucking hell, wait a minute please…" and the phone clatters onto the kitchen bench.

There is silence between the phones while Chelsea grunts, punches, kicks and whooshes. When the sequence ends, she picks up the phone and continues with the conversation like there was no break.

She looks fed-up and pulls the phone away from her face and barks into the mouth piece, "No, she doesn't want to speak to you right now, John. Can you just give her some time to digest everything? She'll come home when she's ready."

She puts the phone back to her ear then she looks up and gives me a patient smile. I'm so indebted to her, fielding this shit for me. Exasperated, she tries to reason with John, "Nah, no John, listen to me please. I'm not letting you in. You'll get your chance to explain everything later. Right now, she just needs a little time. Can you please handle the kids and dinner tonight?"

I think John interrupts her with a stupid question because she loses her temper, "Well I don't bloody know… how should I know that? Make something up. Tell 'em you and Pheebs had a fight and she's driven off in a huff. You'll think of something. Right now, I have to go and console her… yes John, she's all right… I'm hanging up the phone now…bye, yes, BYE!"

Chelsea uses all the force she can to slam her finger on the disconnect button but there is no satisfaction if you don't slam it into a cradle. She walks over to the wall and puts the phone back into the charging socket, then she returns and grabs both of my hands in hers, rubbing her thumbs over my knuckles in a calming gesture, and it works. I don't have a poker face and she can probably see my distress. The vertical lines between my brows disappear.

"He is absolutely freaking out. He drove past and saw your car so when I tried to tell him you weren't here, he jumped down my throat. Either way, I think you should just stay here tonight and handle it all tomorrow.

I withdraw my hands and run them through my hair, squeezing it hard. My scalp is sensitive, and it hurts. The anger leaves me, and I sag in the chair. I'm confused, and my head cold is making me feel even worse. I look down at the table, wondering what the hell I'm going to do. Hot tears run down to the tip of my red glowing nose and drop onto the table in a puddle, and I don't even attempt to wipe them up. Chelsea gets up, I assume to search for a tissue but obviously finding none, she settles for some toilet paper and hands me a length of squares. I must look so wretched when I look up at her to take it because she utters "Oh, darling" and comes over to stroke my back, "Come here, baby, let me hug you."

She takes me into her arms and hugs me while I hiccup and snivel and saturate her shoulder with tears and mucus because I'm gross and ill and miserable and I don't even care because Chelsea doesn't care. We stay like this for what feels like an eternity because I have lost my shit; the cage door is wide open now and I can't rein it in.

2

From A Whisper To A Scream

Phoebe
It is half way through the second day before I finally have the fortitude to make the journey home to face the music. I'm alternately numb and anxious on the journey and pull up at the kerb outside the house. I cut the motor and the ticking of the cooling engine is loud in the silence of the car as I try to control my breathing. I'm nervous and unsure of what awaits me in the house. I think I'm ready to get out of the car, but my heart starts pounding and a cold sweat prickles my skin. I don't want to go inside, I don't want to walk into that room and confront him. I don't want to talk about it, I don't want to hear him explain and I don't want to feel anything. I berate myself for being childish and see movement out of the corner of my eye. I look to the porch and see John standing there, looking uncertain and nervous. He looks wretched. The dark part of me whispers '*good*', and I feel momentarily confident.

Once inside, John sits perched on the edge of his armchair, looking glum. I know he is riddled with guilt and I don't want to prolong this silence, so I just wade in and get straight to the point.

"John, are you gay?"

His eyebrows dart north, and he looks horrified, "Jesus, don't beat around the bush!"

I chuckle but it's a cruel, sarcastic laugh. I am Cruella De Vil and

I want a puppy coat. "Pardon the pun? C'mon John, really? What did you expect my first question to be?"

John physically slumps and looks defeated. There are dark circles under his eyes and he looks unkempt.

"Actually, I thought you would be ranting and yelling. Your calm demeanour is unnerving."

A white-hot heat rushes through me and I'm angry. I don't want to dance around the topic anymore, "Look at my eyes. Look at me! They're red and swollen…I look ridiculous! I've been crying for hours. I just want some answers for now so answer the fucking question, John!"

He looks tortured. "Yes, I think I am."

I have no patience and I am letting none of his regret wash over me. I'm hurt and confused and angry and I want straight answers. "You think? Were you experimenting yesterday or has this been going on for a while?"

"I've been having sex with men for a few years now. I've been coming to terms with--"

"A few years? A few fucking *years*?" My voice is so high I'm expecting glass to shatter. "Are you shitting me right now? We had sex just the night before I found you romping around with a man in a bear suit. Why are you screwing me when you prefer men? You seem genuinely interested in sex with me when we're in the moment so *why are you screwing men*? What the hell are you doing, John?"

John hiccups and his voice changes as he is openly cries "I'm so sorry Phoebe, I really am. I never meant to hurt you and I didn't want you to find out this way."

I want to interrupt and ask how he intended to tell me his secret, but the door has been opened and his words are cascading like magma from an active volcano …and I need to hear it.

"I guess I've known something was different for a very long time. At first, I thought I might be bisexual but then I realised that I was noticing only men and not women. I didn't act on it, I hoped it would just go away and I wished really hard to be normal. Then, I started to wonder how I could love you if I was attracted to men… and I wondered if perhaps it was in my head, you know? I thought I'd just try it once with a guy. It felt really natural but, you know, it's just not who I'm supposed to be. I'm supposed to be John O'Brien, husband and father and heterosexual, but I'm not, I'm something else. I don't want to be gay, I want to be the husband you married, and I want to go back to the way we were but its all wrong. I can't pretend any more, not even for you…but I feel so disgusting."

My resolve is waning, but I don't want excuses from him, I want answers. "Oh, come on, John. We live in a society now where it's mostly accepted except for a minority of arseholes who either don't understand it or have been taught to hate it."

John stands abruptly and stabs the air with a long and rigid finger, "I grew up in a household where homosexuals were considered filthy vermin; you know that! I listened to my father rant about the writings in the Bible and how homosexuals are an abomination, how they should all be put on an island and then blown to kingdom come. How could I be this disgusting thing without thinking there was something very wrong with me? I did what was expected of me and the guilt I felt when I had these desires ate at me like acid."

I'm sorry for John and his awful childhood but I'm miserable and incredibly sorry for myself too and all that I have swiftly lost. My voice is calm and sounds cold and menacing to my own ears. "So, everything we ever had was a lie?"

John looks spent as he stares down at his lap and whispers, "No, not everything. I do love you."

It is my turn to shout and I stand up so quickly that the chair I'm sitting on flies backwards, toppling onto its back. "What the hell? You love me, but you're not attracted to me sexually and you're not *in* love with me, right? Have I got that right?"

"Please try to understand, Phoebe, I never meant to hurt you…"

I cannot be reached, I am angry, and it has all come to the fore, and I don't *want* to stop myself, "No, but you're bringing strange men home and screwing them in *our* bed. *Our* bed, John! Are you wearing protection always? Have you *ever* had unsafe sex with a man then had sex with me days later?"

I can barely hear John's answer as he speaks without looking at me. "No, I've always worn a condom. I've only actively been having sex with men in the last few years and there's only been a couple of times when the condom broke or was somehow compromised, but I got tested and each time it was all right."

I take a calming breath, trying to remove the anger from my voice. As cathartic as the screaming is, it is making my head throb and I remember belatedly that I still have some kind of lurgy and need to take something to ease the symptoms. "John, did you know that one of the questions on the legal document I sign every time I give blood asks if I have recently had sex with a man who may have had unsafe sex with another man? I wonder how many times I have ticked 'no' when I should have ticked 'yes'. Jesus, John! We've been married for almost twenty-one years. I thought we were happy. Then to walk in and find you are not only having an affair; that's one giant bombshell right there, but having an affair with another man? That's two bombshells… and it's almost too much to bear…"

"It wasn't an affair, Phoebe, it was just sex."

"Oh, and that makes it okay? How am I supposed to just carry on with this knowledge? We can't stay married, John, and I don't want to have sex with you anymore!"

John starts wringing his hand "Phoebe, please don't walk out, let's just take this one step at a time, okay? We will go and see a marriage counsellor and get some advice about what we should do"

I'm not feeling merciful. I hiss at him, "Isn't it a little bit late for that? You're gay, you've just told me as much. Do you think the counsellor is going to try to convince you otherwise?"

John pleads "We have two kids, Phoebe. I don't know what to do.

I've never brought a man to our house before, this was the first time. I can't believe you walked in. Why did you walk in? Why did you come home early?"

"Because I'm unwell, John. I have a flu virus and James sent me home. I guess the universe wanted me to find out."

I look at my husband and he looks like a small child explaining himself before the school principal. To my disgust, I feel sorry for him. I still love him, I can't just flick the switch and turn that off, so I sigh heavily, feeling worn out and exhausted. "Okay, we'll see a counsellor and get some advice. I don't know what we should do next either, so I'll take anything at this point. I don't know how we're going to broach this with the kids."

John looks relieved, "I don't know either. I'll take the couch for now and if they ask, we'll just say we've had a bit of an argument."

* * * * *

At 8am I wake and phone James at the office. I complain that I'm still ill. He is considerate and advises me to rest up. Feeling utterly miserable, I lie back down and attempt to sleep. My head cold has shifted to a different stage and my nose has become congested with thick mucus, making breathing difficult. My scratchy throat has morphed into a barking cough, so I sound like a seal. The paracetamol is controlling the headache, but nothing more. I need to drink more water to prevent dehydration but getting out of bed and walking to the kitchen is a task too great, so I close my eyes and hope for sleep. Every time I close my eyes I think about John and our predicament and no matter how hard I try to push it from my mind, it is ever present. I have a dull ache in the pit of my stomach to remind me that hell is indeed a place on earth.

* * * * *

Twenty-four hours later we are at our first counselling session. It is three days following the 'incident'. The Counsellor is a confident and striking young woman with a name better suited to someone in their fifties. Roberta starts the session and she is looking at John. The session is all about John. John explains what was happening in that room when I burst in and he talks about how he felt. It is about him coming to terms with his sexuality, how *he* should proceed. It's as though I'm watching a soap opera about somebody else's life…it's completely surreal. With five minutes to go, Roberta turns to me and asks, "Now Phoebe, how do you feel about what John has just shared?"

I give Roberta a glacial stare and answer, "Numb."

The session is wrapped up on time and I feel nothing. I have just wasted an hour of my life that I will never get back.

During the following two sessions, I feel nothing either; I'm still numb. Roberta continues to try to entice me to speak and share but I feel like she's not really interested in me, like she's just ticking a box and doing her job. I'm starting to dislike her. She is totally focused on John, on his journey and his struggle. I listen to John prattle on about his upbringing, about how he has suppressed his true feelings over the years. I wonder at which point they will remember there are two people in this marriage.

I will not concede that these feelings of omission are all just part of my grieving process for my marriage and so I continue to feel excluded and omitted, even though that is not the reality inside this room. I'm deliberately shutting them out. It is at the end of our third session that I feel a little pinch of anger. I am indignant and hostile. How dare he drag me along to this, the reading of John's life. What about me? All my future hopes and dreams have vanished in an instant. Everything I have worked towards in my life and imagined in my future has to change now. I feel intense bitterness towards him; maybe I'm angry enough to feel hatred at this moment.

Mercedes

Mum is different. She's angry and surly and we haven't done anything wrong. Seth has noticed it too. Last night we had a talk about it in my room because we don't know what the shit has happened. Dad is a little weird too, like he's walking on egg shells around her. He is over-compensating for something and it is making my mind go crazy with what the hell it can be. They've had a fight because when I woke up this morning, Dad was asleep on the couch. I have never seen them have a huge fight before, and if they have ever had a disagreement, it has been sorted out quickly. This has been going on for days. I am sitting on the top step with my backside on the landing when Seth comes out of his room and sits down beside me.

"Hey," he says, like nothing is going on. He is always the peace-keeper and it's not his fault, so I play nice.

"Hey,"

He scoots over and sits closer. He is too close and is not being respectful of my personal space. He's inside my bubble and usually I would tell him to get the hell out of it, but he is just as confused by the going-on in our house as I am. We continue to look down the stairs at the closed front door. Seth whispers, "Are they here, or out?"

I answer loudly, "They're out. They've gone to another counselling session. I heard Mum say all bitchy earlier, 'Oh, we'd better not be late for Roberta, John' when Dad was trying to hurry her up."

Seth looks confused, "Why are they suddenly getting counselling? Since when have they needed counselling?"

I glare at him and spit the words, "How the hell would I know?" with a lot more acidity than I intended. I'm feeling shitty and short tempered. I mentally count the days and realise that my period is due. PMS makes me as bitchy as hell. I don't apologise for biting his head off, it's not my fault that I am female, but I alter my attitude a little and shrug my shoulders and I see in Seth's face that he knows I didn't mean it.

Seth continues to whisper, like he is ashamed to be talking about our parents this way, "I wonder what's happened. I think Dad has done something bad because Mum is really pissed at him. He's bouncing around her like a puppy when she's here but when she's not, he's happy. Yesterday I heard him whistling. I don't get it."

I don't reply because I think Seth was just speaking his thoughts out loud and I have nothing to add. I've noticed Dad's odd behaviour too and it's kind of freaking me out. We continue to sit there in silence until we see two silhouettes through the stained glass at the top of the door, heralding the return of Mum and Dad. We scramble up and into our respective rooms like we've been caught doing something naughty. I have an insane urge to giggle and think that my parents are making me nuts.

I hear Mum's footsteps and she's walking really heavily. She usually tiptoes in the house when she's wearing her heels so she doesn't mark the wooden floors. Today, she doesn't give a shit. I decide to go down stairs to make myself a cup of herbal tea to stave off the looming cramps. I'm all winning smiles and radiating joy as I make my way through the kitchen to the breakfast nook. I flick the switch on the kettle and grab myself a tea cup. "Hi Mum, would you like a cup of tea?"

She turns and glares at me like I asked her something awful. I'm taken aback as she barks, "No!" in my face. My temper spikes and I want to ask her what's up her arse but I remember that I'm premenstrual and she's got something going on, so I say, "Fine."

Then I ask Dad if he'd like one and he bounds over to me like the excited puppy Seth mentioned earlier, gushing "I'd love one, how thoughtful to ask." Involuntarily, my eyebrows knit together, and I feel like I'm Alice and I've just fallen down the rabbit hole. He wraps his arms around me and ushers me away from the tyrannical Queen of Hearts before she can bellow "Off with her head!"

Seth enters the kitchen and makes a beeline for Mum. He doesn't see me flapping my arms wildly and running my finger across my throat to alert him of the crazy bitch standing at the island bench. He leans towards her and gently asks if she can fill in a form for a school trip to the city, which is due in tomorrow. She is as bitchy as hell and yells, "Why are you just giving it to me now if it's due tomorrow?" Her volume dial is turned up to megaphone and I swear all our neighbours are privy to her ranting. I'm a little shocked, frightened even, by her tone.

Seth is shocked to the core and starts stuttering that he misplaced the first one and he went to the office to get a second one today. He is apologising profusely, and I feel a little satisfaction that she's using the same angry tone for him that she wielded on me. Puppy dog Dad briskly walks behind the seething bitch and leads Seth away, placating that he'll sign the form. Seth is still staring at our mother like she's an alien and a long protrusion is going to shoot out of her mouth at any moment and spit vitriolic acid all over him. He looks injured as Dad leads him to the coffee table. Mum is unapologetic. It must be our fault.

I quietly make my tea and get the hell out of the kitchen before she lashes out at me again but I'm not quick enough. As I try to disappear around the corner she yells, "I hope you're not taking that to your room!" I can't think of a response before she roars "No eating or drinking in your room, Mercedes! How many times do we have to have this conversation? You are not exempt from the rules, *no eating or drinking in your room!*"

My mouth pinches and I try to keep myself nice as I mumble, "Mum, I'm nearly sixteen years old." She is having none of it as she gets all up in my business, "You're fifteen, Mercedes and rules are rules."

I want to scream, "What the fuck is up your arse?" at her but I know she will completely blow a valve and lose her shit, so I change tack and try to ask her as nicely as I know how, "Um, is everything okay, Mum?" I sound like a timid kitten; this is not me at all.

Instead of taking a good hard look at herself and pulling her head back out of her arse where it's been for the past week, she rounds on me and yells at me like I'm the root of all evil. "What do you care? You're just bouncing around in your happy little bubble, completely oblivious to anything except what colour lip-gloss you'll wear tomorrow and if that blind pimple will *ever* surface to mar your *'mint'* complexion."

I'm taken aback by her venom and annoyingly, I feel teary. I am not giving her the satisfaction of seeing that she is making me cry so I loudly bang my cup down on the kitchen bench and storm to my room with as much purpose as I can.

I sit on the end of my bed trying to stop the tears, waiting for her to knock on my door and apologise for being a psycho bitch, but she doesn't come. I'm torn between relief that I don't have to forgive her shitty behaviour, and disappointment that she doesn't give a single gram of shit. I hear a gentle rap on the door and it's Seth's head that pops around the corner to check on me. He can see my face and my quivering bottom lip, so he comes into my room without being invited and sits beside me on the bed. I lose the battle and sob like a four-year-old into his top. He rubs my back gently and makes me feel like someone gives a shit.

After I get myself back together, I reach over to the bedside table and take a couple of tissues to mop up the mess on my face. I hear Seth sniff loudly beside my ear and hand him one too without making eye contact. He's trying to keep himself together too, but I know she's really upset him. My hand brushes over my chin and I feel the blind pimple she was referring to and I want to run down the stairs and hit her over the head with something really hard. Stupid bitch!

Phoebe

I'm disgusted by my behaviour. I hate myself but I'm powerless to control my anger. I see that I'm alienating my kids but I'm so deep into this quagmire of shit that I'm exhausted from the daily struggle.

I feel bruised all over by the wrecking ball that John has swung into our marriage but there are no marks on my body. My life has been driven into a ditch and I'm impotently standing on the sidelines watching it all unfold.

We're sitting in a session with Roberta and I'm looking down at my fingers, idly picking at the cuticle and waiting for the session to end. John and Roberta are having an in-depth conversation about John's father, who is a homophobic arsehole. I don't want to sit through this anymore. I've had enough, and I just want to call it quits and go someplace where I can be alone with my thoughts. Roberta pauses mid-sentence and I look up to see that she is looking at me. She has finally noticed me and encourages me to join in the discussion. "How are you feeling today, Phoebe?"

I wish I could turn off this anger, but I can't because I feel hard done by, so I rage at her, "Oh, it's my turn, is it? Do you really want to start with me? I'm not sure I'll be able to stop once I get started. Just saying…"

John shifts his position and looks more than a little worried about what is about to come out of my mouth. I don't give a shit. Roberta is trying to mask her surprise with a well-rehearsed indifference and she nods her ascent. Big mistake, Roberta.

"Well, I'm a little pissed, actually. I come home from work as sick as a dog one day only to find my husband of twenty-odd years' choc-a-block up some guy's hairy arse, grunting like a rutting fucking animal! How do you *think* I feel? I feel shocked and horrified and I feel *ripped off!*"

John winces and Roberta stares at me wide-eyed. But I'm still worked up and it's too late now because the genie is out of the bottle and they should prepare for a little stinging. I glare at John. "That was really confronting, John. I feel like the last twenty years of my life have been a big, fat goddamn *lie!* The moment that door opened, and I saw…whatever it was that I saw, my entire future was just wiped out. My dreams of holding your hand through it all; all of it gone in the seconds it took for me to see what really is. I feel deceived and through no fault of my own, I'm standing in the middle of *your* shitty fucking mess, and I can't step out of it! My feet are glued in the sludge and I'm getting sucked under and you're just standing there, watching me drown! It's not fair and I'm so *bloody* angry."

I am jabbing at the air between us with my index finger to emphasise my point. "I know it's irrational, but I feel like *you* did this to *me*! You lied by omission. You allowed me to think I was beautiful and desirable, you made me think I was *the one* when the whole time I was just a poor second; I was *always* going to be a poor second no matter how hard I tried because I was born a female. I *hate* you for doing this to me!" I feel my emotion burn my eyes as a solitary fat tear breaks free and rolls down my cheek.

Panting from the exertion of my outburst, I shake my head at the both of them and get up to leave. At the door, I turn back and say to Roberta, "I'm sorry for being so crass, for not filtering my raw emotion. I feel so incredibly cheated. I'm not going to come to any more sessions. I'm done". Then I shift my focus to John, "I'm just… done".

I walk out of the climate-controlled room with the comfortable couch and into the Melbourne air. The rain spits tiny droplets onto my face to join the tears streaming down my cheeks. I walk to the tram stop and wait in the shelter, climbing on the first tram that rattles by to take me home. I am tired and drained.

My kids make no attempt to engage me in conversation when they return from school and I don't blame them. I wouldn't want to talk to me at the moment either. I run myself a deep, hot bath, pour myself a giant glass of chardonnay and settle in for a soak and a sob. I have opened the floodgates and I continue to cry for a solid hour. I hear muted movement above me and imagine that Seth and Mercedes are sitting on the top steps, listening to my sorrow as it echoes behind the closed door of the ensuite. They've never really seen me cry, except when my father passed away, so I figure this is really confronting for them. I'm too caught up in my own misery to spare any comfort for them. Exhaustion tugs at me and I wish I could hide away somewhere, alone, and lick my wounds in peace. I don't want to be a mother or a wife or a friend or an employee, I want to feel nothing for a while.

3
Reality Bites

John
I have waited until after eleven to come home because I'm a coward and I don't want a confrontation with Phoebe. I realise that I've actually thrown the kids under a bus by leaving them alone with her and wonder what they've eaten for dinner. I'm still full from my counter meal at the pub and feel a little selfish and guilty. I should have come home and at least cooked the kids some dinner.

I could've gotten wasted but since I had to drive home, I kept the beers to two, resolving that I'll have a shot of whisky before I go to bed. The house is dark and silent as I tiptoe down the hall and into the living room. I'm sick with regret about the whole disaster. The bluntness of Phoebe's outburst today was frightening, and the depth of her despair is palpable. After she left, Roberta and I discussed how I should proceed from this point. As much as she wants to help Phoebe, it is clear that Phoebe doesn't want her help. She suggested that I continue with the schedule of appointments, not only to discuss my progress with the establishment of my sexual orientation and my personal fallout, but also to guide me on how to help Phoebe and the kids move through the next days, weeks and months.

It is inevitable that Mercedes and Seth will have to be told, and that both Phoebe and I should talk to them together, but Roberta has advised that I just need to hold Phoebe's hand through her own war first and make sure she is ready to discuss it with them. She said today's outburst was a good thing and a huge step for Phoebe in moving forward. I was mortified by the crap that was coming out of Phoebe's mouth. I can't believe this shitstorm. Part of me is grateful that it's out now; I was so sick of holding onto this secret, but Phoebe is right, I cheated on her and although it wasn't my intention, I *did* this to her. I should have spoken to her about how I was feeling, but how do you broach that with your wife? It doesn't matter how you dress it up, it is what it is. Phoebe is never going to understand what it feels like to stand in my shoes.

I look through the picture window from the dark kitchen. The giant tree in the centre of our yard is almost devoid of leaves so I can see through it to the train station beyond. The lights at the station are shrouded in mist as fog descends. The station is abandoned, nobody is on the platform and it looks cold and lonely out there, a bit like how I feel at the moment. Why am I being villainised? It's not like I set out to hurt her. I didn't do this to her on purpose. I feel tears well in my eyes and I wish I was made of tougher stuff.

I wonder if Phoebe is still awake and I imagine her tossing and turning, unable to escape her thoughts. I make my way down the hall on the tips of my toes to our bedroom and gingerly open the door. The room is dark, and the smell of Phoebe wafts out and as the light from the hall falls over the bed, I can make out her form. She's lying on her side with her back to me and I note that her breathing isn't deep enough to convince me that she is asleep, but I will let her think she has fooled me. I will take the couch again; returning to our bed is not an option until we've sorted this out. I hope she will be ready to talk in the morning after Mercedes and Seth have left for school. We need to move forward but I have to wait for her to be ready, I owe her that much.

This morning, before meeting Roberta, I rescheduled all my appointments and deadlines for the next two days in the hope that we can speak rationally about the future, but after today's outburst, I'm not sure she's ready.

I decide against the Scotch and just go straight to the couch, the television a dark rectangle on the pale wall. I hear the brakes of a train as it pulls into the station. After a few minutes, the horn sounds and the train takes off; the rhythmic clacking of the wheels on the tracks loud in the silence of the dark house. I wonder who is on the train. Where they would be going at such a late hour. To a job to work the nightshift? To a lover's house? Home after a long day to cuddle up with a spouse?

I lie in the dark with just a throw rug and couch cushion for comfort, listening to my own breathing and waiting for sleep to come. My busy mind is distracting me, thwarting any chance of sleep, so I get up to get the Scotch I promised myself earlier. I wish I could find myself a DeLorean and go back to change the past, just a few days, so I could tell Phoebe in my own way without the horror of the way she discovered it. The number of times over the past three years when I've thought I'll just bite the bullet and confess. After I'd finally admitted to myself that I am, in fact, gay, I always found myself plastered in a bar, telling Phoebe I had caught up with a mate for a beer, instead of facing reality. And now, because I have put off the inexorable truth, my best friend is hurting, and she doesn't deserve it. Pretty soon, my kids will be hurting too.

I silently pad into the kitchen and switch on the lights of the range hood; a cooler and less stark light. It casts enough light over the kitchen for me to locate the bottle of whisky and a glass and pour myself a shot. I wash down a couple of valerian-root tablets with the whisky to help me relax enough to fall asleep. Pouring myself a second measure, I make my way back to the couch and almost throw the whole lot, glass and all, over my head as Seth appears out of the shadows.

"Fuck!" I yelp in surprise as an amber stain spreads across the front of my t-shirt.

Seth reaches out a hand and places it on my shoulder, "Sorry, Dad, just came down for a glass of water. I saw the light on and wondered if someone was up. I didn't mean to scare you."

"That's all right, mate, I just wasn't expecting you. Can't you sleep?"

Seth looks across at the couch and takes in the crumpled blanket and looks back at me. "Dad, what's going on with you and Mum? You've never avoided each other like this, like you have over the last week. Mum doesn't even seem remotely herself. She's snippy and mean and it's just completely out of character. Poor Mercy copped a cruel earful yesterday. She only asked if Mum was okay because she's been worried about her, but Mum just about bit her head off. Dad, what has happened that is so bad?"

I shake my head and mumble, "Look, it's my fault, mate. We didn't have a fight, something has happened, and your Mum is very hurt and confused."

Seth starts to ask questions, so I hold up a hand and cut him off. "I can't discuss it with you yet, mate. I just need to wait for your Mum to feel a little steadier before we talk to you and Mercy about it, but we will, I promise. I can't promise you'll take the news well either but I'm hoping it will be tomorrow, if nothing else to put me out of my misery. Please don't say anything to Mercy, let's just wait for your Mum. Go easy on her, she's had a bit of a shock and she's imploding a bit."

Seth swallows, "Okay, Dad, I'll just get that water and then I'll be on my way.

I watch Seth's back as he fills his glass from the kitchen faucet and then wanders back upstairs. After I hear his door click closed, I turn off the light and go back to the couch, sipping my Scotch in the dark.

Phoebe

My ears pick up the murmur of voices down the hall, but I don't have the inclination to care. Wrapped in my cocoon of doona and sheets, I lie hugging my pain like it's a physical thing. I doze fitfully throughout the night and wake feeling completely bereft of rest. I reach over for my phone on the bedside table and send a quick text to James:

Hi James, still feeling crap. I'll try again tomorrow. P

James responds straight away:

Hey Pheebs. What's going on? Is it just the flu? Are you okay? Anything I can help with? Jay

I sigh before replying:

Yeah, something has gone down here. I'm a bit of a mess actually. I'm not ready to talk about it but I will when it's been sorted out. When I'm ready to talk, I will, I promise. Sorry to be evasive, it's just not great here at the moment. P

Moments later another message pings in:

OK. I'm here if you need to talk. Take your time, we've got you covered. Jay

I'm relieved. I don't have to explain, and he just takes me at my word. I put the phone back on the bedside table and roll onto my back. Staring at the ceiling I feel a pang of guilt that John has spent another night on the couch. As sad as I feel, there are no more tears. It is time to face the music, so I reluctantly get out of bed. I dress in a tracksuit; I'm not going anywhere today. I wander into the kitchen and see Seth and Mercedes preparing their lunches together on the island bench. Seth mumbles a greeting, not making eye contact. Mercedes is cool and aloof. Well that is to be expected, considering how I've treated the poor girl. Forcing cheer into my voice, I return Seth's greeting and walk straight up to Mercedes and wrap my arms around her. "I'm so sorry about the other day, darling. I was awful and you most certainly didn't deserve it. I'm just going through something at the moment and I took it out on you," I look up at Seth over her shoulder "and you too. Sorry, hon."

It is a few moments before Mercedes returns my embrace. I

squeeze harder to convey my regret and cement the apology. When we pull apart, I see tears on her long, dark eyelashes. I step back to give her a moment then turn and embraced my son. I reach up to put my arms around his neck. When did my little boy become this tall man? It feels like only a couple of years ago he was just a toddler, standing on my feet as we waltzed around the kitchen together.

Finishing up, both Mercedes and Seth leave the house for school and I am left with a nervous John. Armed with a cup of hot tea, I make my way to the couch to sit beside him. To his credit, he doesn't shift. Neither of us speaks for a beat, then I start the conversation, "John, I'm sorry about yesterday. I didn't mean to blurt it all out like that. Those first words came out and it was like I'd broken the seal, everything just came tumbling out. It is how I'm feeling but what you heard was just raw emotion. I should have edited it, but my brain failed, and my emotions just ran away with it. Sorry."

I look down at the cup of tea in my hands, hoping that I look every bit as ashamed as I feel. John reaches over and takes one of my hands from the tea cup and gives it a little squeeze. "Phoebe, I can't possibly find enough words to tell you how sorry I am. I know I've hurt and disappointed you, I've changed the whole course of our future, the future of this whole family, but I can't put it back into my pocket again. We have to deal with it now that it's out."

Squeezing his hand in return, I nod, "I know. We have to tell the kids. It's going to hurt and confuse them, but they have to know."

John readily agrees, and I wonder if he's been waiting in the wings because he wants to get it over with and rip it off like a Band-Aid. He looks tormented, battling with his desire not to hurt or confuse his children, but knowing they have to be told. "How do you want to do this? Do you want to tell them you caught me with another man?"

I'm horrified, "Oh God, no! That would put an image in their heads. Let's spare them that, shall we? Why don't we start with you just telling them that you've been keeping something from us all? Tell them you're gay and have been in denial but you can no longer ignore it. Tell them I am hurt and upset, which they will expect and will explain the weirdness that has been us these last few days, and we'll just take it from there." I pause, feeling uncomfortable about what I have to ask, "John? What should we do, you know, about the living arrangements? We can't share the same bed anymore and I think, if you want to… you know, move on, one of us will perhaps have to move out. You can't stay on the couch."

John responds straight away, and I realise that he's been expecting this question. "We'll start a separation. Perhaps you can go into Centrelink and put things in order there and we will work it all out. I could rent a three-bedroom unit and have the kids every second weekend, or something… I don't know. What do you want to do? I'd like us to be amicable for their sake. Seth and Mercy are going to be shocked, and probably angry."

"Let's discuss it with them first, deal with that and then we'll work out the finer details. It's a good idea for me to go into Centrelink and say we're separating as of today's date and get that ball rolling, if you want to go to a real estate agent and see if you can find an apartment nearby?"

"Sounds like a plan."

John looks oddly relieved to be doing something positive. He turns and looks earnestly into my eyes, like he's about to say something he's been rehearsing for a while. "Phoebe, I really am sorry you had to find out this way, but I'm not sure how much longer I would have been sneaking around if you hadn't. Part of me is relieved but another part of me is sad and upset that I've hurt my best friend like this. I love you; I'll always love you. I hope you know that."

What can I say to that? I nod, rise and go to put my teacup in the dishwasher. I take a long hot shower. After I'm dressed, I call Chelsea, to fill her in on what has been going on.

Chelsea has kept her distance, but sending me warm, thoughtful text messages of support; messages that don't require a reply but let me know she is there for me if and when I need her. I find myself reflecting on how much I adore my friend. Chelsea is just about the most selfless person I know. She is the closest I have to a relative.

I wonder how John will go telling his parents. They'd have to be next on the list to be told after the children. That is going to be a hard day. His father will most definitely be disappointed. His knees will bleed from praying; asking God to forgive his errant son and rid him of this illness. He can be such a closed-minded arsehole and his wife will never stand up to him. She will wring her hands anxiously but she will be silent as her husband rants biblically about the evils of homosexuality. How anyone could shun their child is beyond me.

I don't expect that any of us will see his parents after that conversation. There is no room in their hearts for acceptance of this 'disgusting' truth. John will feel the deficit keenly, but his relief at coming out will be evident, as it is even now with just me knowing. I worry how Seth and Mercedes will take the news, though. I guess I will find out soon enough. I gather the paperwork and documents required for the legality of our separation and drive to the nearest centre to set the wheels in motion.

4

The Cold Light Of Day

Phoebe

After we've eaten dinner, the kitchen has been cleaned up and the dishwasher has been stacked, John calls Mercedes and Seth down for a family meeting. I'm nervous and wish I didn't have to be here, but I need to be here for the kids. We sit on the couch side by side facing our children, who are sitting on the couch opposite. Hopefully we're giving off an air of unity and support. John draws a deep breath and starts saying what will change Mercedes and Seth's lives forever.

"Seth, Mercy, I'm sure you've both noticed that something has been… amiss around here of late? I need to explain what's happened and hope you don't take the news too badly or judge me too harshly."

Both Seth and Mercedes look at each other alarmed, and I don't blame them. The news is big, and the soberness of the moment is needed to convey its seriousness. I reach over and take John's hand in mine. He looks at me and our eyes meet. He nods, just once; here goes.

"I need to talk to you about something that's been going on with me. It is going to affect you both and I'm a little nervous about saying it, but there is no easy way to tell you this so I'm just going to say it and get it over with."

John looks down at our joined hands, takes a deep breath and gathers himself. I silently scream at him to hurry up. He looks up and meets the gaze of his children, then wades into battle, "I love you both; I will always love you both. You must know that nothing will ever change that. I hope you will see it in your hearts to continue to love me too. You see, I'm, um… well, I'm actually gay."

An audible gasp escapes Mercedes' mouth and her eyes are wide with surprise. Seth's eyes widen almost imperceptibly, but I see it. His mouth draws into a grim line and he nods ever so slightly. Mercedes puts her hand over her mouth in shock, ever the drama queen, but in this instance, it is justified.

John continues, "I have been in denial for many years, but I have known without a doubt these last couple of years and can no longer ignore it. I love your mum very much, and she's my best friend, but I don't love her the way I should or the way she deserves. It's not fair to any of us to pretend that it isn't what it is. I'm so very sorry."

Mercedes stands up and glares at John with a venomous scowl, then flounces out of the room with a look of complete disgust marring her pretty features. I squeeze John's hand as he hangs his head. He looks up at me and gives me a gentle shrug as if to say, "It's as I expected." Seth swallows hard and stands to address John. He is our calm one, our thinker and our feeler.

"Um, Dad, we're just going to need a little time to process this and then we'll probably have some questions. We're a little bit shocked and surprised at the moment. We didn't see this coming so…"

"I know, mate. When you're ready, we'll talk some more." John is standing to be at eye level with Seth. Seth walks the few steps to him and embraces John and it goes a long way to reassure him.

"This doesn't change how much we love you, Dad; we just need some time to think about it. Like you said, it is what it is, so just give us some time."

Seth looks at me and nods, then turns and walks calmly from the room. John's eyes meet mine. I think we're both shocked at the intensity of Mercedes' reaction but neither of us says so. Seth has taken the news remarkably well, considering. I put my hand on John's shoulder,

"I'm going to go talk to Mercedes before she thinks too much on it, maybe even try answering some of her questions." John nods as I leave the room.

At the top of the stairs I stand outside Mercy's door, wishing I could be anywhere but here. I recall my own reaction to John's sexuality and feel sad for my kids. Gently, I knock on her door and wait in silence for her to answer. I hear only faint sobs, so I very gently open the door and walk over to her bed. In her distress, Mercedes had climbed under the covers and buried her face into the belly of her giant stuffed panda. I feel my heart bruise all over again. I lift the covers and climb into the bed behind her, wrapping myself around my baby girl, gently stroking her silken, dark hair. She turns into my embrace. Her face is red and wet from the grief. I can still see the little girl who used to live in this room. Now she has grown into a young woman but, in her grief, she looks every bit as broken and sad as she had when my father died. I had found her like this then, too, after she had fled the room. Maybe she is incapable of processing shock in the presence of others. On that rainy day, we had lain on this very bed just like this, for what seemed an eternity; the sound of the rain spattering the window and filling the silence. Seth had wandered in and climbed into the bed too, and all three of us had wept for the wonderful man who had been my father and their Poppy.

I hear Seth enter the room now and feel the bed dip as he sits on the end. I look up from Mercedes and our eyes meet. He looks miserable. I am torn between wanting to remain holding my sobbing daughter and wanting to embrace my brave son. I reach out a hand to Seth and, when he takes it, I pull him to me. He lies across the end of the bed, resting his head on my thigh, his hand still clasped in mine. I bring his hand to my mouth and kiss his fingers like I did when he was a small child. Tears run down his face, wetting his cheeks and dripping off his nose onto my leg. Everything has to change now. In the silence left in the room, we can hear misery in the sounds coming from the bottom of the stairs.

John

I sit on the bottom step and sob, unable to hold my anguish in check any longer. I am crying for my children, for my wife and for the future that will be so completely changed from this point forward for all of us. I am crying for me too, wishing I had been born normal, so my family and I would never have to face the cold hard truth of my reality.

What an awful day it is in the O'Brien household. I feel like someone has died. Well, I think derisively, my heterosexuality died today, a role that I have been playing for as long as I can remember. I wonder if I will someday be able to celebrate the birth of my homosexual self? Will there ever be a day when we're all happy again and I don't feel guilt and pain? I put my head in my hands and just let go. My voice sounds foreign even to me as I cry with abandon. This is how we all stay; me alone on the bottom step, Phoebe upstairs in the pink bedroom, holding onto our broken babies until, eventually, the tears ease, fatigue consumes me, and I put myself to bed on the couch where I can't hear them anymore, welcoming the oblivion of sleep.

5

It Is What It Is

Phoebe

James looks up from his laptop as I enter. As I go about setting myself up for the day, I see out of the corner of my eye that he is watching my movements closely; wondering, I guess, what has happened at home and how to broach it. I feel disjointed and distracted and there are dark circles under my eyes. I look straight at him and make eye contact, thinking as I do that he is not good at surreptitious glances. He smiles and raises a hand in greeting. I return his greeting and look back at my PC, I'm not ready yet. He takes the hint and looks away. I hope he leaves me alone and allows me to go in and chat with him when I'm ready.

I feel my stomach clench with foreboding. I really don't want to have the conversation, but it is going to have to happen. I can't ask for a better boss; he is understanding and thoughtful and, above all else, he is a good friend to John and me. He will be shocked when I tell him.

Eventually, I walk to the central kitchen, which services the entire floor, and pour myself a mug of English breakfast tea, leaving the bag in to gain maximum strength. I pour James an Earl Grey, the dingle dangle lasting only a moment to ensure his isn't too strong. I should get back to my morning coffee perk; it's much more bracing than tea. I open the cookie container and place a chocolate chip cookie on James' saucer, then walk into his office. With both hands full, I tap the metal door frame with my toe to gain his attention. He looks up, smiles and motions for me to enter. I walk in and gently toe-tap the door closed behind me. I place his tea on the desk in front of him and sit down opposite. I give him a half-hearted smile then start to relay the events of the past week but for shock value, I just drop it like a bomb.

"My marriage is over. We've just told the kids and they are devastated but not so much that we're breaking up as the *reason* why we're breaking up"

"Oh my God!" James wasn't expecting this, and it shows in his earnest expression, "What happened?"

"Well, it turns out that John is actually homosexual."

"What? Wait, *what*? Where is *that* coming from?"

I don't pause, I just continue like I'm relaying something I saw on the news, like it's somebody else's reality. "You know how I went home sick last Tuesday? I walked in and heard noises, like someone having sex, in our bedroom. I almost kicked down the door because I thought John was having sex with another woman in our bed. You can imagine my surprise when I discovered John in bed with another man."

James rubs a hand vigorously over his face and pulls his chin down; his face becomes elongated and I see the red rims inside his lower eyelids. He can't hide his surprise. "Jesus, Phoebe, I did *not* see that coming. Did you?"

I take a sip of my tea and use the time to arrange my face and calmly answer, "Not even an inkling. He's never exuded any behaviour that would make me think he was anything but the heterosexual man I thought he was when I married him. Apparently, he's known for sure about his sexuality for a few years now."

James runs his fingers backwards through his hair, making it stand up absurdly in spikes like a flustered cockatoo. Slowly shaking his head, he says, "So what now?"

The strong tea has a restorative effect and I can articulate my thoughts. "John has found a three-bedroom unit about a block and a half away, and he's going to move into that. The kids will stay with me for a little while, but they can come and go to either parent depending on how they feel. He's going to furnish both rooms and have toiletries in their bathroom, so they don't have to take anything but their clothes when they visit him. We only told the kids the day before yesterday. The news was not taken well, especially by Mercedes."

"Well I would expect not. What about you, how are you taking this?"

I shake my head and suddenly the tea is not enough; I feel my face droop. Tears fill my eyes as I continue, "Oh, James, it's horrible. I just don't know what to feel. I'm so messed up. I'm worried about how the kids are coping and I know I'm just pushing my feelings to the back and eventually I'm going to have to deal with them. When it first happened, I was quiet and simmering. We went to see a counsellor, like that's going to fix it, to discuss everything about what'd happened and how to deal with it, and even though they kept trying to include me I sort of held them at arm's length; sat there getting really pissy. Then in the last session, I just completely lost it. I yelled and ranted, and I was crass... I used the most horrendous language and references. John and the counsellor were absolutely horrified. I'm embarrassed that I carried on like that, but it just exploded out of me. I can't take it all back; I can't unsay the things I said. I told them I was sorry for the outburst and they seemed okay with it, and I said that I'm just not interested in coming to the sessions anymore."

"Pheebs, you can't deal with this on your own. You really do need to speak with someone about it, someone professional. You're not just dealing with infidelity here--"

I interrupt him because I know what he is going to say, "Oh, I know, this is about my entire life being a lie. Twenty-one years… gone in seconds." I snap my fingers in emphasis. "I think John is a little relieved that it's out in the open. The guilt has been killing him, but I've just got to tell you, part of me died in that room. I've lost something. I'm trying to hold his hand during this whole thing but the entire time I just want to run the other way. I wish I could just escape, get away from it all, you know? I feel like I'm in a fishbowl and everyone around me is watching me tread water."

James reaches across the desk and takes my hand "You know you can take as much time off as you need. Why don't you go away somewhere for a while, just you? The sun will still come up if you take a break."

I shake my head, "I can't. I can't go anywhere; I need to be here for the kids at the moment. Mercedes is kicking and screaming but Seth is so quiet, he worries me. I'm taking the both of them to see someone on Thursday. I think they need to have grief counselling. This is huge and it's sort of like dealing with a death. We all feel deceived and… lost, I guess."

James gives my hand a reassuring squeeze "You let me know if you need some time out, for you, okay? Any time you need to chat, I'm here, I'm always here. Felicity is here for you too."

I would *never* talk to James' wife about my private life. Felicity is lovely, but a terrible gossip.

"Please don't mention this to anyone, including Felicity. I just don't want to have to speak about it to anyone. You can say we've split up but let's not mention John's sexuality. I don't want to be the fodder for the water-cooler conversation."

I refrain from adding, "And I don't want your wife spreading malicious gossip either". James is aware of his wife's information-sharing habits but he can no more change her habits than he could change the weather at whim. He loves her, he is still very much in love with her and it shows. I envy her. I'm reasonably sure it won't be him feeding her the material she gossips about.

He answers curtly like he's just read my mind and I feel my cheeks flame. "Of course."

I stand, ending the conversation. "I'd better get back to it. My desk is a bomb site. Thanks for the chat, James".

I sit at my desk, completely burying myself in paperwork;

anything to distract me from my thoughts for a while. I really need a physical outlet to channel all my negative energy into. I resolve to get up early to go for a run in the morning as I reach into my 'in-tray' and start to prioritise the work files.

John

I walk down the neat concrete-strip driveway, past the carefully manicured garden beds and up the stairs to rap hard on Simon's front door. Maisy answers and greets me animatedly, "Hi John, how are you? If you're looking for Simon, he's in the garage working on that useless piece of crap he calls a motorcycle. How did you know he was home?"

"Hi Maisy." I have turned on the charm, injecting cheer as I lean in to kiss her cheek in greeting. I smell the sweet aroma of baked goods in her hair and I wonder if she's making cookies, her usual fare. "I sent him a text asking if he wanted to catch up for a beer in the next couple of days, and he said he was home today and to pop by so… here I am." I hold up the six pack of beer I've brought with me.

Maisy shakes her head at me, "Men and their toys. Okay, come in through the house, the roller door is closed and a shit to open at the moment." I follow her ample backside through the house and out into the garage, wondering how this plain and frumpy little country girl landed my tall and stupidly handsome friend, who practically had to bash the women off him with a cricket bat in our school years. Eighteen years and four kids later and he's still besotted with her. Half his luck. Simon's normal is so much easier than mine right now.

I can smell the engine oil and petrol before I even get through the door. The garage is cold and unheated and I'm grateful I've remembered to wear a jumper.

Simon looks up from his work as I enter, "Hey, John, how are you, mate?"

"Pretty shit, actually."

Simon stills, "What's up, mate? You look like someone just stole your last dollar."

I breathe out "Where to start?"

Simon uses turpentine and an old rag to clean his greasy hands; the smell is strong.

"Jesus, that sounds ominous." He points his finger at my six pack of beer, "Give me one of those beers and take a seat."

I look around for something to sit on and settle for an old plaster bucket, which I upend to sit on. The relief is instant. "I have a dirty little secret and on Tuesday last week, Phoebe found out about it."

Simon doesn't make a sound, doesn't even bat an eyelid, so I take this as encouragement and continue. "I'm gay, Simon."

Simon's back is as straight as a rod, "What? What are you talking about?"

"Sorry to just dump it like that but there's no easy way to say it except to just say it. I've known for sure for a few years now, but I've been in denial most of my life. You're probably the least homophobic person I know, so I thought I'd tell you first and see how you deal with it. I just need someone to chat to."

Simon is struggling to hide his surprise. "I had absolutely no idea. You and Phoebe looked naturally right for each other."

"Yeah, I know."

"How did she find out?"

"She walked in on me having sex with another man."

Simon's eyes bulge out of his head and his mouth drops open, "Fuck!" he says, "Fuck!" even louder. He takes another swig of beer without breaking eye contact. He says 'fuck' again like it's the only word in his vocabulary and I wonder if I should have just shut up.

Instead, I continue because the cat's out of the bag now. "Went down like a sack of shit. We told the kids the other day and although Seth seems okay with it, Mercy's pissed and won't even look at me. Fair enough, I have to cop that. Poor Pheebs has been so strong but you can imagine how they're all feeling. My whole life has been a lie and they've been caught up in it. I'm going to move out into a three-bedroom unit... half a block from here, actually, so they can sort themselves out a little bit without the white elephant constantly trumpeting in the room. I know it will take a while but I'm hoping Mercy will start talking to me again soon. It's a horrible feeling. At least I don't have to sneak around anymore, or feel guilty for lying about what I am."

"You're gay, John, you're not a monster, mate. Jesus! Ease up on the self hate." Simon raises his index finger of the hand that is holding his beer, points it at me and narrows his eyes, "You know, in year eleven, before Phoebe, there was a time when I wondered if you were a little... confused. I thought you were a bit too attentive to Fraser McDonald, but I thought for sure I would have known about it, with us being best mates and all."

I remember Fraser and how consumed I was by him, constantly looking for him in the year books. "Hah, I had a *huge* thing for Fraser. I thought it was just hormones, you know, confusing everything. Even if I had been able to decipher my feelings back then, I still could never have 'come out.'" I make quote marks in the air with my fingers. "It was the eighties, man! Homosexuality was certainly *not* accepted and *not* the norm around here. Could you imagine my dad's reaction? I still haven't told him. To be truthful, he'll be the last person I tell."

"Yeah, because it will be the last time you see him. He'll treat you like you've contracted the plague." Simon knows exactly how the belligerent prick will take the news. He is, and always has been, an intimidating tyrant to me and I wonder if, on some level, he knew. I was never good enough, would never *be* good enough and the bastard made a show of showering Simon with his affection and admiration in front of me every chance he got. He wanted me to feel intimidated, always preaching 'hell-fire and damnation' that would rain down on the sinners. Mum's a little scared of Dad and although I feel sorry for her sometimes, she should have put me first and come to my defence.

There's no way I would mess up my kids that way. My upbringing has made me agnostic, if not an atheist.

Simon starts talking and pulls me from my reverie, "Are you ready for your dad's reaction?"

"I'm not looking forward to it. He's not even remotely moveable on the subject. He's like that because of his religious beliefs. He's not going to change, not even for his son. It makes me really sad but that's just the way it is, and we'll never see them again. I guess that's why I'm putting it off. Maybe he just doesn't need to know. We could just tell him we're breaking up because of infidelity. As badly as that would go down, I would still be able to see them. I think I will miss Mum most of all."

Simon reaches over and puts his hand on my shoulder. "I know it feels like hell right now, mate, but it *will* get better. Everyone will get over the initial shock and things will come back together, eventually. I just can't tell you how long that will be. The man she caught you with, is he your partner?"

"Oh, God no, just a one-night stand I met in a bar and he sent me a text asking if I'd like to hook up. We met for a coffee and then I took him back to my house and had sex with him. First time I've ever taken someone to the house. You can imagine his surprise when Phoebe burst through the door with a face like thunder, then horror when she realised what was happening. She ran out the door and the guy was horrified that I had a wife and family and they didn't know. He ran like the clappers out of there too."

Simon's expression is incredulous, and I know what's coming. "John! In your *bed*? You *never* shit in your own nest, mate. I can't believe you did that."

I hold up my hands in resignation. "I know, I know. What a terrible way for Phoebe to find out. I'm not looking to meet anyone, so I'll refrain from going to bars until my current mess is sorted out. I don't need the complication and, to be honest, my libido flew out the window when this cluster-fuck happened."

"Wise decision, my friend, sort it all out first." Simon reaches for a second beer and pops the top. I feel relief wash over me and it's cleansing. I wonder if I will ever be able to just be me. It feels like it could be an eternity away.

Mercedes

It's a beautiful sunny Thursday and school is out due to a teachers' correction day and here I am, camped in my room. I'm lying on my bed groaning because my uterus hates me. I want to go downstairs and get a pill to kill the pain, but it would be my luck that I'll run into Dad and I'm still angry at him. I don't want to talk to him and I can't control my temper because my hormones are psyching out and my mood is stuck on 'bitch'.

I'm supposed to be doing homework but instead I'm lying here, seething. Angry just isn't a big enough word to describe it. My uterus stabs me again and I'm groaning once more, distracted from thinking about *him*. I don't want to think about the magnificent chrysalis slowly opening and the hatching of the glorious butterfly; marvelling as it gently extends it wings, free at last. Hell, no! What I am thinking about is how the giant, balding, middle-aged moth downstairs flapped a wing and a fucking atom bomb detonated in the house, and now we're all dodging the falling debris while he stands around looking wounded. Fucking gay? I need to talk to someone about it to get it out of my head, but I don't want anyone to know how fucked up and dysfunctional my family is.

The cramp pinches and throbs in my back and I contemplate crawling out of the French doors and throwing myself off the balcony. With my luck, he'll be outside plucking weeds out of his precious lawn and he'll save me from a certain death, and I'll have to pretend to be grateful when all I want to do is escape his lying arse. Finally, the cramp eases and I can think again. My thoughts return to Dad and I feel betrayed.

What a stupid man he is! Imagine hiding something like that from everyone for forty-five fucking years, and then suddenly deciding that today is the day to tell everyone that you're a fabulous unicorn from the mystical land of fairies singing, "here ye, see my rainbow" as you frolic in delicate leaps and pirouette through fields of poppies, blowing sunshine out of your arse and radiating beauty from your golden hotpants. Piss off! There is no pot of gold at the end of this rainbow, just a giant bubbling pot of 'fuck you', and I don't want any of it. I can't wait to go back to school to get away from this place. I am waiting for him to bugger off, so I can go downstairs and binge eat an entire block of chocolate and half a tub of chocolate spread with a spoon, straight from the jar.

I am pissed off with Mum, too. How can she be taking this so calmly? The bastard came home every day and kissed her, slept with her, had *babies* with her, and all the while he's fantasising about some guy's hairy balls. I feel revolted because he is my *dad*. Ew! I don't want to think about my parents having sex, but now all I can think about is Dad screwing a guy. I shudder at the conjured image. What a nightmare. I don't want to even look at him, let alone talk to him. I'm disgusted with him and the bullshit lies he's been spinning us.

The screen of my phone lights up, heralding the arrival of a text message. Joshua Sangerston! I sit up too quickly and bang my head painfully on the bookcase that juts out from my wall. Ouch! Why is he sending me a message? My hands shake as I read it.

Hi Mercy. Wondering if ur free this arvo or tomorrow... do u want to catch up? Maybe meet at the park?

Holy shit! I can hardly breathe and quickly type a response, hoping I sound cool because I have no idea how to respond to a boy.

Hi Josh. I'm doing homework at the moment (groan) but I can meet u tomorrow arvo at 3 if that works?

I hold my breath as I wait for his reply to come through. My heart is pounding, *that's* the effect he has on me. A moment later I see his response.

Yep, that works. I'll meet u at the swings. See u then.

OK, see u then.

I hold the phone to my chest and sway from side to side, then catch a glimpse of myself in the mirror. I look like I am eleven years old and holding onto a picture of Justin Bieber. I don't care, Joshua Sangerston is cuter than Bieber. He is two years above me at school, in Seth's year, and he is the brother of one of the girls in my friendship group, Monique, who is absolutely mint and my bestie. Every time I go to Monique's house, I secretly hope I'll see him there. He is so fricken hot! When he wears his tight red skinny jeans and a tight t-shirt over that chest and those abs, what's a girl to do? Oh sigh! I can't believe he texted me. I squeal with delight then catch myself and freeze. I don't want Dad to hear me; I need to find my chill.

I have known Josh for at least three years but it's like he just transformed from a gangly, dorky older brother to the hottest thing on the planet. His hair is fashionably longish and messy with natural golden streaks from the sun. He's grown about a foot this year alone, and every time he walks into the room, I feel like all the air is sucked out of my lungs. I sit there grinning at him and wonder if he thinks I'm an idiot. Now he's texting me!

Last Monday, the day before Dad destroyed my life, I was at Monique's house finishing our joint biology project in her room. We decided that we needed a break, so we went down to the kitchen for a snack. We were sipping our milk and Milo (which was really half a glass of Milo with a bit of milk added to wet it a little) and yammering on about all things Harry Styles and we hadn't noticed Josh walk in.

He quietly pulled the chair out beside me and coolly said, "Hey girls, wad up?" I got such a fright that I squeaked in surprise and almost spat Milo across the table. How embarrassing.

Monique yelled, "Fuck off, Josh, and stop scaring my friends!" Monique can be a real bitch to him sometimes. I would never speak to Seth the way she speaks to Josh.

Josh looked hurt and said, "Hey, I didn't mean to frighten anyone. I thought you both knew I was here." He looked at me and half his mouth went up in the cutest smile. I tried to smile coquettishly under my eyelashes back at him but probably only managed to look stupid and slightly touched in the head. I wanted to gush, but I was trying to play it cool. Cool does not come naturally to me and I have to work at it.

"So how are you, Mercy? Watcha been up to?" He flashed me the full megawatt smile and it was all I could do not to fall into a quivering heap at his feet.

My voice, thank goodness, was surprisingly calm as I replied stupidly, "Oh homework, mostly. I can't wait for this term to end. There's just been no time out, you know?"

I don't know how to speak to boys. I have no experience and don't know what I'm doing. My palms get all sweaty and I'm sure my face goes red.

"Wait until next year. It gets worse. The homework is a bitch!" He looked past me to Monique. "Mon, why are you looking at me like I'm a dead, maggot-riddled rodent carcass the cat just dropped at your feet?"

Monique glared at him and hissed, "Probably because you are! Are you hitting on my friend, Josh?"

Josh got all defensive and yelled, "I'm having a conversation for fuck's sake. Do you own her?" He looked pointedly at me and repeated, "Does she own you, Mercedes? Are you allowed to speak to me without her permission?"

I felt my face flush, but it was probably more like beetroot red and ready to set fire to my hair. I didn't want to get caught in the crossfire, but I really like him, so I said, "Nobody owns me, Josh." He floated an eyebrow and the smile became a wicked grin. Everything clenched, and I wanted to fan my face but I didn't want him to think I was weird so I sat there slowly rubbing my hands up and down the length of my glass, catching the condensation… until I realised that I looked like I was wanking the glass and my face went redder still. Mortified, I whipped my hands under the table onto my thighs before they did something else to embarrass me.

I haven't been able to think of anything else… until Dad pulled the pin and threw the grenade into the house. Grrrr! I leap up, carefully avoiding the bookcase, and yank open the wardrobe doors. Hmm, what to wear? Black skinny jeans, the soft pink top with the satin ruffles and the black patent leather ballet flats. Even though it's not until tomorrow I pull out my selection and lay them on the bed. I have to try the jeans on because my period has given me a fluid baby and I don't want to turn up at the park with a grotesque pot sticking out in front of me. I zip them up and they close easily. I don't look as potty as I feel and hope it will stay that way until tomorrow when I see him. I will try not to sit down, or I'll wear a long coat to hide the tummy bulge.

I close the wardrobe doors, lean my back against them and smile lazily. How the hell am I going to finish my homework with my head full of Josh? Oh, dear God, what if he kisses me? Shit! I've never kissed before. I don't know how to kiss. How am I supposed to know how to kiss? Years ago, when I was immature, I tried pashing the back of my hand, trying to mimic what I had seen on television and in movies, but nothing felt like lips would. I am immediately embarrassed for my stupid immature younger self. Who kisses the back of their hand? Hopefully, if he does kiss me, he will know what to do. Perhaps he can teach me. What the hell am I thinking? I need to finish my homework. Returning to my desk, I try to apply myself, so I can finish up and concentrate on how I'll do my makeup tomorrow when I see Josh. Josh, Josh, Josh, Josh, JOSSHHHH! *Back of hand on forehead.* Swoon!

Seth

I sit at the desk in my room, wishing I could be anywhere but here, wishing school wasn't out. The sun is warm and streaming through the windows, but I feel chilled to the bone, like nothing could ever warm me through again. I am worried for Mum, who has had to bear the brunt of Dad's revelation. She is trying to be strong, but cracks are appearing in her veneer. I often hear her crying and feel completely helpless; I have no idea how to fix her. To have spent all those years thinking your husband was attracted to you; that he thought you were beautiful, only to find out he didn't think that at all. Well, maybe he did, but the way you can appreciate the beauty of another being or a painting but knowing he didn't really desire her must feel terrible. Yesterday she went to work, and she went for a run afterwards, she came home and cooked for us, cleaned, organised the uniforms and then took herself off to bed to cry herself to sleep.

Dad moves out tomorrow. His mate, Simon, will help him. I would have liked to have helped but it is a school day and I can't miss even a day. They've rented a small truck to move his stuff. It is sad to see his life packed into boxes and cases, waiting for tomorrow. He hugged me fiercely last night and told me I could call anytime and that he had bought new bedding to make up the beds for the two other rooms in his unit for Mercy and me when we're ready to visit. Mercy refused to open her door to say goodbye, and her response to Dad's rapping on the door was to turn her music up louder. That's cold. Poor Dad.

Mercy is pissing me off. She has become completely selfish and is intent on punishing Dad. It's not like this is a choice for him. He can't help the way he was born. He may have left it a little long to tell us all, but I can understand his trepidation. Dealing with news this big, knowing he was about to change everybody's life in an instant would be a frightening and confronting thing to have to do. But you have to be true to yourself, I am a strong campaigner of that kind of thing. Hating him for his sexuality is just plain mean spirited. It really is the equivalent of hating someone for the skin they're wrapped in. I have seen plenty of that at school with my mate, Brandon.

Brandon has an Aboriginal background, three generations removed on his paternal grandmother's side, but which showed up strongly in his genes all these years later. He is proud of his heritage, but some kids are just born arseholes and there have been times when I've heard kids mumble as Brandon walks past, "petrol sniffer!" or "Blackfella". This kind of insult aimed at his roots is senseless. Brandon has found notes in his locker calling him names too. This one guy, Brent, even threatened to punch Brandon's lights out if he made a move on a certain 'white' girl that he was fond of; told him to stick to the black chicks…like there's a cornucopia of them floating about at our school. Brent Jeffries and his brother Matt are the main perpetrators and are both absolute dicks, with a typical bully's story of an arsehole who pumps himself up by bullying others. It is rumoured that their father is an alcoholic and beats into them. This is how Brent & Matt deal with their shit – they pass the buck and make someone else feel like shit. Everybody has a story.

Sometimes, the name calling has been so bad for Brandon, and so senselessly racist, that he wishes he was dead. I feel blessed that he is comfortable talking to me about it all. What are best mates for? At least while he's saying it to me, he isn't sitting alone somewhere, contemplating his end. We talk about it often and I've asked him to always call me when he feels really low and has those menacing thoughts. I tell him that we can talk it through and that nothing should ever be so bad that he should ever want to escape with suicide, like that's his only option. Brandon has his demons though; the bullying just adds fuel to the fire. There are other means of escape. I choose writing. I write when I'm down or upset, and I write when I'm angry. I don't often feel down or upset but, right now, I'm a little worried and confused about the dad issue.

I'm reasonably popular at school but I'm not one of the 'cool' guys. I'm not ugly but I'm not hot either. I have a pretty good sense of humour and consider myself fun to be around... don't we all? I do seem to be popular with the fairer sex though, and this confounds me. I'm not an amazing footy player, I don't have the skills to play basketball and I don't wear my jeans halfway down the back of my legs with two-thirds of my jocks showing over the top. That's a stupid look. I wonder if those idiots actually ever look at themselves in the mirror. They look like tools. Or maybe I'm a nerd.

I am a little alarmed at the way girls throw themselves at me though, like I'm a conquest, I'm nobody's trophy. Sure, I like sex as much as the next guy, but I don't want it thrown at me like it's meaningless. My mates think I'm mad, saying that if they were in my shoes, they'd be screwing every piece of arse that shamelessly made their intentions clear.

I had a girlfriend for almost a year. Vivienne was my first and only love to date; she took my heart and my virginity. I loved her more than she deserved, and she broke my proffered heart when she screwed one of my mates in a drunken stupor at an end-of-year gathering. So, last Christmas, I found myself down one mate *and* a girlfriend. They can both go and fuck themselves; they deserve each other.

I pull out some foolscap paper and begin to write. I start with a question. "How do I feel?" I tap the pen on my chin, trying to articulate my thoughts. After a moment, I put pen to paper and the words just flow out of me, healing me by means of a therapeutic purge and lending clarity to my thoughts.

My phone quacks, heralding a message. I need to change my alert; the quacking duck was funny for about a minute but now it just shits me. It's Brandon, and he is pissed off. He is sick of the shit and ready to cave someone's head in, he says. Today he is angry as opposed to sad. We both know that it isn't going to happen, but it goes a long way to explain what's going on within him today. I quickly respond with a question:

Do you like the alley or the gutter?

What?

Alley or gutter, dude?

Jesus, I can't even type a text without the punctuation. I am anal, a side effect of being a writer.

the fuck you on man?

Brandon doesn't share my affinity for punctuation, so I mentally add the capital letter and the comma. I've decided I will take him out of his skin for a while.

I'm taking you bowling.

It takes him a couple of minutes to respond. I assume he is over at his house scratching his head.

Finally, he quacks at me: K.

* * * * *

Taking Brandon bowling is a distraction to get his mind off today's upsetting remarks. He was feeling pretty shitty earlier but now I think he is up for a bit of fun. I have managed to score a rolled marijuana joint from a mate, just for shits and giggles. We pull into the car park of the bowling alley and I produce the rolled treasure. Brandon's eyes light up and he's grinning like an idiot.

"You're very resourceful, Seth, my man. Where did you score that baby?"

"I have a friend, who has a friend, who knows a guy."

Brandon eyes me suspiciously. "You know a guy who knows a guy who knows another guy? Where do you get this cloak-and-dagger shit from? Can we trust him?"

"Well, I trust him."

Brandon doesn't look convinced. "It's just that… I've heard that some dealers spray their shit with ice for the buzz and I'm worried, you know? Ice is scary!"

"I'm sensing trust issues. It's all good, mate, and not sprayed with anything. He did warn me that it is strong though."

We light the baby up and on my first drag in I take it deep but find myself coughing and spluttering because my virgin lungs aren't used to having this filthy smoke in them. I suck in air and hate the residual taste of weed in my lungs every time I cough. Brandon is watching me warily, but I shake my head at him that I'm okay and flap my hands to dispel some of the smoke that's making my eyes water. Almost immediately, I feel the buzz, like my head is detached and floating around the car's interior, barely tethered to my body by my spinal cord. I feel my face go slack and my eyes are burning.

I offer the scoob to Brandon, who takes the offending article and pulls a huge lungful. Brandon doesn't smoke either, so he also starts coughing, only during his coughing fit he rips off a fart that I think should blow his jeans off his body. We're both laughing our arses off, and then I get a whiff of his arse gas and I am forced to crack a window before I die from the toxic fumes. The smell is fucking horrendous and I wonder if it's possible to die from smelling farts… then I remember something I read in year eight about the sulphur contained in the fart that makes it smell so bad, and that you can't actually die from it. I am questioning if that is true as I thrust my head out of the window to suck in some cool freshness. I pull my head back inside the car and turn to him, and he's laughing so hard he's crying.

"Did you shit yourself, mate?" It's an accusation and I don't usually use accusations with Brandon; he's hyper-sensitive and often takes things the wrong way, but I'm stoned, and my usual eggshell-walking technique didn't show up for the conversation. He doesn't get his gander up; he's laughing even harder than before and now I'm laughing at him laughing. We're completely stoned on two puffs.

I take the joint back and take another long drag. This time, my lungs are prepared so I hold it in for maximum effect and hand it back to Brandon. I peer at his eyes and they are blood red. Jesus. I pull the rear-view mirror around and look at my own eyes. I point at my image and start laughing. Brandon is puffing on the joint and looks up to see me laughing at myself. He can't even form words. I'm wondering how either of us are going to be able to command our legs and arms to pull us out of the car and walk into the establishment, let alone bowl the ball down the alley. I look at Brandon and he is looking at his watch. It takes him, like, five minutes to decipher what the hands are doing so I'm forced to voice the question, "What time is it?"

Brandon starts up with a high-pitched giggle and I'm looking at him like he's weird. His voice is helium high… he *is* weird. He doesn't take his eyes off the watch, but a few minutes later he laughs the words, "I don't fucking know, man."

It is a full half an hour before we can contain our shit enough to be able to get out of the car and walk. Every step I take shudders through my body hydraulically, like I'm Robocop. I am super aware of how slow I'm moving, and I feel like I need to instruct my body every step of the way. We're walking like we both require a walking cane to assist us, and I imagine my cane will have a big mother of a knob at the end of it, all gnarly and cool looking. I don't share my thoughts, because I'm stoned, but say the rest of the sentence out loud, "It would look so cool."

Brandon turns his head at the pace of a tortoise to look at me, and says, "What?"

I frown at him. Isn't he listening? "My knob would be gnarly."

I realise that I thought the first half of the conversation, but I don't have the patience to finish it because it is taking all my concentration to walk, so I shrug at him and the poor bastard is left confused. Like a goldfish, within seconds he forgets and, still at the tortoise pace, turns his head back to look where he's going.

We walk inside the establishment and my senses are assailed by the smell and noise. The smell of the clown-like leather shoes we have to hire, the smell of cheap junk food (like fries that have been in the bain-marie for hours already and look dried and inedible) colliding with the usual smell of sports venues, which I can't articulate into words. It's so loud. The sound of the balls rolling down the alley and belting the pins at great speed at the end of the alley; the machine re-setting the pins and the balls rolling back up to the top – it all physically hurts my ears. People are shouting above the din and I hope I chill out soon, so I don't keep cringing and hunching my shoulders against it. I look over at Brandon and he's oblivious… and he has a really stupid look on his face.

We walk up to the counter and pay for our game and our shoes. The guy behind the counter eyes us suspiciously, but we must look harmless because he asks us for our shoe sizes and disappears to get them. It takes an eon to lace the shoes up because I'm so stoned, I have to think really hard to get the messages from my brain to my fumbling fingers. Brandon is having trouble too, but his laces are tied… and look like they've been tied by a toddler. The giant loops match the clownliness of the shoes. After we've finished with the clown shoes, and stowed ours in the cubicles, we point and laugh at how stupid we both look. We are both eighteen years old, legally adults in Australia, but we are behaving like six-year-old children.

We walk to our lane and start fumbling to enter our names into the computer when a tall lanky dude walks up and leans in. "Excuse me, I'm a professional bowler and I need to train. Could I play a game with you in your lane?"

I blink up at him; I have no idea what he just asked. Finally, my brain processes the question and I smile and say, "Sure, but I have to warn you, you won't get any competition out of us, we're really bad bowlers." The word 'competition' comes out sounding like 'compishon' and Brandon starts giggling again. I add, "And we've both got the giggles, sorry."

Tall lanky dude raises his eyebrows, then smiles and shoots out a hand. "That's cool, I'm Aaron."

We shake his hand and I ask him to add himself to the computer because my brain can't think how to spell it. Weed has made me dumb.

Brandon is first up to bowl so he stands up and starts to feel the weight of the bowling balls, like he has a clue what he's doing, and picks up the heaviest ball in the rack. He carries it with both hands and walks towards the line at the beginning of the alley, where he tries to gracefully roll the ball. He has the grace of an agitated gecko running on two legs so he waddle-walks and then accidentally drops the ball. It sounds like thunder. The ball starts to roll at the pace of a sloth all the way down the alley. He knocks one pin over. He tries to make his second bowl look normal but hurls the thing away from his body like Hercules and it bounces three times loudly before it skids and slides into the gutter. I'm lying on the carpet, crying with laughter, and Brandon is trying to look cool. Aaron says to me, loudly, "It's your turn, mate."

This is going to be a long night for him; he has not chosen wisely. I don't fondle the balls looking for the right size, I don't give a fuck. I just grab the one in front of me. I try to walk calmly but just before I get to the line, my stupid clown shoes slide out from under me and I land with a splat and the ball nearly breaks my knuckles because my fingers are still inside it. I've managed to slide a quarter of the way down the alley with the ball before it gently slides off my fingers, rolls into the gutter and sloths its way down. No pins for me.

I try to regain my cool composure and reach for another ball, but it's taken me an age to walk back to the rack and my sloth ball returns and clacks the ball I am trying to grab, and almost obliterates my pinkie finger, which got caught between the two balls. I yowl and swear, flapping my hand like it's on fire because it hurts, before I see Aaron glaring at me with a death stare. I manage a half-decent roll this time and turn around to see Brandon excitedly jumping up and down in his seat. He has forgotten where he is, how old he is, and that he's supposed to be cool. It is contagious because when I get a 'spare', I'm giving him a high-five and we're bouncing off each other's chests. We are the personification of stupid youth.

Aaron slides his long, pianist-like fingers inside the holes of his own ball, which he's been polishing for the last five minutes like it's attached to his crotch. He stands before the lane and holds the ball to his chest as he carefully measures the pins and the distance with his eyes, then does a special little run up. During this spectacular display of peacocking, as he leans down to release the ball, Aaron's other leg goes up behind him and across his body and his foot ends up level with his head... but behind it. Brandon and I are wearing our startled emoji faces on the front of our heads. What the fuck is this guy doing? Weird-as-shit Aaron then releases the ball with the aplomb of an expert, and the ball travels with speed to knock down all the pins.

He looks ridiculous but there's a spring in his step as he smugly peacocks back to us. He's so proud of himself I think he might start stroking himself in front of us. Brandon and I are holding onto each other, absolutely destroyed by laughter. Aaron stands up abruptly and retrieves his ball, then hisses, "Fuck off" at us as he exits the area. People in other lanes are turning to look at us because there's way too much volume in our laughter, but nobody looks bothered, they look like they wish they could be in on the joke.

Our game takes a century to finish, especially because each time we get up to have a go, we try to mimic Aaron's geeky leg thing and we're just ruining our games but laughing ourselves senseless each and every time. We're still laughing in the cafeteria afterwards as we critique Aaron's game style.

The weed high is wearing off a little, but we decide to stay for another half an hour or so to ensure I'm okay to drive home. I've already consumed a hotdog, a can of soft drink, a bowl of fries and two potato cakes, and I'm eyeing off the chocolate bars. The weed munchies have turned me into a pubescent teenager in the midst of a growth spurt.

I'm still paranoid driving home. Weed has made me stress out about the speed I'm travelling at. I can't go above the speed limit as that may result in a fine and having to have a stoned conversation with the local constabulary. I can't travel below the speed limit either, because that will draw attention to me and will possibly result in a fine and actually having a stoned conversation with the local constabulary. So, I grip the wheel and think I might bend it because I'm gripping it so hard. Brandon is silent beside me except to utter every few minutes, "I don't know how you're doing this…how are you doing this?"

I don't know how I'm doing this either but I'm grateful to drop him at his door in one piece and make it back home alive myself. I let myself in quietly and tiptoe up the stairs with the stealth of a thief. I get to the second-last step from the top and hear someone in the shadows say, absurdly loudly in the silence of the house, "I was wondering when you'd get home."

I scream and trip up the last two steps to fall in a pile before her, my chin bouncing painfully off her bony kneecap. Mercy laughs and says, "Very cool, Seth."

I glare at her because my heart is in my mouth and she's laughing at me. I acerbically retort, "Why are you sitting in the shadows like a creep?" because marijuana messes with my personality and makes me behave like a dick.

The smile slides from her face and her voice is cold as she says, "I just wanted to know you were home safe." Then she goes back into her room and softly closes the door. I crawl the few paces to my own room, climb up on top of my bed and fall into a marijuana-induced coma, fully clothed and with my shoes still on.

6

Caught Between Heaven And Hell

Mercedes

Josh is sitting on the swings as I approach the park. He stands when he spies me, then walks over to meet me with his easy swagger. His hair is still wet from the shower and I can smell shampoo and soap mingling with his deodorant and aftershave. The smell sends my heart rate off the Richter Scale. His face splits into a wide smile. "Hello, Mercy."

I return his hello with a steadiness in my voice that belies the quaking going on within. I'm freaking out a little with both nerves and excitement. He reaches for my hand and tugs me, sending small shocks into my hand with his touch. He wraps his giant hand around mine so now we're holding hands as he guides me to the bench at the edge the park. I'm silently praying that my hand will be released before it sweats into grossness. He waits for me to sit before he seats himself because he is a gentleman, and my hand dries before it grosses him out.

"So, did you finish your homework yesterday?"

"Yeah, as much as I was going to get done anyway. Of course, there's more today. What did you get up to on your day off?"

"We had soccer training in the morning; coach took advantage of the correction day. We got completely rolled last weekend, so I think he's punishing us, pushing us to our limits to make sure we get up and win this week. I had two free periods this morning, so I knew

I would finish all my homework, and considering the weather was miserable I'm glad I did something productive with it. Right now, I'm sitting here with you."

I feel a little awkward, not sure what to say. I'm grateful that Josh isn't socially awkward and takes the lead otherwise we'd be sitting here like two statues. Josh breaks into my thoughts, "You want to walk up and grab a Slurpee at 7-Eleven?"

"Sure," I chirp. I need to calm down. I don't want him to think I'm an idiot. I feel giddy as he holds out his hand to pull me up. He continues to hold my hand the whole way to the convenience store. I can feel the sweat building between our clasped hands again and I'm marvelling at his control to not pull his hand free and wipe it on his jeans. My hand remains steadfast in his.

* * * * *

Walking back to the park, sucking noisily on our Slurpees, Josh continues to hold my hand. I have to stop for a minute because I slurp too much and give myself brain ache. Josh takes in my pained expression and grins at me. "Brain freeze?" I nod because I can't form words with my head aching like this. Then, like magic, it disappears. He tugs at my hand and we move on, and we're still holding hands.

This is so exciting. I can't believe Josh Sangerston, one of the hottest boys at our school, is holding my hand and is interested in *me*. The wind kicks up the autumnal coloured leaves, scattering them over the carefully manicured garden beds and across the path in front of us. As we pass under the giant tree in the centre of the park, I look up through the branches. They're almost completely bare of foliage and it looks really cool; reaching its woody fingers to the cold autumn sky. Josh stops and, as I turn to him, he takes my Slurpee from my hand, placing both his and mine on the ground at the foot of the tree. He then stands up and leans in to drop a soft kiss on my mouth. I am taken by surprise and stifle a gasp. His lips are cold from the semi-frozen drink, and, as I blink up at him, I'm not sure what to do next or how to even kiss properly.

He takes my quiet look as permission, which it most definitely is, to move forward. He leans down and presses his lips to mine again, using his mouth to part my lips slightly; he tastes like raspberry. He gently kisses me, and I'm doing it too… he's guiding me into a deepening kiss. Holy crap, I'm kissing a boy. Oh wow, it's so easy, it all just happens. Well it helps when the other person knows what they're doing. The tip of his tongue lightly skirts the inside of my lips; I assume he is questioning my acceptance of the tongue. How the hell would I know? I tentatively skate my tongue inside his mouth, too, feeling exhilarated as my tongue brushes his.

Josh pulls away for a moment, smiling disarmingly down at me. I feel like I'm going to faint. He reaches up to tuck a stray lock of hair behind my ear. He moves in for the mother of all kisses, his hands slowly stroking up and down my arms, then circling my shoulders into an embrace. I stand up on my tiptoes and slide my arms around his neck, returning his kiss with all the confident fervour I can put into it. Surprised, Josh eagerly deepens the kiss into something that sends fire in all directions; my body is alight, and I feel poetic, swaying in his embrace. I am light-headed and giddy, and I wish this raspberry kiss could last forever.

When he finally pulls away, he looks blown away. "Wow, Mercy, that was some kiss. Can't say I've ever been kissed like *that* before."

Holy shit! He is breathing heavily, like he's been running, and his chest is rising and falling at a really fast pace, so I see he's just as affected! I wonder, briefly, if he says that to all the girls.

We collect our Slurpees from the foot of the tree and walk to the park bench. We sit chatting amicably for two whole hours before Josh looks at his watch and puts an end to the dreamy afternoon. "I've got to get home. Shall I walk you home first?"

I resist the urge to put my hand to my chest and sigh. I am flattered, accepting his offer. He continues to hold my hand all the way home, oblivious to my clammy moisture issues. He wraps me in another embrace and kisses me softy on the front porch in front of the door, making my heart thump inside my chest. As the sun hangs low in the autumn sky, I watch him walk down the path to the front gate before turning onto the footpath, giving me a wave as he disappears out of sight.

I am that eleven-year-old girl with the Bieber picture again, crossing my arms across my chest in a self-hug. I lean my back against the door and sigh, losing myself in whimsical thoughts of actually dating him.

I hear the release of the door latch a moment too late and stumble backwards into Seth. Surprised, he reaches out and catches me before I fall. "Hey, Mercy, I didn't know you'd gone out."

"Yeah, I just met a friend at the park."

"Oh, cool. I'm off to see Brandon."

Seth's mouth is a grim line. This is an ominous sign that Brandon is having a bad day. "Oh, what's up with Brandon?"

"He's not having a good day. Some arsehole has hacked his social media page and changed his name to Petrol Sniffer! Jesus, you'd think in this day and age people would just bugger off with this racist crap. I think I'm going to have a conversation with his parents. They don't know the extent of this harassment and the effect it's having on him. He says he wants out of this shitty life but I'm not sure if he's just saying that or if he's serious. I'm going to go talk to him, so I've got to go."

He jogs off, yelling over his shoulder, "Hey, tell Mum I'll be back later and maybe you could fill her in for me?"

"Sure. Give him a hug from me," I yell as he takes off at a run. Poor Brandon, some boys can be arseholes! But not Josh, he's cute.

Seth

I am halfway to Brandon's house when my phone quacks and I am reminded that I still need to change the message alert. Slowing to a walk, I read the text message from Brandon:

Hey mate, I've gone for a run. I need to just get the hell out of this room – I'm going mad.

Doubling back, I make my way to the oval. As I approach, I can see Brandon in the distance, lapping the oval. I take a seat on the park bench and watch as he runs. I envy his athleticism; he is built for exercise. He is clearly the best player in the school football team. The way he reads the play, tackles fearlessly, and his amazing marking skills and disposal of the ball are legendary; some people are just born for it. He isn't too shabby on the soccer field either, but the AFL code is his calling. I have seen scouts scribbling furiously and taking photos when they come to watch the matches lately. It is only a matter of time before he's approached by an AFL team to discuss recruitment options in the lower grades.

As I watch Brandon reach the furthest round of the oval, I see several youths step into his path, blocking him. I can't see who it is from this distance. Brandon is forced to attempt to run around them. One of them steps sideways, blocking him from passing and shoves him forcefully in the chest.

I feel revulsion deep inside before I take off at a run across the oval. I've sprinted halfway across when the first punch lands in Brandon's stomach, doubling him over. I'm watching as I furiously run towards him. He takes a kick to the groin, which drops him to his knees, and then the onslaught begins. I can't even see him, just the frenzy of kicks and punches landing on his body. I am screaming at them to leave him alone because I want them to know I'm coming. Seeing me as I approach, the gutless arseholes turn and run away like the pathetic cowards that they are.

Finally reaching Brandon, I fall to my knees beside him and

gently pry his arms open to see his beaten and bloody face looking back at me. I'm horrified and panic a little, but I don't want to show it. This is the worst it has ever been.

"Can you get up, mate? Can you sit?" I am all questions and getting no answers, so I grab at his arms to help him up.

Brandon allows me to assist him into a sitting position. I peer into his face and see that his lips and one of his eyes are beginning to swell, his nose is bloody and he has a huge grotesque lump forming on his forehead where a boot has landed.

I'm shocked and appalled at what I have just witnessed and swear I will take this to the police. I try to sound calm as I ask, "What was that about?"

Brandon shakes his head. He is panting and holding his side. "No reason. They just kept yelling at me between punches and kicks, 'fuck off back to the Nullarbor, Abbo'. What the hell, Seth? I'm just running here. I'm not bothering anyone. Why?... *Why?*"

I have no answers for him because I don't understand why it keeps happening. So, whatever is inside my head pours out of my mouth, "There is no reason, Brandon. They are weak, cowardly, chicken-shit arseholes with nothing better to do than find a target to torment and you're it, mate. They hunt in packs because they're weak and pathetic. They're nothing, Brandon."

Brandon drops his head into his hands and sobs, "Why?" repeatedly. I don't know what to do and I don't know what to say. I'm just standing here mutely watching him in his agony. He looks up at me and he is distraught as he whispers, "It's never going to stop, is it?"

Unsure how to respond, I want to be proactive, so I ask him, "Did you recognise any of them?"

He answers quietly, "Only one, Matt Jeffries."

White heat goes through me and I feel savage. "Well that figures. Screw this, Brandon, we're going after them and we're pressing assault charges. We're telling the school, the police, they are fucking *gone*! I am a witness and I saw it all and what just happened is against the law!"

I take out my phone and start taking pictures of Brandon's face because this evidence is going to bring them down. Brandon looks defeated as he says, "Stop, Seth, I'm not going after them. How much worse do you think it's going to get if I go to the police? Do you think that's going to stop them or just make it worse?"

I sag because he's right. "Yeah, I know," I concede, "but we've got to tell your parents, mate." I am thinking that there has to be a way to stop this from happening. I reach out a hand to him to pull him up. "C'mon, mate, let's get you home and cleaned up."

When we reach his front door, Brandon turns to me, puts his hand on my shoulder and dismisses me. "Thanks, mate. I'm just going to take a soak in the bath and lick my wounds. I need some time alone."

I won't be dismissed, "I'm happy to just hang downstairs and wait for you, man."

There's resignation in his shoulders as he climbs the stairs. I busy myself in the kitchen with the kettle. It looks like I'll be waiting for a while, so I make myself comfortable.

Twenty minutes later, I'm still sitting in the living room, idly flipping pages in a magazine about high-end motor vehicles, when Brandon's mum, Bonny, enters. "Hi, Seth, how are you?"

I stand and embrace Bonny warmly. She is like a second mum to me, "Hi, Bonny. I'm really good thanks, how are you?"

"I'm good, thanks. Where's Brandon?" she queries as she looks up the stairs.

"He went for a run earlier so he's taking a bath. He was set upon by some idiots who knocked him around a bit today. He was pretty upset, and I didn't want him to be alone until we talked it through. That's why I'm sitting down here. He's going to be angry that I mentioned it to you, but you'll see by his face that he's been hurt."

Bonny's eyes widen in alarm. She starts running for stairs, but I call after her, "He's in the bath."

She is still looking alarmed as she says, "How long has he been up there, Seth?"

I look at my watch, "About half an hour? I figured I'd cut him some slack and give him space. He tried to send me home, but I didn't want him to be alone right now, so I told him I was waiting right here until he's done and then we'd talk it through."

Bonny continues to look worried. "Will you come up with me to check on him?"

I hesitate for a beat. This is awkward. "Um, sure, I'll come up with you."

We stand outside the bathroom door listening for any sounds. The echo of a drop of water as it hits the filled bath is all we can hear. Bonny knocks loudly on the door. "Brandon, honey, you okay in there?"

There is no answer. We wait for a few seconds then I knock harder and yell through the door, "Hey, mate, you okay? Wanna give us a yell out or something?"

Still there is no answer. I start to panic and urgently say to Bonny, "He took a nasty blow to the head, maybe he's blacked out or something."

I knock again, really loudly. "Last chance, mate, if you don't answer in five seconds we're coming in, man… and I really don't want to see you naked."

We wait the five seconds and then Bonny nods at me, so I open the door. I see Brandon's head is leaning back against the edge of the bath; he looks to be asleep. Okay, he's not under the water so if he's blacked out, he hasn't drowned. His swollen eye and cut lip stand out like a beacon on his slack features, but the lump on his forehead has gone down and only a little swelling around the bruise tells of its existence. I think of the photos I took on my phone. As we draw nearer, I notice the colour of the water, reddish-pink? It dawns on me what has happened a moment too late, and as I turn and try to force Bonny out of the bathroom door the expression on her face tells me she has already seen – and neither of us can un-see it now.

There is a gaping slash running vertically along both of Brandon's wrists, and the water has made the wounds pop open to reveal ugly yawing gashes. The glint of the razor blade resting at the bottom of the tub confirms the unthinkable. Bonny screams behind me and runs past me to the bath, trying to drag her son's limp, lifeless body out of the tub. She stumbles under his dead weight and half falls into the bath with him. Water splashes over her and the floor. She keeps screaming his name, "Brandon, baby, it's me, Mummy! Please wake up, baby, pleeeeease!" She sobs into his neck. I feel completely numb with shock… this can't be happening. Bonny's awful pleading screams reach me and the moment passes.

I reach over Bonny and feel Brandon's neck for a pulse; there is nothing. The water is tepid; he has been this way for some time. Pulling out my phone, I calmly call triple zero whilst a war of emotion rages inside of me. I am robotic whilst I tell them the address and answer their questions. They advise me that an ambulance is on the way. They ask if he has a pulse and I answer in the negative. They advise that if I choose to start resuscitation that I must continue with it until the ambulance arrives.

I put the phone on speaker and lay it on the floor before turning to help Bonny drag Brandon from the tub. I verbalise what we're doing for the person on the phone. We settle Brandon on his back on the cold tiled floor and I commence compressing his chest, then breathe into his mouth; trying desperately to bring my friend back. I need to save Bonny from looking at her son in this mess any longer. I advise loudly that I've commenced CPR and, as I continue the compressions, I turn to Bonny. "Bonny, the ambulance is coming, and they need you to go and open the front door for them and stand out on the path. You need to wave when you see the ambulance approaching."

She is hysterical and screams, "I can't leave him, I can't leave my baby!"

It almost breaks my fucking heart. I try to reassure her, all the while pumping on his chest, "I'm here with him and I'm going to stay with him. I'm trying to resuscitate him until they get here, okay? You need to let me try." I'm reasonably sure all his blood has exsanguinated into the bath and there is nothing left to pump into his heart, but I have to try, and I am conscious of the seconds ticking by.

I look up to see Bonny still standing over us and I'm horrified that she is witnessing this. I feel cruel as I yell at her to get out when she is in the depths of her despair, but I need to get her out of here. "Go, Bonny, go! I can hear the siren," I lie to her. Bonny reluctantly backs out of the room. I yell, "Go!" and see her turn and run from the room, slipping on the water and almost falling in her haste.

It is a further five minutes of compressing Brandon's chest and breathing into his dead lungs before the paramedics enter the bathroom. The first paramedic through the door takes one look at the bath and Brandon's wrists, then looks at the other paramedic and gives an almost imperceptible shake of the head, confirming the worst. He kneels beside me and puts a hand on my back. "We'll take over from here, mate."

I am done. I stand and take a shuddering breath, then back out of the room, holding Bonny as she sobs fretful tears. Another moment of hysteria takes her, and she breaks free, running to Brandon as she screams, "My boy, my baby boy!"

I pull her back into my embrace, murmuring soothing words in her ear. I stroke her back in an effort to calm her and to allow the paramedics to tend Brandon. I am completely impotent standing outside this room, watching them working on Brandon's broken body. I sat idly downstairs sipping on coffee and flipping through a magazine while my friend bled to death, alone in the bathtub upstairs. Bonny and I step aside as Brandon is carried from the room on a stretcher. Bonny follows them out; eyes huge with fright. The poor woman still thinks there is hope but I know there is none. Part of me has died in that room with Brandon and I am aware that I will never be the same again.

As the stretcher approaches the front door, George, Brandon's father, bursts through the door, visibly alarmed. "What's happened? There's an ambulance outside," he yells.

Bonny runs into his arms and sobs, "Brandon's gone and hurt himself. He cut himself, George."

George is frightened and looking everywhere. "Is he okay? Where are they taking him?"

The paramedic in the front answers soberly, "We have to take him to hospital."

Both George and Bonny run out of the house after the ambulance, leaving me standing at the door, staring after them.

There is an ache in my heart that is physical, as though someone has reached into my chest and has a hold of my heart… and they're squeezing it. I can't breathe properly, and I know this is shock. I am still staring after the retreating ambulance and I feel a single tear roll off my lashes and down my cheek to sit atop my trembling lips; my body quakes in shock. My mind keeps flashing the image of his slashed wrists and the ghastly gaping wounds, and I am startled by the revelation that his wrists now look on the outside how Brandon felt on the inside.

My best mate is gone; my best mate died alone in a bathtub today and I have to walk in this world without him, forever.

7

Let His Tortured Soul Pass Over

Phoebe

I watch my son straighten; see his resolve restore as he prepares for one of the hardest days of his young life. I feel despair for my beautiful boy. So much to bear and such a load to carry. I know he feels blame and it will take time before he can finally accept that there was nothing he could have done to prevent Brandon from taking his own life. Brandon had felt there was no way out, and in that final moment of clarity he knew exactly what he had to do.

Seth told me what happened on the oval that day, the incident that had given Brandon his moment of clarity. He had been fighting his demons for so many years that I've lost count. As sad and heartbreaking as the news of Brandon's death was to me, unfortunately, it was not a surprise when it happened; it was always going to be when, not if. The incident was reported to the police along with the photos that Seth took after Brandon's beating. The police will follow up, but it is too late for Brandon.

The unspeakable emotional carnage left behind by suicide drives us to label it a selfish act, but I know that Brandon wasn't thinking of how this would affect the people around him who loved and cared for him. Brandon just needed to flee his tortured life; wanted the pain to stop and this was the only way he knew how.

I look at my son and he is so dashingly handsome in his dark-grey pinstripe suit. His eyes are red rimmed; he cannot hide his grief. Not only will he be one of the pall bearers carrying the coffin today, but he will also be reading a passage that he has written for Brandon… his last message to his best mate. There is a light knock on the door outside the room and John pokes his head in to enquire if Seth is ready to leave. I wonder if Seth will ever be ready for this day. He tries to smile bravely at his father but his bottom lip quivers and tears course down his cheeks. The pain on his face strikes a chord in me and he looks like a little boy in a man's suit. He shakes his head at John and his voice breaks as he sobs, "Oh, Dad, I can't do this."

The blood drain from John's face as he struggles with his own emotions in an effort to reassure our son. He pulls him into his embrace and Seth sobs on John's shoulder.

"Yes, you can," John soothes, his voice muffled in Seth's suit jacket. He pulls his face away, looks deep into Seth's eyes and says firmly, "Yes, you can. You can do it because you're doing it for Brandon and you *will* get through it," he confirms. Seth emits a tormented sound of anguish, which has me covering my face and turning away. John continues behind me, "It's going to be hard, mate, and it's okay if you fall apart."

I turn to see Seth take a step back, nodding at his father, his mouth set in a grim line. He brushes angrily at his tears, dashing them away only to have more cascade over the burning rims of his eyes moments later. My poor, darling boy.

"Just take a moment to collect yourself, son. Have you got your passage?" John queries. Seth pats the breast pocket of his suit jacket and nods soberly. As we pass Mercedes' room, I knock lightly and ask if she is ready. Mercedes opens the door. Seeing her father, she lowers her eyes to the carpeted floor and passes him without so much as a greeting. I see John wince, but he follows her down the stairs. This is not the time or the place to address Mercedes. This is our time to farewell Brandon. Seth and I follow, making our way down the stairs to the waiting car that will take us to the chapel, within the cemetery grounds.

We have hired a limousine with a driver, so we can all dedicate our attention to Seth for the drive there and back. He is struggling with his loss and we are doing all we can to support him on this journey. As we approach the cemetery, we are momentarily stationary at a red traffic light. I hear Seth whisper, "Don't turn green." I hear it because I am right beside him, holding his hand and there is only silence in the car. He wants to prolong the inevitable. I am sitting beside him silently wishing the light would hurry up and change to green. I am anxious for Seth and I want to say goodbye to Brandon, so my son can start to heal. Watching him struggle with his grief is awful. I can't wear my Wonder Woman outfit today – my powers are useless here and I can't fix my son. The traffic light changes to green and I hear him draw a shaky breath. I squeeze his hand in mine… it is time.

Seth

The quiet interior of the chapel is solemn. The organ music lends soft, subdued tones and is respectfully quiet. I stare at the casket at the top of the aisle as I approach the front pews. Brandon's framed and smiling photograph sits on his school football guernsey, which lies atop the mahogany box entombing him. I take my seat behind Bonny and George and wait quietly. Bonny's sobs are soundless as she buries her face into George's chest, but I see her back shaking. Tears roll down George's face unchecked; they drip onto Bonny's hair. I can barely arrest my emotions, seeing them in such misery. A wave of guilt bubbles up and I breathe hard to control my grief. Mum can see my struggle because she reaches over and grasps my hand, offering support the only way she knows how. She releases my hand, so I can dab at my nose with a tissue.

The five days leading up to this farewell have been agonising. I find myself unable to stop crying. Imagining my future unfold without Brandon is a thought I can't bear to conjure. All the things I have taken for granted over the years flood me in a list of losses... a list of things I'll never hear, see or do with him again; his laugh, his stupid text messages with no grammar, peppered with emojis, his lame jokes that make me laugh because they're so lame, celebrating his best and fairest wins because he's a gun on the football field, hearing about his dates and his awe of the female form, sharing a box of popcorn at the cinema only to marvel when he stands up because half of it is under his arse, getting pissed and suffering his annoying hangover, getting stoned together whilst ten pin bowling, watching movies, watching with envy his graceful lope as he runs a lap of the oval, seeing the look of torture that the racial taunts set in his eyes, helping him fight his demons or talking him down from suicide. I will never do any of this again because Brandon will never be again. He is gone, and the finality of this thought alone almost brings me to my knees.

The last six years have been centred on how Brandon has coped with being ostracised; a new experience inflicted upon him at high school. In primary school, apart from the odd slur, he had pretty much escaped without incident. He had been popular, well-liked by his fellow students and was usually the first selected during sporting activities. I, by comparison, was quiet, awkward, skinny and nerdy. I was always the last to be chosen.

Starting high school was a whole new ball game that neither of us had been prepared for. I was suddenly thrust into the limelight with the attention of girls and the 'cool' group as I reached puberty, put on weight and finally came into my own on the sports track. Brandon, who had previously been the life of the party, was suddenly deemed 'uncool' and shut out of all the groups. There were so many parties and celebrations that I didn't attend because my best mate was not invited; I would protest with my absence, lying to him that I didn't want to attend their crappy parties anyway. You do what you do for those you love.

I look down at my folded hands and wonder whether Brandon would still have taken his own life if he could see what it has done to his parents, if he could see their pain. Here they sit, enveloped in grief with everybody watching on as they wait to farewell their beloved son; their only child. I sit behind them feeling their pain mingle with my own, with everybody looking over at them and at me. I just want to run from the chapel and find a quiet place to give in to the grief that threatens to consume me, to the tears that will not stop filling my eyes and to scream and yell and vent until my lungs are fit to burst.

Every time I've given in to the emotions over the last few days, I've thought that surely, I will feel better afterwards, but I haven't, and I don't. For hours I've lain still on my bed waiting for the tears to dry and the heaving convulsions in my chest to subside, but the pain will not abate, it continues to ebb and flow in waves until I am reduced to a lifeless nothing inside the shell of my body. I've wondered, during those painful hours, how I will ever feel anything but this pain again. 'Time heals all wounds' is the quote, but I just can't fill the cavernous chasm that has opened up inside me. Time might make the pain more bearable, but the chasm is always going to be there, like a great gaping hole in the centre of my universe. I wonder, at this moment before our final farewell, why he didn't confide in me and let me talk him down that one last time? Or, better still, why couldn't I have run up those stairs and checked on him sooner?

I have to stop this guilt. It is self-indulgent and totally pointless, but, today, I allow myself to wallow in it, feeling culpable for my friend's early demise, even though the voice of reason conveys otherwise.

The minister steps up to the lectern microphone and begins the formal proceedings in a sombre voice. Bonny's sobs become audible as the minister commences his sermon. George pulls her in tighter and strokes her back. Mum takes my hand in hers again, soothingly rubbing her thumb over the back of my knuckles. I draw comfort from the gesture as I dab at my tears with my other hand.

"Family and friends, it is with a heavy heart that we gather here today to farewell Brandon; much-loved son of Bonny and George, grandson to Myra and Stanley, nephew to Vernon, close friend to Seth, and well-loved and respected member of the community."

The sermon is short, followed by two readings from the Bible and the eulogy, read by Uncle Vernon. The lump in my throat swells as the eulogy ends and a slideshow of Brandon starts up to 'The Circle of Life' by Elton John, taken from *The Lion King* soundtrack. *The Lion King* was Brandon's favourite childhood movie. We watched it so many times as children and we still watched it every time it came on television, both of us struggling not to cry when Mufasa dies, even as young men. As the music ends, the Minster quietly calls on me. It's my turn to publicly say goodbye… to have everyone in here stare at me as I swim in the fishbowl. I don't want it to happen, I want to run far, far away as fast as I can… but I have to do this for Brandon, so I pull myself together.

"We would like to welcome Seth to the front now, to say a few words." The minister stands back from the lectern and waits for me to make my way to the front. I steady my breathing as I stand and make my way forward to begin the arduous task of delivering this final message to Brandon, without falling apart before everyone.

I walk up the two steps to stand before the lectern; the paper with my message and poem quivering as my nerves and grief combine to make my limbs shake. I look over the people gathered in the chapel; so many that they are tightly packed into seats, with two rows of people standing behind the pews. I can see the entire football team standing in the back, their dark suits covering most of their football guernseys, only a little peeking from beneath their lapels. All eyes are cast on me and I draw a steadying breath before unfolding my paper and reading my message. My voice sounds robotic and foreign to my ears, like I am on autopilot.

"Brandon and I have been friends since we were about five years old. We met at a playground near our houses and almost came to blows over who got to the horse-on-a-spring ride first. I think I was the one who backed down; Brandon had a huge sense of justice and a fierce temper on him." I pause as a few people chuckle around the room; Brandon was notorious for his temper.

"He eventually finished riding the horse on the giant spring and walked over to me with purpose, asking if I wanted to have a go on the see-saw with him. I was quiet and shy and not very good at making friends so having someone actively seek me out was something I wasn't used to or expecting. I jumped in with both feet. We played in the playground for a couple of hours until our respective parents took us home… and that was that. Christmas came and went, and we didn't see each other again until we started primary school the following January. Brandon was in my class and plonked himself beside me at the table. I asked him his name and he pointed to his name tag saying, 'Derrr'. I felt indignant and told him I couldn't read yet but since he was so smart maybe he could read my name and I pointed to my tag saying, 'Derrr' back at him. He looked down at his lap and sheepishly admitted he couldn't read either." Another chuckle reverberates around the room.

"We became such good friends. We were inseparable, always. Sure, we had our fights, what kids don't? There would be a shove and a grunt and then we'd find ourselves in stitches, laughing at each other. We never went more than a couple of days without talking. I honestly thought we would be mates for the rest of our lives. Well we were, I guess. I didn't expect my best mate to make that choice himself."

My voice breaks and I am mortified as a strangled cry breaks free and I almost whisper, "I miss him so much," but the microphone in front of me carries it all around the chapel and I see so many heads bow as they struggle with their own emotions. I take a deep breath and continue; my voice steady again.

"Every hour of every day, I miss him. I want him back, but he just didn't want to be here. He just couldn't hold them back anymore, so he gave way to his demons and let them take him away." I look at the casket. "I wish… I wish so much that things were different, Brandon, and that we had been enough to help you fight those demons." I am breathing hard with emotion and I feel a tear slide down my cheek to plop onto the folded piece of paper in my shaking hands. "But we weren't enough and now you're gone. You will never grow old; you will never even know what it is to be twenty-one. You will remain for all eternity just eighteen years old… forever young." I am whispering again, barely audible as my lips quiver and my voice betrays me.

I pause to recoup some of my equilibrium, gulping air and balling my hands into fists. I look up to see Bonny and George staring straight at me, into my eyes. Their tears have ceased momentarily as they listen to my words. For them, I continue, "I have written a poem for Brandon." I unfold the paper, flattening it out on the lectern with my hands, taking the time to find my calm. The words on the paper have blurred where the fallen tear soaked through, obscuring part of the poem. It doesn't matter… I know it from memory because it is written in my heart.

"Through years of mateship shared,
our lives, our hopes, our dreams,
we laughed, we joked, we just hung out,
spent hours sharing memes.

Then in high school; it all changed,
the demons came to play,
we talked it through, we fought them off;
you lived another day.

There came a fateful moment,
forever etched in mine,
the hill too steep, the feat too great;
you found your end of time.

I wish I could have saved you,
been enough to change things,
but I wasn't, and I couldn't;
you got your Angel wings.

You're gone and I am lost,
and there's this pain that will not cease,
I hope wherever are, that you're smiling,
and finally at peace."

Silence fills the room and I feel the minister place his hand on my shoulder. As I step back a pace he returns to the microphone. "Let us have a minute's silence in respect for Brandon."

In the silence that follows, Bonny's sobs echo around the small chapel. I glimpse Mum look up at me as I bow my head, clasp my hands in front of me and feel my shoulders shaking as I silently try to contain my grief. After the minute ends, the minister continues, "It's time to say farewell to Brandon."

I take a step towards the casket and gently place a hand on top. "Goodbye, mate," I whisper, only to him. The minister removes the photo and hands it to Bonny to hold as the congregation stands to walk respectfully behind the casket. I walk to the front and take hold of a handle, and five members of Brandon's football team join me to wheel the casket to the waiting hearse. Bonny and George walk behind us, and, as the congregation shuffles to join the throng, I hear both of them sobbing.

After the door to the hearse closes with Brandon inside, the minister stands at the rear of the car and addresses the waiting group, "Now we will proceed to the gravesite. It is not far from the chapel, so we will walk behind the hearse."

Mum slips her hand in mine as we walk behind Bonny and George's hunched forms. Mercy takes my other hand and I take comfort in their gestures. Bonny's sobs have reduced to hiccupping gulps as she struggles to keep her grief in check. At the gravesite, I am again called on to carry the casket to the burial site. We stand waiting for the minister to direct us to the green strips upon which the casket will sit, suspended, as the last prayers are shared before Brandon is lowered into his final resting place.

I look down into the dark abyss with its broken, rough edges of dirt and try not to think about the worms and other bugs that will consume my friend. I wonder how cold it will be down there, deep in the earth. A shudder moves through me, which has Mum looking deep into my eyes with a questioning look. I nod, to reassure her. The casket is heavy, and my arms start to shake a little as we wait for direction to place the casket down. Finally, we get the nod and we all step forward to place the casket as gently as we're able down onto the green hammock.

It feels like an eternity passes before the minister completes his last words, followed by the Lord's Prayer. The motor whirs and the casket is gently lowered into the blackness. Bonny takes a deep breath as she is handed a white rose.

I hear her agonising voice say, "Goodbye my baby boy. I'll see you when I get there. Save a dance for me." She leans down to release the rose. I imagine it will float down and fall soundlessly onto the casket, but it doesn't. As she opens her hand over the yawning grave, the rose drops like lead, rocketing down the few feet to land on the casket with an unexpectedly loud *thunk*, which startles me and makes half the group around me jump. George takes a rose and gently tosses it onto the casket, and even through I'm expecting it this time, the sound is still loud enough to make me clench. Next, I'm handed a rose and I hold it to my chest for a moment before tossing it in.

An unseasonably warm wind blows against us and the sun sits high in the cloudless sky above. It beats down, turning our faces and necks red, belying the sadness of this day. A thunderstorm would more befit this moment rather than this joyous autumn day.

The minister advises that refreshments are being served back at the chapel now. As the group moves towards the chapel, Bonny's wretched sobs slowly grow quieter as she walks away, while I stay a little longer. I look around to ensure that I'm alone with him. I look down into the darkness at the casket far below. I reach into my breast pocket and take out my written poem; the teardrop stain making the ink a beautiful kaleidoscope of blue and purple. I wonder what Brandon would call the colour. Blurple? Or plue? He'd go with blurple because it sounds funny and he'd say it in a stupid voice, too. I chuckle at Brandon's colour choice; the colour I imagine he would choose because I will never know. I can't ask him. He's gone. Shit! I take a deep breath and kiss the folded note, dropping it into the hole and hear it gently thud against the wood.

"I'll see you later, mate," I whisper, then turn to walk back to the chapel.

8
Hot Café Guy

Phoebe
Sitting across the table from Chelsea, in a café just a block away from my workplace, I am listening with rapt attention as she animatedly relays where, on the scale of cuteness, the hot café guy falls, and how he came to ask her out.

"So, I'm sitting there sipping my chai latte s-l-o-w-l-y so I can maximise the time I get to look at his cute butt, when he wanders over and starts chatting with me. I just happened to be wearing my *Doctor Who* tee..."

This peaks my interest because I love *Doctor Who*. "Ooh, which one? The one with the daleks or the tenth doctor?"

She frowns at me. "Tenth, of course. Anyway, he asks if I'm a fan and looks straight at my boobs. I was momentarily taken aback until I realised, he was looking pointedly at the doctor, not my boobs. 'Absolute Whovian!' I say, and he tells me his favourite is the fourth because he used to watch it as a little kid. Then, Rachel, the café owner, calls out that he can take his break now, and he looks at me and says, 'Mind if I join you?' Oh my God! My stomach flip-flopped, and it was all I could do not to pant 'yes please' at him. He sat down opposite me and we spent his entire half-hour break talking about *Doctor Who*, because we're both geeks."

I feel a rush of excitement for Chelsea. Finally, a guy she can relate to. She's been withering in a drought of men for so long that I can't remember the last time she got some action. Chelsea continues, retelling the incident, so I pull myself back to the now to listen raptly; her joy etched all over her sweetheart-shaped face.

"Then he asks me out on a date!"

"Yes!" I lean over and high-five her, oblivious to the stares of other patrons.

She bounces up and down in her seat. "Holy crap! I'm so excited… and nervous. I *really* like him, Pheebs. He's hot and cute and big and manly and my loins are quivering at the very thought of some attention."

I almost lose my eyebrows in my hairline because she has no filter in today and is as crass as ever. "Jesus, Chels, calm yourself, woman!"

"Sorry, I'm a little nervous."

She regains her composure and continues in a monitored tone, "I've made an appointment at the hairdressers, so my hair can look fabulous." She swishes her long blonde locks like she's in a shampoo commercial. "I'm heading there in about half an hour."

"Where are you going on your date?"

We are interrupted by Chelsea's tics. When the series finishes, she continues, "Oh, we're off to Rocky's Bar & Grill. We're just having a casual dinner."

I don't have to dance around Chelsea, so I ask the unmentionable, "Are you worried about the tics?"

Her Tourette's was nowhere near this debilitating until she was in her early twenties, when they became severe. Sometimes her Tourette's lies quiet for months at a time, but it always returns. The syndrome is uncontrollable, but the tics occur more often when she is stressed. She can feel them coming and suppress them for a few minutes until she's in a position to 'release' them, as she calls it. Going on a date never ends well for her as getting to a bathroom to de-stress or release the tics is not often easy.

I am reminded of one particular occasion when she turned up on my doorstep afterwards, inconsolable. She was totally besotted with a guy she'd met at the cinema, of all places. The tics had been quiet for a while and she'd managed to go tic-free for the previous two dates, and was looking forward to the end of the evening with this particular chap. She relayed, sobbing on my shoulder, that most of the evening had gone smoothly. After their meal at a local restaurant, she had asked him in for a little nightcap and they had ended up in bed. As she was nearing her climax, she felt the tics start up. He was completely unaware that she suffered from Tourette's and mistook her grunts as pleasure.

As he was thrusting with fervour, he took a blow to the throat as her fist tried to beat her chest. He was still processing that when she kneed him in the groin with her leg. He rolled off of her in agony while her tics kept progressing. Her state of distress had her repeating "whoooooooooooooosh" multiple times, and the more she tried to control them, the higher her pitch soared. The last few sounded like a fire engine wailing, so she had said. Then, because she was in a state of distress, the whole lot started up all over again and she was helpless to stop them. By this stage, the poor man was hurriedly yanking his pants on. Before he took his leave, he turned to look at her, gyrating on the bed in the throes of the tic set, and yelled at her in voice pitched high with anxiety, "What the fuck is wrong with you?"

She managed to utter, "T-t-t-Tourette's" between ticing fits, but the words were lost on him as he made his hasty exit. Chelsea *really* liked him, and she was hoping she could get him to like her enough to be able to handle the Tourette's when it surfaced, but it seemed she wasn't meant to have that man. He just made her feel weird, like the rest of them. She was low for a long time after that and it has taken years for her to gain enough confidence to accept a date. I'm beyond happy for her. I refocus on her as she answers my question.

"Ah, now that's the thing, he already knows about them. I've had a few in the café already and during a big one last week I could see him looking at me then mumbling to Rachel. I assumed he was thinking I was a freak, but I think he was asking her what the hell I was doing over here. Rachel would have just explained that I have Tourette's. He still asked me out, Pheebs, knowing I'm a freak!"

I get angry when she does this, so I bark at her in angry tone, "Hey, you are *not* a freak and I don't like it when you say that!"

She gets defensive and retorts, "Well, surely it's okay if I'm labelling myself?"

I change my tone; 'angry' is patronising and pisses Chelsea off. "You're not a freak, Chels, and I'm excited for you. I want a full report tomorrow please. Except for the sex… actually, tell me about the sex too. I want to hear it *all*!" Chelsea giggles like a delighted child.

"When he first started at the café, he was so shy. Like, he'd barely make eye contact with me when I placed my order. Then, as I continued to come in and get the same thing every day, sometimes with, sometimes without the muffin, he started looking at me and he'd blush, and I was like wow, he's nervous, that's soooo cute. Then he started looking directly into my eyes and he'd say, 'soy chai?' I'd say, 'Yep' and he'd say, 'muffin?'" Chelsea waggles her eyebrows.

"Ew!" I say as I pull a disgusted face. Chelsea revels in my discomfort.

"Ha! Look at your face." She points at me like I can actually see my own face without a mirror, so I give her a withering look. She continues with her diatribe. "He'd just bring it over when it was made and place it in front of me. He was all polite and shy and cute as hell. Then last Thursday, something changed. He started mentioning the weather, like I give a shit, but hey, when a cute guy starts talking about the weather, you suddenly get all interested. Hell, he could have started a conversation about the rate of hair growth of a yak's right nut and I'd be showing interest."

This makes me laugh. She steeples her fingers under her chin and looks heaven-ward. "Oh, *please* be an animal in the sack," she prays.

"What's his name?"

"Gavin."

I went to school with a Gavin so now I'm picturing his face. I change the direction of the conversation, so I can get school Gavin out of my head. "What are you going to wear?"

She pops up in her seat like a meerkat, suddenly excited about the topic. "I'm thinking those white jeans, they hug my arse and make me look like I actually have one, and maybe my electric-blue silky top. What do you think?"

I feel my top lip curl up. "You shit me," I counter, "I'm trying desperately to minimise my curves and you're wearing clothes to give you some. Hardly seems fair."

Chelsea guffaws. "Don't be so hard on yourself. You've lost a stack of weight since you discovered John's little 'hide the sausage' secret."

I groan and visibly shrink in my seat. Chelsea looks at her watch. "I'd better get going before I miss my appointment."

"Remember," I warn, "I want a full report …and don't leave *anything* out."

She stops at the door and runs back up to the table. "Oh my God, I meant to ask how Seth is. I got so caught up in myself and my date, I'm sorry."

"Don't be sorry, it's an exciting time for you. Look, Seth is not in a great place but he's managing. He's seeing a grief counsellor to make sure he stays on top of it all."

She is satisfied with my answer. "Well, give him a hug from Aunty Chelsea."

"Will do!" I call after her.

* * * * *

Walking back to the office, I feel a light drizzle misting down on me. Great, my hair will look like a frizz ball when it dries. All the time I spent grooming the fuzz with a hair straightener this morning was all for naught. Curse this Melbourne weather! James is sure to bring out some afro references when he sees it. I hope Chelsea has an umbrella as I want her fabulous locks to hold until she has dinner with cute Gavin.

I feel good, maybe even a little happy; a feeling that has been missing since John's indiscretion and all that has occurred in its wake. I don't want to read too much into my elation. I will take it for what it is. Baby steps, I remind myself, I need to take baby steps as I progress forward. If only for a few minutes, I feel like I can manage and that is a magnificent thing.

9

Existing In The Void

Seth

It's been two weeks since we buried Brandon, and I think I'm slowly going through the different phases of grief. I can't remember them all, but I know that sadness has been with me for the entire journey. It takes an age to fall asleep each night, but when I do it's a wonderful and blissful escape. When the alarm wakes me in the morning, for a few magical moments all is right with my world… then I remember, and the dull ache in the pit of my stomach throbs and my world skews on its axis again. I'm supposed to be writing but I can't make myself do it. I'm not ready and more than a little frightened of what will come out onto the paper. The mind is a strange place and sometimes when I write, I'm surprised by what comes out of the vault inside my head. I'm the king of hiding behind my smile. The guilt has come to play again. I try to rationally push it from my mind.

Mum and Dad have insisted I see a grief counsellor. They both offered to come with me, but I don't want that. I need to do this alone, so I don't have to edit my answers. Sometimes I don't want to go because he makes me confront feelings that I want to leave buried. It's easier to cope when you build a wall and hide behind it, but, unfortunately, my 'emotional bucket' is full to overflowing so if I don't empty some of it out, it will start to dribble out of its own accord. My counsellor's name is Alan. He is quiet and speaks little. At the beginning he spoke of himself, a lot, which I thought a little odd until it dawned on me that he was trying to share some of himself to make me feel comfortable enough to share some of myself. That's clever, of course, I will feel better talking to him if I feel like I know him.

It took me a while to open up. It feels weird and foreign to be talking about my feelings and it took me time to let go. Then, sometime in the fourth session, I pulled the walls down and now I can't shut up. I panic sometimes when I look at the clock and see we've gone over, and I try to finish the session up, but Alan says I've paid for an hour's session and if it goes over that hour, I'm not to concern myself, and that he will decide when it's over.

So now I try to surreptitiously glance at the clock because sometimes the session is painful, and I just want it over. Instead of going on about the time, I just tell him I don't want to talk about that anymore and he lets me move on.

Sometimes I cry, sometimes I speak through clenched teeth because I'm angry that Brandon took his own life, sometimes I laugh when I recall some of the antics we got up to, and sometimes I feel numb. Alan is more verbal during the happy talks, contributing to the conversation, but when I cry or get angry, he asks pointed questions and guides me through it. He says it's okay to feel angry but that I shouldn't let the emotion consume me. Anger is the new emotion that has come to play.

The last session was hateful, and I was embarrassed by what came out of my mouth but trying to keep a lid on it is proving harder than I'd anticipated. I'm angry at my best mate for depriving himself of a future with him, I'm angry that I've been robbed of a lifelong friendship that I feel I deserved, angry that after all the times I managed to talk Brandon down from breaking point, that he cheated me out of helping him this one time. Brandon had known that it would be either his mum or me that would find his lifeless body, yet he did it anyway.

Now, every time I close my eyes, I see my dead mate. I see the ugly slashes across his wrists, the awful pink of the bath water that he bled into, the razorblade winking in the fluorescent light, resting on the bottom of the bath. I feel the coldness of his lips and chest as I tried fruitlessly to bring him back with CPR, and I see the slack look of death on his unresponsive face. I can't stop seeing that.

Alan explained that during these episodes of helplessness, the victim ceases to think of anyone or anything except escaping and stopping the pain. He had crossed the point of no return and just wanted out. That doesn't really make me feel any better. I remember he had repeatedly said to me on that oval as he dripped blood all over the grass, "It's never going to stop, is it?"

My jaw clenches when I think of the arseholes who made him feel this much desperation. The bell sounds and startles me out of my reverie. It is the end of third period and I have just spent an hour in the library completing homework. As I cross the courtyard, perusing my timetable, I look up to see Matt Jeffries walking towards me, laughing and joking with his friends. He has managed to avoid me around the school because he feels guilty, I presume. His usually smart mouth has been annoyingly silent. The ire in me rears up and I can't help it. I walk straight up to him and smash his books out of his hands with the back of mine. I throw my own down violently and shove Matt in the chest. "Why don't you fight *me*, arsehole?" I goad him. Matt holds up his hands in supplication and shakes his head, backing up a little. "No, man, I don't want to fight you."

I can't stop it; the rage is uncontrollable. "Why is that, Matt? Is it because I'm *white*? Well guess what, arsehole; you *are* going to fight me today."

Matt is defensive, still walking backwards, and I see so much regret in his face, but I am indignant and too angry to allow it to make a difference. His friends back away; they can see murder in my eyes. He is stuttering in panic as he walks backwards. "Look, I'm sorry about Brandon. We were just doing it for a laugh, you know? We didn't think he'd go home and… and kill himself, man."

That's it; I lose my shit. "Doing it for a *laugh*? You were *relentless*! You were *always* pushing him around. What do you think happens when you just don't let up on somebody?"

Breathing hard, I lose control and I know how I feel is irrational, but I feel powerless to rein it in. I hear Matt hiccup and his voice brakes as he cries, "I'm sorry, man. I wish I could go back and change things, but I can't. I've got to live with his death for the rest of my life."

I do not want to feel sorry for Matt. I funnel my anger to sit atop the pity and the rage takes over as I scream, "Hey *fuck you*!" with so much volume that the entire basketball court full of student's silences and turns to watch in awe. I can feel their eyes boring into me, but I don't care, this is my moment to avenge my friend and right now I think that vengeance will be mine. I feel a cackle bubble up in me. This should be an indicator that I have become totally deranged, but it's too late to put a lid on it.

I launch myself at Matt, shoving him to the ground. I straddle him and start raining punches onto his face. I'm not a fighter and I've never hit anyone before, so I'm surprised to feel like I'm punching a wall. The bones are hard, but it is satisfying so I just keep punching… I can't stop. It is a surreal moment and time is suspended.

Hands grab me under my armpits from behind and pull me off. I am trying to yank myself free of whoever has pulled me off of him; I'm not finished pummelling my fists into that face yet. I hear a man's voice yell in my ear, "Knock it off, Seth" and recognise Mr Roberts, my science teacher. "You wanted to draw blood? Well you drew blood, now calm down! Look at what you've done to Matt's face and your hands," he yells, his face an unnatural shade of dark red.

Matt's face is a bloody mess and blood is pouring from his nose and his split lip. One of his eyes is beginning to swell and the soft flesh over the rim of his eye socket has split and is oozing blood. Jesus, I can't believe I did that to another human. I am caught between screaming and crying. My chest is heaving with emotion and my knuckles are beginning to throb and burn. I look down at them and see that on two of my knuckles the flesh is almost shredded. That must be where I connected with Matt's teeth. Mr Roberts frogmarches me to Principal Scott's office and shoves me none too gently into the seat outside. He knocks firmly on the door and enters. I look down the hall and see Miss Eider assisting Matt into the sickbay area. No doubt his parents will be called, and Matt will need to attend hospital. I can hear Mr Roberts and Principal Scott discussing the incident; then I am called inside.

Principal Scott's mouth is a thin line, his expression clearly displaying disappointment. "Seth, what on earth is this all about? This is not like you, not like you at *all*."

I am silent. Principal Scott continues, "I know you've been through a lot with Brandon's passing, but randomly punching students is not how we deal with things here."

I glare coldly at the Principal and snarl, "Did you know that Matt and his little gang of weirdos bullied Brandon *all the time*? They even *cyber*-bullied him. That day, the day Brandon topped himself, Matt and his mates shoved and taunted him in the park where he was running. I was there, I *saw* it! Matt and his gang are *responsible* for Brandon's death! I'm a *little pissed off, Sir*!"

I cannot believe these rude and disrespectful words have come out of my mouth but if Principal Scott is shocked by my outspoken rudeness, it doesn't show on his face. He looks understanding and sympathetic. "Seth, I have only recently been made aware of these incidents in the wake of Brandon's death, and we are looking into it. We have started the process with the police, Matt's parents and Brandon's parents, even though they don't wish to press charges. Hitting another student is not how we deal with these kinds of incidents at school. There is a process in place for bullying and strict guidelines need to be adhered to."

He sighs, "Seth, I'm sorry about Brandon, I really am. He was a talented young man and I am very saddened by his passing, but you need to find a way to deal with your anger. You know Matt can press charges, don't you? You assaulted him before an audience of fifty or more students."

I look down at my hands. I feel no remorse and that shocks me. This hatred in my heart is foreign to me. I wanted to make sure Matt felt the weight of responsibility for Brandon's death, as he should, but I wonder if he will ever really know what he's done. He may not have actually pulled the trigger, metaphorically speaking, but he most certainly put the gun in Brandon's hand. Bonny wants me to let it go, to forgive Matt like she has, but I just can't move on, not yet. Every time I see the little bastard's face, I just want to smash it in. My anger is alarming.

* * * * *

I arrive at the counselling session with Alan in the afternoon. When he sees my bandaged knuckles, he asks if I want to talk about it. I shake my head in the negative, so he lets it slide. We shift topics and stay in a safe place for a while, but he keeps looking at my knuckles and I'm forced to talk about it. I tell him what happened and how good it felt smashing Matt's face. Alan is calm and doesn't look disgusted or horrified by my actions. He has his 'psychologist' mask on.

He benignly looks at me and asks if I attend a gym. I tell him I do, and he advises that I should take up boxercise or boxing lessons. He talks about the positive effect of endorphins after exercise and adds that boxing will benefit my need to pound and punch. I tell him I'll look into it. I shelve it for now; I'm not interested in talking about it anymore. I'm feeling surly and disjointed and Alan sees this because he changes topic again and asks about the mood in the household. He knows about Dad because that's one of the first things that came up, so we stay on safe ground and I tell him we're mostly okay, but Mercedes is behaving like a spoiled brat. He tells me she will come around in her own time and that everybody handles shock and change, especially the big one that has resulted in Dad's news, differently, and I should cut her some slack. I want to vent at him but recognise that I'm in a shitty mood, so I shut up and nod at him, plastering a pleasant smile on my face to hide behind.

I look down at my hands now. My knuckles will be an array of healing scabs and bruises over the next few days. I'm dreading having the conversation with Mum and Dad. I think I might go home and write. I'm ready to write but I know I will write with anger. I'll try to get some of that onto the paper and read it back to myself because I need to get it out of my head.

* * * * *

When I get home, I go straight up to my room and start to write. I am writing furiously when the lead in my pencil snaps and tears a rent in the paper. I am a little frightened by my inability to quash these angry thoughts that just keep floating through my head. This is not who I am, and it is not how I behave. I am becoming a thug. I am turning into Matt Jeffries.

I remove my phone from my pocket and scroll through my contacts until I find the gym. I make an appointment to meet with a personal trainer. I am going to listen to Alan and take up boxing. Tonight I will talk to mum and dad and explain my hands. They need to know.

Mercedes
Pulling away from our kiss, I look deeply into Josh's eyes. My heart is beating like crazy in my chest. I look at the little hollow below his Adam's apple and see his erratic pulse; he is feeling it too. He slides his warm hand up my top and inside my bra, running his thumb over my nipple. I'm embarrassed as I feel it harden under his thumb. Despite the embarrassment, I like how it feels when he touches me there.

We are lying in the park under the big old liquid amber tree on a bed of brightly coloured autumn leaves. There is nobody in sight; we are completely alone. I am lying half across Josh's chest, controlling the kiss, but Josh rolls me over and lies on top of me, kissing me hard and deep. Something is digging painfully into my hip bone. I pull away to speak. "I think your phone is digging into my hip." But as I slide my hand between us, I feel the object causing me grief is actually Josh's erection. I'm mortified, and I yank my hand out

Josh reddens. "I can't help it, I'm really turned on."

I am flitting between feeling flattered and horrified at this frank admission. I decide to cover his embarrassment because he can't hide his arousal, so I reach up and grab his face with both of my hands, pulling him back down to me again. Wiggling my hips, I slide under him, so his hardness is pressing into the soft part of my belly rather than my hip. Josh takes the gesture as a green light for… something, so he launches into another kiss that has me seeing stars.

My phone pings as a message arrives. I pull away from Josh to look at my phone. It's Monique asking when I am coming over to see her, rather than her brother. I groan and roll my eyes. Taking in my eye roll, Josh queries, "What's up?"

I sigh. "Oh, it's nothing. Monique is just getting bitchy with me because I come over to see you and not her. She keeps saying she's lost her best friend to her brother. I can't help it; I want to be with you."

Josh rolls off me and onto his back. He runs a hand through his hair in frustration. "Why is she being so needy? Is she normally like that? She needs to get herself a boyfriend… or a real problem." He flaps a hand at me. "Don't worry about it."

It's not that easy, I think. Josh doesn't understand how girls are and ignoring the situation certainly won't help it. Sometimes I'm jealous of how easily boys handle their annoying mates.

"Well, I have to worry about it because when we're at school everyone in the group is pissy with me, and they make snide remarks about how when *they* get a boyfriend, they'll still remember their friends." I look pointedly at him. "When are you out next?"

Josh looks confused. "Tomorrow night… footy training. Why?"

I look up at my fractured view of the beautiful cloudless sky; the dappled light streams through the remaining leaves and gnarly bare branches of the giant tree we're lying under. I love this park and I love being in it with Josh, but bloody Monique is ruining it.

"I'll call over tomorrow night after school and spend some time with her, maybe try to get back into her good books. I'm sick of the comments and the cold shoulder. If I choose a night you're there, she'll think I came to see you, so if you're not there that should make her happy."

I sit up and type a text message to that effect to Monique, only to have her respond, lightning fast with:

What? When Josh is busy you've got time for me? No thanks, Mercedes, I don't play second fiddle to anyone. Don't bother. Sit with someone else tomorrow, we don't want to be your 'part-time friends' anymore!

I read the text and sigh. Girls are so much hard work. "Great, now none of them are talking to me."

Josh looks at me sympathetically. He stands and reaches out a hand to pull me up. "Come on, we'll go to my house and see if we can smooth things over."

I beam up at him. He is the best boyfriend in the world. We walk the short distance from the park hand in hand and neither of us unclasps to wipe away the sweat. When we arrive at Josh's house, it's empty. There will be no smooth-over conversation today. Josh pulls me with him to his bedroom. We lie on the bed, kissing and fondling, when Josh pulls away, breathing heavily. I'm alarmed because I have zero experience. "What's wrong?"

"I have to stop, Mercedes, I'm getting way too turned on so…"

He lets his voice trail away as he looks at me. I feel brazen as I state matter-of-factly, "Well then, let's have sex."

"What?" Josh's face whips around and stares at me in shock. He's not sure if he heard me correctly. He ventures, "Did you just say, 'let's have sex'?"

I feel my bravado desert me and the fear trickles in. I mutely nod.

Josh turns his back to me and I watch his back muscles move as he runs a hand through his hair.

"I don't know, Mercy. We're both virgins. I've never done it before and I don't even know how I'm supposed to do it." He turns and looks at me sheepishly. "Well, I know what to do but I don't know how to make you happy. It's supposed to hurt girls the first time."

I am brave all over again. "I want you to be my first. I'm almost sixteen, Josh, and I'm sure it will only hurt a tiny bit."

A look of disappointment crosses Josh's face and I see his shoulders sag. "I don't have a condom."

I imagine a light bulb lighting up with a 'ping' above my head. "That's okay, my period is due next week so we'll be fine. I'm pretty sure I can't get pregnant at this stage of my cycle. I remember reading it somewhere on the internet. My cycle is like clockwork, right down to the hour."

Josh leans over me, kissing me gently on the mouth. He looks suddenly nervous. "Are you sure about this? Please don't do this if you're not ready. I don't want you to feel like you have to do this. If you're not ready, I can wait, as long as you want me to, okay?"

I have made up my mind and there's no going back now. "I'm sure, Josh."

I want to please him, so I reach up and loop my arms around his neck, pulling him down to me. We kiss enthusiastically until we're both panting. I reach down and unfasten my jeans, pulling them down and then kicking them off my feet. Josh stands and begins unbuttoning his own jeans. I am so nervous that I feel myself shake a little. He looks down at me lying on the bed in my underpants, and he looks like he wants to dive on top of me. He pulls both his jeans and his trunks down and stands before me with an enormous erection against his belly. I feel shy, and, as I peek at his genitals, I have to stifle the giggle that bubbles inside me. Nerves always make me giggle. I look at the size of his erection and feel terror as I wonder how in God's name that giant thing is going to fit inside me.

Josh reaches down, loops his fingers through the band of my knickers and gently slides them down my legs before dropping them on the floor. The cool air swirls around me and I feel immediately embarrassed by the giant thatch of pubic hair on display. I wonder if I look normal or if I'm particularly woolly. Perhaps I should start shaping my bikini line...or removing it altogether. My face heats up with embarrassment. The bed dips as Josh lies down beside me, sliding his hands inside my top to gently massage my breasts while he kisses me into a pant again. I feel reckless as he rolls on top of me, gently pressing his erection against my pubic hair. I am breathing hard, but I think it is more from fear than desire.

Josh looks at me intently and whispers, "Are you sure, Mercy?"

He needs reassurance because he's nervous too. I nod, not daring to speak because I am sure my voice will shake. He hovers over me and uses his knee to gently nudge my knees apart. I don't know what the hell I'm supposed to do so I just try to remain calm and hope he knows what he's doing. The head of his erection nudge my resisting flesh and it goes nowhere. I don't know how to allow him in.

Josh rolls to the side, opens the drawer in the bedside table and removes a small bottle of lubricant. Kneeling up, he puts a small amount in the palm of his hand and massages it over his erection. I feel embarrassed, but I can't tear my eyes away. My face tightens as I imagine him using the lubricant to masturbate, and I want to squeak and hide under the covers.

Hovering over me again, the pressure of his erect penis is strong but as it nudges me again, this time the tip of it goes inside a little. Josh pushes a little harder and manages to get a little way in before I tighten my knees at his hips. The burn is tremendous... it really, *really* hurts. Josh tries to apply more pressure to get further in and tears start to roll down my cheeks. Josh stops pushing, he looks alarmed. "Hey, you want me to stop? It's really tight and if it's hurting that bad, I'll stop. I don't want to hurt you."

I choke out a sob. "No, I am going to try to relax and then when I say 'Go', I want you to push as hard as you can and just get the worst of it over with. Please?" I am sure that after the first time it will start to get better.

Josh looks at me, unsure. I nod at him to let him know its okay.

"Okay," he breathes. He has all his weight on his arms, hovering and waiting for me to relax. I close my eyes, slowly counting backwards from five.

When I get to one, I open my eyes and gasp, "Go!"

Josh pushes hard into my unyielding flesh. It feels so incredibly tight and I am sure that it is tight around him. I wonder if it is hurting him too. Finally, something gives and he slides into me, right up to the top of his shaft. It hurts more than I could have imagined, and I give an involuntary yelp. Josh stills. I look at him, the pain is probably etched on my face, but I want it over.

"Keep going, I want the first one to be over," I hiss at him.

Josh thrusts out and into me and, annoyingly, I keep gasping. Josh looks like he's in agony, so I ask if he's okay. "It's hard to maintain an erection when my girlfriend has her eyes screwed shut, and tears are running down her face."

"I'm sorry," I sob.

But Josh shakes his head. "I don't want to hurt you, but I can't help it."

Closing his eyes, Josh thrusts back and forth. I see something change in his face. He starts to look sleepy as he whispers in my ear, "I'm going to come."

Thank God. He thrusts into me one last time then stills as, I assume, he empties inside me. I watch his face flit between pleasure and pain and wonder what he is feeling. The pulse at his throat is erratic. He looks down at me. "Are you okay?"

I nod, glad the horrible ordeal is over. As he pulls out of me, I hiss through my teeth, but I have to admit it isn't as bad as it was at the beginning. It feels weirdly rubbery down there and the burn has gone.

I catch a whiff of something raw and weird smelling and I don't like it. I wrinkle my nose as I deduct that I am smelling semen. Josh reaches under his bed for a box of tissues and, again, my face burns. He hands me a couple of tissues and goes about cleaning himself. I wipe myself as best I can without soap and water. It feels slimy, like egg whites. Gross. I see that the semen on the tissue is pink as it's mixed with my blood. I stand to get dressed. I look down and see blood on the sheets. I gasp, horrified that I have made a tell-tale mess. "Josh, there's blood."

"That's okay, we all have to wash our own sheets in this house. I'll change them later. Want to go into the kitchen and have a coffee?"

All I want to do is go home and have a bath and wash the stinky stuff off of me. Josh sprays the room with deodorant. He can smell it too. "No, I think I'm going to go home."

I feel awkward. Josh grabs my house keys and leads me from the house.

"I'll walk you home, then." He walks me right up to the front door where he kisses me gently. I return the kiss and hug him hard to my body.

"Are you okay?" he whispers in my ear. He is worried that he hurt me. I nod. I can't articulate my feelings. I'm teary and unstable and I don't want Josh to see me break down. I wonder if this is premenstrual hormones or the emotions of losing my virginity.

"Can I come over on Thursday to see you?"

"I'd love that. Thank you for being so gentle."

"I'm really sorry it had to hurt."

"It's okay." I turn and enter the house. I feel both grownup and young all at once. My emotions are all over the place, so I decide I will run a bath and have a soak and a think.

10

When Opportunity Knocks

Phoebe

I am sure my frustration is evident to everyone around me as I slam my clenched fist down hard on the desk. My computer has completely shut itself down in the middle of a lengthy letter… again. Since the issue began last week, I've been compulsively saving my documents every few minutes, lest I lose my work when the computer decides to shit itself. Now I am silently congratulating myself for my paranoid actions when I sense a presence behind me. I turn to look over my shoulder and squeak out a startled cry when I see James beside me. He is wearing an expression of concern. "Have you actually spoken to IT about this?"

I frown up at him. "Do you honestly think I'd be putting up with this piece of shit,"—I gesture with my chin at the dark computer screen in front of me— "without alerting the propeller heads about it?"

James raises his eyebrows at my derogatory description of the IT staff. I continue with my frustrated rant, "Rafael came to look at it on Friday afternoon and said he needed to replace the whole thing. I could have told him it was a worthless piece of shit, but he insisted on pulling the casing off the hard drive and seeing for himself. He called this morning to say he'd ordered a new one, that it has arrived, and he will install it after 12pm today. In the meantime, I've been trying to finish this letter to accompany the Buchanan report."

"I assume you saved your work on the network, right?"

It takes effort not to retort with a pissy tone, "Of course, why?"

"I have to go into the boardroom to join the directors' meeting, so you can use my PC, which I know works perfectly fine, without having to pull your hair out in the process. Just give me five minutes to finish an email then it's all yours for about half an hour or so."

I'm elated with this news and I'm sure it is written all over my face. I just want to finish this letter, so I can go and eat. "Great, I'll pop in and finish the letter in five minutes. Then I might go out and grab a bite to eat for lunch, if that works for you?" On cue, my stomach rumbles conspiratorially, loud enough for James to hear.

James grins and nods. "No probs." As he disappears into his office, I get on my hands and knees and crawl under the desk. Locating the cords, I unplug the dying dinosaur that is my computer and lay the cables on my desk, ready for the IT technician. Afterwards, I enter James' office. He stands and reaches for his notebook and a pen, then brushes past me with a cheery wave as he makes his way to the boardroom.

It takes a grand total of about ten minutes to finish the letter and print it. Quickly binding the report, I place the newly typed letter on top for James to sign and leave it in the middle of his desk. I swing by my desk to retrieve my handbag and make my way out of the office for half an hour of solitude while I eat my lunch.

The sun is warm and welcome as I exit the office. My desk is not near a window, so I am almost always surprised by the weather. I turn my face up to the sun and enjoy a moment of warmth before making my way to the corner café for a sandwich. The thought of queuing and jostling with indecisive crowds at the food court, then having to find a space in the grassed area to eat, feels too hard today. I choose the café with its open windows and quiet corners. I find it more appealing and begin to salivate as I approach the entrance. To my dismay, the café is already crowded but I spy a single seat in a breezy corner, which draws me in like a moth to a flame. Gustav, behind the counter, waves at me as I sink into the seat with a sigh.

"Ham and salad on rye?" he calls across the busy room. I smile and give him a thumbs-up gesture. The sandwich arrives minutes later and is everything it promises to be. I groan in satisfaction and munch quietly as I stare out of the window.

When I return from lunch, there is a distinctly male backside protruding from the space beneath my desk. Concluding that it belongs to the IT technician, I wrinkle my nose in distaste at the three inches of hairy crack bulging above the band of his boxer shorts. I look up to see James gesturing for me to come into his office. Without even pausing to deposit my handbag, I continue into his office and take a seat opposite him, asking, "So, how was the meeting? Boring as usual?"

James looks eager to share. "Actually, it wasn't. Have you ever met Ryan MacGillivray? He heads up sales in Australasia. Tall, good-looking chap."

I try to place him; no joy from the grey matter. "I've heard the name, but I can't conjure up a face to go with it. Why?"

"He's here from England, although I think he might be Scottish. He's been here for a few years, but I can't remember how many straight off the cuff." James looks down at his desk and ponders. "Yeah, a few years. Anyway, a position has opened up back in London so he's going to go back there. His wife and kids have already left and gone back. If I remember rightly, his wife is a gorgeous little thing. Blonde and petite and a little flirty. Really cute though."

I muster up extreme patience as he digresses. I don't care about whoever he's talking about and I'm waiting for him to tell me the relevance of the guy and his 'really cute' wife. "Anyway, he needs someone to travel over to the UK with him and set him up with everything, and to get him ready to transfer all the Australasia stuff over to Nick Hartley, who will be taking over his position here. He has to travel pretty soon, so he will need to finish his position from London. We need someone from this office to go over with him. Evelyn, his current assistant, can't go so they're trying to find someone else. Given the shitstorm you've been in lately, I thought it might be a good opportunity for you if you just want to take some time out and sort yourself out for a while."

I'm suddenly interested in the guy and his 'really cute' wife. "You don't have to go, I just thought it was a good opportunity for you. It's for about five and a bit weeks and all expenses will be paid. Basically, it will be like a mini European holiday that you don't have to pay for… except you work on the weekdays. The firm is happy to tack on a couple of weeks to ensure you get some downtime and your weekends will be yours."

In my mind, I'm going over all the questions I need to ask. "If I say yes, when will I be leaving?"

"In about three and a half weeks. Would that be enough time for you to get yourself organised?"

I want to scream, "Yes!" but I keep myself nice. Instead, I ask, "What about the office here? Who will take care of you while I'm gone?"

"Do you remember I said I was going to Thailand for a spell? Well, we booked the flights last week. We're off for about six weeks, and, since it's our slow time, I thought of you when the email came through to all managers this morning. They asked me to join them in the directors' meeting to discuss it and I said I'd speak with you."

I refrain from leaning over to fist-bump him. "James, it sounds like a perfect opportunity, but I need to speak with John and the kids to make sure it will work for them too. As appealing as it is, I can't just take off and leave them all behind while I 'find' myself in Europe. Can I let you know tomorrow?"

James waves at me and says, "Sure, no problem." I'm elated and hope the family jump onboard with me on this one. I really need some time out and this is just the answer.

Ryan

I sit at my desk and stare at the photo of Logan and Annabella. I'm desolate and miserable. I have a few weeks to get myself in order before I can go back home and see them. It feels incredibly unfair that it was Catherine who screwed around and ruined our marriage, and then when I caught her at it, she blamed me, said it was my fault because I had dragged her over to this godforsaken country and had then gone off to work every day, leaving her at home bored out of her head with two children to entertain. This isn't strictly true; I took her to weekend barbeques with colleagues and their families, I introduced her to the neighbours on either side of us and two doors up, who also had young children. Then there were parents at the kindergarten that Bella attended and other parents they had met at the pool where the children had swimming lessons.

Catherine was constantly out with the kindy and swim mums, drinking lattes in cafés or catching up at their houses. After Logan was born, she was even harder to keep at home, so half the time I would arrive home to an empty house and an empty fridge and had to duck out to the supermarket to find something to cook for dinner. I had to employ a cleaner to do the housework because she was never home, and then I had to organise to drop my shirts off at a drycleaners because she flat out refused to iron them, and I didn't have the time. She went shopping all the time and spent money like it grew on trees, but I didn't mind all that; I wanted her to be happy and she seemed truly happy. She hadn't complained about loneliness, so I could only assume she pointed the finger back at me because she didn't like feeling guilty.

Besides, she knew exactly what she was getting into by coming to Australia and was more eager to get here than I was. It was Catherine who talked *me* into taking the position because she wanted to go to Australia where it was warm and sunny. We'd just come off the back of an unseasonably hot English summer and she touted that she was Aussie summer ready if he was. So, I accepted the position at her nagging, and four years later I'm in this quandary. I've really found my feet here and I'm really sad to be leaving, but I need to be near my children. There is nothing else to do but follow in her wake back to England.

It's been four months since I caught her cheating and it still burns to think about. I had attended a conference in Adelaide, which finished half a day early, so instead of hanging around I caught an earlier flight back to Melbourne and arrived home to find my wife enthusiastically performing fellatio on the neighbour from two doors up. Apparently, she had left the children with the wife whilst she 'popped out for a spot of shopping', but instead had popped back home for a quickie with the husband. I stood at the door in shock, not sure what to say or do when Robert caught sight of me standing silently in the entrance and uttered an, "Oooh, fuck," before yanking his cock out of Catherine's mouth.

"What the fuck is going on?" I'd bellowed, when I finally found my voice.

Startled and clearly not expecting to have to explain herself, Catherine looked at me blankly, and then stated, "It's not what it looks like."

Surprised by her comment, I shook my head and yelled, "Oh, so ye weren't just sucking Robert's cock? I didna just see Robert's cock in yer mouth just then when I walked in?"

She had the audacity to retort, "Don't be vulgar, Ryan."

The patronising tone had me indignant. "No, Catherine! You were just sucking another man's cock in our living room – it is *you* who shouldna be so vulgar."

I turned to glare at Robert then growled, "Robert, get the fuck oot of my house, right now!"

Robert pulled his underpants over his limp dick, zipped himself up and hurried from the room with his tail between his legs. He squeezed past me, leaving as much space between us as he could; I heard his back scrape against the door frame as he slithered out.

He was possibly expecting me to throw a punch. I certainly felt like punching him, I was angry enough to do it, but I'm non-confrontational by nature so I let him pass. I wanted him out of my house. Catherine turned to me with a face like thunder, angry at *me* and hissed, "This is *your* fucking fault, Ryan. How about taking care of your wife? Don't give me a reason to go looking for it."

I was so shocked that she would shift the blame onto me that I was momentarily silent. This is how spoiled bitches behave. I somehow managed to keep my anger reined in. "Catherine, I've never given you reason to go looking for someone else. I don't ask much of ye. I work five days a week, that's what normal people do. It's a full-time position, it's not like I can take a few hours off in the arvo to pop home to stick it to the missus. I don't complain about ye spending, I got us a housekeeper so ye don't have to do housework, I get my shirts laundered and pressed elsewhere, ye're out all day doing whatever, but I don't complain when I have to come home and cook a meal fer the family. I just want ye to be happy. I dedicate my entire weekends to making sure you get to sleep in and that we have family time. If ye were unhappy, ye sure didn't mention it to me. It's not like I'm unavailable to ye. This is *not* my fault, Catherine, *you* fucked this up."

"Well fuck you, Ryan. I'm sick of this marriage, I'm sick of this country and I'm sick of *you*. I'm going home and I'm taking the kids with me."

I could no longer contain my anger. "So yer answer to fucking me over is to behave like a spoiled bitch and run home to mother... taking my kids away with ye. You're un-*fucking*-believable!"

Good to her word, she booked a flight back to the UK and took my babies with her. I was powerless to stop her. She has uprooted my family and now I have to follow her back to the UK. I'll only be able to see my children every second weekend, as per the outcome of the video-linked conversation between my lawyer and her lawyer. I completely understand why men feel so betrayed during a separation and divorce. We definitely get the raw end of the deal. God knows how much poison she's pouring into the little ears of my children about me while I'm a million miles away.

I phone them every Saturday night and I'm allowed to speak with them briefly before Catherine elects that my time is up. Then I have to wait another week to hear their little voices again. Our calls always start with excited voices, but they always end in tears when they have to say goodbye to me, and I'm pretty out of sorts for hours afterwards. I vow to myself that I will change that when I return. I need to move forward and remove the bitterness, or it will change me. To be truthful, I really miss Catherine. Not only have I lost my wife, traitorous and deceiving bitch that she is, but I've lost my best friend and confidant, too.

I called Jonathan and Theresa, my dearest friends who work in the London office, and explained what happened. As upset as they are that Catherine has mistreated me and returned home with our children, they're glad I will be coming home and have promised to help me find a fabulous apartment to settle into.

Right on cue, an email pings into my inbox with a picture of an apartment that is up for rent within walking distance of the train and office. It comprises 3 bedrooms and a study/fourth bedroom, has an excellent living area, a large kitchen/diner and is the penthouse suite with a cute little view and a small balcony. In the email, Jonathan states that he and Theresa will meet the agent at the apartment after work tomorrow, and, if they think it's suitable, they will arrange for a virtual tour to be sent through to me. It fits with my budget, so I'm a little buoyed by the news. Now all I need is the assistant from James' office to agree to come and help me set up in London, and then I will be set to finish up and leave. I just want to be home to see my kids.

John

I down my fifth Scotch for the afternoon, but instead of feeling relaxed and happy, I'm sad. The part of me that is celebrating the fact that I can finally be what I really am has been suffocated by the part of me that has watched my family splinter apart. The whole scenario is painful, but I toy with the idea that it isn't forever, that the wounds will soon heal and we will all find the love we had before I dropped the "G" bomb.

Wandering back into the study, I glance at the preliminary drawings on the drafts board. I have recently started spending more time working from home, since moving to the apartment, than in the office. My manager is fine with that as long as the work is completed on time and is up to my usual standard. It usually is but I hit a snag in my architectural flow when midway through the front-facing view of the design of a building at the local state school when I got up to make myself the first Scotch. An hour or so later and I just can't commit anything else to the drawings in my current state of inebriation and emotional funk.

Firing up the laptop, I shoot an email to the school principal stating that I need extra time to complete the preliminary drawings due to unforeseen circumstances. I apologise for the delay and hope she will understand that I need to ensure the drawings are completely correct before submitting them for her perusal. Within a few minutes I hear the ping of an incoming email. Returning to my inbox, I notice a reply from the principal already. I'm relieved that she's agreed to a two-week extension.

I accept the extension of a fortnight with the true grace of one who's just had a prayer answered. After fist-punching the air, I hear the distant hum of my phone vibrating on the coffee table in the living room. I dart into the next room and grab it, noting who it is before I put it to my ear. "Hey, Pheebs." I cringe as I hear myself call her Pheebs like nothing has happened.

"Hi, John. I was wondering if the kids and I could join see tonight. I have something I want to run by you all."

This is great. I haven't seen them all in over a week and they haven't seen my unit yet, so I'm excited. I try to keep the excitement out of my voice because I don't want to sound desperate. "Sure, do you all want to come over here and I'll cook dinner?"

"Works for me."

"Do you think Mercy will want to come?"

"I'm not going to ask her, John, she'll be there. I really do need to discuss something with all of you. She'll have to suck it up for tonight."

I'm not sure if I want her dragged over here kicking and screaming, but I don't think any of us have a choice, so I agree, then add, "Is everything okay, Phoebe? This sounds a little last minute. Has something happened?"

"No, not at all. I've just been presented with an opportunity and wanted to run it by all of you at the same time."

An opportunity? What the hell kind of opportunity. I play it cool. "I'm intrigued. Okay, how does six o'clock sound?"

"Perfect, I'll see you then."

I hang up and reach for my car keys… then put them back down again. I'll have to walk to the supermarket because I've had too many drinks to drive. As I lace my runners, I think about consuming water when I get back so as to get myself a little more sober before they arrive. I grab my wallet and jog to the supermarket to buy ingredients for dinner. I'm actually looking forward to having all of them around my little table in my new unit. The kids aren't ready to stay with me but tonight I can at least show them that I have bedrooms set up for them and assure Phoebe that I'm serious about having them every second weekend when they are ready to stay with me.

Mercedes

I'm in Josh's room, wrapped up in his post-coital embrace. That sounds so weird, even to my own ears… like only adults should have this moment of spent delirium. I just had the weirdest period ever. It was almost a week late, I didn't get any cramps and I only bled for a couple of days… and it was a really light flow.

Sex the second time still hurt a little, but nowhere near as much as the first time. If it gets a little better each time, it should be fine soon, and I'll be able to enjoy it too. Josh didn't have a condom again but that's okay because you can't get pregnant a couple of days after your period. I'm pretty sure I read that somewhere, so I told him it was fine but that he has to remedy it before next time. I don't want to risk it actually being a problem.

As I'm lying here wrapped up in Josh, listening to his heart gently thrum in my ear, I can feel his semen run out of me and it's all I can do not to shudder. Ew! I whisper that I need to get up and get a cloth because it's gross, but he whispers, "Just another minute." He sounds far away, like he's in the distance. I shift my head and look up at him and he seems almost childlike. There is a faint smile on his mouth and his eyes are closed – oh yes, I just took him there, yes, I did. I'm congratulating myself and decide not to worry about the semen, it's his bedding that's going to get the stain on it.

I have to go home but I don't want to walk out into the kitchen when Monique is out there. Eventually, I tell Josh I need to clean up and go home. He pulls himself out of his stupor and gets me something to clean myself with. We dress quickly and dart past the kitchen unseen. Then he walks me home because he is a gentleman. I like the way my hand fits in his. I like the way he smells of both deodorant and aftershave. I like the way his hair kicks up over his right eyebrow with a cowlick that gives his face a model-like quality. I like the way it feels when he hugs me tight. I like how soft his lips feel when he kisses me and how it sets me alight all over. I like the feel of his weight on me when we kiss and have sex, and I like that I can make him blissfully happy.

As soon as Josh walks away, I turn and enter the house. Straight-away, Mum is at me. Apparently, we have to go to Dad's house for dinner. Fucking hell. I don't want to see him, and I tell her so. I'm still angry at him for screwing up our family. I vow to myself that she will not force me and cross my arms over my chest in defiance. I want to hurl foul language in her face, but I know that it will go down like a sack of shit. She tells me to stop behaving like a petulant child and says she's not asking me, she's telling me.

I scream at her at a thousand decibels, "You're ruining my life!" because I don't want to be forced into doing something I don't want to do. I'm almost sixteen years old. When am I old enough to make my own decisions and choose not to go places I don't want to fucking go? She starts crapping on that she has something she needs to discuss, blah, blah, blah, but I'm not listening anymore because she has pissed me off. I yell, "Fine!" at her because I want her to shut the hell up.

I spy Seth over her shoulder and he's looking at me like he thinks I'm behaving like a child too. I'm ready to tell him to go fuck himself but I remember what he's been through recently, what Mum's been through too, and decide to pull my head in. I stomp upstairs because I'm still pissed off… they've just ruined my beautiful afternoon. Selfish shits, the lot of them!

Phoebe

Mercedes is harder to force into the situation than I anticipated. A simple request has turned into a full-blown "you're ruining my life" whine that ends with me yelling, "Mercedes! I am *not* asking you. We are going to your father's house for dinner tonight and you are going to stop behaving like a spoiled little brat. I have something that I need to discuss with *all* of you and whether it's here or there, we're all going to be at the same table at the same time having this conversation! He offered, I accepted, and that is that. We will be leaving at 5.45pm and you *will* be ready to leave at that time. Do I make myself clear?"

That gets me a "Fiiiiiiinnnnne!" and I see that her eyes are bright with unshed tears. She turns on her heel and stomps up the stairs like a five-year-old in the middle of a temper tantrum. I groan and throw my hands up in frustration, then go in search of a good bottle of red to take along with us.

Despite the eye rolling and fiercely crossed arms, we all make it to John's unit on time. I am impressed by the brick façade. It is neat and modern and, as first impressions go, I like it.

John answers the door on the first knock and welcomes us in with a convivial smile, and mouth-watering aromas waft from within. I give him a perfunctory kiss on the cheek, which feels awkward and weird, and walk inside. Seth hugs his father hello but Mercedes brushes past John and stands inside, arms still crossed over her chest. I stifle my eye roll. "Hello, Mercy," he tries.

Mercedes glares at him like a petulant child. I glare at Mercedes until my eyes almost dry over and she responds with a meek, "Hi." Even though the greeting is forced, I see that John is delighted.

Seth breaks the tension. "Mmm, smells great in here, smells like roast," he states hopefully.

John beams at him. "Well sniffed out, it's roast pork. It's still a little way off. Come in and I'll give you a tour of the place."

He leads us down the hall and into the living room. I note the room is decorated tastefully with minimal and modern furniture. From here he leads us to the two guest bedrooms, which he has set up for Seth and Mercedes respectfully. Both rooms have a queen-sized bed, which meets with approval from Seth. John has put a Tinkerbell quilt cover on Mercy's bed. Mercedes looks at John and says, "I'm almost sixteen, Dad."

"You're never too old for Tinkerbell, honey."

Mercedes smiles, then remembers herself and replaces the smile with a scowl but not before John sees it. This softens the hard lines on my face. John continues his tour with the bathroom that Seth and Mercy will share, his own bedroom and ensuite at the end of the hall, adjacent to his office, and then ends with the kitchen where the delicious aroma of roasting pork and vegetables fills the unit. To Mercedes' horror, a loud rumble sounds from her stomach and I have to try really hard not to laugh. All eyes immediately fall on her and, to hide her embarrassment, she mumbles, "I'll set the table," and makes off towards the dining table at the other end of the room. I pat John's shoulder as I pass him and follow in Mercedes' wake to find the cutlery.

Roast pork is always John's specialty and a particular favourite of Mercedes. This is well played by him because I can see some of the ice melting in Mercy's glacial stare. After a hugely satisfying meal, we are swaying in our seats, weary from being full, and I need to go lie on the couch and pop the top button of my jeans. I stifle a belch and bring up the topic I need to discuss with them all.

"So, the reason I wanted to talk to you all is… I've been offered an opportunity to go abroad for a number of weeks."

There is a chorus of questions. "Well, there's a guy in our office who is moving to London and they need someone from here to go over there to tie up the loose ends for the handover, and to help him get settled. They will pay all the expenses and put me up in a nice hotel. James is going away, and I'll be at a loose end, so he thought of me and put my name forward at the directors' meeting today. I told him I need to talk to you guys before I can commit to it."

John looks taken aback, and almost barks at me, "Who is this… guy?"

"I don't know, I haven't met him yet. His wife and kids have already gone over so he's keen to go soon."

John visibly relaxes at the mention of the wife and kids. My mouth tighten at the jealousy he has just displayed. How dare he get jealous

– I've never cheated, he did that… he is the shit in this relationship. I keep my temper in check for the sake of the kids, but Mercedes is glaring at John with disgust. I continue, thwarting a flare up, "It's for about seven and a half weeks and, to be truthful, I would really like to say yes to this offer."

Mercedes complains, "Well, what about us, what are we supposed to do while you're gone?"

I want to reply to her that I don't give a flying fuck but that is irresponsible. I am a parent first, human being second. "I thought, if it's okay with your dad that you could stay here while I'm gone?"

I look hopefully at John and see he's delighted with the suggestion. Mercedes scowls and Seth breaks into a huge grin. "I think that's a great idea, Mum. It's a little closer to school and I'm really liking that room you've set up for me, Dad."

"Works for me," John agrees.

"Fine!" snaps Mercedes, folding her arms in obvious disagreement. I can tell that she really wants to scream, "No!" but she knows when she's beaten. I'm reasonably sure she's been missing her dad, even if she won't admit it, and I think this is a great way to force a reconciliation between them. I'm sure it is closer to Monique's house too. I voice this in an effort to bring her willingly across the line.

Mercedes looks a little convinced, "Yes, I think it is closer. Anyway, it's closer to school too so…" she leaves the sentence unfinished.

"Okay then, I guess I'll tell James that I'll go. Then I should probably meet the guy I'll be helping while I'm over there. Maybe he and his wife can advise me of some nice places to visit on the weekends." Excitement bubble up in me. This is going to be so good – to just get away from this mess.

John brings me back to the now. "When will you be leaving?"

"I'm not completely sure but I've got about three weeks before I go. I'd better check that my passport is in order. My God, I can't even remember when I used it last. I don't even know where the damn thing is."

I look at John, he is the organised one. "It's in the filing cabinet in the study. They're all in the one spot under 'travel' I think. Let me know if you can't find it and I'll pop over and have a hunt around for it."

Relief floods me. "Will do."

"I think you'll be fine though; didn't we have to update yours for the trip to Thailand in 2015?"

He has the memory of an elephant. "Yes, we did too. That's great news, I hate the paperwork and photos… Ew, I remember that photo. I look like *Jabba the Hut* in it."

"No, you don't," John counters, "you're always so critical of yourself."

Of course I am, the older I get, the worse I look. "I hate photos of myself and in that one I'm particularly chubby, my hair is stringy, and it looks like I've aged ten years. My jowls are really saggy, and I look like a murderer. I liked the one before."

I hate that every ten years my licence photo morphs into an uglier alien than the one from a decade before.

"Mum stop it. There has been ten years in between the two photos, of course you look older. You *have* aged ten years. The photo is fine," Seth soothes. He's right. Anyway, who gives a shit. It's not like anyone except the officials at customs are going to see it. I don't expect to be 'picking up' at the airport.

"Right, I'll take my laptop and set up Skype, so we can talk face to face every few days. The only problem will be the time difference, but we'll work that out. Do you think you'll all be okay without me?"

John answers too quickly. "Of course. We'll all miss you, but we'll survive. We're all big kids now."

I see him wink at the kids. Seth laughs but Mercedes turns her face away to hide her smile.

John loudly places his hands on the table. "Right, well that's settled. Who's up for dessert?"

I float an eyebrow. "You made dessert?"

John looks playfully wounded. "Of course, I did, lemon meringue pie."

"Yesss!" Seth punches the air then high-fives John.

Mercedes thaws a little and mumbles, "Just a little slice, then."

I relax. That went well. I stand up to help with the pie. I'm suddenly hungry for something sweet, like I haven't just eaten my own weight in pork.

11

Coffee And A Chat

Phoebe

A cold wind sneaks in through my unbuttoned cardigan; the effect is instant and millions of tiny goose bumps cover my décolletage. I look down at the tops of my breasts and wonder if I've worn the wrong thing. I don't want to appear suggestive, but this dress makes me feel good about myself and I want to come across as confident. Apart from revealing a little bit of cleavage, it's pretty tame.

I'm nervous but I don't know why. What if he turns out to be an arsehole and I have to endure him for eight weeks? We spoke on the phone yesterday and I was delighted to hear that he has a Scottish accent. I imagine he will be short, fat and balding with a sprinkling of red hair, but James said he was tall and good looking… although I'm sure James' appreciation of men differs somewhat from mine.

Yesterday, when Ryan and I spoke, he said he had spare rooms in his apartment, so I could stay in one of them if it was easier than finding a hotel. Then we could go to work together. I accepted this offer, of course, because there was no way to say no without sounding rude, but I wonder what his wife will think of me lobbing in for a couple of months. That would shit me to tears if the situation were reversed. I'm hoping he cleared it with his wife before he put the offer to me. If I cook sometimes for them and I bugger off on the weekends, maybe it won't be so bad.

Before he hung up yesterday, he asked what I look like, so he could keep an eye out for me at the café today, and I'm sure he meant height and hair colour but for some reason I described myself as short and rotund with cow-poo-coloured eyes. What the hell did I say that for? He gave a little nervous chuckle and now he's probably looking for a whale with cow-shit-coloured eyes. I said this *after* he offered for me to stay with him, so he is probably thinking I'm a nut bag and *he* has to endure *me* for eight weeks. I will redeem myself today and show him I'm normal.

As I make my way down the street, I spy the coffee shop across the road but since I'm halfway between two sets of lights and loathe walking the distance to either to cross legally, I decide to dart awkwardly into the middle of the road. I am almost taken out by a tram as I wait for the last of the cars to pass so I can cross. The tram driver angrily rings his bell at me and I resist the urge to raise my middle finger at the impatient prick. I smile winningly at him instead The icy glare he gives me could freeze a sunbeam. When the road is finally clear, I finish crossing and make my way to the café.

❦

Ryan
As I sit at a table by the window with Evelyn, I look for Phoebe, who we'll meet today. When I asked her to describe herself yesterday, she said she is short and rotund. I look at Evelyn; she's a portly woman who would have commanded the description of handsome over any other. I'm wondering what rotund means. Perhaps she is really, really fat. I don't give a damn, I just hope she's good at her job and makes the transition in London flow. It's a pity Evelyn can't come across with me; she's the perfect assistant. Evelyn has been my PA for the past four years and is efficient beyond measure. She has an unexpected frankness and a wicked sense of humour.

I look out the window and see a woman pick her way across the road, annoying a tram driver who is unable to continue without running her down. She smiles up at the tram driver and is pisses him off even more. A grin tugs at my mouth. Her tight-fitting black dress falls demurely below the knee, with a neckline that complements the ample bust peeking over the top. A thin black cardigan, which looks completely useless, flaps in the breeze caused by the passing cars. Her bright-red, shiny heels add a bright splash of colour to her outfit as her matching lip colour adds a bright splash of colour to her face. I'm drawn to her as she hurries across the last stretch of road towards us.

"Do you think that's her?" Evelyn says beside me.

"I hope not, look at that rack! Besides, she described herself as short and rotund, whatever that means."

Evelyn throws back her head and lets out a baldy laugh. "Haven't I told you not to walk around with a loaded pistol? She *is* short and although she's not quite rotund, she certainly has curves." She says this with envy.

A gust of cold air follows the woman into the warm café, bringing brightly coloured leaves through the door, scattering over the tiles. She scans the seated patrons until her eyes travel to Evelyn and me. She walks over to us, stands before me and thrusts out a hand. "Hi, I'm Phoebe O'Brien, you must be Ryan MacGillivray."

Jesus, it *is* her. I awkwardly stand up and take the proffered hand to shake in greeting. I try to calm myself. Her hand is surprisingly warm given the cool wind she escaped moments before. Her handshake is firm and confident but doesn't hold the bone-crushing assertiveness that reeks of bra burning and feminism gone mad.

"Hello, Phoebe, nice to meet ye" I gesture at Evelyn beside me. "This is Evelyn, my assistant."

I sit down as she reaches across the table and holds out a hand to Evelyn in introduction. "Hi Evelyn, nice to meet you."

My eyes travel to her ample bust as she leans over towards Evelyn. As she seats herself, the café door opens to allow a new arrival and another gust of cold air breezes over us. Phoebe shivers slightly and goose bumps cover the cleavage peeking out of the dress. Percy stirs down south and I cross my legs, looking out of the window in an effort to gain control over my testosterone. I can't believe I offered to have this woman stay in my spare room. I'm going to have to walk around with a magazine perpetually covering my crotch.

※

Phoebe
My breath catches in my throat when I spy Ryan. James said he was a good-looking chap, but he is ridiculously handsome. My heart-rate picks up when my eyes come to rest on his; dark brown like chocolate mud-puddles, bordered by long dark lashes; he has bloody baby giraffe eyes. He is very tall, and although his legs disappear under the table, one pokes out the side; long and athletic. His hair is light brown but the sun washing over him through the window shows a chestnut hue. I imagine his beard, if he grew one, would be reddish.

He speaks with a sexy Scottish brogue that almost makes me swoon. I wonder if he owns a kilt and that has me wondering what he would wear under it. I blush and hope they can't see it. When the door opens and allows the cold air in, Ryan's eyes travel to my chest. A lustful expression flits across his face. I pointedly smile at Evelyn to give him a moment to gather himself, then turn back to Ryan.

He flags a passing waitress, who hurries over to take my coffee order, all the while trying really hard not to look at Ryan. Her eyes keep darting to him as she hurriedly scribbles on her pad, then she hurries off. Ryan is oblivious. Turning his attention back to me, he speaks of the six-week role in London, what will be required of me and the people I will be working with. He describes the location of the office, the apartment and the proximity of local tourist attractions. My coffee arrives, temporarily breaking the conversation. Hating awkward silences, I start asking questions. Ryan turns his attention back to me as I ask what kind of outerwear I should bring along. He chokes on his mouthful of coffee, spluttering into a napkin, and his face reddens; he looks suddenly sweaty. Both Evelyn and I look askance at him.

"I'm sorry, what did you ask?" It dawns on me that perhaps he thinks I asked about underwear; I did say it rather quickly. He looks embarrassed. As if I would ask him about my knickers, Jesus!

I refrain from frowning at him and speak slowly, "I just asked what kind of outerwear I should bring. I don't know the weather in London and I know your spring and summer seasons are nothing like ours."

He looks mortified and I think I'm bang on with my suspicion. I watch him gather himself to answer, but a soft smile plays about the corners of my mouth, which I think conveys that I know exactly what he thought I'd said. He blushes again because he sees that I know and he's trying to pull himself together. Evelyn is looking at him and then me like she is trying to decipher the secret conversation. He looks down at his coffee as he answers, "Weel, ye should probably bring a light coat or jacket and some tops like ye're wearing noo."

I look down at my unbuttoned cardigan, noting that the single button I had fastened over my breasts has popped apart. I refasten it as Ryan continues, "It will be mid-spring then early summer while you're there. Our summer is more like an Australian spring or autumn. Londoners call any series of days where it gets consecutively over twenty degrees a heat wave. Having lived through no less than four Australian summers, I can tell you it will not be like that over there. I've become quite used to the warmth here and how mild your winters are. I'm not looking forward to the British seasons or the drear of London weather."

His eyes are drawn to my fingers as I fasten the button in the centre of my breasts; I know that the material is stretched so tightly across my boobs that the button hole is stretched to a wide oddly shaped hole. It only holds for a second before the button pops back out and the cardigan springs apart again. I keep talking and see Ryan's hands involuntarily clench and unclench as I continue the conversation, having given up on my cardigan. I don't want to draw any more attention to my boobs, so I leave the cardigan alone. "When will you get there?" I ask, drawing his eyes up to mine and away from my boobs.

"About a week before you, I think. I've got some loose ends to tie up here over the next few weeks, then Evelyn and I will begin packing up my office. I'll have to hand all of my Australian clients over to Nick Hartley, so they will be the first things to be packaged up as we'll need to do the transference with client meetings and lots of discussions. I can't just throw the poor bugger in at the deep end. Unfortunately, I'll have to do most of the handover from London."

His cheeks dimple as he grins at me and my breathing escalates. My heart thuds painfully around in my rib cage and I sincerely hope these two can't see my obvious state of infatuation.

Evelyn leans forward. "I've been putting a package together of the things you will need to know and the kind of things you'll be doing over there. The package will include contacts in London, contacts here and all the things Ryan will need your help with to set up over there, just so you can be prepared before you get over there. I'll have finished putting it together next week, so I'll have it sent up to your floor for you. Just so you know, you can call me to discuss anything when you get over there, just be mindful of the time difference."

I am relieved that she is so helpful. "Of course! I'll have a fair idea of the time difference for when I can talk to my kids back here. Thanks so much, Evelyn, that's really helpful."

She beams at me. "Perhaps we could meet for another coffee and chat a few days before you leave for the UK, just in case you need help with anything."

I almost sag in relief. "I'd really like that, thank you."

The conversation morphs into one of a more personal nature with Evelyn asking me about my children; their age, which schools they attend and who will be taking care of them in my absence. Ryan leans back in his chair and watches quietly as I gesticulate with my hands.

I feel the weight of Ryan's eyes on me and wonder why he's staring.

I nervously lick my lips. The more he stares the more I nervously licking them. Evelyn thankfully asks Ryan about his children. We are both looking at him and waiting for him to answer but he is still looking at my mouth. Suddenly, because we are silent and looking at him, he jolts and says, "What? Sorry, I was just thinking about… what did ye ask?"

Evelyn repeats herself slowly, like he's stupid. I think she is wondering what is going on with him. I get the feeling he's not usually this distracted.

"We were just discussing the age of your children. Annabella is five and Logan is three, is that right?"

"Almost. Logan is not quite three yet. His birthday is about two days after I get back." He looks at me and smiles as he speaks of his son. "Logan was born here in Australia. He's at that age where he's into everything. He pushes all my buttons. Annabella mother's him and frets over him. She's my wee worrier."

His expression is suddenly sad; I deduce that he's missing his children. I wonder what it would take to make his smile return. I catch myself and stop dreamily looking at his mouth. Evelyn is watching both of us and her expression screams that she feels like a third wheel. There is sexual tension between us because I don't have a man anymore with sex on tap whenever I want it, and Ryan's wife is on the other side of the world and perhaps he needs to acquaint himself with his hand.

Evelyn asks who will be taking care of James in my absence. "James is actually going on a six-week holiday to Thailand with his wife, so it will only be for a week either side of his holiday. It won't be too bad, and I'll make sure everything is covered before I leave." After a pause I add, "I'm really looking forward to this trip but I'm going to miss my kids."

Not wanting the conversation to venture into current affairs within my household, I pointedly look at my watch and state that I have to leave to take my son to football practice. The reality is that

Seth can drive himself there, but I need an out and I need to get away from those sad eyes.

Ryan hands me an envelope with my travel information, and politely stands as I gather my things. "I'll see you in London," he says.

"See you then." I wave farewell to both Ryan and Evelyn and walk back out into the cool air. The soft hush of the door slowly closing behind me is broken by Evelyn's voice, "She's lovely."

And Ryan's reply, "Aye, she'll do," before the door soundlessly mutes any further conversation.

I don't want to dart across the road in front of them, so I walk up to the traffic light and cross like a good pedestrian. I sit in the car for a few minutes to get myself together before driving home. I open the envelope Ryan handed me and look at my itinerary and other travel information and let out a squeak of excitement.

12

Girl Talk

Phoebe

Sitting opposite Chelsea in our favourite café, I watch my friend excitedly relay her date with her new beau, Gavin. "I was so nervous. I had the tics going off all over the place all afternoon but when he rang the doorbell, they just… stopped. I opened the door and he had flowers… flowers Pheebs."

"Ooh, what kind?"

"They were yellow roses, but they were such a deep colour that they were almost orange. I took a photo, look…"

I wait patiently as Chelsea scrolls through the photos. She flips the screen to me, but I barely have time to register the picture before she pulls it away from me again and continues to flip through the pics. "And I took one of my hair too – check it out!"

This one she allows me the time to view properly. "Oh wow, Chelsea. Look at those curls. Oh, I'm so jealous. Did the curls hold?"

She bounces in her seat. "Yes! And when I opened the door and he saw me, he was like, 'Oh wow, you're beautiful'. I was so gobsmacked that I wanted to cry. I haven't had someone call me beautiful in forever! He was wearing a tight pale-blue tee that was really firm around his chest and biceps and these really tight jeans… Oh my God, his arse!" She flaps a hand at me. "Sorry, I digress. So, we went out to this restaurant. His car was just a run-of-the-mill commodore sedan, but it was clean and neat, and I suspect he cleaned it especially."

"Of course he did. He didn't want you to see the wrappers from Macca's and the empty KFC buckets strewn everywhere – stale chips between the seats."

Chelsea pulls a horrified face, "Ew! Don't even go there! No, I think with a body like that he eats healthily and goes to the gym a *lot*."

I interrupt, "Come on, I don't give a shit about any of this, tell me about afterwards when he took you home and scratched your itch."

Chelsea beams at me, raises a long finger in the air and says, "Honey, he stayed the night and we were scratching itches aaaall-niiiiiight-long. I had the tic thing happen at the breakfast table and he just waited them out and then said, 'You okay?' and I said, 'yep' and that was that."

She is like a teenager as she gushes, "Oh, Phoebe, he is amazing, and he is so good in the sack. I swear he was a woman in a past life because he knows what a woman wants, you know? We're going out again tomorrow night. I'm so excited."

Her voice actually squeaks the word 'excited'. I'm not alarmed by the over-share, this is classic Chelsea and she doesn't feel the need to edit anything when she's around me.

"I'm so happy for you, Chelsea. It's been a long time coming but now it's your turn to stand in the sun. You go girl!"

She swipes a hand through the air. "Okay, so that's me done. What's new with you?"

"Well, actually, I have news too."

I relay the events of the past few days. She is excited for me. "Oh my God! What did he look like?"

I excitedly blurt, "He is pretty, but he's off-limits – he has a wife and kids. He did offer for me to stay in his spare room though, so she must be lovely. I don't know that I could handle someone else staying in my house from another country for eight weeks or so, but that's just me. James said he remembers her and she's a petite, blonde little stunner. Of course she is, beauty attracts beauty," I say flatly. "Anyway, the point is that I will be able to get away for a little breathing room.

And then I can sort myself out. I don't know that I want another relationship for a long time anyway. John was my one and only. There was nobody before him and we were just so familiar that I don't know how to do the single thing. I don't want to go to bars or nightclubs, I don't want to be set up and I will never swipe right. I just can't imagine myself with anyone but John and I can't imagine kissing someone else let alone having sex."

Chelsea brightens. "Well, since John wasn't actually behaving normally, if you know what I mean, perhaps the next guy will really tick your boxes. Make you *love* sex."

"What do you mean? John still ticked my boxes – I had no idea he wasn't heterosexual. I'm so confused by everything. All I know is that my entire sexual experience is John. He was my first kiss and my first for sex."

"Well, I have lived the life of a whore. I've had quite a few guys and they're all different. You just adapt and compromise and if you don't like the way one guy does it, you don't have to stay with him."

This doesn't wash with me. "Chelsea, I'm not one to just have sex for the sake of having sex. I have to feel something for the guy."

"Well, maybe you'll feel lust. You don't have to have relationships with everyone you have sex with."

"Well *I* do! I mean, I know I don't literally have to do that but that's who I am. I can't imagine just having mindless sex. I guess I'm just a little scared of the unknown."

Chelsea reaches across the table and takes my hand in hers. "Yeah, I get it. Your whole world, everything you knew has been ripped out from under you. You're not sure how you feel and you're a little frightened to take those steps. Perhaps we should just get you a sex toy for the interim, something to get you over the line while you wait for Prince Charming to gallop up on his noble steed."

I gasp. "Hell, no! I don't want something like that hanging around my house for my children to see. I'm not that desperate, yet!"

"Oh my God. I'm not saying you need to hang it on the wall on display. You hide it. Do your kids usually go through your wardrobe and cupboards?"

"No, not usually, but if I don't have one there then they can't find it. I would die if they found something like that in my house."

Chelsea looks surprised, "Wow, for a grown woman you're quite the prude, aren't you?"

I'm burned by her remark. "Oh bugger off, Chelsea. Just because you're getting some... don't judge me!"

"Mmm-hmm, and when I didn't have Gavin, I just used my 'friend.'"

Now I am astounded. I look at Chelsea, completely surprised by the confession.

"Does that bother you?"

Now I feel old and completely out of touch. "Of course not, I just never imagined..."

"Ew! You don't *get* to imagine... ever!"

I put my hands up in surrender. "Easy, I'm just saying I'm surprised that you have one. I apologise, of course you do. It's normal and there's nothing wrong with it... it's just not for me. Did you get it from a sex shop?"

She shakes her head. "Nope, ordered it online. Actually, when it arrived, my dad collected my mail and handed it to me with the letters on top."

My jaw drops open in horror. "Holy shit! What did you do?"

Chelsea frowns, "What do you mean what did I do? It was in a brown cardboard box. It's not like they send it in a clear box with the name of the website written all over it! They're discreet."

I feel prudish and unworldly. A whole other world exists that I know nothing about. It's like I've been living in a bubble for the last twenty-five years. How am I ever going to meet a guy? How will I know what to do with someone else? I'm old now and certainly not in my prime. It's going to be harder than ever. I think perhaps you only get one chance at love and I used mine up on a rainbow unicorn.

13

Soaring With The Eagles

Phoebe

Always fretting and panicking at the last minute, I mentally go over my checklist for the zillionth time since my taxi departed for the airport forty minutes ago. It's only eight weeks but it's like I'm fleeing a war zone and leaving my family unarmed and alone in their own battles. Mercedes is bitter and angry and refuses to talk to me, Seth is still trying to deal with the emotional fallout left in the wake of Brandon's suicide, and John is trying way too hard to compensate; overzealous in his efforts to patch things up with Mercedes and offer support to Seth. But run away is exactly what I've done. I need time to think; time to deal with the gravity of the situation and perhaps start to heal. I just need some time to be me. I will go to work, come home from work and just 'be'. Eight weeks of that is exactly what I need.

As the taxi pulls up to the curb at Melbourne Airport departures, I retrieve my wallet and pay the driver, then root around in my handbag for the airline ticket information and my passport. The driver has already removed my case and hand luggage from the boot and placed them on the path.

Shouldering my handbag and hand luggage, I reach down and grab the handle of my case and start to walk inside in search of the airline check-in, grateful for the wheels on my luggage. Thankfully, the queue is small, and I'm processed almost immediately. I'm pleased that I have a window seat. Then I set off to join another queue for customs. This line is longer, and I find myself worrying about what I may or may not have remembered to pack. I'm not used to travelling abroad on my own and more than a little nervous about how I will manage at the other end.

The internet advised that the distance to London is 10,497 miles (or 16,893 km), which is approximately twenty-four hours' flying time. At least there will be a break in between as my flight will stop over in Dubai. Hopefully, this will keep me from going stir crazy. I have brought some pills to help me sleep, but although in theory this should work, sleeping in a sitting position is uncomfortable and I expect to be awake for most of the flight, if not extremely uncomfortable. I'm going to be so sleep deprived when I arrive in London.

Finally, emerging on the other side of customs, I find that I have time on my hands. I walk into a newsagency and choose some trashy gossip magazines, today's newspaper and a suspense novel for the flight. I stow these in my bag, walk into a café and sit down for a coffee. Opening the newspaper first, at last I start to repose; losing myself in current affairs until it is time to board my flight.

* * * * *

Seated and belted in, my overhead luggage stowed and my reading paraphernalia in the back pocket of the seat before me, I settle in for the long flight, and try to watch the air hostess prattle on with the safety spiel as we are pushed back from the airport gate. I'm happy with the window seat and hope for a quiet passenger to sit beside me. Silently cursing my choice of jeans for the trip, the waistband digs annoyingly into my stomach. There is a kafuffle in the aisle and a man falls face first into my lap, then profusely apologises for his impromptu crotch dive. Enter the passenger from hell.

I feign great interest in the view out of the window; I want to be left alone. After the plane levels out and the Captain has finished greeting the passengers, I order a wine from the drinks cart and pick up my novel. The chatty gent to my left starts asking me a myriad of stupid conversation-starter questions, to which I give single-word answers in the hope that I can give the guy a hint without being rude. Unfortunately, he is either a dolt or not easily swayed as he continues to attempt to engage me in conversation. I smile and turn to look out my window and he finally gets the message. I look down at the brown hues of the earth below, glowing red in the late afternoon sun. Central Australia is both beautiful to look at and boring at the same time; I see both beauty and barren nothingness in the landscape below. I return to my book and lose myself in somebody else's pain for the remainder of this leg of the flight.

By the time we touch down in Dubai for the stopover, another day has dawned back in Melbourne and I rise wearily to my feet to be herded from the plane for the two-hour interval. I decide that when I reboard, I will take the sleeping pill and pass the rest of the time in oblivion. I need to get a little rest before I arrive in London, lest I look and sound like a zombie when I meet Ryan at the other end.

When the time comes to reboard the flight, I'm pleased to discover that I've been upgraded to Business Class. The change of comfort level is fabulous but given the number of hours I will be lounging in this position, I pop the sleeping tablet anyway and settle in to watch a movie until I am overcome with tiredness.

The subtle change in air pressure wakes me from a peaceful slumber. I rouse just before the Captain announces that we have commenced our descent into London. It is early May and mid-spring here, so I am hopeful that the weather will not be too cold. Moments later, the Captain announces that the temperature in London is a mild and sunny fourteen degrees… fourteen! That is a cold winter's day in Melbourne. I shudder and hope I've brought enough warm clothes to keep me comfortable during my stay, recalling Ryan's comment that a week in the low twenties is a heatwave in London. Brrrr!

14

London Calling

Phoebe

Having retrieved my baggage, I make my way through the long line at customs, then join a throng of people heading for the taxi stand. As I head for the exit, I spy a tall, thin man in a suit holding a sign with my name on it. Smiling and waving at him, I head towards him and greet him. His serious expression splits with a grin and he quickly takes my bags and begs that I follow him. Directing me towards a waiting black car, I wonder if he has the right Phoebe O'Brien. The suit deposits the luggage in the rear of the car then opens the back-passenger door for me, introducing himself as Samuel. I clamber in as I thank him over my shoulder then promptly lose my footing and fall into the car, landing awkwardly on Ryan's lap. I blink up at his surprised face, and instantly begin apologising… completely formal in my stress. "Oh, Mr MacGillivray, I'm so sorry. I didn't see you there."

What the hell is wrong with me? I'm such an idiot. Immediately, I realise that my hand is wedged at the juncture of his thighs, so I try to stand up as I whip the offending hand out of his crotch. In doing so, I belt the back of my head painfully on the roof inside of the car before falling like a sack of shit into his lap again, this time with my face on his thigh, dangerously close to his member. My face is flaming and I'm uttering all manner of expletives as I back out of the car on my hands and knees, fall backwards and land in a pile of arms and legs on the pavement outside the car. I want to teleport to somewhere else. I don't even know what just happened.

Recovering himself, Ryan shoots out of the car and extends his hand to me as I'm in the process of trying to right myself. I am absolutely mortified and wishing really hard that the ground would swallow me whole, right this second.

"Phoebe, hello! Oh, God, I'm so sorry, this is totally my fault. I was on the other side of the car when we pulled up and I just assumed Samuel would bring ye to that side, so I scooted over to this side. Of course, ye weren't expecting me to be sitting there."

His accent is heavily Scottish, and he runs the fingers of his other hand through his hair in what looks like a stress habit. I take his proffered hand and scramble to my feet, trying to be normal. This is not a natural state for me and I have to work *really hard* to pull it off. I am giggly because I'm nervous and I feel like an idiot!

"Actually," I admit, "I wasn't expecting you to be here at the airport at all, so it wouldn't really matter where you were sitting. I'm terribly sorry about that."

I gesture lamely at his crotch and he looks down at himself and back up at me. I am screaming "fuck!" loudly inside my head. Why am I looking at his crotch? I look at it again as my brain screams at me to stop it. Ryan stands aside, angling his crotch away from my eyes, and ushers me into the car. Ryan glares at Samuel, who is struggling to hide his enjoyment at the awkward situation, before I manage to seat myself in the car without doing something else stupid.

Samuel contains his mirth long enough to apologise to Ryan. Ryan shakes his head at him as he continues his conversation with me. "Of course I would meet ye. Ye don't think I would actually leave ye to make yer own way out of Heathrow, do ye? And please call me Ryan, Mr MacGillivray is my grandfather. Even my father goes by Donny Mac. Now tell me, how was ye flight?"

I regale him with tales of the flight and the unexpected pleasure of my elevation to Business Class.

By the time we pull into the apartment complex it is twilight and I can't really see the surrounding neighbourhood. Like a mind reader, Ryan states that he will take me on a tour of London tomorrow if I'm rested and up to it, as its way too dark to see anything at this hour. I realise that I haven't eaten anything for about eight hours and I am ravenous. To my horror, my stomach makes a loud protest at my thought, which makes the situation clear. Ryan asks unnecessarily if I am hungry. My stomach rumbles again in answer and we both laugh.

The elevator is silent as we rise up the levels to Ryan's apartment. I have a fleeting image of a scene from *Fifty Shades of Grey* that makes heat rise to colour my face. Ryan looks at my face and smiles. He raises his eyebrows at me and utters, "Fuck the paperwork, right?"

Surprised, I burst out laughing and the tension is somewhat eased. The elevator doors open into a hall. A few feet away, Ryan approaches a door with his keys at the ready. I look left and right and see no other doors except the fire exit at the very end. I wonder at the size of his apartment.

Ryan swipes his hand over the wall just inside the door to light the entrance. Then he stands back to allow me to enter first. After a couple of steps, I see the elevated entrance steps down into the rest of the apartment. To my right is what I assume to be a coat closet, which Ryan promptly confirms by opening it and hanging his jacket inside. He holds out a hand to me. I shrug out of my coat and wait for him to hang it. "Come on, I'll give you a tour."

Two steps in, past the cloak closet, we step down and into the open-plan living area. Straight ahead is a sizeable kitchen with an eight-seater dining table to the left of it, with glass doors leading out to what I assume is an outdoor balcony or veranda. To my immediate left is a large, open living room. The largest TV I have ever seen dominates the far wall; it looks to be about 110 inches in size but suits the size of the room. The coffee table is sturdy, and squat and it sits atop a beautiful large white shag-pile rug. The most inviting thing in the room is the lounge suite.

Exhaustion tugs at my shoulders and the lounge looks incredibly inviting; it is a physical struggle not to plonk myself down onto it straightaway. So far, the apartment seems obscenely clean. I wonder where the toys are, the knick-knacks that make up a family home. Perhaps his wife is a neat freak and completely anal about mess. I worry for the children and silently hope they have a playroom somewhere in the house where they can let go.

Ryan ushers me out of the living room and turns me around so we go back past the kitchen and enter a long hall. The first door we come to, on the left, Ryan stops at. He opens the door to reveal a large-sized bedroom with a queen-sized bed, decked out in simple white bedding with a glossy satin trim, a sizeable double-door built-in wardrobe, a small armchair strategically placed on an angle in the corner, and a small ensuite with a shower, toilet and a single basin. A double window takes up most of the far wall, black in nightfall. Ryan walks over to the window and presses a button beside the architrave and a muted hum sounds as blinds quietly cover the windows. "This is yer room, Phoebe. I hope ye'll be comfortable here."

"Of course, I'll be comfortable," I politely respond. "It's huge."

The next door reveals a room about the same size containing two single beds. One has blue bedding and one is adorned in lemon. The blue bed has a doll in the middle and the lemon one has a bear. There are toy boxes on the far wall under a window and a small blackboard on an A-frame. There is a chalk-drawn picture of a large circle with giant scribbled circle eyes and a huge smiling mouth. Arms and legs jut out of the sides and underside of the head. I am reminded of how Seth drew people like that and smile at the memory.

Ryan turns to me and states matter-of-factly, "This is where my children sleep when they come to visit every second weekend. I hope ye'll be okay with that? They're well behaved and not at all obnoxious."

Ah, so that's why the house is so neat. The children live with their mother. Ryan and his wife have obviously separated. That explains the invitation to stay at his apartment; nobody else is here to care. "Of course, I'll be okay with that. My two were children once too, you know." I smile up at him. "I look forward to meeting them."

Ryan opens the next door to expose a large bathroom complete with a sizeable bath, which contains many bath toys. I notice a toilet and a double basin. A little step resides in front of the toilet and a vinyl child's toilet seat rests against the wall. "If ye want to take a bath, ye can use this one."

He gestures to the last room at the end of the hall and states, "That's my room at the end there," but he doesn't take me inside.

A doorbell chimes back out in the apartment living area. Ryan looks at me confused for a second before remembering. "Ah, that will be Samuel with yer bags. Shall I ask him to put them in yer room for ye?"

"That would be fabulous, thank you."

Fabulous? Why am I channelling my mother-in-law? My stomach gives a loud protest. I look at Ryan and apologetically smile. "Sorry, we're very noisy today."

"Pizza?"

I'm hungry enough to eat a horse. "That sounds great."

After directing Samuel to my room, Ryan walks to the phone on the kitchen wall and hits a button. "Hi, Lydia? It's Ryan. Do you think I could order a couple of pizzas to be brought up to the apartment?" He listens for a moment then covers the mouthpiece, looking at me. "Any allergies? Likes? Dislikes?"

"Oh, I don't like pineapple, and I'm not a fan of the hairy fish but I'm up for anything else."

Ryan pulls a face. "Hairy fish? Anchovies?"

I nod, smiling because he deciphered my description. He returns to his call. "Sorry, Lydia, could we grab a House Special and maybe a Capriccioso? Hold the anchovies. Aye, put it on the tab. Ten minutes... cool."

He smiles and asks, "Wine? White or red?"

I like how he assumes the answer is yes. I refrain from doing my happy dance in his kitchen. "White, please."

He walks to the fridge and after extracting a bottle of chardonnay he holds it up in a questioning gesture. I nod enthusiastically, no point hiding the fact that I'm a bit of a lush. Ryan pours me a glass and hands it to me. He walks to the kitchen counter and unscrews the lid on a bottle of red, which he pours for himself. I take a sip of my wine and almost dissolve in ecstasy. It is cool and crisp and has such a deep aftertaste that I follow it directly with a second sip.

He takes a sip of his own but quickly puts it down and rushes off to see Samuel out of the apartment. They talk amicably by the front door for a moment, but they are too far away for me to hear the conversation. After closing the door, Ryan walks into the living room and sits on the couch, groaning in relief as he does so. He looks at me and smiles, "Want to join me?"

I put my glass on the bench, bend down to remove my heels, put them neatly against the wall by the hall entrance then make my way over and sink into the couch beside him. "Phew, what a day."

"Do ye suffer jetlag?"

"Well, I've never travelled a substantial distance before – this is my first long distance trip."

"Oh, where have ye travelled?"

"Well let me see, Fiji, Thailand, Fiji, Fiji again and then Thailand again… Fiji and Thailand, it seems."

"Okay, so what is yer preference of the two?"

"Oh, definitely Fiji. When I go to a beach destination, I just want to relax and rejuvenate. I don't want to go shopping every day in the markets, and I certainly don't want to haggle for label rip-offs; I don't want to have to pay extra for every service and I don't want to walk along a lovely beach dotted with things that have washed up overnight… like a toilet seat, a TV, or half a couch. I just want someone to cook for me, I want somewhere clean and I just want to lay about and be pampered."

"I'm with you, I dinna like hagglin' or the bustle and I struggle with the depraved side of some parts too. The prostitution that is thrust in yer face is alarming. There's a smell about the place too."

"I know; its sewerage! I mean how can they create a resort in paradise with views to die for from all six of the pools but leave the sewerage drains open with only grates covering them? Oh, and the cats! Cats and kittens everywhere! Climbing all over you because they're starving. I'm a cat lover and I absolutely adore the little things, so I struggle with it."

Right on cue, a pure-black, long-haired cat with stark golden eyes pads into the living room, sits at Ryan's socked feet and meows loudly. "Phoebe, this is Lucifer. Don't be taken in by his calm countenance now – he's completely mad."

Ryan leans forward and scratches Lucifer affectionately under the chin. Lucifer starts purring loudly, reminiscent of an outboard motor. I can't resist so I sit forward and reach out a hand for Lucifer to sniff. Ears back, Lucifer sniffs and licks at my fingers before jumping onto the couch between us. He sits like a statue of regal splendour before shooting out a foot and grooming his undercarriage. The doorbell chimes and startles the cat; he leaps from the couch and lands metres away near the kitchen, tail wagging in agitation.

While Ryan attends to the door, I walk into the kitchen and begin opening cupboards in search of dinner plates. Locating the crockery, I stand between the dinner table and the living room and wait for Ryan to direct me further. He spies me then gestures back at the couch. "We'll just eat here, if ye like. I don't suppose you're a *Doctor Who* fan?" he asks hopefully as he reaches for the television remote.

I am delighted. I rush to the couch to join him. "Yes, the new series doesn't come out in Australia for another month at least." I slap my thigh. "Of course, you get it here – it's filmed in bloody Wales. What episode are you up to?"

"Oh, it only just started, last Sunday. So, you're a Whovian then?" Ryan seems pleasantly surprised.

"Oh, dear God, no! I am merely an avid fan."

"My wife… sorry, estranged wife, hates it and I had to watch it in the downstairs room at our last home, far away from her and with the volume at a 'sensible level.'" He makes quotation marks in the air. "The sound of the theme song almost drove her batty. Favourite Doctor?"

"Tenth. Tennant is also my favourite British actor."

"Really? He's my favourite Doctor too."

I venture, "What did you think of Capaldi?"

"I think he was great. He's a Scot, that's cool, and he's really chilled for an old guy. I didna like those sonic sunglasses in his first season though. I'm excited for this female doctor."

The Doctor appears on the screen and Ryan un-mutes the volume. He leans forward and opens the lids on the pizza boxes. Handing him a plate, I peer at the pizzas and feel my mouth fill with saliva. I delicately extract a slice, slap it on my plate and sit back to enjoy.

"Mmm," I moan in rapture as the flavours dance on my tongue and finally slay the hunger pangs, while the Doctor Who theme song sounds.

15

A Sight To Behold

Phoebe

The joyful song of birds comes to me in waves as I drift in and out, dozing. Eyes still closed, I stretch languorously and slowly rise to the surface from a deep sleep. I look up at the ceiling and experience a moment of panic. My heart beats erratically within my ribs. I can hear the muted tones of a television somewhere in the distance above the roar of rushing blood in my ears. After a moment, I sit up and recall that I am in Ryan's apartment in London. I glance at the clock on the bedside table and see that the digital display says 1:03. Perplexed, I frown at the clock and perform a sanity check on my watch. My watch, which I set to London time when the plane touched down at Heathrow, also states 1:03. Then the penny drops. It is 1:03… in the afternoon!

Leaping out of bed, I run out of my room, down the hall and into the living room, completely forgetting that I'm wearing pyjamas and fluffy socks. I'm freaking out.

"Ryan, why didn't you wake me? I'm so sorry, I overslept. Aren't we supposed to be in the office right now? Oh God, I'm sorry I overslept!"

I know that I am blathering in my panic but can't articulate my thoughts into a sensible sentence. Ryan's eyes travel over my pyjamas and back up to my face. He smirks. "Hello, Phoebe, I trust ye slept well?"

Why is he so calm? And why is he smirking? "Too bloody well, why didn't you wake me?" I ask again.

"Given that you flew from Australia to London, I'm not surprised in the least that ye overslept. And what kind of a guy would I be if I expected ye to appear at the office today? Besides, I'm showing ye around today, remember? Last night ye were so deep in sleep on the couch that it felt like a crime to wake ye."

With a sinking feeling, I remember Ryan shaking me awake and leading me to my room the night before. I wonder if I was snoring. I was curled up in a ball and not lying on my side so chances are I sounded like a wounded bull. Too tired to care about anything except sleep, I spent a grand total of two minutes on my face and teeth before climbing into bed and drifting into a sound coma. I wonder at my appearance and see him smirk again before he erases it. I probably look like a scarecrow and my morning breath could possibly peel paint.

"Okay, just give me a few minutes to have a shower and change and we can go."

Ryan holds his hands up in a calming gesture. "Hey, there's no rush. You go and have a shower and I'll make ye a pot of coffee. Ye can have some toast to tide you over and then, after we've been oot and aboot, we'll go and have an early dinner at one of the restaurants around the corner."

I utter a brief thank you and spin on my heel to jump in the shower. I catch a glimpse of myself in the mirror over the sink. I have smudged mascara under both eyes from the hasty ablutions last night, and my hair is a riot standing in all directions around my head like Medusa's nest. I couldn't possibly look worse if I tried.

When I reappear, my hair is brushed and glossy, my makeup has been reapplied and I look half decent again. I hope this image eclipses the last one in his memory. I can smell freshly toasted bread mingling with the strong earthy aroma of coffee. Ryan looks up from his paper and points at the coffee pot. "Help yerself."

Beside the coffee pot is a mug with a spoon, a carton of milk, a plate laden with toasted bread, some softened butter in a small dish and an array of spreads from jams to a can of something that looks like pureed spam. Electing to sweeten my morning with strawberry jam and steer far, far away from the spam spew, I hastily prepare breakfast… brunch.

Lucifer pads into the room and performs a figure eight around my legs. The familiar feeling of feline adoration makes me miss our beloved cat, Charlie, who met his maker three days before last Christmas. The thought of Christmas makes me long for the familiarity of home and hits me with a pang of guilt at having abandoned my family in the midst of upheaval. The reasonable part of my brain reminds me that I'm also badly affected by the home situation and the time away will give us all some much-needed healing time.

Pushing my emotions aside, I grab my toast and coffee and sit opposite Ryan, almost tripping over Lucifer as he continues his weaving all the way to the table. When I am comfortably seated, Lucifer lets out a bellowing "Meow". I look down at him to see what is amiss and see that he is standing upright on his two back legs, looking for all intents and purposes like a little bear. Aww, he's so cute and I want to squeak at him. I look askance at Ryan, but he is engrossed in an article in the paper. I run a finger over the top of the toast, scooping a finger full of jam and butter and surreptitiously lower my hand under the table for Lucifer to lick.

Lucifer is most pleased with the jammy-butter and starts purring and uttering little 'meeps' as he licks. The sound is a sticky, whirring, meeping suck-fest that is so loud that Ryan lifts his gaze and looks at me. I guiltily grin back at him. He moves his whole body sideways and glances under the table at the source of the noise. He pops his head back up and queries, "What is he eating?" *Inquisitive*.

"He's just licking my finger." *Not guilty*.

"Really? So, he's just licking yer skin?" *Suspicious*.

"There may or may not be a little jam on my finger." *Innocent*.

"Are ye trying to win over my cat?" *Distrustful*.

"I've already won; he loves me." *Smug*.

"Ye know he is loyal to me, right?" *Insecure*.

"I am a cat whisperer." *Superior*.

Lucifer leaps onto the seat beside me, puts two paws on my thigh and rubs his head industriously against my shoulder. Ryan narrows his eyes at the cat and mutters, "Traitor." *Defeated*.

I reach down and stroke Lucifer's lustrous fur.

"Good boy," I whisper. *Champion*.

* * * * *

As it is already afternoon because I snoozed half the day away, Ryan opts to show me just the nearby sights and places I may need to know. First, we walk to the train station. Ryan hands me an Oyster card, explaining that it's the card required to travel by train in London. "Ye put money on the card and use it as travel currency."

"We have a similar system in Melbourne."

We board a train, swiping our cards as we pass through the entrance gates, and head out of the station in the direction of central London. We exit the train at Covent Garden. After a brief walk, Ryan points to a building across the road.

"That's the office. I walk some days but mostly I drive in and park in the parking spaces beneath our offices. As a manager I have a reserved parking space but its pot luck if yer name isna hanging over one of the spaces. It's walking distance from the apartment, only a matter of blocks, but I dinna wear heels." He grins at me before continuing, "Ye probably want to take the train. Ye can come with me if I'm going to and from the office but I often have late meetings or need to go oot of town overnight. I wouldna recommend walking home on yer own in the dark. Keep yerself safe. Ye saw how close the station is to the apartment and it's well-lit, but ye never know."

I am grateful for his advice. As least I know that if I don sneakers, I can walk in to the office on the mornings that he is out of town.

Ryan continues, "Tomorrow, if ye're up to it, we'll go in and you can meet the team and familiarise yourself with the office layout and your workstation. Of course, if ye're still really jetlagged, ye can stay home for another day, but I'll have to head back into the office tomorrow. I can only wrangle so many days of sympathetic leave."

Ryan is smiling at me and I notice his dimples. I smile back. "I'm pretty sure I'll be fine. If anything, I think I'll have a little trouble maybe sleeping at night, but I should be fine during the day."

Ryan points out that a city block away from the office in the opposite direction is the fresh food market and supermarket. He advises that I can go there in my lunchbreak if I need food to cook at the apartment or supplies, or even to purchase lunch as there is a deli as well. He mentions the name of a butcher that I won't recall and compliments the quality of the meat he sells. He also mentions an excellent fruit and vegetable stand but adds that there are a few each of butcher and chicken shops, fish shops, dried fruit and legume stands, and a variety of sweets shops housed in the building as well. I turn back to look at the sign adorning the market; 'Covent Garden Market'. I make a mental note to visit it and familiarise myself with the local produce in the next week or so, but the task feels daunting – the market is huge.

"Many of our staff walk to the café a block away to get some fresh air and clear their heads as much as to seek a change of cuisine that's palatable."

His cheeks dimple at me again. The light is beginning to fade as afternoon morphs into early evening. Ryan mentions that we are two blocks from the apartment and asks if I want to walk back or take the train. The evening is clear and cool and I'm enjoying the outdoors, so I suggest we walk. A few streets from the apartment, Ryan stops at a Thai restaurant and asks if I'd like to have an early meal since we missed lunch. Ravenous after the two slices of toasted bread, I nod excitedly. It is 5.45pm and the restaurant is already half full, so we enter and prepare for a tasty meal. Craving seafood, I am already perusing the menu in search of a red curry with prawns. Ryan orders Pad Thai, a boring choice given the cuisine on offer, and an entrée of mini vegetarian spring rolls to start, which he promises to share with me. I order the red curry.

Our conversation flows easily. He tells me about the area surrounding our apartment complex and I'm interested to hear there is a park with a running track nearby. Seeing my interest, he also advises that there is a gym within the complex, which he assures me I can use with the small keychain fob attached to the apartment key that he keeps forgetting to give me.

* * * * *

Walking back to the apartment, I take in the beautiful night lights of the city. It is a crisp night with not a breath of wind. My mouth is still zinging from the heat of the red curry. On the walk, I ask, "So, how many staff work at the London office?"

"Last count I think it was four hundred and sixty-one. It's our largest office."

"Phew, and I thought the Melbourne office was big."

"Well it is big, this one is just bigger. Melbourne is our second-largest office, but it falls under Australasia and encompasses New Zealand and Indonesia too, with only small offices in some major cities to keep things going on the ground. The thing with Australia is that although the country size is vast, the geographical positioning of the cities is huge. So, when you're in charge of all of Australia, you're flying from city to city. The demographics are a completely different ballgame than they are in Europe and the UK. Trying to explain that to the boffins in London was nigh on impossible so I had them fly out there in the first year to show them first hand where they all were; drove them to appointments, flew them to the different states and only now do they understand the figures. I'm sure all the other managers are feeling a new appreciation for the demographics lesson."

I stifle a yawn that pops up out of nowhere.

"Sorry, I'm probably boring you."

I'm embarrassed. "No, not at all, I think the time differences are really messing with my head. I'm insanely tired all of a sudden. I feel like I'm going to stumble, I'm so tired."

Ryan takes my elbow and steers me into the foyer of the apartment block. I didn't realise we were so close. "I'll walk you up, so you can go to bed and rest. I'm not ready to turn in yet so I'll pop back down here to the bar for a drink."

I yawn noisily and drowsily nod, literally too tired for words. Opening the door for me, Ryan bids me goodnight. I turn and thank him politely before stumbling in exhaustion to my bedroom. Lucifer follows me to the bathroom and sits on the toilet as I go about my night routine. He pads after me as I enter my room to change into pyjamas, then, as I settle into the welcoming comfort of the sheets and duvet, he pounces onto the bed and curls up in the hollow between my breasts and knees. Lucifer purrs contentedly, and I can feel my breathing become deeper. I stroke his soft silky head and the effort is more than I can manage. My hand drops beside him wearily and within minutes I'm drifting off into deep sleep, borne out of pure exhaustion.

16

Training For Madness

Ryan

There is no madness when she wakes this morning. I hear her humming in the shower as I add the filter and coffee grounds to the coffee maker. When she wanders calmly out of the hallway and into the kitchen dressed in office attire, Lucifer follows in her wake. He doesn't dart past her and trip her up as he does with me in the mornings, ravenous for his food. He walks slowly behind her like she is his queen. He looks up at her adoringly and I am disgusted in his fickle heart. He is my quiet companion who sleeps with me and expects nothing in return except gentle petting and food. I tell him all my secrets and although he appears aloof, he still makes me feel loveable and sane. He didn't come to bed last night and I wonder if he spent it with her. Today he makes me feel rejected and I decide to wait until the last minute before opening a can of food for him. I don't want to appear desperate, even though I am.

She looks nothing like yesterday when she came tearing out of that room in the middle of the afternoon, flapping about in front of me, pointing to her watch and panicking at the time… raving like a lunatic. Her face was laughable with smudged makeup and sleep creases etched into her skin, framed by crazy, frizzy hair. Her flannelette pyjamas and fluffy socks made it hard for me to keep my shit together. In that state of vulnerable disarray, I found her quite appealing.

She is beaming at me. "Good morning, Ryan. That coffee smells good enough to drink! May I have a cup?"

I beam a smile back. "Of course, help yourself. There's bread in the freezer for toast, all those spreads in the pantry and cereal too. Milk is in the fridge."

She opts for the cereal and pours herself a small bowl that wouldn't keep Lucifer satisfied, then completely drowns it in half a bottle of milk. I have to look away because I don't want to frown at her. Each to their own, I think to myself, but it is all I can do not to utter, "Have some cereal with your milk!" Amazingly, she doesn't slurp when she's eating it. This is the polar opposite of Catherine, who ate her muesli with a couple of tablespoons of yoghurt for moisture, and almost made me gag because I imagined it would be all dry in her mouth and stuck to her gums. I nearly succeed in making myself gag at the memory. I think I make a small noise because Phoebe looks up at me and asks if I'm all right. I'm mortified.

Lucifer leaps onto my lap and I forgive him instantly because I also have a fickle heart. He is purring loudly and rubbing his face all over me. I stroke his sleek fur from the top of his head to the base of his spine and his purr gets louder. Lucifer is hungry and loves me more because I am the keeper of the food and the deliverance of joy in a bowl. I decide he can have milk today instead of the expletives because I'm happy that he's wandered back to me.

I offer the paper to Phoebe. She accepts it and loses herself in the headlines. I hear her molars crunching on the cereal flakes. Lucifer goes up on his hind legs, so he can love me more. He extends himself to full height and I use the nails on both of my hands to scratch his adorable face. I forget that I'm not alone with him and bury my face in his fur and nuzzle him. I look up to see Phoebe staring at me with a hint of a smile playing on her lips. I smile back at her and rise to feed Lucifer because I'm embarrassed by my behaviour. Lucifer runs after me and almost trips me up as I make my way to the laundry to give him sustenance. He is purring and meowing and making crazy with my legs in anticipation. I head to the bathroom to brush my teeth and see a goatee of Lucifer fur dangling from my chin, stuck to my smoothly shaved skin. I look like an idiot and Phoebe saw it. I am emasculating myself.

Phoebe

The elevator doors open to a plush office setting, which appears to be a giant rectangular floor space surrounded by glass offices. In the centre is an expansive area with desks forming another rectangle. I take all this in as I follow Ryan, though his long legs take giants strides, which have me almost running to keep up. My walking stride is pretty fast but wearing high heels makes for the comical clip-clop of a goat walking on two legs when I rush. As I follow in his wake, I notice how his firm backside moves in the smooth material of his suit pants.

Ryan stops before a tidy desk and I almost run into the back of him. I imagine myself wedged in his butt crack and a giggle bubbles in me. "This is where ye'll be sitting, just outside my office, which is just across there."

He points to a glass office adjacent to my new desk. His desk is facing me on an angle and I think that he will be on display in that office. He won't even be able to scratch his balls without me seeing. All this glass is supposed to give an air of transparency, but it feels fishbowl-esque. "This is Theresa, she's going to help you get started. Theresa, this is Phoebe."

I am pulled out of my wayward thoughts as Theresa stands up and walks over with her hand outstretched. I shake her hand firmly. "Nice to meet you, Theresa."

"Welcome, Phoebe. Thanks, Ryan, I'll take it from here."

"Right, thanks Theresa. Get back to me at about 1.30?"

"Sure."

With that, Ryan turns on his heel and walks purposefully to his office. Again, my eyes are drawn to his backside, but I don't openly stare this time.

Turning back to Theresa, I take comfort in her warm smile and immediately relax. Theresa takes me through my login details to start up my computer and the various packages that I'll be using during my six-week stint.

The introductions around the office are good except for one guy, Howard. He sits in an office opposite Ryan. I can see into his office from my desk, too, but only when I'm standing as the small petition blocks most of my view when I sit. When we enter his office, Howard looks me up and down. His eyes fix on my face and he's wearing a scowl. He stands up and continues to glare at me. Howard is tall and overweight with serious man boobs on display through his tight striped shirt. He wears nothing under the shirt and I can see copious amounts of hair matting over his stomach. He stands erect and looks down his nose at me.

I speak a polite greeting to him but after barking a gruff hello at me, he walks out of his office in the opposite direction, leaving Theresa and me awkwardly standing alone in his office staring after him. I'm surprised by his rudeness and I look at Theresa, who looks every bit as surprised as me. I shake it off and we continue with the tour of the office, which takes a good couple of hours as people stop to chat. We eventually return to our desks at mid-morning. I smile at Theresa and say, "You know, I won't remember any of their names, except that Howard guy. He doesn't like me."

"Yeah, I don't know what's up with him. He's not usually like that. I'll have to ask the others about him. That was really weird."

Theresa shakes off her puzzled expression and changes topic. "Anyway, grab your coat and bag and we'll go check out the market and grab a coffee."

* * * * *

The market is a bustling sea of bodies. There are butchers calling out their specials and fruiterers pedalling their wares, but Theresa pushes past them all to get to the back where she shows me, in her words, the finest butcher, the most excellent poultry man, the favourite fishmonger and the top greengrocer of the lot. As confused as I am, I take it all in then decide to think about what I can cook Ryan and me for dinner. I ask Theresa, "Do you know if Ryan has any allergies or dislikes?"

"Yeah, he's a little fussy with seafood, but only because he doesn't like the taste of it."

Okay, not allergic but doesn't like seafood. Good to know. "I might start with something simple. I think, since he's allowing me to stay in the spare room, that I should show my appreciation somehow. I'm sure he'd appreciate a home-cooked meal he doesn't have to prepare himself or order from downstairs."

Theresa smiles. "I think Ryan would love that."

Deciding on a simple meal of crumbed chicken, crispy baked potatoes and steamed broccolini, I purchase the ingredients as well as a ham and salad sandwich for lunch.

Theresa eyes my packages and asks what I'm making. I tell her, and she jokingly asks what time I'd like her there. I hope she's joking because I only have enough for two, so I laugh back at her.

Theresa and I walk away from the market and sit on a nearby park bench to eat our lunch. She tells me that she's married to Jonathan and that he and Ryan are close mates. Ryan reports to Jonathan; and Ryan is Jonathan's sounding board. She advises that we will most likely see a fair bit of each other because Ryan and Jonathan are almost inseparable. "When he and the family went to Australia, Jonathan was inconsolable. It took months to drag him out of his funk. They emailed each other constantly. I'm upset about what Catherine did, the stupid bitch, but I'm glad he's back. Jonathan is so excited to have him home. He was bouncing around like a four-year-old when we heard the news."

I want so very badly to ask what Catherine did but it's inappropriate to ask about my boss and gossip about their close friend, so I stifle the questions.

Back at the office I take up some fridge space in the central floor kitchen with my food purchases and label the bag. Inside, I place the keys and fob that Ryan has finally remembered to give me, so I remember the packages before I leave the office for the day.

The remainder of the day passes quickly as I have many tasks to perform, most of which involve understanding a photocopier that is a computer and requires a degree in engineering to operate. Leaving the office before Ryan, who is tied up in a meeting, I fetch my food from the fridge and make my way to the train station. Back in the apartment, I start making dinner. I put tiny little bits of chicken in a small bowl for Lucifer and hope that it's early enough that it doesn't spoil his appetite for when Ryan returns and feeds him.

Ryan returns as I'm removing the chicken from the pan, moments before I dish up. Timing only a man can manage. "Perfect timing. I've seriously just finished cooking."

Ryan says he's delighted with the meal and grateful that he didn't have to throw something together himself after the long and arduous management meeting that bored the brains out of him, and he gladly offers to clean up afterwards… I gladly let him.

Feeling that all is right with the world, I have another early night to restore my lagged brain and drop straight into a deep sleep.

17

Howard The Horrible

Phoebe

It's late morning and I'm halfway through a memo. Half the floor is away at a training course on a different floor of the building. It's quiet in my nook. The intercom crackles so I sit back and wait for an announcement, but I'm surprised to hear a conversation taking place. "How are you, darling girl? Are you holding up?"

"Oh, Howie, it's been terrible. I've been missing him so much and he just won't hear me out. He won't even let me explain."

Everybody, including me, looks up to the roof where the intercom continues to share the conversation. I wonder if 'Howie' is Howard on this very floor. The stuck-up rude bastard took an unmistakable dislike to me upon introduction a few days ago. I am completely perplexed as to why this should be.

The conversation over the intercom continues. "So, have I got competition with this one from Australia? She's actually staying at the apartment, I hear."

It dawns on me that they are talking about me. "Oh God, no! No competition at all! She is fat and ugly. That's why she's staying there; there's no attraction."

I stretch myself tall, elongating my neck, and look directly into Howard's office. He has the phone to his ear. It's him all right and he *is* talking about me and Ryan, and everyone can hear. What a shit-head.

"Oh my, she's looking at me now with sad puppy eyes like she can lip read. I hope she can lip read. Stupid bitch." The mousy voice on the other end of the phone giggles; I can only assume it is Ryan's estranged wife. Why are they being so bitchy? I haven't even met this Catherine woman. Humiliated, tears sting my eyes and brush at them angrily as I sink back down into my seat. I hope the idiot realises he's on loudspeaker soon, so I don't have to tolerate this insulting diatribe for a minute longer.

Across in his office, I see Ryan glance at me. He stands up. He has the phone to his ear and is glaring at Howard's office. He sits back down and continues to look at me, trying to gauge my reaction. Howard resumes his conversation, "Just you bide your time, honey. He'll remember what a catch you are and come crawling back to you. He'll forgive you. It was only one little naughty, well that he knows about anyway. Don't worry about this other one, she's not a threat."

Catherine giggles. "Good. She'd better keep her mitts off my man. I don't care what I have to do but I'm going to get him back! It's his fault, really. What was I supposed to do when he left me home alone in a strange country with nobody to talk to? What did he think was going to happen?"

Ryan ends his phone call, stands up abruptly and stalks across the expanse of carpet towards Howard's office. He has a thunderous expression on his face as he bursts through the door, startling Howard, who jumps in fright and yelps like an injured puppy.

Everyone on this floor can hear Ryan over the intercom as he yells, "Hang up the bloody phone, Howard, NOW!"

"Who was that?" Catherine squeaks. "It sounds like Ryan."

Howard looks nervous. "Yeah, I've got to go, sweetie. I'll call you later."

Howard replaces the phone and stands, looking uncertain. Ryan's face is an angry shade of puce and even without the intercom he is still yelling loudly enough to be heard outside Howard's office.

"You were on the bloody loudspeaker, you stupid git. We all

just heard your entire conversation over the intercom. Go into the boardroom and wait there!"

Jonathan exits his office and locks eyes with Ryan. Ryan looks royally pissed off. He nods at Jonathan as he continues towards the boardroom in Howard's anxious wake.

I dart into the ladies' room. I'm horrified to have heard myself described so cruelly. Is that really how I'm perceived? Am I that awful? Trying to stop the tears from coming, I breathe tremulously and, widening my eyes, dab a tissue under my eyelashes to catch the unfallen tears. To my surprise, Ryan enters the room. Spinning around, I press my backside to the sink nervously. I'm all kinds of messed up.

"Phoebe, I'm sorry ye had to hear that. I dinna know what the bloody hell is going on with my ex and this arsehole, but he's committed an offence that commands an instant dismissal. We have a no-bullying policy here and it's in his contract. He'll be asked to clear his desk and leave immediately. What a prick! Are ye okay?"

"Yeah. It was a little confronting hearing him describe me like that. I've barely said two words to him and he's been so rude to me. I'm going to go and continue with whatever I was doing before that... happened."

"Ye know that nobody thinks like that about ye. That was Howard being a knob. I'd better go give Jonathan some support while he does the deed. What an arse!"

Ryan leaves the room and I'm left standing at the sink, wishing I was back home in Australia. I need a Chelsea hug. I take several deep breaths to restore order and balance, then return to my desk to continue with my work. About twenty minutes passes before I see Howard storm out of the boardroom and into his office. Amanda from the mailroom enters and places a cardboard box on his desk; fleeing without making eye contact with the fuming Howard, who immediately starts to fill the box with his personal items. Ryan appears at my desk and sits on the edge.

"You okay?"

"Yeah, I'm feeling a little guilty that Howard has to leave. How long has he been with the company?"

"Five years. He started aboot a year before I moved to Australia. I'm gob-smacked that he's carried on like this. I kenned he was friendly with Catherine, but I couldna have imagined the two of them plotting like this. I'm shocked Catherine was so bitchy, considering she's never even met ye."

Jonathan pops out of the boardroom and walks up to Ryan, asking for a moment. They both move to the far wall to stand near a row of desks, empty due to the training course, and hold a quiet conversation, which I presume is about Howard the horrible. I look over at Howard and notice him glaring at me with glacial hatred. I am uneasy under his hostile glare. He stalks out of his office holding a box of possessions, and directly up to my desk. My heart rate kicks up a notch. I don't want to hear his abuse first hand. I take comfort from the fact that Ryan and Jonathan are standing somewhere behind me, and I rise and come around my desk to face him. Howard's face is a mask of hatred as he spits his words at me. "I hope you're fucking happy, you fat slut. I'm fucking fired because of you."

How am I to blame for him getting fired? He got fired because he's a dick and everyone heard him being a dick. I'm defensive but my tone is a little apologetic. "Howard, how is any of this my fault?"

He almost takes my eye out with his finger as he jabs it close to my face. I pull back in reflex. "Don't you dare speak to me!" he fumes. "How fucking dare you!"

Before I can respond, he shoves past me and the edge of the box he is carrying knocks me into the petition and my head hits hard. Howard either doesn't know the box has connected or he doesn't care; he continues to storm towards the elevators. Tasting blood, it becomes apparent that the inside of my mouth has split against my teeth. Dazed I sit back in my seat, watching the scene unfold before me in a dream-like state; powerless to contribute anything sensible with my addled brain.

Ryan's face is red with ire again as he storms toward the elevator and yells at Howard, "What the fuck is wrong with you?" Howard looks my way and is unapologetic, "that was an accident." Ryan tells him to get the hell out of the office and returns to me. "Are you okay?"

I wait for Howard to leave before speaking. "Um, I think I'm just going to sit here for a bit, Ryan."

Ryan takes a seat on the desk and puts his finger under my chin to lift my face. He reaches over and pulls a tissue from the box on my desk and dabs at the blood on my lip. "Just a little cut, I think," he mutters. He takes a huge breath and looks at me with apologetic eyes. "I'm so sorry about this, Phoebe. I'll get yer coat and handbag. We'll go back to the apartment and change and then we'll just go to the bar and have a drink and try to make sense of this ridiculous state of affairs."

I get shakily to my feet and allow Ryan to slide my coat over my shoulders. I look up into his earnest face and, to my disappointment, my bottom lip quivers. He sits back down on the desk, pulls me into him and wraps his arms around me. He holds me in his embrace while I struggle to keep myself together. He runs his hands over my back in soothing circles until my laboured breathing slows and I just want to stay like this for eternity. Finally, I pull back and extract a tissue from my pocket and dab at my eyes, embarrassed by the tears.

Ryan stands and brushes a stray lock of hair behind my ear. The sweet gesture feels foreign. John never knew what to do when I cried but Ryan makes me feel feminine.

"Let's go." He sighs. Touched by his gentle manner, I allow myself to be led from the building. Passing Theresa on our way to the elevator as she returns from her training course, Ryan explains that there's been a bit of an altercation and that Jonathan will explain it all. He asks if she and Jonathan will join us for a drink in the bar below Ryan's apartment in about an hour. Theresa nods at Ryan then turns to me and hugs me warmly. I give her a defeated smile before turning back to be led to the elevator.

18

Stuffing Turkeys

Phoebe

Ryan unlocks the door to his apartment and gently pushes it open. He stands back, ever the gentleman, to allow me to enter. The apartment is warm and bright with light from the early afternoon sun. It doesn't match my mood. I feel delicate and emotionally bruised. I want to go into my room and climb under the covers and stay there until I feel better, but Ryan wants to go for a drink. I should probably take the distraction, so I'll go and get changed.

Two steps in and past the cloak closet, I stop and stand motionless, staring at the scene at the bottom of the entrance stairs. Ryan's house keeper, Helga, is lying on her back on the tiled entrance floor without a stitch of clothing on. Another woman, with a shock of unnaturally red hair, is performing oral sex and using a giant sex toy; the girlfriend is also completely naked. Her backside is up in the air and her hairless genitals are at a most unfortunate angle, looking like a turkey about to be stuffed. Too shocked to utter a single sound, I continue to gawp at the scene until Ryan almost falls over the back of me as he rounds the corner. I turn to look at him and I can see by his expression that he has taken in the scene. The colour drains from his face.

He grabs my arm and yanks me back around the corner, unceremoniously shoving me into the cloak closet and throwing himself in after me. He pulls the door quietly shut, shrouding us in darkness.

The closet is barely big enough for one person let alone two, so I find myself pressed up against the back wall with my face buried in Ryan's chest near his armpit. A little dazed, I'm surprised to notice the crisp scent of his deodorant, the spicy overtones of his aftershave and the gentle aroma of his laundry detergent. My brain provides this pleasing sensory distraction for about a second.

My hands, still holding my handbag and umbrella, are down at my sides and there is absolutely no room to move inside this space. Ryan's hands rest on my shoulders like it is absolutely normal to be standing this close in the confined space of a closet in the middle of the afternoon. I wonder vaguely why this shit keeps on happening to me. First John, and now this on the entrance floor. I can hear Ryan gulping air as he tries to steady his breathing, but I can hear that his heart is racing. As my ears become accustomed to the silence of the dark closet, the moaning and loud directives, peppered with expletives from the other side of the door, continue unabated. Helga is not a quiet lover. "Oh yes!" Helga bellows, her German accent is strong in her lust.

My face feels hot and I'm mortified for the girls on the outside of this door, who have no idea they can be heard. Shallow breathing into Ryan's shirt, it's all I can do not to hyperventilate myself into a faint.

Lucifer has discovered us because he is a super sleuth. There is all manner of fucked up going on outside of this closet, but he has detected Ryan and me with his keen sense of smell. He meows outside the closet door. Ryan's heart beat rises and throbs in my ears as he realises we could be discovered soon if the little feline shit doesn't go away. He meows again, and I can hear his claws scratching as he tries to open the closet door with his furry little paw. My heart feels like its fit to burst through my chest and I really don't know what to do. What if Lucifer succeeds in opening the door and the two girls see us? It will look like we are both partaking in some weird act of voyeurism?

Deaf to Lucifer's meows, Helga is yelling now, obviously nearing her climax. I'm embarrassed by the noises and completely freaking out at our predicament. My mouth makes a small whimper of its own accord into Ryan's shirt as I hunch my shoulders up in an effort to muffle the ecstatic cries echoing beyond the door. Ryan is also distressed by our quandary and hisses, "Fuck!"

He opens the closet door abruptly, taking Lucifer by surprise and causing him to leap a somersault into the air comically before scurrying down the hall with his hair on end. Ryan yanks me after him and we quickly leave the apartment. He quietly closes the door behind us so that only a quiet 'snick' can be heard as the latch clicks in. Still clutching my hand, we run down the corridor, past the elevators and towards the stairwell. I'm flying two metres at a time between each bounding step as Ryan pulls me along behind him. He hisses at me over his shoulder, "We'll take the stairs. I'd die of bloody embarrassment if she came oot and saw us standing there. She'd know we'd seen... *that*!"

He has fallen into a thick Scottish brogue in his distress, which makes the words come out without fine-tuning his inflection. He takes the stairs two at a time as he runs as fast as he can, trying to put as much distance as possible between us and the pornographic scene in his apartment. I'm still wearing high heels and stumble on a couple of occasions, barely righting myself each time before we turn at the landing and continue down the floors. How I don't sprain or break an ankle is nothing short of miraculous.

When we reach the ground floor, we burst through the exit door and into the glass foyer beside the ground-level bar and restaurant. Upon exit, we're both pacing, and I am shaking my hands like I'm trying to rid myself of something evil. Ryan clutches his head, leans back against the wall and groans. I start ranting because the day's events have finally tipped me over the edge.

"Holy *shit*! What the fuck was all that about? How embarrassing. Sorry to be swearing, Ryan, but, *bloody hell*!"

Ryan is just as shocked as I am. "Och, dinna apologise. If I live to be a hundred, I'll never rid myself of that monstrous image. Holy God!"

"Well, I've got another one of those stored in the memory bank. What is going on with people? There must be something wrong with me; I'm so bloody straight and boring!"

Laughing, Ryan says, "What? What does that mean?"

"Oh, don't mind me. I'm just *freaking out!*" I can't stop behaving like I'm nuts when these stressors keep occurring in my every day. Why me? Why is the universe conspiring to make my life so atypical? I feel sorry for Ryan because he's caught in the maelstrom surrounding my life. He tries to calm me, but I can tell he's losing his cool too.

"I think we're both freaking oot. Let's just grab a bloody drink and try to calm the hell doon." He pushes through the glass doors into the bar. Waving at the waitress, he holds up two fingers, then a moment later holds them up again, then points to a table in front of us. She nods and turns to do his bidding. Obviously, Ryan frequents the bar regularly because she knows exactly what he wants two of.

As we approach the table, I can see the bar stool is really high. I am grateful to discover a footrest rung so I don't actually have to perform the vertical splits and pole-vault onto it. I hoist myself into the seat like a small child and glance at Ryan, who has already seated himself because he's tall, and he is grinning at me. I frown, "What?"

"You're really short."

"No shit, Sherlock!" He floats an eyebrow and I'm immediately embarrassed by my rude outburst and feel my cheeks flame in response. "Sorry," I mumble, and I'm saved any further embarrassment by the arrival of our drinks. Two straight shots of whisky are placed in front of me and two before Ryan.

He holds out his glass to me and states, "Bottom's up." I close my eyes to dispel the image of the bottom that we've just witnessed 'up' and clink my shot glass to Ryan's before throwing back the whisky in a single gulp. So much for bravery; the whisky burn flies up my nose and has me gasping in surprise as my eyes water. I resist the urge to choke, which will make the whisky drizzle out of my nose. The cut in my mouth burns like fire, which makes for a rather eye-watering event. I peer at Ryan through glassy eyes and cannot mistake the mirth in them.

Recovering my equilibrium somewhat, I smile up at him and throw back the second shot just as the elevator bell sounds. Looking over at the doors, I spy Helga's girlfriend, who I recognise by her flaming red hair, exit with a recycled shopping bag slung over the wrist of one hand. I whip my head around to Ryan and hiss at him, "Shit, duck down!" as I grab the menu off the table and hold it up to slouch behind. Ryan, spying the girl exiting, immediately slouches down with his head close to mine, as if he's considering the menu along with me. I can't help it, I start to giggle nervously, which sets Ryan to laughing. Both of us are laughing so hard as Helga's girlfriend leaves the bar that we're oblivious to the people around us.

Ryan

Phoebe and I look up to see Jonathan and Theresa standing in front of us. Jonathan extends a finger and pokes at my chest. "What's that?"

I look down and see the perfect imprint of Phoebe's lips in the flaming red colour that she's still wearing, with a dark, bloodied edge to it. I look at my puzzled friends and sigh. "Oh, where to start——"

Phoebe interrupts, "Oh, let me tell this. I'm good at putting people in the picture."

"Do you really think they deserve that?" I can feel hysterical laughter bubbling somewhere near the surface.

"Well, if we had to endure it, they can hear the telling of it, surely?"

Frustrated, Jonathan says, "Just bloody well get to the point, already!"

Phoebe holds her hands up in a calming fashion. "All right, keep your shirt on! We went back to the apartment to quickly change and come down here to meet you two for a drink, right? Obviously, that didn't happen." She gestures to our unchanged attire. "We walk inside the apartment and the first thing we see is Ryan's housekeeper, naked and in a very compromising position with her girlfriend, right on floor of his apartment." I'm laughing so hard that my eyes are watering. Theresa has never seen me laugh this hard and she's not hiding her surprise.

Jonathan sits forward and slams his hands on the table. "Oh my God! Are you serious?"

Phoebe continues, "I know! So, Ryan's way of dealing with it was to pull me out of there and shove me into the cloak closet and dive in after me. There is only enough room for a couple of coats in there and nothing else."

I defensively counter, "Hey, not my fault, I panicked!"

Phoebe is amused. "Hmm, well Mr 'Cool-In-A-Crisis' stood there with his chest pressed against my face, hence my lipstick mark on his shirt there. It felt like we stood like that for an eternity. I'm not sure if he was trying to keep me silent or suffocate me but nothing was detracting either of us from hearing what was going on outside that door!"

Theresa starts to snicker, but Jonathan's face has gone beetroot purple. Phoebe apologises for being descriptive.

Embarrassed, Jonathan explains, "I'm just not used to such plain speaking."

I have to come to her defence because they really can't know how horrendous it was. "Oh, trust me, Phoebe really held back. Nay words in the English language could describe the carnage of that scene."

Theresa puts a hand to her mouth to stifle another giggle. "That's terrible, Ryan. What are you going to do? You can't let her back in to clean the place, surely."

"I don't know what the hell to do about it. Just before you two came over, we saw the other girl leave. That's why we were hiding behind the menu. I want to leave plenty of time for Helga to vacate the apartment, so I don't have to see her. Then I'll have to think of something to tell the cleaning company so that I can have her replaced with someone with a few more scruples!"

We end up eating an early dinner with Jonathan and Theresa and eventually talk about Howard's awful behaviour. I'm embarrassed by Catherine's involvement in the phone conversation and upset that Howard's behaviour left Phoebe with a cut mouth. Her bottom lip is still slightly swollen, and I feel a pang of guilt that this happened on my watch.

Phoebe

With trepidation, I stand behind Ryan as he opens the door and pokes his head inside. Both of us glance at the floor where the act took place. I look up at Ryan. "I'll grab the mop and bucket; you grab a towel."

We mop the entire tiled area with disinfectant and dry it off but we both avoid stepping on the area for the remainder of the evening until it dries.

I look at my watch. "Bugger! I was supposed to Skype-call Mercedes about fifteen minutes ago. Do you mind if I disappear for a bit?"

"Not at all, I'm going to have a shower anyway… try to rid myself of the horrors of the day."

As soon as I log in and answer the Skype call, I'm greeted by Mercedes, glaring back at me with a face like thunder. "What took you so long? I've been sitting here for ages waiting for you to answer."

I'm exasperated. Why do teenagers think the whole world revolves around them? "Mercedes, I have had a really shitty day. Please don't start with a pissy attitude, I've missed you."

Mercedes looks contrite. I ask her how she has been, and she relays the highs and lows of her week with much animation, then she gushes at me. "Mum, I went on a proper date with Josh."

"Monique's brother?" I didn't see that coming. She emphatically nods. I consciously keep my smile big because Mercedes looks happy.

She puts her hands under her chin and looks like a young girl in love. She pauses for a moment then draws her face closer to the camera. "Mum, is your lip swollen?"

I run my finger over my lip and feel that it is still a little puffy. "Long story, honey. Why don't you tell me about Josh."?

She takes this as consent to gush and her excitement is tangible. "So, you know he's Monique's brother and I'd seen him a couple of times in the park before you left. Well, he's in Seth's year but he's still seventeen. He's not turning eighteen until the end of the year. He is so cute, Mum. And he holds my hand and he smells so fine!"

My God, Mercedes is only fifteen. I don't know if I want her dating a seventeen-year-old. I have to try really hard to hide my panic. I make a mental note to ask John to keep an eye on her. I don't want her having sex at fifteen. She's just a kid. I'm not a fan of Monique. She is shallow and full of her own self-importance. Although polite when she comes to our house, I can see through her. I don't like the way she speaks to my daughter and I don't like how Mercedes has started to behave. I hope her brother is nicer to my daughter than she is. I tune back in to Mercy.

"I had my first kiss," she squeaks. This upsets me, and I struggle to hide it. I missed it, I missed her first kiss. I feel guilty for not being there.

So, I ask the question all good mothers should ask. "Is he a good kisser?"

I expect her to be horrified by the question and yell "gross" at me, but she sits in close to the camera and whispers, "He is such a good kisser. I was so nervous because I've never kissed before, but it was so good that I thought I'd die of happiness." She pauses for a moment, then says, "To be honest, I kissed him before you left but we were hardly speaking, and I didn't want to share him with you then."

I'm a little hurt by this news. The horror of the weeks preceding my departure reminds me that neither of us was up for that kind of discussion. She holds her phone up to the camera in her PC to show me his picture, and excitedly blurts that he is her boyfriend and they're a 'thing' now. He is very good looking. No wonder my daughter is falling all over the place. She's so young and vulnerable, and I'm worried she'll jump in feet first and get her heart broken. If and when that happens, I hope I'm back home, so I can console her. I'm sad that I can't be with her sharing this over a cup of hot chocolate, so I change the subject because my time is limited, and I don't want to waste it feeling like I'm missing out.

"What's everyone else been up to? Are you and Dad okay?"

She reluctantly changes the direction of the conversation. "Yeah, he's been okay. At first, he was just trying way too hard and it was annoying me. He's backed off a little now. We're still a little polite around each other but I'm sure it will change. Josh came over for dinner last night and Dad made roast chicken, which is Josh's favourite. Dad likes him and called him 'an upstanding young man.'" She executes finger quotes in the air.

That makes me laugh. "He sounds like Grandpa!"

I'm so happy to hear they've moved on from the uncomfortable situation I left them in. I'm relieved that John has met this boy, too, and approves. I assume he would tell me if he had a problem with him, so I send my guilt packing and sit back to listen to the goings-on in the household without me. When Mercedes finishes transmitting the news, she sits forward and whispers, "So, what's he like? Is he cute? What's the wife like?"

I don't want to have this conversation with my fifteen-year-old daughter. My twenty-year marriage only ended weeks ago and its way too soon to be moving on let alone discussing it with my daughter. "Mercedes! He's a lovely man and his wife doesn't live here, he's separated. Besides, I'm most definitely not his type."

"How do you know you're not his type?"

"Well, going by his ex-wife, only recently separated I believe, she was described to me by a girl in the office and it appears he likes tiny, petite, quiet blondes that could fit in my handbag; girls who speak the Queen's English, albeit with an acid tongue. I couldn't be any further from that description if I tried. Having said that, he is quite the gentleman, a quality lacking in a lot of men, and we get along really well. He's got a great sense of humour. Besides all that, he looks like he'd be younger than me. I'm no cradle snatcher." There, that should put a cork in it.

"Oh, Mum! You're both old so age differences don't apply."

Old! I am in my forties! Mercedes giggles at my horrified expression. It's been a long time since I've seen my daughter so relaxed and happy. She is usually uptight and trying really hard to act exactly like the Barbie doll types she socialises with. This is a welcome restoration of her natural personality and happy disposition. I playfully quip, "Oh shut up, you!"

She takes me back to my earlier comment. "What do you mean by 'acid tongue'?"

"I overheard her speaking badly about someone today and it wasn't nice. She's quite a bitch."

I can hear Ryan calling me and my face pales because I have just been making disparaging remarks about his ex-wife. His voice gets louder as he nears the door. "Phoebe? Phoebe, are you there?"

I look at Mercedes and pull a face. Mercedes giggles again. "That's Ryan. I'll get him in here and introduce you."

I stand up and run out of the door to catch Ryan before he goes to the other end of the apartment looking for me. Unfortunately, he enters the room as I am exiting it and my face bounces off his chest. Stumbling backwards, I back into the half-open door, which propels backwards and rebounds off the wall behind it, then comes back to hit me in the back of the head. Ryan utters an "Oooh, shit!" as he continues his momentum into the room. Falling backwards into the room, windmilling my arms in an effort to stop from falling. Ryan is falling forward and reaches out with his hand to try to grasp me before I actually land on my arse. His hands grab a handful of my shirt front as I land and there is a distinct 'ripping' sound as the material of my shirt tears seconds before impact; Ryan lands heavily on top of me.

After several seconds of stunned silence, we're laughing hysterically. He rolls off of me and lies on his back. We have had so much shit happen in a single day that we've completely lost control. I sit up and spy another perfect lipstick imprint in the middle of his clean t-shirt, which I point at and continue to laugh like I've lost my marbles. Ryan points at my torn shirt as his eyes fill with tears of mirth. I wonder if it's actually possible to die laughing. Both of us are jolted back to reality by Mercedes, who I have forgotten is witnessing this ridiculous series of events.

"Um, yoo-hoo! If you two have finished literally rolling around on the floor laughing…"

I leap up and introduce Ryan. "Oh, sorry. Ryan, this is my daughter Mercedes. Honey, this is Ryan."

"Hi Ryan. I see that shit is still happening to Mum all the way over there."

"Hi Mercedes, nice to meet ye. Oh, ye've got no idea how much that statement resonates with today's events. We've had a day from hell!"

Mercedes' smile reaches all the way up to her eyes. Ryan turns to me and says, "I'm going to bed. I'll see you tomorrow. Nice to meet you, Mercedes."

"Likewise." Mercedes beams at him.

"Oh, why were you calling me before? Did you need something?"

Ryan's face registers a memory. "I was looking for Lucifer and wondered if you knew where he was. I've just seen him outside the door."

On cue, Lucifer pads into the room and leaps onto my lap as I resume my seat in front of the laptop. Ryan waves a hand and disappears out of the door. "Goodnight."

I turn my attention back to Mercy. "Mercedes, meet the handsome Lucifer." Lucifer begins to settle himself on my lap, massaging my legs and purring loudly. His face is the epitome of bliss.

Mercy squeaks at the monitor, "Oh look at him, he's soooo cute!" Then she whispers, "So is Ryan, for an old guy."

That gets her an eye roll. Exhausted from the emotion of the day's events, I bid Mercedes goodnight, promising to Skype with her in a couple of days when Seth can join in. I miss him too. Lucifer follows me into my bedroom and makes himself comfortable on my bed. I make it through two-thirds of a page of my novel before I realise that I have dozed mid-chapter. Turning off the light, I slip into an easy slumber within seconds of being horizontal.

19

Charitable Behaviour

Phoebe

Slowly rising through the fog and surfacing from sleep, I have a few minutes before the alarm goes off. I sit up in bed and look around me. Except for Lucifer snuggled beside me, I am alone in my room in Ryan's apartment. Lucifer stretches his front paws and his body quivers next to mine; he looks blissfully happy. He meeps a hello at me. Running my hand down his sleek coat, I whisper hello back at him.

I recollect that today is the charity event that everybody in the office has been talking about this past week. The entire London office and their families attend the annual event and thankfully, due to my late arrival into the country, I am exempt from participating in the event and have completely missed the draw. The event this year has been dubbed 'Onesies for Kiddies', so I imagine we'll all get a good laugh out of some of the costumes. All proceeds collected will be donated to a children's charity of the event organiser's choice; someone in Human Resources, I recall.

Ryan raps his knuckles on my bedroom door. I sit up and call out that he can enter.

He pops his head around the corner of the door, his expression concerned. "What's up?" I query.

"I just had a call from Simon in Finance. They've only got two hours until the charity thing happens and two late withdrawals of the selected participants. Marcus has stomach flu and can't stop puking or shitting and Amy woke up this morning with a migraine. Neither of them can participate or even attend so Simon's called an emergency meeting to come up with a solution. After much deliberation they called me on a conference call and asked if you and I can step in. I'm really not keen on the idea but they're desperate. I assume you can ride a bike so, do you think you will be okay with this?"

Taken off guard, I can only stare at him with an open mouth. My brain is screaming "No!" but my stupid mouths says nothing. He raises his eyebrows, waiting for an answer. I don't want to be a party pooper.

"Um okay, I guess I can do it if you're going to do it."

"Great, thanks" and he disappears, quietly closing the door as he leaves. Shit, what have I just signed up for? Shit, shit, shit, shit, SHIT! A moment later he is back. I'm still sitting in the exact position he left me in, listening to my brain scream the same expletive over and over. He walks in and sits on the bed, almost toppling me into him as the bed dips.

"Thanks for saying 'yes'. They're very pleased with us."

Nervously, I ask him what I will have to do. "I've just asked Simon the same question. The long and the short of it is, they'll dress us up in funny onesie outfits and we will have to cycle around a set track. You *can* ride a bike, right?" I nod mutely at him. He looks relieved, "Okay, good. So we will ride around this track in our ridiculous getup, which will probably take 20 minutes or so. The whole track will be lined with the office staff and their families, cheering us on. Afterwards, there will be an awards ceremony, all in good humour, and then, there will be a fair at the end point with carnival rides and fairy floss, a petting zoo and loads of food and drink marquees. It should be fun. My kids would have loved it, but Catherine wouldna let me bring them because it's not my weekend".

I don't know what to say to that. Ryan feels the weight of the silence, "The only catch is that we've got to be quick. They need us to get there early to get ready so… sorry Phoebe".

"Okay, say no more. I'll see you in the kitchen soon."
Ryan leaves the room and quietly closes the door.
Shit!

Ryan

I am an arsehole. I have thrown Phoebe under a bus. It's not ideal; neither of us wants to be making a dick of ourselves but what can we do? After Howard's hissy-fit the other day, she is the last person that I should be asking to endure this. Now I feel like a real shit.

Her room smells like her and I like her smell. It has been such a long time since I have been intimate with a woman that pornographic thoughts are almost consuming me. I'm still standing outside her door like a creep, listening. I can hear the shower running and I imagine her with a soapy cloth, lathering herself. I imagine her wet breasts, glistening as the water cascades over them and down her belly.

Lucifer meows loudly on the other side of the door and startles me. I almost leap in fright. My erection deflates. Lucifer thrusts a paw under the door and his claws pierce my toe. I stifle a yelp as I whip my foot away from his sharp little claws. There is silence in her room, so I deduce that the shower has stopped. In panic I run from the door towards the living room like I've been caught. I realise that I need to take my own shower and time is limited so I spin around and walk briskly down the hall to get to my own room. As I pass her room, the door opens, and Lucifer darts out and almost breaks his little neck as he collides with my shin. Fuck, his head is a hard nut; my shin is throbbing! He sits back on his haunches and shakes his head. Poor, little man. I reach down and pick him up. As I straighten, I notice Phoebe is standing in her doorway with a fluffy white towel hugging her wet skin. She has another towel wrapped around her head like turban. All the blood in my body floods my crotch and I turn away in embarrassment and mumble something indistinct as I head to my room. Closing the door, I lean back against it, one hand on my beating heart, the other holding my confused cat. Lucifer yowls at me and I get a whiff of his disgusting cat-breath. His breath is so bad that it makes me gag. I make a mental note to mix some teeth cleaning pellets in with his dry food to fix this problem. He meows again, and I hold my breath so I don't smell his stinky kitty breath. Putting him down, I open my door ajar to grant him an exit. When I look up, Phoebe is still standing in her doorway wrapped in her towel, looking at me. My face flushes as my dick stands to attention again, like it's fourteen and can't be controlled. I smile and wave, because I'm awkward, and shut the door. I head for the bathroom for a shower; I need to get Percy back under control.

Phoebe
An hour later and we arrive at the charity event location. We're running late because we had not expected our taxi to encounter a fender bender two cars in front of us, which has delayed us by ten minutes. Ryan has spent the last few minutes of our hasty trip fielding frantic calls from Simon. As we run up the back stairs, Simon greets us at the top and hurries us into separate rooms.

I am unceremoniously plonked into a swivel chair with my back to the mirror, opposite the door. A blond girl with frizzy yellow hair, a bright pink smile and a makeup bag slung over her shoulder, enters the room and immediately starts applying powder to my forehead and cheeks. She doesn't say hello, doesn't speak at all so I don't say anything. I can't even smile because I don't want makeup on my teeth. The blonde is applying all manner colours from a bright pallet on my face and I realise this is not going to be everyday makeup. She chews gum like a cow chewing cud throughout the entire prep-up. She hasn't spoken a word to me, but she keeps smiling. As she is applying the last few touches to my face, she squats down beside me and states in a gust of minty breath, "I'm going to get your onesie. You can turn around and see your face now."

As she disappears from the room, I swivel my chair and gasp in surprise. She has painted my face in an array of bright colours that scream at me. I have little rainbows on my cheeks which sparkle with glitter and the artistry is really beautiful. She returns a few moments later with a giant white onesie with a silver probiscus. I stifle a groan; white is going to make me look like fat little witchetty grub. Her smile is bright as she holds the costume out to me. "I'll pop out for a few minutes and let you get your kit off and climb into that, then I'll pop back in and make sure it's all done up properly."

After she exits, I strip off my clothes and quickly get myself tangled in the onesie. The more I try to hastily get into the thing, the more entangled I get. I take the damn thing off and start again. There is a rap on the door, "Are you ready yet?"

I almost scream at her that I'm still trying to get the onesie on, but she enters anyway. She smiles at me and advises, "… sit down on the chair and put your feet in first. It's Phoebe, isn't it? I'm Carly, I'm from Finance."

"Hi Carly," I smile up at her and do as advised and of course it works. I recall my aunt used to say, *'less haste, more speed'*. Carly helps me get my arms in and snaps the studs closed from my waist all the way up to my neck. She pulls the onesie hood up over my head and turns me to face the mirror. I am a unicorn. The onesie is enormous so the material balloons around my ankles and wrists. Carly squats in front of me and wraps the onesie tight around my calves and ties it. I assume this is for safety, so I don't get all caught up in the spokes or chain of the bike. Carly hands me white ugg boots. I look a little ridiculous but decide not to take myself too seriously.

As I set out of the room, Ryan is standing in the hall waiting for me. Ryan's face is painted perfectly as a lion. His face is surrounded by the mane on his lion onesie. The onesie is way too small and ends half way up his calves and wrists respectively. He has long yellow socks and tan coloured ugg boots.

He takes one look at me and bursts into laughter. I march over to him and he stops laughing abruptly; he thinks I'm going to sock him. Instead, I take his hand and lead him into my room and stand him before the mirror. Ryan is not laughing anymore. He looks ridiculous too. After a moment of silence, we both burst into fits of giggles until Simon storms in and tells us to get our arses out of here and to the bike shed, already.

The day is sunny but a little cool. I am grateful for the warmth of the onesie. Carly is standing beside a pink bike with bright coloured streamers puffing out of the ends of the handle bars; the seat cover is a bright rainbow. So much work has gone into this event. Ryan has a giant bike with yellow fur wrapped around all metal parts. There are others dressed in various different onesies retrieving their bikes. I spy a clown, a dog, a cat, a giant bird, a horse, a giraffe and a cow. As we walk our bikes towards the starting line, the crowd starts to cheer, and it builds into a roar. Hundreds of people line the track and there are children everywhere, excitedly cheering and waving. We all wave back at them enthusiastically. The cheer gets louder.

The official puts a megaphone to his mouth and holds a starting gun in the other. "Ladies and gentlemen, domestic and farm animals, clowns and mystical creatures, on your marks, get set, GO!" he booms into the megaphone. He shoots his gun but there is no sound. A red flag pops out the end and drops to reveal the word 'BANG'. After a giggle, we all awkwardly get on our bikes and take off. Ryan shoots to the front followed closely by the clown. A commentator calls the race over the speakers like a horse race and it has the crowd in fits of giggles.

The children are squealing with delight as we cycle past them. The adults are laughing as the commentator continues to hilariously call the race. The track is flat, and the laughter is making it hard to breath and ride fast. As commentator draws us all in with his hilarious race call, the cheering is so loud that the commentator has to shout the finishing names to be heard over the din.

We are all panting and breathless but we're grinning like crazy. The children are screaming with excitement as we jog a lap of honour, dishing out high-fives to their eager hands stretching out from their little bodies hanging over the fences. After the lap of honour, we re-hydrate before we're called to stand on the podium to receive our medals, presented by the CEO. The crowd cheers during the presentation, after which we return to the rooms to shower and change into our civilian clothes again.

As we wander to the fair ground, Simon sidles up and thanks us for stepping in at the last minute. After he leaves, Ryan steers me to the alcohol tent and buys us both a wine. Jonathan and Theresa join us, and we chat as we wander to the food marquees for lunch.

"How did you draw the short straw? We didn't know you were participating," queries Theresa.

"Neither did we. It was last minute; two contestants had to pull out for medical reasons, so they asked us."

Theresa quirks an eyebrow, "Lucky you. You know you looked ridiculous, right? You wouldn't catch me in that get-up. You're a bloody good egg doing that."

I grin at her and wink, "it's all about the brownie points."

We are spoiled for choice in the marquee but because we're famished, we fill our plates with a variety of lovely dishes. We find a table a little away from the noise and bustle of the fair ground. We sit chatting for a few hours as the sun and wine makes us a little drowsy. Before we leave, we all have a go at the carnival games and Ryan wins a duck shooting game. He selects a stuffed unicorn and presents it to me, much to the joy of Jonathan and Theresa.

After the big lunch, we're not hungry for dinner so we return to the bar below Ryan's apartment and enjoy some more wine and share an antipasto platter. We chat for hours and it is a lovely end to a surprisingly enjoyable day. I've decided I'll put the unicorn against the pillows on my bed to keep Lucifer company.

20

Gently Doth He Kiss Thee

Phoebe

Still buzzing from the charity event, and wide awake at eleven in the evening after a hot shower, I put some soft music on low volume and wander into the kitchen. After pouring myself a chardonnay, I hoist myself up onto the kitchen bench and start sifting through my text messages and social media. I take a moment to stretch out the tension that has built in my shoulders as Ryan enters the kitchen. I thought he had gone to bed, so I worry at his sudden appearance and start to remove my posterior from the kitchen counter. Ryan holds up a hand. "Nay, stay there."

"You don't mind? It's a habit I got into at home and it's a hard one to break. I'm not ready for bed yet so I thought I'd just stay up for a while and have a glass of wine… try to get tired. Do you want me to turn the music down?"

Ryan shakes his head. "It's fine, really. I didn't hear it until I came down this end of the house with the same intention. I might join you in a drink, I'm wide awake too. What a day."

He reaches into the top cupboard above me and takes down two shot glasses and a bottle of single malt whisky. He gestures at me, asking me with his dark-chocolate eyes if I'd like to join him. I nod mutely at him. Catching the scent of his aftershave as he moves beside me, I close my eyes and inhale the bouquet of him. My abdomen tightens. He hands me a glass and advises, "When ye throw it back, hold it in yer mouth for ten seconds before ye swallow it."

I do as he bids and find that, in doing so, the sharpness of the alcohol leaves a nice tingling buzz around my gums. Ryan leans in and pours me another shot, but this time he instructs me to hold it for twenty seconds and to keep my eyes closed. He tells me to focus on the sensations inside my mouth. As I hold the amber liquid within my tightly clamped lips, I marvel at the buzz and velvety qualities of the single malt, admiring his expensive taste in liquor, as it smoothly sets my mouth alight and delicately burns before I swallow. Concentrating on the heat in my mouth as the molten liquid silkily slides over my tongue, I sense, rather than feel, his mouth before he gently presses his lips to mine. I swallow the remaining whisky and gently part my lips because I want him to deepen the kiss. He merely changes the angle slightly and gives my lips another soft and warm brush, inviting, seeking consent.

I whisper, "May I open my eyes?"

"Sure," he murmurs against my mouth.

I become aware of the soft and gentle tenor of Jeff Buckley as he croons his haunting rendition of 'Hallelujah'. Ryan's face is still close, his warm breath and aftershave making for a heady concoction for my senses. Leaning forward, I gently return his kiss, inviting him in, enticing him to give just a little more.

His hands are on either side of my hips on the kitchen counter. I wonder if this is more to keep himself upright than to bring us comfortably face to face.

Ryan
I can taste the whisky on her breath and smell the soft scent of her soap; I feel it all the way down into my jocks. She moves her soft lips to gently part mine, deepening the kiss without urgency. I want to press myself against her, to kiss her mouth hard and steer her towards

the bedroom but I don't want to break the soft spell she has woven between us. I let the kiss gently recede, pulling back to lean against the kitchen counter adjacent to her. I notice she is breathing heavily; I have affected her. My voice is hoarse as I whisper, "I should go to bed before I disgrace myself."

She smiles serenely at me, reaches for my hand and pulls me in again. I allow myself to be pulled back in and I kiss her deeper, with a little more passion, but still withholding the urgency. She runs her hands up and over my chest, around the back of my neck and her fingers weave into my hair, pulling me down harder so that I find myself standing between her thighs, lightly touching her all over. It adds another dimension to the kiss, which has my pulse racing, and I sound an awful lot like I've been for a jog. I can feel myself getting very aroused and the need to press myself hard against her is alarming, so I pull away abruptly, feeling flushed and out of control.

"Jesus," I hear myself gasp. "I really have to go to bed. Sleep tight." I turn to leave and almost run from the room but not before I see her eyes wander down to my crotch; she has spied my arousal straining against my pants.

I make it to my room, gently close the door and, for the second time today, I press my back against it. I don't want to be attracted to her. She is only here for a matter of weeks and I can't get emotionally or physically involved. I'm a little confused by my inability to remain unaffected by her. I wish I hadn't asked her to stay here, I've made a rod for my own back.

21

To Carry A Burden

Mercedes

Searching the fridge for something to fill my delicate stomach, my jaw shudders as a wave of nausea washes over me. I have felt this way on and off for a couple of weeks now and wonder if the virus I suspected I have is actually something worse. My heart thuds hugely in my chest as I wonder if I could be pregnant. Surely, I didn't get pregnant after only two times. How crappy would my luck be? I put a calendar alert in my phone to remind me to call by the chemist to grab a pregnancy test kit on the way home from school so at least I can take that off my list of things to stress about.

I can't find anything alluring in the fridge that doesn't make my stomach lurch, so I close it and rustle through the pantry until I find a dry biscuit to nibble. Hearing the kettle reach boiling point, I get out a coffee cup, but the thought of coffee makes my stomach flip-flop. I return the coffee mug and take out a tea cup instead.

As I wait for the camomile tea to brew, I mentally count back the days since my last period and freeze when I remember. The concern steps up to real fear when I realise that I haven't had a period since we last had sex. How could I have missed this? Oh my God! My stomach shudders and make a run for the bathroom. I retch over the toilet bowl and actually follow through with a little bit of puke, which is mostly fluid and a little bit of the undigested biscuit. I think I might go to the chemist before school and get the test over with because now I'm actually worrying myself sick.

The thing about sex with Josh is that I enjoy the feeling of him being on top of me, I like being naked and I understand about the desire, but it still hurts. Even the second time, he was incredibly gentle with me and continuously asked me if I really wanted to do it. I'm blessed that he's so thoughtful and caring. Some of my friends, when they were still my friends, were pushed or railroaded into having sex, but Josh is legitimately the best boyfriend.

I feel a twinge of regret that I don't have those girls as my friends anymore. Now I sit alone or go to the library during lunch and recess to avoid their bitchy words. I guess one positive is that my homework is done on time and I'm up to date with my revision. The negative is that I feel ostracised and alone. I can't talk to anyone about my wonderful boyfriend or my first-time having sex, or even the crap going on with my parents because I've got no one. I'm completely alienated.

Back in the kitchen, I sip my tea. I feel a little better after throwing up and hope the icky feeling goes away soon, but I can't seem to drink the tea; it's making the nausea return. I really hope that I've concocted this whole pregnancy nonsense inside my head and that the test shows up negative. My worry is not helping the situation, so I decide to put my shoes on, grab an apple and go directly to the chemist to collect the test kit first. The sooner I know for sure, the better I will feel.

I dart into the loo for a nervous piddle before I leave. I check my look in the mirror and accidentally bump my boob with my forearm, and it hurts. I feel like I've been punched in the boobs. I wonder if I'm actually finally getting my period and all this worry is for nothing as sometimes my boobs get tender around my period. I unbutton my school dress to look at the poor things reflected in the mirror and see they are almost bulging over my bra. I look down at my suddenly full bra. My boobs are big!

* * * * *

Within fifteen minutes I've grabbed the test kit from the chemist and I'm attempting to pee on the stick, without peeing all over my fingers, whilst hovering over a toilet bowl in the school bathrooms. This is ridiculously awkward. I promise myself that I won't look at the stick until the two minutes is up, so I pull my knickers up, close the toilet lid and sit on it, watching the seconds go by on my watch. After the two minutes, I take a deep, steadying breath and look at the stick. Two bars… the test is positive. Shit! I abruptly stand and start pacing within the small cubicle. Holy crap, I'm pregnant. The shock hits me and I'm forced to sit down on the toilet lid again.

What the hell am I going to do? Who can I tell? Who *is* there to tell? There's Josh… actually, there's only Josh that I can tell. Oh God, what will Josh say? Will Josh leave me? Am I going to lose him too? Shit, shit, shit. I'm too upset to concentrate so I zip the peed-on pregnancy stick in my pocket, stuff the packaging back into my bag to dispose of later and walk to my first class. I'm unable to concentrate during the entire first period so, after the bell, I make my way to sickbay to tell the nurse that I'm feeling unwell and to ask if I can call Dad to collect me.

Dad arrives shortly after to take me home. We're sitting in the car in the car park, and he looks deeply into my eyes and asks, "Are you okay, sweetheart? You look a little peaky."

I feel utterly miserable. I'm sick from the pregnancy, but I have a different kind of nervous sick feeling going on now that I know I'm pregnant. I'm a little scared to open my mouth to speak because the nausea has returned. I manage to mumble, "I just don't feel well, Daddy. I don't know what's wrong, but I feel really crap." I'm aware that I sound like a little girl, but I feel icky and I just want him to take me home.

Dad reaches over and puts the back of his hand on my forehead. "You feel a little clammy but you're not burning up."

The nausea sweeps over me in a dizzying wave and I quickly open the door and vomit beside the car. When I finish, I pull myself back inside the car, shut the door and close my eyes, trying to slow my breathing. I just want to be home in bed, but I don't want to endure the car ride to get there. I hope to God I don't vomit all over myself on the way there. I open the car door again for another purge.

John

I am waiting for Mercedes to stop hurling outside of the car door. I hope she doesn't have a stomach bug that will have me doing the same thing within twenty-four hours. I really don't need to get sick – I need to focus on the school design plans that are due soon. I feel immediately guilty for my selfishness. My poor girl looks pale and sweaty and I need to get her home and comfortable as soon as she stops chundering outside the car. I hope she doesn't spew all over the front seat. I look into the back seats for something to give her to puke into and find an old towel that I keep in the car for when Seth plays footy in the mud and rain. I drape the towel over her lap and tentatively ask, like she's made of glass and will break should I change my tone, "Are you okay for me to take you home now, honey?"

Without opening her eyes, Mercedes nods her ascent and I start the car to take her home, deciding some chicken noodle soup would be perfect to settle her churning tum. When we arrive, I help her to her room, remove her shoes and tuck her into bed like I did when she was a child. She's too ill to even change into her PJs and crawls into bed in her uniform. Fluffing her pillows, I try to make a show of caring for her because sometimes just knowing somebody is there for you is enough… her eyes are still closed. She is probably wishing I would bugger off and leave her alone. I go into the bathroom and wet a facecloth to drape over her forehead, telling her I will go and make her something to settle her stomach. She manages a small smile but still looks a little peaky.

I return an hour later with a bowl of soup and some crusty bread on a tray. To my surprise, she wolfs down the whole bowl and the bread and lies back down, as if exhausted by the effort. This perplexes me. I sweep her hair, damp from the facecloth, back from her forehead and gather the tray and empty plates to leave her to her rest. Maybe it wasn't a virus or perhaps it's already run its course.

I wonder if perhaps she's worried about her upcoming exams or if the girls at school have been giving her grief again. She is prone to bouts of anxiety during times of stress that can sometimes result in vomiting. Phoebe and I have talked with her about seeing a professional who can provide tips and breathing exercises for high-stress times but so far, she's not been agreeable to that path.

The bitchy girls are bothering me, though. Just last week I heard her sobbing in her room, and, as I hovered outside listening with an ear to the door, I could hear her complaining to Josh on her phone about the girls in her group who've been nasty of late. I hope she doesn't make up with those girls. They are bitchy and venomous. Neither Phoebe nor I were pleased when she hooked up with this group. Our sweet girl started showing signs of the same bitchy behaviour and it is completely out of character. I can't fix this for her though, I have to let Mercedes find her own way out of this one. I reassure myself that she is learning some life skills and how to deal with difficult or insidious personalities, but it doesn't make me feel any less impotent as I stand by and let her work her own way through it.

I walk away from her door and allow her the rest she needs. The chicken noodle soup should perk her up a little. So far, she has kept it all down so I cross my fingers. I have put a bucket beside her bed should her stomach not find the soup agreeable. Hope for the best, prepare for the worst.

Mercedes

After Dad closes my bedroom door, I look at my watch and calculate that it will be lunchtime at school now. I send a brief text to Josh:

Hey babe, I'm home from school. I'm not feeling well today so Dad picked me up. I puked so I think I might have a virus or something. Can we maybe catch up tomorrow instead? M xoxo

I lie back on the pillows and wait for his response. I don't have to wait long as a couple of minutes later a reply pings and I open his message:

Sure baby, I hope you're feeling better soon. Rest up and I'll text you tomorrow. J xx

I really need to buy myself some time. I have no idea what to do. Maybe twenty-four hours of thinking will make a difference. I really miss Monique. In any other circumstances, I would go straight to her and we would toss it around together. Now I've sabotaged my relationship with all my friends because I chose Josh. I wish Mum wasn't a million miles away in another country. I really need a mum hug and she would know what to do. But can I even tell Mum and Dad? They will surely fly off the handle at this news. Nobody wants their fifteen-year-old daughter to be pregnant. What about school? What about the child? How the hell will I be able to care for a child when I'm still basically a child myself? What a mess I've gotten myself into… and I've dragged Josh into my mess with me. The internet lied… you can get pregnant straight after your bloody period.

Tears slide down my cheeks and onto the sheet that I've pulled up to my chin. How am I supposed to deal with this? Maybe I should start by telling Josh. He is two years older than me; surely, he'll have some idea what to do. Then panic clenches my belly again because the poor guy is completing his final year of high school and I don't want this to screw it up for him. He's really studious and working so hard to keep his grades up; I don't want to be the reason it all goes to hell.

How is he supposed to concentrate on completing the year when he is expecting to become a father in the near future? Have I set us both up for failure because I screwed up with my cycle? I rationalise that I can't make any decisions on my own, we're both in it and I owe it to Josh to be upfront with him. If he runs screaming for the hills then I'll just have to deal with that, too, but I have to start somewhere and, let's face it, I didn't get myself knocked up all by myself.

He's going to be so pissed at me because I assured him when he couldn't produce a condom for that second time that we'd be fine with my period having just passed a few days before. Then I completely forgot about it and hadn't even realised that I'd missed the next period.

* * * * *

It's been twenty-four hours and I hear the ping of an arriving text.

Hey babe, how are you feeling today? Wanna catch up? J x

I still feel delicate but it's Saturday. I'm rested and ready to share so I send a reply to Josh:

Hey, let's go for a walk in the park today.

The response is quick:

Sure, I'll swing by in five minutes.

Sliding my phone into my back pocket, I put on my shoes and shove the pregnancy test strip, which I've wrapped in a tissue because of the gross pee factor, into the pocket of my hoodie, then I walk outside to wait for Josh. I spy him jogging down the street and my heart-rate picks up because at the moment, he is my world. Immediately, a sense of relief flows through me; I no longer feel alone in this ordeal.

We walk the few streets to the park hand in hand. I'm safe and secure when I hold his hand as I breathe in the familiar smell of his aftershave mixed with washing detergent on his windcheater. Josh senses that something is up and appears to be waiting for me to start the conversation. I decide to wait until we are on the park bench before I start.

"Josh, I know why I'm sick."

A look of concern crosses his face, so I press on before he can interrupt and before I lose my nerve. "Do you remember the second time we did it? Had sex, I mean?"

Josh looks relieved. "Of course, I do, it was only like, a few weeks ago. What about it?"

Then I watch the colour drain from his face – he knows what I'm going to tell him before I say it out loud. "Oh my God, you're pregnant."

Here it comes. I wait for him to vent and rant and throw his arms up in the air and accuse me of trapping him. He doesn't say anything else; he's waiting for me to elaborate.

"Yes. Well, it was over a month ago. I took the test yesterday and it has two bars." I reach into my hoodie pocket and extract the test stick, waving it in front of his face. "See? Pregnant."

Josh waits a beat then says the accusation very gently. I promise myself that I will not lose my shit. I have taken him by surprise and I will give him time to let this sink in. "I thought you said you couldn't get pregnant."

My gaze drops to my lap because I feel guilty and responsible for this mess. I want to cry but Josh deserves my strength right now. My response is not defensive, it's babbling out of me because I want him to forgive me and I don't want to be in this alone.

"I thought I couldn't get pregnant a couple of days after my period but apparently I could… and I did. My period has been like clockwork since I was twelve… every month on the dot; never a day late. I don't know what the hell happened, and I don't know what to do. I'm so naïve, it's all my fault. I think I need to start with a doctor, but I don't know if I should tell Dad first or if parents actually have to be there since I'm not an adult… I just don't know."

Josh reaches for my hand because he is just a beautiful, forgiving person and I do not deserve his trust right now. "What do you want to do, Mercy?"

I blurt out my biggest fear and it comes out sounding like a wretched babble, "I can't kill it! I just can't do that. I understand if you want to walk away from me now and I know I said it would be fine because my period had just finished but it wasn't. It's my fault, I know that. I don't know what happened, but the fact of the matter is, I'm going to have a baby and I don't know what to do."

Josh looks hurt and offended. "My God, Mercy, what do you think of me? I'm not leaving you, I still went ahead and had sex with you knowing we didn't have protection. I'm stupid and naïve too, both of us are. I know the facts and I should've been strong, but we went ahead despite the risks. No matter what, I'm not going to leave you. I love you."

To my horror, a sob escapes me like a dog bark! I'm an emotional train wreck and Josh just said he loves me. In the middle of this shitstorm, Josh just told me he loves me. Tears are sitting on my eyelashes and I fight the blink reflex because I don't want them to cascade down my cheeks, dragging my mascara with them so I end up looking tragic. Josh just said he loves me.

The sun hits the tears as I look up at Josh and a kaleidoscope of brilliant light bursts across my vision. I'm trying so hard not to cry and I don't want to sob when I say this, so I whisper, "I love you too." He squeezes my hand, clasped in his, and brushes his lips over my knuckles. I sag in relief. He's not going to run, and I am not alone.

"When did you find out?"

"Yesterday. I've been feeling icky for days and I wondered if my period was coming when I suddenly remembered that I didn't actually have it last week when it was due. I went straight to the chemist before school and got the test, then did it in the girl's loos at school."

"Ew! Why did you do it there, of all places?"

"Because I didn't want to be late for school, but then after I bought the test from the chemist, I didn't want to wait until I got home again so I just did it and then went to class. I was sick with worry by recess, so I ended up in sickbay and asked them to call Dad to collect me. I actually threw up outside Dad's car, so he legitimately thought I was ill with some kind of virus. He probably disinfected the whole front seat thinking I had something that he was going to contract."

"What do you want to do?"

I shake my head. "I don't know what to do." I look up at the earnest expression on Josh's face. He's so beautiful to look at and I can't keep it to myself, so I gush, "I really do love you."

He leans down and plants a soft kiss on my lips. I hiccup a sob then give in to the turmoil, unleashing all of my pent-up emotions on his shoulder. Josh runs his fingers through my hair soothingly and lets me cry. We stay this way for a long time until I get myself under control. Finally, Josh says, "We have to tell our parents. Can you ask your dad to pick you up from my house tonight and we'll tell them both together? Hopefully they don't yell at us. I'm doing year twelve and don't even have the means to support myself, let alone you and our child."

"Maybe I can have the baby and then give it up for adoption?" I don't know if that's what I want but it is an option I'm putting out there.

"Do you think you'd be strong enough to let it go after you've been living with it growing inside you for nine months? My God, why did we take this chance?" Josh wonders aloud.

We stay on the bench, me resting my head on his shoulder and him gently stroking my back in rhythmic circles, both of us lost in our own thoughts, both of us circling the same disturbing reality.

* * * * *

Dad arrives at Josh's house at seven in the evening as requested. We're at the table and we hear the door open; Dad is greeted by Josh's mum, Jennifer. She invites him in and, as he enters the kitchen, he looks about and sees Matthew, Josh's dad, and Josh and me sitting at the table with a solemn expression. Dad suddenly looks wary.

"What's up guys?" He goes for cheery because that's Dad's go-to expression. He's about to feel the smile slide from his face. I guess now he will know what it's like to be hit by an unexpected bombshell.

Matthew replies, "We're having a meeting, apparently. These two probably feel the need to confess their undying love for each other." He points at us, laughing loudly, and Josh tenses beside me at his father's patronising tone.

Dad laughs nervously; he looks at my face and I'm pretty sure he can tell that something serious is about to be discussed. I wonder if he thinks I'm going to throw the whole 'Dad is gay' conversation around the table, like I'm *that* arsehole.

Josh draws a deep breath, looks at me for a moment and, on my nod, begins to say what has to be said. "I want you all to remain calm."

Straightaway, everyone shuffles in their seats. Seven words and they're all sitting up like they've each got a rod up their arses. Josh continues, "I'm just going to come out and say it because it's not the type of thing you can gently lead into and we just don't know what to do so... here goes... Mercedes is pregnant."

Matthew reacts first. He is glaring at Josh with anger like he magically did this all by himself. "What the hell, Josh? Mercedes is fifteen years old. What the bloody hell is going on here? What were you thinking, Joshua?"

Josh holds up placating hands, trying to calm his upset father. "I know. We thought we both felt ready and we thought we would be okay but we're not and we screwed up. We can't undo that, but we just don't know where to go from here, so some helpful advice would be great."

Dad looks at me and his disappointment is clear. I look down at my fingers, which are clasped tightly in my lap because I don't want to feel the weight of that gaze. I think I would rather he be angry than disappointed.

Jennifer says, in a low tone, "I'm a little surprised at you, Josh. I thought you knew about basic prevention. If you're old enough to do the deed, then you're old enough to deal with the consequences."

I look up from my clasped hands and see she is glaring at him. I want to scream at her to leave him alone but instead I say, "It was my fault. I'd just finished my period and I thought we'd be safe but, obviously, we weren't." A look of incredulity crosses Jennifer's face at my naïve statement.

Matthew queries, "Again, what were you thinking? Neither of you is equipped to be parents at this time. You can't seriously be entertaining the idea of having it, Mercedes?"

I feel his glare on me and I squirm under the intensity of it. I give him my sternest gaze and say, clearly, "I can't and won't have an abortion, I'd never be able to live with myself. That's just not an option. I really don't know what to do but that is not on the table."

Dad stands up to leave. "I think we need a little time to let this all sink in. How about we all go our separate ways tonight? The way I see it, the first step will be to go to see the doctor and have it all confirmed. After that, we will do a little research and I'll talk with Mercedes and you can talk to Josh, and then we will regroup in a couple of days when we have more information. Whatever we all decide to do, it's a little late to start the shame game; let's just move forward and come up with a solution."

God, I love my dad. He is telling them to pull their heads in and not start yelling or pointing the finger. At this pivotal moment in my short and really screwed-up life, he is my hero and I can almost see his cape flapping behind him as he stands tall beside me.

Matthew rubs his hands vigorously over his face because he's freaking out. "Yep, and I'm a little shocked and angry at the moment so anything I say will just be negative. Let's do that. I'll give you a call in a couple of days, John, and we'll talk about this further when we've had a little time for the news to sink in and you've got confirmation from the doctor."

Josh's parents and my dad start walking towards the front door. I turn to Josh for a reassuring hug because it's been a huge day and I'm drained. As I'm doing so, I spy Monique over his shoulder, standing in the doorway with a scowl on her face. Was she listening all the time? The scowl makes her look ugly, as if someone has taken a knife and slashed it across her face. She continues to glare at me and shakes her head in disgust. I'm pretty sure I won't like what is about to come out of her mouth. "So, you're a stupid bitch *and* a slut."

Typical of Monique to lay the boot in when I'm already down. How did I miss her friendship? Josh comes to my defence and rounds on her. "You want to know what a bitch is? Go take a look in the mirror. There's a bitch for you. You and your girlfriends have treated Mercy like shit, so you don't get to comment."

Monique's face turns an ugly shade of dark pink and she spits at him, "Fuck you, Josh. You had to stick your dick into one of my friends, didn't you? Now you've just ruined it for everybody. Oh, and baby is having a baby, how very tragic. You're really stupid, you know that? And you know what else? You two deserve each other. You can have her – she's damaged goods now anyway." She looks me up and down like I am despicable, her back stiff and disgust written all over her face as she abruptly turns and storms upstairs.

Stung, I turn away from Josh and stalk out of the house to climb into the car next to Dad. I wonder if Dad is going to lose his temper with me when the car door is closed but instead, he reaches for my hand and gives it a reassuring squeeze. My heart constrict and it's all I can do to stop myself from crying in front of him like the fifteen-year-old child that I am. I risk a glance and he's looking at me with all the love and forgiveness I need. I wonder if Mum will be forgiving of my screw up.

I look up at Dad and ask, "Can we keep this from Mum until she comes back? I don't want to ruin her trip; she needs this time to sort herself out."

He gives my hand another squeeze and says, "Of course we can, sweetheart." I squeeze his hand back then reluctantly pull my hand from his, so I can buckle my seatbelt.

22

The Panty Shimmy

Phoebe

I blink awake to a knock at the bedroom door. Rolling onto my back, I stretch and groan. "Yep?" I mumble, my mouth and eyes still glued shut with sleep. The bed is vibrating so I look over at Lucifer and he has the unicorn in a bear hug beside me and he is beating the shit out of if with his back feet. Ryan calls to me on the other side of the door.

"Are you nearly ready, Phoebe? I can't be late."

"What?" I jerk awake and reach for my phone, the timer is running, and it's been a stupid number of hours. What the hell? Sitting up, I look at the time at the top of my phone and leap out of bed. I inadvertently set the timer instead of the alarm last night. It is 7.30am! Ffuuucckkk!

I'm sure Ryan can hear me banging about in my room, uttering expletives. I yank the door open and panic yell in his face, irrespective of my morning death-breath, "My alarm didn't go off! Give me five minutes, okay?"

Ryan takes a step back. I'm not sure if it's my *dead-budgie-in-a-cage* breath or because I haven't respected his personal space. I must look very undone, but I can see by his eyes that he likes what he sees. What is it with men getting all aroused by a woman's freak? He nods and takes another step back. I close the door in his face because I'm freaking out. I yell another expletive when I catch my image in the mirror. My hair is a riot of untamed knots, frizz and curls, my face is lined with the creases of sleep and my pyjama bottoms are twisted so that they're absurdly tight on one thigh and a baggy sack on the other. The poor bastard is probably thinking he's definitely going to be late because a woman's five minutes is very different to a man's five minutes. I am going to pleasantly surprise him because I'm sure he is thinking that he didn't sign up for this shit.

I spend two minutes in the shower, almost tearing my hair out in my haste to wash and condition it. As I hurriedly dry myself, I slip on the suds at the bottom of the shower recess and land with a colossal, thunderous whump that sounds like an elephant has fallen through the ceiling and has surely registered on the Richter Scale. I rub my tender rump, the red welt already spreading over my derrière. I can hear Ryan banging on the door asking what the hell the noise was. Mortified, I yell, "I'm okay, just slipped. I'm nearly done."

The hell I am. Yanking on my underwear, which is gripping my undried thighs and rolling into a cylindrical nightmare, I hear the tear of material, but I pay this no mind because I'm bloody late. I hurriedly zip my skirt, button my shirt and apply my makeup and, in my haste, poke myself in the eye with the mascara wand. My eye starts watering profusely, raining black tears down my cheek. I want to scream and vent as I dab the tears with a tissue. I grab a brush and hair tie so I can fix my hair in the car, and run out of the bedroom.

True to my word, I enter the kitchen after five minutes. I'm hopping on one foot as I fit a heel on the other, then bracing myself on the wall as I fit the second heel. My hair is a wet mess and my left eye is red and watery, but I'm here and Ryan won't be late. He takes in my appearance and I can see he is trying to stifle a grin. I want to hit him over the head with the brush I'm holding but I choose instead to collect my bag and coat and look pointedly at him. He is still looking at the wet chaos of hair hanging and dripping all over my shoulders and I'm grateful that I'm wearing black so the red of my hair colour leeching from the tangled mess, which continues to run for a month after colouring, doesn't stain my clothes. "I'll do my hair in the car."

Ryan frowns, hands me a coffee, and asks, "What happened to your eye?"

"A casualty of my haste. I don't perform well under pressure."

"I beg to differ," he counters. I look up to see him smiling appreciatively at me. I want to tell him to bugger off, but I keep myself nice. It's not his fault I'm stupid. My eye continues to stream tears, all the way to the office, leaving one side of my face devoid of makeup. My hasty braid is rough and skew-whiff but at least I have tamed the wet mess. As I'm applying the lipstick, Ryan fails to adequately break for a speed hump. My hand darts across my face and my lipstick skids up my nose, trailing bright-red lipstick from the top of my lip right inside my nostril.

Unable to contain my anxiety, I yelp, "Fuck!" loudly. Ryan apologises but I can see he is enjoying my fluster. "Stop laughing at me!" I growl, and he manages to contain his mirth.

I search my handbag frantically for a tissue to no avail. We pull into the car space and get out of the car. I point to my mouth then turn and walk off, calling over my shoulder, "I have to go to the restrooms to fix my face." Ryan takes the stairs to the ground floor where he'll catch the elevator up to the sixth floor. I make a beeline for the loos.

When I get into the bathroom, I put my face close to the mirror and groan. There is a red line of lipstick going straight into my nose. No wonder Ryan couldn't help but laugh; I look comical. My left eye is still red, squinty and watering, the lipstick line looks like I've been attacked with a knife, and there's a loop of hair that has failed to make the braid properly which is stuck up on top of my head like a shark fin. I am astounded that I can look so ridiculous. My hair is all over the place and even though I've removed the excess, the lipstick has stained my skin.

I walk back out of the bathroom and head for the elevator and see Theresa, who is walking towards me. She smiles tentatively. She is not used to seeing me dishevelled, and for a moment she looks a little worried. The elevator doors open and I stalk in after her.

I think I'd better explain myself, so I start with, "The alarm didn't go off. Sorry, I'm having a shit day."

Theresa smiles at me, clearly stifling a giggle. "Is now a good time to ask you what you're doing on Saturday? I meant to ask you the other day, but I didn't actually see you."

"Ask me what?"

"Do you want to come horse riding with me at my cousin's farm? I'm assuming Ryan hasn't got anything planned for you."

"Okay, sure. I don't think Ryan has anything planned but I'll ask him later today."

"Have you ever ridden a horse before?"

"Of course, heaps of times."

"Great, I'll pick you up at five thirty. Don't forget to set your alarm." Theresa winks at me as the elevator doors open on our floor.

I process what she's just told me. I call after her, "Five thirty? In the morning?"

"It's a fair drive. I'll call you when I get outside your apartment block."

"What should I wear?"

"Just some old jeans. It's about being comfortable. My cousin has boots and riding hats, so you just need to dress sensibly."

I smile at her. "Now let's hope my day gets better."

"Don't jinx yourself, honey, it's only just begun."

The day does not get any better. The scanner deems all my document 'infected' with a virus, which it refuses to send to my email address; instead, storing them in quarantine, which I cannot access without the help of the IT department. Fed up, I decide to ask for help.

As I am walking down the hall, heading towards the IT department, something snaps and stings my hip. I stop awkwardly mid-stride and feel my knickers shimmy down my thigh to pool at my ankle. Shit! I kick my foot up in the air, flicking the knickers off the end of my shoe and into the air in one fluid movement, which I deftly catch in my hand before anyone can see my predicament. Unfortunately, as I flick my leg up, the split at the back of my skirt tears open all the way up to the zipper and my shoe flies off the end of my foot, bouncing loudly off the glass of the conference room door. Every person in the conference room turns abruptly at the sound. Their eyes widen as they see me staring back at them with a horrified and shocked expression on my face. I hobble over to the shoe to retrieve it and notice that there is a rent in the leather, which has made it gape. My face is flaming and my knickers are scrunched in my hand, which also holds the wrecked shoe, my other hand clutching the back of my skirt together over my bare arse. I smile at the group apologetically and wonder if I should explain myself. How can I explain how my shoe bounced off the glass?

I stand rooted to the spot, feeling like a complete idiot. I spy Ryan and he is smiling broadly at me. He winks, and I want to teleport out of the hallway. I turn on my heel and limp the rest of the way to the IT department, retrieved shoe in hand and spinning my skirt on the side so the split is on the side rather than the back. I snarl an order at the IT guy, like it's his fault my day is buggered, and stalk away.

I return to my desk, pilfer the stapler and make my way to the restrooms where I put my knickers back on, the snapped side tied together in a knot, and staple my skirt back together so I can make it through the rest of the day without flashing everyone. I gingerly sit down, mindful of the staples, and wish I could just go back to bed and start the day again.

My phone starts buzzing. "Phoebe speaking." The propeller head, who is assisting me with my IT issues, asks me to go to the scanner and try to scan my document again and report back with the results. Hanging up the phone, I exhale heavily, and my sigh makes it all the way to Theresa.

"Are you okay?" she queries. I give her a run down of the knickers and skirt issue and she laughs until her eyes tear up. I'm not glad to be the joke. I return to my desk to spy the IT guy approaching… I forgot to test the scanner. I almost lose an eyeball in my exasperated eye roll.

At 4.45pm, Ryan calls to tell me he'll be held up for another hour or so and that I should take the train home. Oh, fabulous. I limp on my destroyed shoes to the Underground. As I make my way to the platform, I see the train I am supposed to board pull into the station. Shoving my umbrella across the top of my bag, I awkwardly run as fast as my fucked-up shoes can carry me and follow the man in front of me through the train doors just as they're closing. As I enter the train, I put my bag and brolly forward and follow bodily after it. Unfortunately, the gent in front of me stops the moment he makes it into the train and is not expecting the point of my umbrella to stick him in the backside as my bag enters.

He emits a high-pitched scream, like a startled woman, causing all the commuters to stare at him and me, and runs to the other side of the carriage, his hands guarding his backside against my wayward umbrella. The doors close with the flap of my jacket enclosed between them before I can pull myself completely through, so I have to ride to the next station with my back pressed up against the doors like an idiot. The entire train full of commuters is looking at me like I've escaped from the lunatic asylum. I stand uncomfortably at the door, laughing to myself because I cannot believe how badly this day from hell has panned out.

I am grateful to finally stagger through the door of the apartment. I press my back to the closed door and feel my shoulders droop. To my surprise, I hear the key rattle in the lock and as I pull away from the door, Ryan walks through, literally moments after me. I glare at him with pursed lips, looking pointedly at my watch, then return my glare to his face, which is now displaying an apologetic smile.

"I thought you had to stay back," I skewer him with a look.

"Sorry about that. Rex looked at his watch and called an end to the meeting. You had left the office already so I just… came home. Sorry."

On a sigh, I drop my bag, umbrella and coat on the floor of the entrance and remove my broken shoes in utter exhaustion. Ryan's eyebrows rise when he sees the state of my shoes. I drop them onto the floor next to my bag. I am defeated and beyond caring so I ignore his expression of surprise.

"Should I ask how your day was?"

"Not unless you want to walk with a limp!"

Ryan walks around me and into the kitchen, pouring a measure of wine and returns, handing me the glass. I accept it gratefully and take a long sip. Sitting down on the step, the staples pop at the back of my skirt as I sag in relief, but I don't care.

After a few moments, I recover myself and start to explain the bloopers that have filled my day. During the telling of the flying shoe, Lucifer innocently wanders in front of me as I demonstrate the flicking kick. The poor unsuspecting feline is suddenly sailing through the air. I race after him, horrified, and find the startled cat clinging to the drapes, his hair on end and his whiskers twitching. After coaxing him down, I hand him to Ryan to pet and console, but he's laughing so hard his eyes are watering. I retire to my room to shed my torn garments and soak in the bath before dinner.

I can feel Ryan's eyes watching my retreating form and I don't even care what he can see. I'm sure he can see my torn and staple-studded skirt exposing my bare backside, one cheek of which will now be sporting a huge bruise from this morning's shower fall. I hear the digital beeps of numbers on the phone and assume he's ordering dinner.

* * * * *

I slide into the bath with a sigh of pure ecstasy, sliding all the way down so that I'm almost completely underwater, except for my nose. I breathe deeply and then sit up. I see that my hair dye, which I applied in Melbourne the night before I departed, has leeched out and coloured the bath red. Shit! When I return to Melbourne, I'm definitely going back to the warm chocolate-brown hair colour that doesn't run everywhere. As vibrant as this red is, it's a mess that never ceases to run, even after a month of hair washing. Sliding back down I submerge myself to lie at the bottom of the bath again, then close my eyes and begin meditating silently to calm my frazzled nerves while breathing through my protruding nose. I can hear the hum of the overhead exhaust fan and the heating click on to add a second layer of hum, but what I fail to hear is Ryan's knuckles, gently rapping on the door. I am yanked from my luxurious languid state into a sitting position by a forearm and open my eyes to Ryan's face inches from mine with a look of pure horror masking his features. In my panic I yell at him. "Ryan, get out! What are you doing?!"

Ryan's face is inches from mine and he is panic screaming, but the water is still sluicing off my hair and over my ears, so it takes a moment to hear what he's yelling.

"Where did ye hurt yourself?"

"What? What the hell are you talking about?"

"I was knocking on the door and ye didna answer and then I popped my head in and the bath is filled with blood. What the hell have ye done to yerself?"

I sag and want to cry in relief. My legs are pressed together and my arms are protectively hiding my breasts. "Ryan, the bath water is dyed with my hair colour!"

"What?"

"I said, the bath is filled with my hair colour. I haven't hurt myself. This is hair dye."

Embarrassed, Ryan steps back and runs his fingers through his hair, "I'm sorry, Phoebe, I called several times but ye didna answer so I opened the door and peeked in, calling yer name. I could see the tops of your knees but I couldna see any movement in the bath. I pushed my head in a little further and yer whole body was completely submerged, even your face. Yer hair flowing around yer face like Medusa. I mistakenly thought ye'd hurt yersel', so I dived in here and wrenched you up. I'm sorry, I thought, um. Right, I'll go then."

Ryan retreats from the room. I am staring at the door in his wake, thinking how articulately he explained himself in his stressed-out state. When will this fucking day end?

I rise out of the bath, dry and dress myself before walking into the living room. Ryan looks at me and sinks low into the couch. "I'm sorry, Phoebe, ye didna answer, and I saw the colour of the bath and I thought…"

The poor guy feels awful and I owe it to him to let him off the hook. "I'm sorry that happened, Ryan. I can't imagine how it looked. I'm sorry I panicked you." I hope that goes some way to help us both move on from the episode. I'm not sure how much of me he saw but I'm guessing it's more than I would have liked.

Ryan self-consciously shrugs and sips at his wine. "I ordered pizza for dinner and came to ask if ye'd like a wine in there."

"You saw me naked."

"I saw ye naked… but I didna see ye naked. I was flipping out, so I really only saw your knees… and your, um… I saw your knees and your hair, floating around your face."

"Like Medusa. You said it was floating around my face like Medusa. I'm sure the rest of the vision will come to you – little bit by horrifying bit."

"Why will it be horrifying? I noticed your belly button is pierced."

"Because I'm forty-two years old and I've had children and everything on my body sags and droops. My belly button has been pierced for eighteen years – I should probably remove it before my stomach swallows it."

Ryan grins at me. "Your belly jewel is sexy."

The doorbell sounds, heralding the arrival of the pizza. I make my way into the kitchen to pour a glass of wine. He thinks my belly jewel is sexy.

23

Lady Madonna

Mercedes

The steady release of bubbles from the aquarium in the waiting room of the medical centre where I sit with Dad is both harmonious and unnerving at once. It is intended to be a soothing and comforting sound, but it is setting my nerves on edge as I anxiously pick at a cuticle. Dad's knee is bouncing nervously as he waits with me to be called into the doctor's small rooms. The door swings inwards and a patient exits the rooms, making her way to the reception desk. The receptionist talks to the patient in muted tones. The cuticle peels further than I'd intended and blood wells in the nail bed. I suck in my breath because it stings so I absently put the finger into my mouth. The doctor steps out of his room and calls my name. Both Dad and I stand and follow the doctor into the room, and he closes the door behind us. My heart is thumping and I'm nervous because I don't want to see the look of disappointment in our family doctor's eyes. After we comfortably seat ourselves, Doctor Hanson greets us familiarly. "Good morning Mercedes, good morning, John. How are you both?"

We both answer in unison that we're good.

"Now what can I do for you Mercedes?"

My voice shakes as I state the reason for my visit. If the doctor is disappointed or surprised, he masks it with an air of non-judgemental professionalism that goes a long way to calm my nerves. Dad remains silent as the conversation continues.

"How old are you now, Mercedes?"

"I'll be sixteen next month, on the nineteenth of July."

"Okay, and how did you come to this conclusion? Did you miss your cycle, or have you taken a store-bought pregnancy test?"

"Well both, I missed my period and so I took a test to see if that was the reason. I actually thought you couldn't get pregnant a couple of days after a period, but I guess I was wrong."

Doctor Hanson raises his eyebrows. He probably thinks I am an idiot and he's probably sick of dealing with idiots who do stupid things without thinking about the consequences and then they end up in his rooms discussing options. He keeps the 'you're an idiot' tone out of his response because he's professional.

"You absolutely *can* get pregnant at any time during your cycle and you should never have unsafe sex, even when you have your period. The fertile cycles in women's bodies can be very different. Ovulation often occurs between day twelve and day sixteen and if you have regular cycles, pregnancy usually doesn't occur however, if your cycle for some reason becomes irregular, it is entirely possible to fall pregnant at any time as no one knows the exact day of ovulation."

I try not to look too dejected when I reply, "…but you could usually set your clock by my period. I have never been late, ever, in almost four years." My brain throws a memory at me that my last period was almost a week late. I decide not to voice that. I wish Dad wasn't in the room because I don't want to talk with Doctor Hanson about having sex when Dad is here but it's not like he doesn't know now, so I continue.

"It was our second time and we didn't have protection, but I thought since I'd just had my period that we would be okay. He wasn't comfortable with not using protection, but I convinced him it was okay. This is all my fault."

The guilt of this situation that I have got us both into makes me feel anxious and upset. Tears start to roll down my cheeks and plop onto my clasped hands, which I am wringing in my lap. I feel small and embarrassed and I want to be anywhere but here. Dad reaches over and takes one of my hands in his for moral support. Doctor Hanson leans forward and put a reassuring hand on my shoulder. Both of these men are not judging me at this moment and for that, I am grateful. Poor Josh is at school waiting to hear from me.

"Mercedes, it was an error in judgement that came with some really big consequences. Laying blame or making yourself sick with guilt is about as effective as hitting your forehead on a wall to solve a mathematical equation. It will not resolve a thing. Now let's confirm that you are in fact pregnant and then we will discuss options after that, okay?"

He reaches into a draw at the side of his desk and pulls out a sterile plastic jar with a bright yellow lid, which he hands to me. "I will need a urine sample for testing and I need you to take the sample mid-stream. Do you remember where the toilets are near reception?" I nod my head and take the jar from Doctor Hanson, heading out of the door to the toilets. Great, why can't I just provide an uncomplicated pee sample? Instead I have to do some pelvic floor gymnastics to grab a mid-flow sample. As the door closes behind me, I hear Doctor Hanson address Dad. Their tones are low, so I can't actually hear what they're saying but I hope he isn't berating Dad for my stupid behaviour.

✧

John

As soon as the door closes behind Mercedes, Doc Hanson turns to me and I'm waiting for the patronising tone that I know is coming.

"She's very young to be having sex, John, and surprisingly naïve. The test she's already done is more than likely correct, you should know that going forward."

I sink a little in my seat because I feel somewhat responsible for some of the mess. If I hadn't been having sex with a strange man in our bed, Phoebe wouldn't have found out and then the whole family wouldn't have been in the eye of the storm when it hit the house. In response to my fraudulent behaviour, I suspect Mercedes ran into Josh's arms and probably had sex despite being too young, breaking the rules to get back at me.

Unfortunately, the whole thing backfired and now we're in this predicament. I scrunch my eyes tight and try not to sound too beaten when I answer, "I suspect that the test is correct. We've been going through a crisis in our house lately and I'm sure she sought comfort in the arms of this boy. We both knew she was seeing him, but it's only been a couple of months and I was hopeful that Phoebe would be back from the UK before they took things to this level. I didn't see it coming because I've been caught up in the crisis and not really watching. If anything, I've been super lenient to make up for the crisis. She's not all that naïve; she just made a stupid decision that, as you say, comes with big consequences."

Doc Hanson is immediately conciliatory. "I didn't mean to judge, that's not what this is about. I'm a little concerned about her age. Does she have any idea which way she wants to go with it?"

"She will *not* terminate the pregnancy. She has stated rather emphatically that termination is not an option, so I guess we'll encourage her to place it up for adoption afterwards or find a suitable family during the pregnancy."

"What does Phoebe have to say about all of this? It must be hard being on the other side of the world while all this is happening."

"Actually, Mercedes has asked that we keep this to ourselves until she returns. We've recently separated, and she is taking an eight-week working holiday in the London office, so she can clear her head and think rationally about which way she wants to go from here."

"Oh, I'm sorry to hear that, John. It can happen to the best of us, I suppose."

Not willing to go into detail right now, I reassure him, "We're still friends, but our dynamics have changed, which has made our differences irreconcilable, I guess." Sure, they've changed… my differences relate to the gender I'm attracted to and Phoebe doesn't have the necessary equipment.

The door opens and Mercedes walks in, places the specimen jar on the desk and takes her seat next to me. Doctor Hanson opens the lid of the jar and inserts a thin strip into the pee. He then takes the jar and strip over to the basin and empties the jar. He looks closely at the strip then throws it in the bin and returns to us.

Mercedes

"Okay, I've confirmed that you are pregnant, Mercedes. I can only go by the dates you provided and using those dates, you're about six and a half weeks along, which will make your baby due around 24 February. "Do you know what you want to do, Mercedes? We need to discuss your options."

"I won't terminate it. I'm definitely going to have the baby but I'm not sure what to do after that."

"All right, I'm going to give you a referral letter for a gynaecologist to give you a more accurate idea of how far along you are. She will want to do an ultrasound to check the baby's health and to make sure all is well. She will be able to give you a better idea of your due date going by the size of the foetus." He hands me an envelope with the gynaecologist's name on it. He puts a sticky note on top of the envelope with a website address on it.

"When you get a moment, go onto this website, which will explain what options are available to you and how to go about setting your chosen path into motion. Good luck, Mercedes, I wish you well on your journey, whichever path you choose. Please don't hesitate to pop back to see me should you have any concerns or queries. I will send an email to the gynaecologist, so they will be expecting your call. You will receive a referral letter for an obstetrician in the mail and that will be your next appointment. Make an appointment to see her a few days after you've seen the gynaecologist."

With that, Dad and I walk out of Doctor Hanson's rooms, and, as Dad pauses to pay at the reception desk, he hands me his keys and I continue on to the car.

Dad climbs in and sits behind the steering wheel shortly after. I let out the breath I've been holding onto. "So, I'm going to be a Mum."

"So, you are. Where to now, honey?"

"Take me to school, Dad. I've got my uniform in my school bag. I'll be able to make it by the end of recess if we go now."

"Okay, love, if you're sure."

I give another sigh. "Yeah, sure. I'm as ready as I'll ever be."

* * * * *

As I exit the toilet block, where I've changed into my school uniform, I make my way to the lockers. I see Monique and Charlotte at the top of the stairs. Of course, they don't let me pass without insulting me. "Oh look, here comes the slut." Monique spits the words at me with a look of disgust on her face. Right now, I want to punch that horrible face. Instead I sigh and continue walking, calling over my shoulder. "Really mature, Monique."

Tears threaten but I straighten my spine and strut past them like they're insignificant in my world.

"You're nothing but a cheap whore. I hope you die in childbirth, whore!"

"Whore, slut!" echoes Charlotte. Cool, let's make a chorus out of it, shall we?

As I approach my locker, I spy Josh lurking in the hall, no doubt waiting for me. I quicken my pace and almost throw myself into his arms. On a sob, I cry, "I'm pregnant, I really am pregnant."

Josh is comforting, of course. "It's okay, babe, we'll figure this out. I'll be there as much as I can."

I draw back and look into those beautiful sparkling eyes on his earnest face and whisper, "I really love you, you know that?"

Josh gives me his heart-stopping lopsided smile. "Is that your hormones saying that?"

I shake my head and beam up at him.

"Is it just the pregnancy that's got you upset or something else?"

"No, I saw Monique and Charlotte at the top of the stairs and they slut-shamed me."

"They *what*? Are you *serious*?"

Josh makes to tear down the stairs to say God knows what to his sister, but I grab his arm and shake my head at him. "Some people are just not worth it. I know she's your sister, but I've seen a side of her since you and I hooked up that is nothing short of evil. Never in my wildest dreams did I imagine she would behave this way, but you just never know with some people. I'm just going to stay away from her and the other girls – they're toxic and I need to take care of myself."

Josh is still scowling in Monique's direction. "She's a fucking bitch! I'm going to say something to her and I'm going to do it in front of Mum and Dad. They need to know what kind of bitch they've raised. Monique has never been like this before. I can't understand why you and I hooking up has made her so nasty. She has some serious issues."

The bell sounds, calling an end to recess. I reluctantly pull out of Josh's comforting arms. "I've got to go. I've already missed the first two classes." Then I remember what subject I have next and groan. "Oh God, I've got a double science with Monique. God help me!"

Josh kisses the top of my head and leaves me to grab my books from my locker for my next class.

As I walk in, I make my way to the back of the room, and the low hum of chatter stops, and all eyes turn to me to watch my progress. Excellent, Monique has been slut-shaming me to the whole class. I catch Monique's eye and she glares at me with all the hostility she can gather. I match her glare with equal hostility. I may be ostracised, but

I won't be walking around with my tail between my legs. Monique can go to hell, I decide.

"Slut!" Monique hisses at me as I pass her. I want to hiss something back at her, but I choose to smile at her instead. Her face looks even angrier and I am expecting steam to start shooting out of her ears. Her reaction gives me great pleasure.

I take my seat and notice most of the girls in the class are looking at me. The girls with Monique look at me with disdain but most of the others in the class just seem to be curious. The boys appear awkward and unsure of how to behave with the news. Thankfully, they choose silence. I endure the remainder of the day as best as I can, using all the strength I have to keep myself from sinking to Monique's level.

Seth

It's late afternoon and I've come home from school during my free period to study. I'm drowsy because I was up late last night revising for this morning's test. I'm not sleeping well at the best of times, so I'm not surprised by my lethargy. I'm trying to look over my notes for tomorrow's chemistry practice exam and the words are swimming on the page. I decide lying down for a few moments might actually be more beneficial than trying to force information into my head when I can't actually absorb it.

Lying prostrate on my bed, I put my ear buds in, listening to some music on low volume. I choose country because I don't want any strong beats to disrupt my relaxation. My thoughts turn to earlier this morning when I ran into Brandon's mum, Bonny, as I made my way to school. Lately she looks drawn and the dark bruising under her eyes tell tales of her insomnia. When she hugs me, she clings to me really tightly, because she misses her boy and she can't hug him anymore. I don't mind her affection, but it makes me feel guilty that

I'm here and he's gone. I hug her tighter because she needs it. We made plans to meet for a coffee on Saturday morning because she needs to talk to me.

Their house is on the market as the ghosts of Brandon weigh heavy on them, and she says they need to move on because it's making George sick. She said that every day after work she comes home to find him sitting on Brandon's bed, clutching a photograph of their smiling son to his chest and sobbing. It's slowly killing him, and she needs to get him out of there before she loses him too. Hearing their plight makes my chest ache and opens the emotional wounds that had finally started to scab over. I push Bonny from my thoughts because I need to relax. Concentrating on the music in my ears and the sound of air going in and out of my lungs, Keith Urban croons about making memories and in this relaxed state I feel like I'm floating.

I am looking at a surface that I can't quite make out. I'm floating. I'm on a tropical beach, that's what I'm looking at below; it's sand under water. I'm snorkelling in Fiji. I know this because I've been here before and I recognise it. I don't know how I got here. I can see the ocean floor beneath me fall away from the underwater coral cliffs. Brightly coloured fish swim lazy loops near me and I'm lured by their beauty. Far below, I see bull sharks circling and I'm oddly unaffected; I don't feel threatened at all. I'm floating on the surface, moving with the ebb and flow of the water, and the view below moves as I'm rocked by the motion of the sea. Spreadeagled, arms and legs akimbo, my breathing is regular. My snorkel is making the air intake sound tubular. The tide must be coming in because my view seems to move backwards a little and I am hovering over the underwater cliff edge.

There is something floating between me and the sharks below, but I can't quite make out what it is. It's too far away. Whatever it is floats higher towards me. I think that perhaps it is another person. As it rises, I think it's definitely a human as I can see the halo of dark hair floating about its head. Unless its seaweed. Maybe it is seaweed around a spherical object. Whatever it is, it seems to be getting closer. I wait for it to slowly rise higher, so I can see it. Yep, it's a person. I wonder where their mask is. How are they breathing under here? There is something beautifully tranquil about this person. It's a guy; I can see his genitals now peeking out of his pubic hair. Way to go man, be free and completely unrestrained. He is floating towards me. There is something oddly familiar about him, but I can't pick what it is.

I look at the hair floating about his head and realise that it's Brandon. Oh, it's Brandon. I've missed him so much and I have to try really hard not to swim to him; I have to wait for him to float up to me because I can't breathe underwater like Brandon seems to be doing. As he floats closer, his face comes into view and he is not tranquil at all... his face is tortured, and he is screaming. Why can't I hear him? He is screaming, and I can't hear what he's saying because we are underwater and it's just noise bubbling out of him.

I panic because I need to get to him to hear what he's saying but I'm scared of drowning. The water around him is darkening. It's changing colour from crystal clear to bright red. There are ugly slashes on his wrists. The water is making them pop open and blood is pouring out of them. The red colour around him is blood. Brandon is bleeding to death. His voice is muffled by the water, but I can hear his voice screaming; I just can't make out the words. He sounds desperate, he's panicking, and I watch him mouth the words. He is screaming at me to help him. He has somehow cut himself and he's bleeding to death and he is crying out to me to help him.

I can't move. I am commanding my arms to swim down to him, but nothing is happening. I scream back at him, but my words are subdued and undecipherable underwater. I am thrashing my head around trying to make the words be heard but he can't hear me. He is only about a metre away from me, but I can't reach him. My arms won't move, and he is begging me to help him... I can't help him. He is screaming to me and he's terrified. Finally, my arms move, and I reach out for him, trying to take hold of his hand to save him. Our fingertips are centimetres away from each other, but I can't get to him. I shake my head in frustration and scream bubbled reassurance as hard as I can. "Brandon! Brandon I'm coming. Wait for me!" but Brandon starts to sink away from me, dropping further down into the murky depths below us, and within moments he is lost to me. I am terrified, I don't want him to go and he's so frightened. I scream his name one last time as loud as I can.

I wake up. My scream echoes around my silent room. For a couple of brilliant moments, I think it was all a dream and I will call Brandon... then I remember that he really is dead, and this is my subconscious mind trying to deal with it. I try to pull the threads of the dream to the fore, so I can unravel it and analyse it. I leap up and scribble what I can remember before it is lost to me.

There is a gentle rap of knuckles at my door and Dad's voice asks if I'm okay. I didn't realise he was home already, and I tell him I'm fine; that I'd dozed off and had a dream. Dad opens the door and pokes his head around it. He looks concerned. "Sorry, Dad. I had a bad dream about Brandon. I'll be okay."

Dad pulls a face that tells me he's sorry for me, but he doesn't know what to do about it or what to say. I tell him that I have these dreams often and I'll call Alan to talk it through then I'll go to the gym and box. The boxing has helped me keep on top of the anger, just as Alan said it would. I don't actually want to talk it through with Alan, I want it to go away. But like a sore that you just can't stop picking at, worrying the edges until it bleeds again, I go over every detail of the dream and pick it completely to pieces. All I get out of it is that I wanted to save Brandon, but I couldn't... or didn't. I know that I still feel guilty and even when I rationalise that I couldn't save him because he didn't want to be saved, the feeling still remains and sneaks into my dreams. I call Alan's rooms and make an appointment.

I hear the front door open downstairs and Dad withdraws his head. I follow him out to the landing and look down at Mercy in the entryway, hanging her coat on the stand by the door. She looks exhausted, so I call down to her and ask if she's okay. She makes eye contact with Dad and gives him an imperceptible nod. I wonder what that was about. She has stopped hating him suddenly and there is something between them that I don't know about.

She climbs the stairs like she's elderly and sits in the middle of the top step on the landing. Dad sits on one side of her and reaches around behind Mercy to pat the other side for me to sit. Mercy looks at me and her eyes look troubled. I stow my curiosity and sit beside her, waiting for her to tell me whatever she has to tell.

I take her hand in mine and she tells me it all and I don't interrupt because it's a hard tale to tell. I am absolutely stunned by her news. Our family is just getting blown apart. What have you done, Mercy?

24

Out Of The Mouths Of Babes

Phoebe

I take off at a great pace. As I jog past Lincoln's Inn Fields, I see up ahead that the gate is open. It's not usually open until later in the morning and I wonder if a grounds keeper has accidentally forgotten to lock up. It doesn't matter because I'm taking advantage of it and follow a couple of fellow joggers straight through the gate and onto the running track. This is part of a larger running loop through the London streets and parks and I am loving it. This morning, I feel reckless.

The early pre-dawn light lends an eerie quality to the track. I'm taking great loping strides and feel like I could run a marathon. I am a gazelle on the plains, leaping and bounding with abandon. It is warmish, for London, and a light breeze fans my hair. I imagine how my fabulousness looks as I jog my way along the track. There are quite a few people out running this morning; I'm not alone in my quest for fitness. I pass an Asian woman shuffling at a pace slower than my walking pace and feel a burst of energy. Sprinting past her, she is lost in my wake and I imagine a vapour trail behind me; she disappears in my cloud.

I feel suddenly uncomfortable with the dense foliage surrounding me in the dim light. It has gone from eerie to creepy and I can hear little noises off to my left. I convince myself that small nocturnal animals are foraging for food before they settle for rest. A twig snaps loudly behind me and I'm suddenly panicking. My bladder chooses this moment to alert me it is full to bursting and release is imminent. I ignore the small alarm going off in my nether regions and hope the dam wall holds a little longer.

I'm reasonably sure someone is behind me, so I pick up my pace a little. My eyes are wide open. I'm freaking out and trying hard not to look as though I am. I see toilets up ahead and my bladder starts throbbing with joy but my mind screams 'sexual assault haven' so I Carl Lewis-sprint past the bloody thing and my bladder is not impressed. I curse my old and disappointing pelvic floor. I'm sure that only a few years ago my pelvic floor muscles were honed, I could have popped an array of ping pong balls during a nude performance of the Can-Can. Now, as I make my way through my forties, holding a half cup of water is an achievement.

I hear the bastard behind me gaining. Jesus Christ I'm freaking out and somehow veer off the track. Leaves and branches are slapping me in the face so I'm waving my hands above my head like ET chasing Gertie and I think, in my terror, that I'm making the same nonsensical sounds ET makes. It is getting darker as I venture further off-track in my panic and I want to turn around, but my pursuer is closing in. Out of nowhere, a tree appears in front of me and I don't see it until I smack my forehead against its hard and unyielding trunk. My head bounces painfully and I stumble backwards in shock.

I lose balance and windmill my arms in an effort to pull myself upright and inadvertently smack someone in the mouth. He grunts loudly in surprise, so I turn around and see a tall man in spandex before me and completely lose my shit. I panic scream in his face and it sets him off so we're both screaming at each other like crazy monkeys, but no one is flinging any shit. Then, my bronchial tubes swell, and I can't breathe. I pat myself down and realise that in my dash of madness I've lost my asthma inhaler and I can't for the life of me get any air into my lungs. I'm wheezing like an elderly smoker with emphysema and feel my nostrils suck flat as I try to suck in air.

I can no longer scream at him. I'm hissing and whistling through my mouth and he has such an odd look on his face. I wonder if this will be my last memory before he kills me.

My head spins and then the worst happens... my bladder releases. Hot piss runs down my thighs and into my shoes. The smell of urine is offensive to my senses. The man takes a step back and looks into my eyes. "Are you okay?" he asks. "You look like you're going to faint." My legs give way and I slide down the tree trunk and land with a wet splat in my urine-soaked knickers and pants. I no longer care if he is going to attack me. "Go ahead, rape me," I scream, but all that comes out is a wordless wheeze. All I care about is getting air into my lungs.

He reaches into his pocket for what? A knife? He pulls his hand free and he's holding an asthma inhaler. Tears of relief burn my eyes as he proffers the lifesaver. All my germophobe fears take a hike and I don't give a shit if he has gonorrhoea of the throat. I shove the germy end into my mouth and suck hard, inhaling the beautiful aerated gold. Moments later, precious oxygen floods my lungs. While I'm waiting for the dizzy to dispel, he explains that he was chasing after me to tell me I'd wandered off the path and was running in the wrong direction. He waits for my breathing to regulate then holds out his hand to pull me upright. My shoes squelch and I get another whiff of urea. I wish I could magically teleport out of here, but I have to take myself home with my legs.

By the time I make it back to the apartment, my thighs feel raw. My top lip is smarting and feels swollen. I take off my soggy sneakers and clothes and bag them to contain the odour. I leave them in the laundry tub and tentatively poke my head outside to listen for Ryan. The apartment is silent except for the sound of the shower in Ryan's ensuite, so I nudie-run down the hall to the safety of my room. I have a rash all over the inside of my thighs from my pee. I press my bum against the cold door and look up at the ceiling and I wonder at life.

* * * * *

The phone on my desk rings as I'm buttoning my coat to leave the office for the day. The handset screen says its Ryan's mobile. "Hi Ryan, are you nearly ready to go?"

"Actually no, I've got to stay for a meeting, sorry. I've just popped out to call you. Are you going out tonight?"

What? Yeah, sure, I'm going out for a night on the town. "Where the hell would I go on my own on a Friday night in a strange city? No, I'm going to be staying in. Why do you ask? Do you need me to do something for you?"

His tone is sheepish, "Well, yes. It's a huge favour, I know, but I have my kids coming over this afternoon because it's my weekend with them. I don't think I even mentioned that to you, sorry Phoebe. I'm just wondering if you could be with them for a couple of hours?"

I wasn't expecting that. "Of course. Do you want me to make them some dinner?"

"I usually take them out for dinner on a Friday night, but I won't be home for a while."

"Surely they eat early? They're young, right? I'll make something. Don't worry, I've got this." I pause for a moment before asking, "Is Catherine dropping them over?" My stomach clenches at the thought of seeing her.

Ryan is emphatic, "No, thank God. Her mum will drop them over, her name is Margaret. Catherine refuses to drop them over and for that I'm grateful. Don't tell her I'm not there though, tell her I'm in the loo or something. The last thing I need is a black mark against my name. Thank you, I owe you, Pheebs."

"Pah, think nothing of it. Now bugger off so I can get out of here and get to the apartment in time." I replace the receiver and turn around to see Theresa looking at me. Like an excited child I blurt, "I'm going to meet Ryan's kids tonight. I'm so excited." Theresa's eyebrows go up. I leave her with that startled expression and walk briskly out of the office toward the station.

At the apartment I quickly change into jeans and a light jumper and start preparing vegetables for the children's dinner and a chicken and leek pie for Ryan and me. When I'm done with the preparations, I go into the laundry to retrieve my washed clothes and sneakers after my run this morning and hang them on a small clothes horse in my bedroom; my sneakers over the duct. I wander back into the kitchen to check on everything, feeling fidgety and absurdly nervous. I almost squeak in alarm at the sound of the doorbell.

I open the door to a respectable-looking older woman who oozes class and position. She is holding the hands of two smiling cherubs. I thrust out a hand in greeting. "Hello, I'm Phoebe, you must be Margaret." The children push past Margaret and into the apartment, their second home every other weekend. Margaret looks me up and down and then shakes my hand and returns my greeting, "Hello, Phoebe. Is Ryan in?"

She probably thinks I'm the help. I try not to stutter as I tell a bald-faced lie, "He's just got home and is taking a shower, I think." I look convincingly down the hall towards the master bedroom."

Margaret buys it and seems eager to leave. "Oh, well tell him I said hello and remind him that I'll collect them tomorrow at about twelve thirty after lunch."

She waves goodbye to her grandchildren and makes her exit. After closing the door, I turn around and squat down before the children, thrusting a hand out to Annabella. "You must be Logan." And then to Logan I say, "Now you must be Annabella."

The children squeal with delight, and Annabella corrects me. I make a play at being stupid and slap my palm to my forehead in feigned stupidity; my forgotten bruise throbs in protest. I roll my eyes in pretend idiocy and to Logan I say, "Oh, so you're Logan?"

Logan giggles. "Yes, and she'th Bella." He points a chubby finger at his sister.

"Right, got it now! I'm Phoebe, it's nice to meet you both."

"How do you know my daddy?" queries Bella.

"I work with your daddy. I'm from Australia. I've just come across to this office to help him settle in, so I will only be here for a little while. Your daddy said he had a spare room, so I could sleep in it instead of a motel. So here I am." You can tell that to your bitchy mother, I think uncharitably.

Logan's dimples and lisp are adorable when he speaks. "We uthed to live in 'straya. Now we came back. We lived in a houth."

"I know. Your daddy told me all about it. I live not far from where you used to live. Just a quick drive in the car from your street. Come on in and let's put your things in your room."

When we return to the living room, Logan says, "Where is Daddy?" I hope he didn't hear my lie to Margaret earlier.

"Daddy will be home soon. He had to finish a very important meeting so I'm going to be spending some time with you before he comes in, okay?"

Bella starts dancing on the spot but Logan grumbles, "Aw, but I'm hungry."

"Well I'm making something for dinner and it won't take very long at all to cook. Do you want to pop up to sit at the bench while I cook it?"

The children run into the kitchen area and scramble onto the stools at the breakfast bar to watch as I put a pot on to melt the butter and start browning the veggies. The meal cooks in fifteen minutes, during which time I have established that Bella is in kindergarten and will be going to school next year and Logan attends day care twice a week where he has started to make new friends and learn to play in group activities.

When the meal has cooled sufficiently, I place a bowl of the chicken noodle stew in front of them. They look at the bowl and then at me, not pleased at the sight. Uh oh.

"What is this?" says Bella politely.

"It's chicken noodle stew. Try it. It was my kids' favourite when they were about your age."

"You have children?" Bella asks. I love how she's incredulous.

"Yes, I do. I have a boy and a girl too, but my son is the eldest and my daughter is the youngest. Mine are almost all grown up now."

Bella dips her spoon into the bowl and takes a tentative mouthful while Logan watches intently. Her eyebrows lift, and she exclaims, "Hey, this is really yummy!" to which Logan responds by thrusting his spoon into his bowl and shovelling the entire meal down. I give him a second smaller serve, which he almost finishes.

While the children dine, I finish making the pie and put it into the oven.

When they've finished, I say, "Now, which movie should we watch?" I pick up my personal favourite. "How about *Finding Nemo*. Do you both like that one?"

They both bounce in excitement. Bella takes the disk from me and carefully places it in the open DVD tray. I plonk myself on the couch and they climb up to sit either side of me.

Lucifer pads into the room and, after sniffing at the children's feet and having them in fits of giggles at his silly expression and his wet nose as it tickles their bare toes, he hops onto my lap and starts kneading my thighs. As the movie begins, both of the children snuggle down close to me. The barracuda scene builds, and Logan's little fingers dig into my arm. I look at him and he has his eyes squished tightly closed. Bella reaches across me and takes his hand for support. This gesture is adorable. Bella peers up at me and whispers, "Logan is afraid of the big scary fish that eats all the other babies and Coral, that's Nemo's mummy." I nod at her and put my arm around both of them. I completely lose myself in the movie because I miss these moments in time with my own babies.

❦

Ryan

The ping of the elevator sounds as the doors open and I exit into the deserted hall. I'm hurrying because I've left Phoebe alone with my kids for way too long and I've imagined all sorts of scenarios with them whining about not liking what she's cooked or that they're bored. The meeting went for an eternity and I almost yelled at Paul from finance to make a bloody decision already. After all the negatives he threw at us, the stupid prick decides to postpone his answer for another fifty-six hours. Of all the nights, the stupid indecisive arsehole. As soon as the words were out of his mouth, everyone around the table leapt out of their seats and practically ran out of there. Just because that boring bastard doesn't have a life, we shouldn't have to endure a three-hour meeting on a Friday afternoon when we all just want to get the hell out of the office and start our weekend. Boring knob.

I gently open the front door and tiptoe into the apartment. It's quiet and orderly. Nobody turns to look at me because all their attention is on Bruce the shark as he rattles off the motto in the 'Fish-Friendly Sharks' support group. The pang of guilt dissipates and is replaced by relief that Phoebe has managed without me. I tiptoe to my room to change and get ready to join in the fun. As I walk past the kitchen, I see the Disney character bowls, Bella and Logan's favourites, with remnants of dinner in them, still sitting on the bench. I peer inside and see the remains of the eaten meal. Are those vegetables? Good Lord, how the hell did she get them to eat vegetables? I dip a finger into Logan's bowl and taste the cold splodge. It is surprisingly tasty. Sniffing the air, I pick up the scent of something else and look into the lit oven to spy a pie baking. My stomach rumbles loudly in anticipation as I continue past the kitchen and on to my bedroom.

After changing, I sneak up to the couch and lean my head over, greeting them in a deep and creepy tone, "Good evening."

Not one of them had heard me enter or sneak up to the couch, so all jump as one in surprise. Lucifer reacts the harshest, hissing in surprise before launching himself from Phoebe's lap, and by the look on her face, painfully clawing her thighs in the process. This was not my intention. Hands on their chests and hearts in their mouths, all three of them lurch forward and turn to glare up at me. I stand up in surprise; I hadn't expected that reaction.

"Sorry guys, I didn't mean to frighten you all. I won't be trying to be clever again."

Bella and Logan leap up onto the couch and dive into my arms. It brings me so much joy to see their little faces glad of my arrival. Phoebe reaches for the remote to pause the movie, then walks to the other side of the room to retrieve a panicked Lucifer, who is cowering under the dining table; his wagging tail fat and fluffy, his ears flat in ire.

"Have you eaten without me?"

"Yes!" Logan and Bella shout together, then Bella adds, "Phoebe made chicken noodle stew and it was yummy."

"Where's mine?" I playfully whine at them.

"It's for little people and you're a big people!" giggles Logan.

Bella corrects him, "Big *person*, Logan."

"Person," he parrots.

"I made a chicken and leek pie for us, knowing you would be a little late. It won't be ready for a while yet. Would you like to join us? We're watching *Finding Nemo*."

I find my enthusiasm for my kids, and because I'm grateful to Phoebe for fixing this stuff-up, I respond, "Oh, yes, please."

"Yay!" shouts Logan as he scoots over to make room for me. Phoebe asks Bella if she would like to sit beside her daddy, but she politely declines, stating that she is comfortable. I see her reach for Phoebe's hand and put her own firmly inside. I make eye contact with Phoebe and mouth "thank you" to her. She waves it away with a flip of her hand.

Phoebe

I'm conscious of his thigh pressed against mine and it stirs something deep within. I have a little room on the other side of me, between

Bella and me, to move over, but the familiarity of it warms me and kicks my heart-rate up, so I stay put.

As the movie resumes, a scary part starts up where Bruce the shark gains a whiff of Dory's blood, which turns him into the crazed hunter he is programmed to be.

Logan starts to fidget in his seat. "Oooh, this is the scary part, Daddy. We have to all hold hands now."

The cute little man leans past Ryan to look at me with an earnest expression. "You have to hold Daddy's hand now, so he doesn't get frightened."

I stifle a giggle as Ryan holds out his hand for me to hold; his expression is complete innocence. I take his hand and feel the blood drain from my face and the breath catch in my throat. I am conscious of his scent and the warmth of his hands, which are… *huge*. My mind takes a wayward path replaying the old adage "big hands, big…", then I have to mentally drag myself back to the moment. The scary scene ends and Logan all but deflates in relief as he lets go of Ryan's hand. I wait for Ryan to let go of my hand, but he continues to hold it in his. Engrossed in the plot, neither Bella nor Logan can see that we're still holding hands. Ryan begins to rhythmically run his thumb over my knuckles, making concentration nigh on impossible. It's all I can do to keep my breathing regular. We remain this way until the movie comes to an end. Ryan looks at me and reluctantly relinquishes my hand and I'm sorry for the breaking of the spell.

The children chatter excitedly with Ryan as I check on the pie and deem it cooked. I dish up our meal and quickly throw a salad together. As a reward for eating their vegetable meal without fuss, I spoon ice-cream into bowls for Bella and Logan, so we can all sit at the table at the same time. Bella relays the songs she has been learning in kindergarten about spring flowers and even shyly sings a little bit. She is rewarded with applause and cannot contain her pleasure. I'm amazed that she already knows the alphabet and can write the names of everyone in her family. Logan talks about his favourite book at day-care, and succeeds in confusing us all in the telling, which is interspersed with fits of giggles and much exasperated eye rolling from Bella. It isn't long before Logan yawns and mumbles, "Daddy, can I have a bath in the morning?" It is way past his bedtime.

"Sure, you can, little man, but remember Grandma Margaret is picking you up at lunchtime because you two have your cousin Bartholomew's sixth birthday party."

Disappointment shadows Bella's face and she looks to be fighting tears. Ryan reaches across the table to take her hand and quickly adds, "But ye'll be back again in two weeks and we're going to Poppy's cottage in Scotland."

"Really? Why, Daddy?"

"Well, it will be Daddy's birthday soon, so we'll go there and stay for the weekend. Won't that be fun?"

Bella looks across at me. "Will you still be here?"

"Oh yes, I'm staying for a few more weeks yet. We'll see each other again before I go back to Australia."

Bella brightens and stands up from the table, helping Logan to do the same.

Ryan says, "Now you two go and put on your pyjamas and brush yer teeth." Bella looks at me, "Can you please read us a bedtime story, Phoebe?"

I'm surprised by the request. "Sure… but doesn't Daddy usually read you the story."

"That's okay, he can listen today. We sit on Logan's bed because his is against the wall and nobody falls off."

"Right, okay. Who gets to choose the story?"

"You, of course," Bella says. She reaches for Logan's hand and tows him stumbling down the hall to their bathroom.

Ryan and I both stand and collect the plates and take them into the kitchen. As I start to rinse the dishes and stack them into the dishwasher, Ryan sidles up behind me, reaches over and turns off the faucet. I turn and look at him, bewildered. He is standing so close to me that I have to lean back to look up into his face. I wonder if he can see my lip and forehead. They both still feel swollen and bruised from this morning's encounter with a tree. He doesn't mention my mouth, so I assume he can't see it.

He puts his hands around my waist and hoists me onto the bench, then proceeds to lean in and kiss me enthusiastically. I stifle a yelp because my mouth still hurts but I'm so pleasantly surprised that I kiss him back. When the kiss ends, and he pulls away, I'm blinking up at him, warmed through. My heart is racing, my cheeks feel hot and I'm flustered. He exacerbates the situation by placing those large warm hands either side of my face and drawing me in for another kiss that has my senses reeling. The thud of children's feet coming down the hall makes us spring apart. He yanks me off the kitchen bench and spins me around to face the sink before they come bolting in, excitedly exclaiming that they're ready for the story.

"Right, Phoebe and I are still cleaning up the dishes so you two go and pop yourselves into bed and snuggle under the covers and we will be in shortly."

Ryan looks awkwardly at me. "Sorry, that was very forward."

I don't want him to think he can't do *that* again. "Nothing to be sorry about… that was nice." I feel shy as I look up at him, but he smiles at me and the awkwardness dissipates. My heart is still racing, and the heat is making me feel flustered again.

He puts me out of my misery. "Why don't you pop into the room with the kids and help them choose a book. I'll finish here and join you soon." He covers the leftover pie in cling wrap and puts it in the refrigerator. As I leave the kitchen, he takes a cloth to the benches, so I hurry down the hall.

I all but run into the children's bedroom, my discomfort in the kitchen borne of desire not embarrassment. Walking into the small shared bedroom of Bella and Logan is a welcome distraction. "Where's this book selection I get to choose from," I chirp. Bella motions with her arm at the array of books she has spread out for me to select from. She is the most organised young girl I've ever met.

I look over the selection; so many of the titles reminiscent of my own children's bedtime. *The Faraway Tree* was always a favourite for Mercy, but it requires numerous nights to read so I skip past that one. *The Very Hungry Caterpillar* is maybe just a little too young for Bella. Then I spy the much-loved Dr. Seuss' *Green Eggs and Ham*. I scoop up the book and hold it up to my audience.

Logan claps excitedly, all evidence of his earlier sleepiness has deserted him, and he looks eager to begin. Ryan rounds the corner and we all pile onto the little bed. I sit in the middle with the children snuggled on either side of me while Ryan lounges on the end. As I begin to read, I completely forget my audience as I fall back into my old reading style that I adopted for my own children years ago. I use different and silly voices as I read the dialogue of the characters, to the delight of the children. I can almost recite the book by rote, I have read it so many times, and the words flow out of me with ease.

When the story ends, Logan looks drowsy again and rewards me with a sleepy smile. He holds his arms up for a cuddle, so I bend down to embrace his little body. He plants a wet, sloppy kiss on my mouth. I turn to Bella and whisper, "Goodnight, Bella." She peeks up at me through her curls and smiles shyly. I stand up to take my leave so Ryan can say goodnight to his children in private.

As I near the doorway, Bella calls out to me and leaps into my arms. "Goodnight, Phoebe." Her embrace is fierce, so I tighten my hold on her little body.

Returning to the living room, I sit on the couch beside a wary Lucifer and reach for the remote. I am flicking through the programs when Ryan re-enters. He closes the hall door, leaving us separated from the children. There are a couple of movies that are about to commence on several channels, and I ask Ryan what he'd like to watch.

As he rounds the side of the couch, plonking himself down wearily,

Lucifer leaps to the floor and pads away in disgust. Ryan looks after his retreating form and utters, "What's got his furry pom-poms in a twist?"

"You scared the shit out of him before and he's holding a grudge."

We select a movie and Ryan gets up to fetch us both a drink. I'm looking forward to relaxing in peace. He flicks off the light switch with his elbow on his way back, hands me a wine glass and stretches out on the long end of the L-shaped couch.

Ryan looks a little uncomfortable, despite his relaxed form, and I'm not one to dance around a subject so I just knock it on the head straightaway. "Are you okay, Ryan?" He looks at me and I see his cheeks pink. Well that's cute.

He smiles. "I'm fine."

I continue to look at him until he turns to me again. I raise my eyebrows in an 'out with it' expression and he's forced to speak his mind. "Weel, ye're a guest in my hoose and I think I overstepped the mark. I dinna want ye to feel uncomfortable around me."

I'm surprised by this admission; it's not what I was thinking. "Did I pull away?"

Ryan looks to be bereft of a response. I stand, walk over to him and stretch out beside him on the L-shaped couch. I take his wine out of his right hand and put it in his left and place my hand in his free one. There, that should dispel any notion that I want to run. He looks closely at my forehead. "What's that?" He points to the middle of my forehead and I reach up to feel what he's pointing at, and the throbbing pain reminds me of my encounter with the tree this morning during my panic-bolt through the scrub. I tell him about my run this morning, omitting the part where I wet my pants.

Ryan laughs, and I feign a glare. "Are you laughing at me?"

"Yes."

The opening scene of the movie starts, and Ryan withdraws his hand from mine and puts it around my shoulder, so I can snuggle into him. He is warm, and he smells divine and I find great comfort in the simple act of resting my head against his chest as I relax, sipping my wine and watching the movie. Ryan has chosen light and flippant romantic comedy and it proves easy to watch.

Halfway through the movie, Ryan sits up and removes my glass from my hand and places it with his on the coffee table. I'm a little puzzled until he turns into me and gently kisses me, inviting, not taking. As the kiss deepens, I find myself sliding back until I am lying on my back with Ryan lying on top of me. I can feel his arousal pressed against my hip as his hand finds my breast under my tee. So much for not throwing himself at me.

He slides his hand inside my bra and measures the weight of my breast in his hand; his thumb gently stroking my nipple until it puckers hard against his finger. I'm heady with arousal. I rhythmically thrust my hips against his and move with him in a heated dance of mutual arousal that leaves us both panting and a fiery heat igniting between us. His erection is pressing against me and a thrilling heat is burning south. The desire to have him is almost unbearable. A loud cry sounds down the hall, jolting us apart and out of our trance. Logan cries out again, I recognise his little voice.

"Shit!" Ryan breathes as he sits upright and tries to right himself. He stands abruptly and utters, "I'm sorry, Phoebe, I have to go to him. He has nightmares."

"Of course! By all means…" I find myself stuttering.

Ryan is gone for a long time. The movie has ended, and I have long since finished my wine, so I turn off the television and take both our glasses into the kitchen. I'm weary and exhausted from the early start and the long day, so I decide to call it a night. I check the front door is locked, turn out the lights and make my way down the hall. I poke my head into the children's room on the way to my own and see, in the low glow of the night light, Ryan stroking a now quiet Logan back into a comfortable sleep. He looks up as I enter, and I don't want to wake the children, so I quietly whisper, "I'm off to bed now, Ryan. I'll see you tomorrow?"

"Sure, goodnight, Phoebe," he whispers back, the heat of the moment before completely extinguished and I see regret in his eyes.

Hastily removing my makeup and brushing my teeth, I change into pyjamas and climb into bed. I lie in the dark listening to the recurrent tick of my watch on the nightstand, wondering at the lust and burning desire fuelling my body and his. His mouth is soft and gentle, ardent and commanding all at once. I feel a familiar tugging in my loins when I recall the way we engaged in fully-clothed sex; rocking and riding each other like horny teenagers in a stolen embrace. I wonder where it would have ended up had Logan not woken. I know I would have jumped at the merest suggestion of sex, but I wonder if he would have wanted to go there so soon.

It's a long time since I've felt this kind of desire or attraction. Before my world with John imploded, our pre-sex dance was a familiar one where I danced my part and he danced his and, between us, we danced out the same choreography for twenty-three years, sometimes out of duty because he didn't always arouse me. This is a new dance with a new dance partner and I wonder if we'll ever get to the crescendo. He makes me feel sexy and desirable and I wonder at all the years I've been dancing this same dance with the wrong partner. How had our normal felt so right when it was so absolutely wrong? Does John feel this when he's with another man? This longing and need?

John was sweet and comfortable and familiar, and I knew him well. I had loved him, and when he looked at me, I thought it was love staring back, but now I know that it was all wrong. He looked at me like I was a great friend, not a lover, and our dance was a means to an end, at least for him. That knowledge dredges up the pain of our 'now', and it makes me feel a deep sadness that momentarily eclipses my new-found excitement. Now that I have just this small part of the new dance with Ryan, I think of the way he looks deep into my eyes with unrestrained lust and kisses me with so much passion and substance, like he wants to ravage my body, to please me and take me all the way, and that he would enjoy the journey with me; not just find his way there and hope I found mine along the way. A tear rolls down my cheek and soaks into the pillow.

My mind wanders to Ryan's situation. Forced to move and only see his children two days out of every fortnight and then, sometimes, to have that cut short because something else falls on his weekend with them. Poor Ryan. Forced into an impossible situation. As I think of him, I picture his face. Lean and chiselled, his mouth soft, his bottom lip full and inviting.

I stow my wayward imagination and try to run through some relaxation techniques that will relax me enough to finally close my eyes, banish Ryan and his inviting mouth from my thoughts and invite sleep in.

25

Neigh You Say?

Phoebe

My alarm intrudes on a very steamy dream that leaves me aroused and a little disoriented. Seconds pass before I realise the noise that awoke me was not the alarm but my phone ringing. Answering the call, I mumble "Hmm?" into the receiver, expecting an Australian accent because who the hell else would be calling me at this obscene hour. Theresa's voice booms into my ear, "Phoebe! Tell me I didn't wake you?"

"Theresa? What time is it?"

"It's five thirty."

"Why the hell are you calling me at five thirty on a Saturday?"

"Didn't you set your alarm?"

"Why would I set my alarm for five thirty on the weekend?"

"So, you forgot. We're going horse riding today at my cousin Felicity's farm, remember?"

Shit! I did forget. My stomach sinks as I recall the conversation. For the second time this week I leap out of bed and run for the bathroom, my phone to my ear as I kick off my pyjama pants, whip off my top single-handed and turn the shower faucets on.

"Shit, I completely forgot. I'm up. I'll jump in the shower and be down in ten minutes."

Theresa cheerily replies, "I'll be waiting." How annoyingly happy she sounds. She's obviously a morning person.

I don't even bother washing my hair this time. After the briefest of showers, I yank on jeans, a tee, socks and sneakers. As an afterthought, I run back into my bedroom to retrieve a hoodie. London is not famous for hot mornings.

I race into the kitchen as quietly as I can so as not to wake Ryan and the children, grab an apple for breakfast and leave Ryan a brief note on the kitchen counter. Phone in hand, keys in my pocket, I slip out of the door. It's dark outside and the birds are still slumbering; an offensive time to be up and about on a Saturday. As I approach the car, I am tying my hair into a ponytail, a fitting hairstyle for the day's event, and startle Theresa when I knock on the passenger window.

"Wow, you're quick. You don't mess around do you?"

I shake my head at her; my mouth full of apple. I leap into the car and we take off.

The sun takes its good old time rising but when it finally does, it is a clear and sunny day.

Theresa interrupts my peaceful thoughts. "You said you've been riding before, so can I assume that because you're an Aussie you were practically born on a horse?"

I frown at her. Really? "God no! Why would you think that? It's not like I grew up on a stud farm. I was raised in suburbia. I've just been on a few horses in my life. I like horse riding. Don't confuse 'I've been on a horse before' with 'I was in *The Man From Snowy River*', that's not how it works in Australia."

Theresa looks confused. "The man from where?"

"*The Man From Snowy River*. It was the most popular Australian film until *Crocodile Dundee* happened."

Theresa shakes her head. "Never heard of it. I've heard of *Crocodile Dundee* but not that one."

I shake my head. "My point is, Australia isn't just one giant outback adventure. We don't all spend our weekends getting pissed at ute musters, droving herds of cattle over the Nullarbor or with our arm up to the shoulder in a cow's arse checking for calves. I live in

Melbourne, a very large city. You have to go looking if you want to go horse riding. That's like me assuming that because you live in London that you whinge and complain a lot and only eat cold pork pies."

Theresa frowns. "Why would you assume that?"

I'm exasperated, it's like having a conversation with an alien. I flap a hand at her, "Never mind."

"Okay, my bad. Sorry." Theresa looks abashed, and so she should. "The only reason I ask is because the last time I was there, the woman who runs the horse-riding adventures for my cousin gave me a really slow horse. I didn't even get to canter. I was hoping you could call ahead and ask for us to get a couple of horses with a bit of spunk."

"Oh, right. I may have overreacted. Sure, tell me the number and I'll call ahead."

Theresa hands me her phone and directs me to call Felicity. I call Theresa's cousin and mention who I am, and Felicity forwards the call out to the stables. After requesting a couple of horses that will canter, Theresa rewards me with an ear-to-ear grin, holding up her hand for a high-five. Okay, let's behave like we're seven years old then. I give her a high-five and her smile gets even bigger.

* * * * *

Twenty minutes later, we turn into the driveway and make our way to the parking lot near the stables. As we get out and stretch, a short guy with a thick thatch of silver hair approaches.

Theresa leans in to my ear and whispers, "That's Lachlan. He takes the trail rides. Conversation is not his strong point, but Sherry will come along too and she's a regular *Chatty Cathy* doll."

Theresa makes the introductions; I thrust out a hand to shake hello.

"So, you're Phoebe? I have your horse here. His name is Lightning Bolt, he should make you happy. Theresa, Thunder is your horse today."

Theresa and I exchange alarmed glances and I wonder what the hell she has gotten us into. After finding suitable boots and a firm-fitting riding hat, we both mount our horses with trepidation. Three other women arrive and after a brief pause while they find boots and hats, all five of us sit comfortably in the saddle whilst Lachlan runs through the rules. A slight young woman with soft brown curls walks out of the stables and makes her way to the posse. She introduces herself as Sherry and describes the terrain and trails we are about to travel on during our two-and-a-half-hour trail ride.

Sherry mounts her horse and leads us out of the stable yard, through the gate and onto a trail. As we make our way through the gate, our horses take off at a bolt, startling both Theresa and me, as we were not prepared for the sudden pace of a gallop.

I dig my knees into Lightning Bolt's ribs in an effort to keep myself upright. I rein the horse into a canter and Theresa's horse, Thunder, slows at Lightning Bolt's lead pace. Sherry canters up level with us and smiles before taking the lead. For the next hour, both of us have to work hard at controlling our horses, who just want to run like the clappers at every opportunity. We pause to wait for the rest of the group to catch up and Theresa breathlessly apologises for making me call ahead, which has landed us two crazy horses.

As the path narrows, we are forced to ride single file. Suddenly, a rifle shot rings out nearby, startling the horses. One of the horses in the group panics and rears up on its hind legs, depositing the rider on the ground, before bolting ahead; the reins dangling and stirrups bouncing off the horse's sides. Sherry stops us and jumps down to help the rider up. Apart from a bruised derrière, the woman is unharmed. Sherry turns to me and yells, "Go get the horse, quick!"

What? Shit! Now I have to act like I *was* in *The Man From Snowy River*. Bloody hell! I kick Lightning Bolt into a gallop and chase after the terrified horse. A fallen log blocking the path means my horse has to jump. Having never jumped before, I hope the hell the horse knows what to do. I'm just clinging on for dear life, gripping the pommel of the saddle because I think my life might actually depend on it and I don't want a broken neck. Lightning Bolt leaps over the fallen log and continues at a death-defying pace without breaking his stride.

Through a creek and back up the other side, we continue this pace and I'm so freaked out I don't have time to panic, I'm just going with it. I spy the spooked horse up ahead. It has slowed its pace; its initial fear dissipating. As the horses draw near level, I lean to the side of my horse and reach for the dangling reins of the riderless horse beside me. I have no idea if what I'm doing is correct, I'm just doing it because I'm shit scared and Sherry thinks I perform horse stunts in my spare time.

Securing the reins, I right myself in the saddle and finally slow my horse to a walk. Turning the horses around, we walk up the bank and around the fallen tree. This was an unexpected adventure I could have done without and I think it has taken years off my life.

Sherry takes the reins of the skittish horse and urges the fallen rider back into the saddle. Theresa is beaming at me when she sidles up alongside my horse. "That was pretty cool," she gushes.

I'm embarrassed by the attention, so I underplay the moment, mumbling a lame response in the hope that Theresa will drop the subject. She continues to look at me with open-mouthed awe and I'm uncomfortable in her admiring gaze. My face heats up with embarrassment, so I kick my horse forward to continue with our ride.

The remainder of the ride is uneventful. My thighs and backside are quivering from the effort of holding on whilst reaching for the reins of the bolting horse, and the insides of my thighs are smarting from chafing. I'm looking forward to finishing the ride, getting back to the apartment and soaking myself in a hot bath.

We stop for morning tea at the top of a winding ridge at about the halfway mark of our journey. Fresh scones, jam and whipped cream are produced from a basket strapped to the back of Sherry's saddle. Picnic plates and plastic mugs are handed out and steaming hot tea is poured from an ancient thermos. The hot sweet tea and fluffy scones are restorative. The group refers to the fallen rider's bruised bottom with lewd jocularity. She laughs along at the jokes good naturedly.

The second half of the ride is mostly downhill. Theresa and I both have our horses under control; however, as we approach the homestead, they pick up their pace and the two of us let them have their heads. The trail here is reasonably flat so the galloping pace is thrilling, and Theresa makes me promise that I'll come and ride again with her before I return to Australia. I'm not sure I'm up for another adventure of this type in the next few weeks and I say as much, but it has been a fantastic day riding with Theresa.

On the drive home we laugh about our crazy horse antics and the poor fallen rider's bruised backside. "Next time, you can make your own calls and you can have the nutty horse."

I bid Theresa farewell and take the elevator up to the apartment. When I enter, Ryan is making a sandwich at the kitchen counter. I am conscious that I smell… horsey. My tee is smudged, my fingernails are dirty and there is a large quantity of dust on the seat of my jeans.

"How was it?"

"Don't ask," I moan as I all but collapse onto a kitchen stool.

"Are you hungry? I can make you a sandwich while all the stuff is out on the bench."

I get a whiff of my horsiness and decide against his thoughtful offer. "If it's okay with you, I think I might have a soak in the bath. I'll grab a sandwich afterwards when I don't smell like a stable."

"Knock yourself out. Before you go, I was wondering if you'd like to come with us to Dad's cottage in a couple of weeks? The kids, Dad, my sister and my brother will be coming. It's in Dunkeld, Scotland. We're going to catch a train to Inverness and then drive to Dunkeld in a minibus. Just thought you might like to see a little more of Britain whilst you're here."

"Sure, when are we going?"

"Monday after next is a public holiday, and I spoke to Jonathan about taking the Friday and Tuesday off too, so we'll go Friday and return Tuesday late afternoon, if that works for you?"

"I'd love to. Thank you for thinking of me. Can you let me know how much I owe you for the tickets and my share of the minibus hire, accommodation fees etcetera?"

Ryan frowns at me. "It's not that much, my treat, and the accommodation is my Dad's cottage so…" His voice trails off and he looks a little awkward before he resumes, "I know you're here for a little longer than the temporary position requires, so maybe we can explore more of England before you go back to Aus, another weekend without family. I'd love to show you some countryside if you're inclined?"

"Okay, if you're sure, that sounds great. Well… I'm going to de-stink."

In the bathroom, as I strip, the inside of my thighs burn. I can see the skin has chaffed right off in a couple of places. When the bath is fully drawn, I add a little musk oil and step in. Lowering myself into the water, my breath catches when the water laps at my tender thighs. I hiss in a breath and bite my lip, waiting for the sting to abate. As I lower the rest of my body into the water, I groan in ecstasy as the soothing warmth envelops my aching body. I swirl the water around my tortured thighs, rhythmically moving my hands in circles. A groan escapes me as the hot water relaxes my muscles. I reflect on the morning's ride and feel a little chuffed about how I handled myself in that crisis. I really like Theresa and I can imagine having a great friendship with her. She's my kind of person.

I wonder at the sudden invitation to join Ryan and his family on their holiday. I hope the family will be okay with me joining them. I haven't met them yet but I'm hoping to do so before next weekend. Unfortunately I won't be able to kiss those gorgeous lips for five whole days while we're away.

26

Crack-A-Toe

Phoebe

With Ryan out of the apartment early and away for the day, I plug my iPod into the stereo and turn the volume up loud enough to hear it clearly in my room as I ready myself for my day in the office. Reflecting on the steamy kisses Ryan and I have been sharing, I wish I could discuss it with Theresa… but then she will discuss it with Jonathan, as couples do, and then it will get back to Ryan that I've discussed us, and because men don't usually understand a woman's need to share, that would be that… *finito*.

I don't want to jeopardise what is currently bubbling my blood, so I decide my best bet is to continue to diarise everything I'm thinking and feeling in my electronic journal, which is password protected at least, so it doesn't have to be edited. I re-read my last entry. I could easily waste the morning away daydreaming about Ryan, but I need to get a move on.

I have decided on fire engine red knickers and matching bra. Who cares that nobody else gets to see them; at least I will know why there is a spring in my step today. I throw my shirt on, but I won't button it up until I have my skirt and pantihose on.

Whilst I'm dressing in my room, I'm singing loudly to a song that I particularly like, and I can only reach the high notes if I sing it really loudly. No one is here so I belt out the tune like a maniac. There's that saying, 'Sing like nobody is listening' …don't mind if I do.

Ryan

I have re-entered the apartment searching for my mobile phone, which I thought I had left on the kitchen counter along with my tablet. I can't find the damn thing and I'm searching everywhere for it in a hurry because Jonathan is lingering somewhere downstairs waiting for me.

Phoebe's iPod is plugged into the speakers and is playing exceptionally loud. I can hear her singing along somewhere up the other end of the apartment. She has a nice singing voice. She has a nice mouth. Her mouth is all I can think about lately.

As the song soars, I hear Phoebe belting out the song from way down the hall and it makes me smile. My phone is not here. I open cupboards and look on every surface, but I can't find it. Finally, I spy it peeking out from beneath some papers on the corner of the bench. I hear a thump down the hall and a yelp, followed by expletives. I wonder what she's done to herself this time.

Phoebe

I am halfway through the second chorus and, as I waltz out of the room, I stub my toes on the door jam, almost tearing my pinkie clean off.

"Aaahhhh shit!" I yell, and I can't stop the flow of expletives because it bloody hurts. "Aah FUUUUUCCCCCKKKKK, *Jesus!*" Gripping both sides of the bedroom door architraves, I cover the injured digit with my other foot and groan in agony, waiting for the pain to abate to a dull throb.

"What'd you do?" I hear Ryan's voice yell above the song.

I scream in alarm and spin around, startled to see him standing at the end of the hall. I have completely forgotten my state of undress.

"What are you doing here? I thought you'd gone early this morning." Oh God, how embarrassing.

"I just came back to get my phone. I left it in the kitchen."

His eyes are crimped at the corners… the bastard is laughing at me.

"It's not funny. I really hurt my toe. It's a wonder I didn't rip the bloody thing off!"

Ryan raises his eyebrows. "Geez, talk about exaggeration. I'm sorry, ye looked really funny standing there half-naked, yelling expletives. I'll kiss it better for ye."

I look down at myself and see I'm not dressed but I don't care. Desire is pooling in my belly as I watch his progress down the hall and up to my doorway. He gets down on his knees and gently presses his warm, soft lips onto my glowingly red toe. He kneels up and his face is directly in front of my cleavage. My breath catches in my throat. His eyes rise to meet mine, but he doesn't stand. I can feel the electricity surrounding us both. Gently, he kisses my décolletage and completely steals my breath away. I want more.

We're both breathing hard, reflecting our mutual desire. I lower my mouth to his because I can think of nothing else but feeling his lips on mine. There is nothing gentle in my kiss. I drop to my knees and Ryan deepens the kiss as he presses himself against me. I lower myself until I am lying on the carpet and Ryan is on top of me. I can feel his turgid need pressed against my pelvis and it is making my breathing laboured. His hands are caressing my breasts and I'm pressing my pelvis into his, almost aching in my need. I am desperate to have him inside me, so I throw caution to the wind and, feeling brave, I whisper, "I want you inside me," hoping it doesn't scare him away.

In between gulps of air, Ryan says, "But Jonathan is waiting for me downstairs. I'm supposed to be getting my phone and going back down."

Coincidentally, his phone starts to ring. I grab it from him and see that it is Jonathan, so I urgently whisper to Ryan, "Go along with me, okay?"

"Okay." Ryan looks confused.

I'm still panting so I work it into my spiel. "Hi, Jonathan, God, hang on." I pull the phone away from my ear and start yelling, "Ryan I've got it… it was in your jacket pocket." Ryan looks startled, but I continue and hope he catches on, "Here, I'll hand you over." I feign a giggle as I pass the phone to Ryan.

"Hi, sorry mate, couldn't find the bloody thing anywhere. I think Phoebe just found it in my jacket." He winks, and it makes me pant. I want to rip the phone out of his hand and throw it away. He is so gorgeous at this moment!

I point to the phone and mouth, "Say you need to powder your nose."

Ryan's eyes widen in alarm, then he floats an eyebrow but says as I have suggested, "Listen, er, I've just got to powder my nose."

I yell near the phone, "Oh, Jonno, you know what that's code for. Get yourself a coffee mate, it'll be at least 15 minutes."

I hear Jonathan groan and Ryan disconnects the call and throws the phone on the floor. As he hurriedly unbuttons his pants and pulls them and his jocks down, his erection springs free and I admire him in breathless anticipation. Reaching up to the bedside table, I feel around until my fingers find the packaging of the condom I pocketed yesterday at the shopping centre, handed out by some poor dweeb dressed as a giant banana. As I tear at the foil packaging, the overpowering sweet stench of banana surrounds us.

I pant, "I'll explain later," kissing him hard as my hands get busy between us, sliding the condom over his rigid phallus. I slide my knickers down and kick them off; I don't care where they land. Lying back down on the carpet, I pull him with me. I run my fingers through his hair and knot them, I want him so badly I can't contain myself.

What transpires next is nothing short of a primitive coupling.

There is nothing gentle, sensual or sweet between us as we both give in to our need. He thrusts into me with such fervour that it surprises the breath out of me. Within moments I feel my orgasm approaching and I'm embarrassed and horrified by how swift it is. "Oh Ryan, I'm sorry I can't… ah, hold… on. JESUS!" It is only seconds before the tingle and scalding sensation spreads through my body as the orgasm rips through me.

Ryan thrusts once more, then groans and hisses breath through his teeth as he collapses on top of me, spent. We both draw apart and gaze at each other apologetically, knowing that what just happened should not have been so convulsive and animal.

Ryan moves up onto his elbows and forearms, staring down at me. He looks unsure what to say after such a brief but satisfying burst of lust. His face looks apologetic. "I have to go."

"I know, and that's fine." He pulls out of me and sits up as I run into the adjoining bathroom in search of some tissues. His awkwardness is palpable, and I feel a twinge of guilt at having put us both in this position. I try to convey that I'm fine with him leaving straightaway in an attempt to dissolve some of the awkwardness. I hand him some tissues and slip on my knickers, bending down and kiss the tip of his nose.

"I'll see you later then." I give him a winning smile and I hope he doesn't feel like he's just been used as a human sex object. I escape the bedroom and retreat into the bathroom, closing the door behind me; giving us both some space to deal with what comes next. I lean against the closed door, shut my eyes tightly and wish it was possible for me to turn back time. My face is flaming, and I'm mortified. Shit, I can't believe that just happened. I feel idiotic and awkward and I wonder what the hell Ryan is thinking. There is silence on the other side of the door and I wonder if he is looking at the closed door thinking I'm weird. Of course, he's thinking I'm weird, I ran off and closed the door without saying anything. I'm agonising over everything I just said and did, and I want to go back and change it somehow. Who climaxes seconds after starting?

❦

Ryan

I look at the closed door and wonder what to make of her reaction. Have I offended her? Should *I* be offended? It was so hot and fast that I'm reeling. I didn't expect it and feel like a heel just leaving straight after having sex with her. I can hear her breathing on the other side of the door and hope she's not crying. Shit. I don't know what to do but Jonathan is downstairs waiting for me and I have to go.

I quickly dress and lace my shoes then stand looking at the door stupidly. I look down at my wringing hands and feel like an idiot. I finally yell at the closed door, "I'll speak with ye later, Phoebe."

There is a pregnant pause and I hear her stop breathing in there for a moment. Then she replies, "Okay, Ryan, have a good day." Just like that, like nothing has happened. I don't know what to make of it. I'll give her a call when my brain kicks back in and I can actually form sentences.

I duck to my ensuite and clean myself properly with a wet face cloth, then I check myself in the mirror. My hair looks mussed and an awful lot like I just had sex. Jonathan is going to take one look at me and give me a knowing wink. Shit. I repeatedly run my fingers through my hair to put it back how it was but I need hair product to make it go back down. Phoebe's fingers have knotted my hair and made it all stick up in spiky bolts. I run back down the hallway and have to dart back into Phoebe's room to retrieve my phone. Jesus, imagine if I ran out without it a second time… bloody hell, get a grip, Ryan. I run out of the door and stand impatiently shifting my weight from one leg to the other as I wait for the elevator. Finally, the bell heralds its arrival and I allow my breathing to regulate on the ride down.

Jonathan is looking at me, a frown on his face when I climb into the passenger seat. "Jesus mate, that was a quick shit."

What? What the hell is he on about? Then a penny drops, and I realise he's referring to our lie about me powdering my nose. I smile at him and quickly reply, "Yeah, drop and burn, mate." I'm impressed by my quick wit today.

Jonathan gives me a stupid grin and I know he's not pissed. He sniffs the air and wrinkles his nose. "Did you have a banana smoothie?"

What? Oh shit, the condom. My face burns and Jonathan frowns at me again. "Um, no, but I think Phoebe may have been making one. The bananas were really ripe so…" I trail off, not knowing how to finish that sentence. Jonathan looks at me again and frowns. My face burns and I just want the interrogation to cease.

The car is filled with the shrill sound of an incoming conference call and I'm saved further embarrassment. I sink into the seat and try to think of a coherent message I can send Phoebe when I get a chance.

*

Phoebe

It's after lunch when I hear the ping of a message on my phone. I pick it up to see a missed call and message from Ryan. Shit! My phone is on silent. Stupid! I call my message bank and listen to the message carefully.

"Hi Pheebs, it's Ryan. I um… ah, I just wanted to touch base with you about this morning. I hope you don't feel weird about it. It sort of happened so quickly that I just don't know what to make of it all. I am usually a little more attentive and I apologise for just diving in, so to speak. I don't know what's wrong with me lately. Um, look, just let me know that you're okay with everything. Just send me a text. We can talk more when I get back if you want, or not… if you don't want to. Shit! Anyway, I'll speak with you soon."

Oh, poor Ryan. I type a text message because at least with a text I can think about what I want to say:

Hi Ryan. This morning was a lot faster than I would have liked but, unfortunately, my lust far outweighed my ability to control it. I am not usually so forward or impatient and I don't usually get to the finish line so quickly either, but it's been quite a while and I think I channelled my inner strumpet this morning.

I press send then slam the phone down on the desk. Out of the corner of my eye I see Theresa look over at me, possibly wondering at my mood this morning. I'm fidgety and distracted and I'm sure it's not lost on her. I'm still staring at my phone when a message pings.

I like the strumpet. You can invite her back any time.

I respond quickly:

I'll get her number.

He's lightning fast on the phone keypad today.

I've got to go shortly. We're about to go into the boardroom to meet with a very important twat who landed this role because his daddy is the director. We'll do this presentation and waste an hour of our time and he'll tell us to go fly a kite anyway because he's a twat.

I expect smoke to float out of my phone keyboard at the speed of my fingers as I type:

He sounds like a twat. Why are you bothering at all then?

Another message pings and out of the corner of my eye, I see Theresa turn in her chair and look at me again.

The original meeting was with his daddy but he got a better offer to take a yacht trip with a group of bikini models for a photoshoot, so he palmed us off to the twat.

Okay, well go shake hands with the twat... make sure you wash your hands afterwards though. Ugh!

See you later... PS – What was with the banana condom?

Horrendous, I know! A giant banana handed me a couple yesterday in the mall. I must have looked desperate. It's all I had though, so I apologise for the fruity latex.

Jonno asked me if I'd had a banana smoothie. Nearly laughed out loud... except I was too busy blushing.

Haha. Banana smoothie! Okay, well I'll see you when you return tonight then.

Ok, bye.

Crisis avoided. My shoulders sag in relief. Next time, I'll make bloody sure I'm a little more restrained. I need to get some normal condoms. I make a mental note to go and get some in my lunch-break. Walking around smelling like a banana-flavoured anything is a no-no.

Theresa can't help herself, she has to know what's going on. She drags her chair over to my desk and point blank asks me what's up. I try to brush her off, "What do you mean?". She narrows her eyes at me with a 'give it up' look so I tell her Ryan and I had a weird moment this morning and I was worried about it, so I texted him to check it's all okay.

Her interest is piqued so she scoots in further and breathes at me, "Oooh, what happened? I had a text from Jonathan earlier stating that Ryan is a little 'off' this morning, whatever that means. What happened that was so awkward?"

Shit! I don't want to go into it because I'm embarrassed, and I don't want her to tell Jonathan and then he'll question Ryan... so I try to pass it off as a mini-argument, but she is looking at me blush and she's suspicious. She's glaring at me all squinty eyed when suddenly she hisses, "Oh my God! You had awkward sex this morning! I want details! Tell me everything and don't leave a single thing out."

Mortified, I try to pretend that she is way off topic, but she can see my blush and I'm stammering my reply, so she nails me with a glare that makes me feel like a worm wiggling on the end of a hook. I give up on fabricating a bullshit line and just blurt, "I can't tell you because you'll tell Jonathan and he'll ask Ryan and Ryan will know I've said something to you and that will just make everything so much more awkward than it already is."

Theresa hasn't listened to a single word I said in that confusing sentence. She gets a firm grip on my shoulders and hisses, "Details!"

Bloody hell. I tell her with as little detail as I can, but she is mentally filling in the gaps as I speak. She interrupts my vanilla interpretation of our encounter with, "Did you guys use a banana-flavoured condom?" How the hell could she possibly know that? My wide-eyed horror gives affirmation to her query and she whispers, "…because Jonathan said Ryan stunk like bananas. He thought it was a smoothie, but I know Ryan is a toast and jam or muesli kinda guy. Now it makes sense. So, how was he?"

I don't want to talk about this with Theresa and I say as much. Thankfully, the phone rings and I'm off the hook.

* * * * *

When Ryan returns later in the evening, I'm sitting on the couch in front of the TV, eating a cup of instant noodles. I'm a little embarrassed by my laziness.

"Oh, hello Ryan. I didn't know you'd be back this early, so I didn't cook anything, sorry. I've just poured some hot water into a noodle cup. I have another one if you want it?"

"Hi there. Nay, it's okay. Jonno and I grabbed a late lunch on our way back so I'm not really hungry. I could murder a beer, though."

He removes his shoes and walks to the fridge to retrieve a beer, then joins me on the couch. I put my half-eaten noodle cup on the coffee table and turn to him. I need to make this right because I need to end this awkwardness between us.

"Ryan, I'm really sorry about this morning. I almost attacked you; I'm really not usually like that. I just got so insanely, um... when you were kissing me, and it's been so long since I felt that fire... and then you were lying on top of me and I just wanted you so much that I threw all common sense and decorum to the wind. And then when it was over, I was embarrassed and felt like a harlot so I... ran and hid in the bathroom."

Ryan looks at me for a beat, then smiles. He leans forward, places his beer on the coffee table and reaches for my hand, stroking the back of my knuckles. He gently lays a kiss there before replying, "I could hear you breathing heavily in the bathroom and I wondered if you were perhaps crying. I thought I'd upset you. It was all so fast, and I certainly wasn't expecting *that*. I was pretty worked up myself... it's been a long time for me too, so I get why it happened. It's not how I would have planned it to go... I'm all for spontaneity but that was madness. It was amazing, but it was weird too. I think maybe because I had to run out the door seconds afterwards, the guilt got to me."

My cheeks flame and the embarrassment returns. I look down at my lap and wish I could erase the encounter and start again. I hope the awkwardness doesn't hang around too long. I still have a good four weeks here to endure.

Ryan leans forward and gently presses a kiss to my lips. I close my eyes and lean into him, tasting the beer, cool on his lips. He pulls me into an embrace and slides his body over the length of mine. He kisses the hollow beneath my ear and runs his tongue gently down the length of my jaw. He drops tiny soft kisses down my neck and deepens it at my throat, forcing my pulse to quicken and my breathing becomes laboured once again. A groan escapes me, and I experience the same desire to have him plunge into me again and I try in vain to rein it in.

"Ryan, I'm there again, already. It's embarrassing. I don't know what's wrong with me. I really don't."

Ryan's eyes are dark with desire on me. "Oh, I'm there too but I'm a guy, we're always there. I don't usually get this reaction from women though."

"Women… plural?"

"Okay, I've never had this effect on a woman, *any woman*, before. What do you want me to do? We don't have to do anything at all if you don't want to."

I remember that I forgot to get normal condoms, so I sheepishly say, "I only have one more condom and this one is banana, too, same as this morning. I forgot to get some."

Ryan smiles at me and stands, reaching for my hand. He pulls me up to standing and his lids look heavy with arousal. He smiles lazily down at me and murmurs against my mouth, "Let's go make a banana smoothie."

A giggle bubbles out of me as I follow him down the hall and into my bedroom. I stand before him and loosen his tie, pull it free and drop it. I unbutton his shirt, letting it hang loose and open. Sliding my hands up and over the planes of his chest, I take my time exploring his body. Ryan reaches behind his neck and pulls the shirt up and over his head, like guys do, discarding it on the floor. He reaches for my tee and gently eases it over my breasts and raised arms, depositing it with his shirt on the floor.

My hands fall to his waist as I loosen his belt and pull it free of the loops on his pants. I slowly unbutton his pants, unzip the fly and let them fall, all the while our eyes are locked and I'm forcing myself to go slowly. I unbutton my own jeans and push them down my thighs, stepping out of them to stand in just my underwear before him. Ryan reaches behind my back and deftly springs the clasp of my bra open. His eyes leave my face as his gaze travels to my chest. He sits quickly on the bed and pulls me to him. I straddle him and feel his hardness press against my crotch. He gently kisses my breasts; my nipples harden. My pulse quickens, and my belly tightens as he begins to gently gyrate against me.

I stand to reach for the condom as Ryan sheds his trunks. As I wrestle with the condom wrapper, he slides my panties down; kissing my belly to keep the yearn burning and starts a small fire between my thighs. As I straddle him, we both emit small moans. We rock and roll our way to a heady climax; our kisses are fierce, and our pace is quickening until we both succumb to the fire and fall spent onto the bed to gasp in sated release.

I roll towards him and mumble against his chest, "That was better."

He sounds exhausted as he replies, "Hmm…. much better."

We lie this way for some time before finally redressing and going back to the lounge, where we cuddle up on the couch and watch meaningless television in companionable silence. Lucifer is curled between us purring in his kitty heaven.

27

To Appease The Soul

Seth

The silence of the library is destroyed by the ringing of the bell to signal the end of fourth period. I gather my books to make my way to the lockers. As I walk towards the exit, I see Mio packing her books. Her hair is dark and lustrous and is so shiny that it looks like liquid onyx. I want to run my fingers through it. She is so incredibly delicate, and I find myself drawn to her quiet beauty. I can't walk by without greeting her because I want to see her alabaster skin up close.

"Mio, hello."

She startles a little but recovers. "Oh, hello, Seth. I didn't know you were in here."

"I was on the other side beside the computers."

"Hiding, were you?"

I chuckle. "Yeah, you're a scary girl."

Curious about her name, and I want to keep her talking a little longer, I ask, "Mio, I've always wondered. What does your name mean translated into English?"

"Well, the name comes from the Japanese word 'Mi' meaning beautiful combined with 'o', meaning cherry blossom."

"What a perfect description of you."

Mio blushes and looks beautiful. "Oh, I don't know about that."

I like to see her alabaster stained red. "Well I do… and *I'm* the beholder."

Mio awkwardly packs up her books. She looks shyly at me. "What does Seth mean?"

"Oh, mine has a stupid meaning. It's 'placed' or 'appointed' in Hebrew. I mean, what the hell? I don't think my parents chose it for its meaning. They just liked the sound of it."

Mio giggles delicately and I love the sound as it tinkles out of her. She stands holding her books and we walk to the lockers. The area is extremely loud, made especially so by a gaggle of noisy girls making their way to the courtyard. One of them shouts "Hi, Seth" and wiggles her fingers at me. Mio raises an eyebrow and I'm embarrassed. She delicately excuses herself and makes her way to her own locker. The entire group of girls giggle like primary school kids as they move on down the stairs. I frown after them. I still feel like the awkward nerd I was in primary school. I like Mio's quietness and that she doesn't behave that way.

As I make my way from the lockers, I spy Matt Jeffries. Matt's eyes connect with mine, and then he spins on his heel and walks back the way he came. The sight of Matt no longer heats my blood or incites violent tendencies within. My counselling sessions have moved me past that stage and I know that Matt was just a direction to point my anger. I've finally honoured Bonny's wishes to let it go. Matt is most likely beating himself up every day for the terrible path Brandon took that day.

I sigh and then run after Matt. I call his name as I approach, and he spins around and yells, his face tortured in some kind of agony, "You know what, just hit me. Just do it, man. I'm not running away, I deserve it."

I hold up my hands in surrender.

His voice breaks with emotion, "I can't take it back. I wish I could, I wish I could go back in time and undo what I did but I can't! I have to live with that every day for the rest of my life so just take your best shot and then let me go."

I swallow hard and try to make amends, "Hey Matt, I just wanted to say I'm sorry about what happened that day outside the library. I don't want to hit you and I don't blame you. Nothing is going to bring Brandon back, he's gone. I just wanted to say you don't have to walk the other way, I'm not angry anymore."

I hold out my hand to Matt as a peace offering. "Let's call it a day, mate. Let's just move on."

Matt looks suspiciously at my outstretched hand. He gingerly takes my hand in his and looks tormented as he blurts, "Can you ever forgive me?"

"Yeah, I can. Brandon had other demons. And you need to forgive yourself too. I got some grief counselling and it has really helped me. It's a long road and I'm only a little way down the path, but I'm on the *right* path now."

Matt looks relieved. "I've been seeing the counsellor here at the school. My mum made me do it and it's actually helping, but I can't get away from the guilt."

"Guilt is like cancer, mate, it will eat you up inside if you don't come to terms with it."

Matt nods, he already knows this. We walk together out of the building to sit under the large oak to eat our lunch, talking amicably for the first time in forever. I find the conversation healing after so much anger and turmoil.

* * * * *

After lunch I have double biology. I groan at the thought of the coming SAC test, which will count towards my final ATAR score at the end of the year, and the ridiculous amount of information I need to absorb about cells. The microscopic little bastards are so detailed, and my brain hurts from the saturation of information. As I sit down, Mio pulls out the chair beside me and plonks herself down.

"Hello again." She smiles shyly.

I grin back at her. "Hello there 'Beautiful Cherry Blossom.'"

Mio looks skyward and groans, "Oh dear God, why did I tell you that?"

I grin stupidly at her. "Because I asked."

"Because you asked. Is it 'placed' or 'appointed'?"

I dramatically throw my head back and repeat her words, "Oh dear God, why did I tell you that?"

Mio giggles again and the sound is beautiful. "Because I asked."

I don't want to break this spell, so I venture, "Are you allowed to go out after school?"

Mio frowns at me. "Of course, are you?"

"Well my parents aren't strict, so yes."

Mio counters, "My parents aren't strict either. Did you just assume my upbringing, Seth?"

My face flushes with embarrassment. "Yes, yes I did. My bad. Wanna grab a coffee some time?"

Mio grins back. "I'd like that."

I got it all wrong. Mio isn't shy at all.

Mercedes

It is the end of fourth period and I don't want to deal with the slut-shaming, so I nibble on my sandwich as I make my way to the library to spend my lunchtime in solitude. I'm looking forward to the weekend, feeling lighter just knowing there is only two more classes before I can leave this place for a break. School has become a battlefield and it's making me weary. My nausea abates a little as the food hits my stomach, but I can only really cope with bland food. My vegemite sandwich is not appealing but the first few mouthfuls stop my mouth from filling with saliva, and I don't feel the need to purge. I place my hand protectively over my stomach. At six weeks, the baby is the size of a lentil. I wonder what I will look like when my stomach pops out

I'm petrified of giving birth. I don't know how I'm going to push a baby out when just having sex hurts so much. I'm really scared that it will ruin my girly-parts forever. Will it end up like throwing a sausage through an open door when it's all said and done? I've looked up some stuff on the internet and all I seem to find are horror stories. And that awful day when I accidentally hit 'images' and saw the most horrifying images *ever* and wonder how I'm going to push this baby out without tearing myself to pieces in the process. I'm staying away from it for a while; I'm just going to focus on getting through each day.

Josh was cute last night when he put his hand on my tummy. I looked at him and said, "It's the size of a lentil."

The tips of his ears went pink with embarrassment, so I reached for his hand and kissed his palm. I don't want him to feel silly. "I'm not going to feel anything for about another ten weeks… *you're* not going to be able to feel anything for months. I only know this because I looked it up yesterday."

The gynaecologist has organised an internal ultrasound in three weeks, just to make sure everything is okay in there. I'm not looking forward to it because they have to go in through the outside… interuterine. Ugh! Josh seems completely unperturbed by it. Of course, he does, it's not him being violated.

I've almost made it across the courtyard. I see Seth leaving the library with a pretty girl. Seth looks completely besotted with her. I make a mental note to ask him about her when I get home from school this afternoon. I can't finish my sandwich and I don't want to risk shoving too much into my fragile stomach, so I fold it back into the cling wrap and slide it into my pocket.

I don't quite make it through the library doors before I hear Monique yell loudly, "Slut alert!"

I roll my eyes at her immaturity and continue into the building to a chorus of laughing and jeering girls. I choose to ignore them and pretend I don't hear them. I wish I could change schools. I feel completely alone. Josh spends his lunchtimes in revision classes to ensure he keeps on top of his subjects. He wants so badly to make it into the field of veterinary, so his final score needs to be high to be accepted into the universities he'll apply to.

Seth is aiming to be a paramedic, but he is studious, and it all comes easily to him. I don't know what I want to do so my path is not clear to me. Choosing my acceleration subjects for this year has led me nowhere, but I've got biology as my advanced subject and I'm finding it so hard. Seth has been helpful because he's completing the second year of biology this year, so he helps me with revision techniques. I've just left a double biology class, so I choose to spend this lunchtime revising what we've just learned.

Intently reading over my notes, a shadow falls across the page and I steel myself for some more slut-shaming before I lift my gaze, a banal expression fixed on my face. I'm surprised to see Genevieve standing next to the table. Genevieve shares my biology class and is in most of my other classes; she is looking down at me. She takes a huge breath before mumbling, "May I join you?" I am startled by her voice because she is usually painfully shy and quiet in class and rarely speaks.

Genevieve has rich auburn hair and the palest of pale skin, which is swarming with freckles. As she blushes, her face lights up with embarrassment and flushes an extreme red. Her body has started to angle away from me, like she is regretting her decision to ask me if she can sit here, and she is expecting rejection. I smile up at her as calmly and politely as I can and reply, "Of course you can, Genevieve."

She blushes again and pulls out a chair. It strikes me that I've never seen her with another person. Although this is her first year at our school, she has failed to make friends, and I feel a sense of guilt that nobody, including me, has reached out to her. This could be because I've been self-absorbed and in a group of self-absorbed bitches until recently. I am ashamed that I've been so easily caught up in the 'it' crowd. Genevieve sits and looks awkwardly at me. I see her take another big breath in before she blurts, "How come you don't sit with

Monique anymore?" She is almost flinching, like she thinks I'm going to bite her head off.

I arrange my features as I reply, "I started dating her brother. Since then, she has shown that she is awful and is a bitch." I pause before adding, "I'm sure you've heard by now that I'm pregnant? She takes great joy in slut-shaming me."

Genevieve nods her head so hard I think her eyes might roll in her head. "You were never mean to me when they all said stuff about my hair and freckles. You looked down at your feet, like you didn't agree with what they were saying. I always thought you didn't belong in that group."

I feel shame again that I stood by and watched Monique and the other girls verbally bully Genevieve. "Genevieve, I silently bullied you by staying mute. Having been on the other end of Monique's acid tongue, I know how it feels to hear that kind of abuse day in and day out. It's awful. I'm sorry I didn't stand up for you."

Genevieve is surprised and her face flames again but this time, in delight. "That's okay, I don't blame you. Maybe the two of us can sit together in class… and ignore her together."

I'm rescued from the hours of classroom loneliness stretching out before me and I have to look away, so she doesn't see my eyes brimming with grateful tears. My raging hormones are making me soft. Her hair is a beautiful shade of auburn and I tell her so. She beams at my compliment. I don't want to feel awkward, so I ask, "So tell me, why did you only start at our school this year?"

The words gush out of her as she explains that her parents moved down here from Perth just before Christmas as one of her mother's changed jobs.

"I have two mums," she explains, and she is clearly proud of both of them. "I was really badly teased in primary school about my two mums because it's not the norm, you know? By the time I got to high school, it was old news, and nobody gave me grief anymore. I had some really good friends in Perth and it was hard to leave and then start again in a new state and a new school. Both of my parents have been stressing about my inability to make new friends here, and they're really beating themselves up, but I've told them I'm fine. I've been waiting for Monique to find out about my parents, so she can add that to the list of taunts."

I tell her that we've just found out that my dad is gay and how upset I was with him for lying for all these years. I also tell her I was horrified and angry and embarrassed all at once, and I couldn't tell my friends because they would use it against me. "I behaved like a petulant and spoiled child and I feel really bad about the hard time I gave my dad." It feels cathartic to say it out loud… to not feel shame about it. I tell her how wonderfully supportive he's been during this surprise pregnancy and I tell her about Mum on the other side of the world. It just feels so good to not feel alone, to be able to share something with someone who is not judging me, not retaining everything I tell her to use against me in the future.

I type out a text to dad and ask if I can have a girlfriend over after school and, of course, he replies that he'll make a batch of cookies for us to eat… like I'm seven years old. I love him, and his cape is flapping loudly in the breeze. I ask Genevieve over after school and she's delighted. She seems pretty happy, like me, to not feel isolated and alone.

28

The Vampire Slayer

Ryan

Surreptitiously, I slip my head into her room and I'm disappointed to find her gone from the apartment so early. I need to borrow her eye makeup for a party this afternoon. I *hate* themed parties. I feel like a thief steeling into her room and groping her stuff without her say so.

My cousin, Connor, decided on a Vampire-themed lunch barbecue for his fortieth birthday celebration, because he's still aged ten in the head. After much thought and a stupid amount of internet research, I've decided to go as 'Vincent' from the 2011 version of *Fright Night*. I've managed to scrounge some obscenely tight vinyl pants from Connor's older brother, whose taste is questionable and wanders into the eccentric. As he was rummaging through his closet for the vinyl pants, I almost yelped in horror when he pulled some chaps and a tutu aside to access the pants. Today I'm grateful for his weird taste in clothing.

I found a long vinyl coat in a pre-loved clothing store two blocks from the apartment, and purchase a long black wig, fake stick-on tattoos and a fake moustache and goatee online. I had hoped Phoebe would be around to help me with the makeup and to put it all together. She must have either gone early to the gym or for a run... bugger!

As I curse myself for not mentioning it the night before, I wander to the small table under the window to search the drawers for something to use as eyeliner. Her laptop is open on the table and, as

I bump it, the screen lights up. I only glance at it briefly but my name jumps off the screen at me. I find myself reading what appears to be a diary. She is describing, in great detail, the awkward sex we had a couple of mornings ago.

We had sex on the floor of this room this morning. It wasn't even sex, it was the epitome of a quick screw. I thought I was home alone because Ryan had gone to work early so, of course, I was singing at the top of my lungs. I accidentally kicked the door frame and almost tore my toe off. Swearing like a sailor and hopping around the room like an idiot because it hurt like a bitch, it was as I was jumping around like this lunatic in nothing but my knickers and bra that Ryan asked what had happened. I got such a fright, which he thought was hilarious. He was supposed to be out of the apartment and I wasn't expecting him to be there. Anyway, he kissed my sore toe, which made me sigh and then he kneeled up and kissed the tops of my boobs bulging out of my bra. Well, that undid me. I was panting like a bitch in heat and almost used him as a human dildo. The poor bastard didn't know what to make of it. It took a grand total of three minutes for me to crow... God, I don't even know what I said (screamed??) in the throes of ecstasy. It's been so long since I've been that aroused. What a desperado! I was so mortified. Then I ran into the bathroom and hid behind the door until he left the apartment. WTF? He probably thinks I'm completely bipolar. To add insult to injury, the only condoms I had were those two stinky banana ones handed to me yesterday by that idiot at the mall. So, we basically screwed like wildebeest in a banana fog. Shoot me now!!!!!

I catch myself snorting with laughter. She has a way with words. Guiltily, I continue reading.

Ryan and I texted during the day, I feel a little better now that I've sort of explained... I'm not looking forward to seeing him when he gets home tonight – it's going to be awkward.

Okay, so it worked out okay. I didn't even cook a meal, had a noodle cup for dinner thinking he'd be back at around 9.30pm. So now I feel like a total arsehole. If it wasn't his apartment, he'd have run screaming for the hills by now. Anyway, I apologised for riding him like Pharlap and told him it's never happened before. Ten minutes later I'm back in the saddle, albeit a little less crazy but still in the banana fog, messing up the sheets on my bed. Twice in one day, it was nice after the drought. He's got a huge dick.

Huge dick? I have *not* got a huge dick… I'm average. Her ex must have a micro dick. I like how that makes me feel… her thinking I'm well-endowed has got me peacocking and I'm almost strutting around her bedroom. A pang of guilt bounces through me for reading her diary but I quickly push it out of my mind as my watch beeps the hour and brings me back to the reason I'm in here creeping around her room. I move to the bathroom and feel like a pervert as I go through the cupboards of the vanity. Finally, I locate an eyeliner in what appears to be a makeup bag nestled amongst tampons and a million bottles of girly stuff. I apply the stick to my top and bottom eyelash line and hope for the best. I look ridiculous – I am not good at this. My hand is not steady, and I wonder at the dexterity of women who apply this every day.

Fucking Connor, why can't he just have a normal barbecue like everyone else – minus the dress-ups. I have to run back to my room to make up the time I spent faffing about looking for eyeliner and reading her diary. I squirm and wriggle my way into the faux-leather pants and kid myself that it's because I've got a big dick. I position and reposition the wig until I think I look the part. The stick-on tattoos and fake facial hair are easy to apply so I make it out of the apartment and out the back way to the underground car park with only twenty-five minutes to spare.

Phoebe

"Sure, so what time will you all be here?"

Beth, Ryan's sister, is at the same birthday party that Ryan is at and she's managed to sneak out to call me and confirm our dinner arrangements.

"Och, I think about 5.30pm, will that work?" Her heavy Scottish inflection is not disguising her delight. Earlier in the week, I picked up the landline in Ryan's absence and spoke to a startled Beth. I explained that I am not, in fact, his new girlfriend but here briefly from the Melbourne office in Australia, helping Ryan settle into the London office, and that he offered me the spare room instead of a hotel suite.

Between us, Beth and I decided to surprise Ryan with a birthday dinner the day before his birthday. As it's a Sunday, I offered to throw something easy together. Who was I kidding? I've been cooking since yesterday. I made the minestrone last night, convincing Ryan that the recipe was best made the night before and that it was for us to eat tonight, when Jonathan and Theresa will pop in for a quick bite. I then worded Theresa up with a text message, so she and Jonathan don't ruin the surprise. I had obviously sounded convincing because he didn't question me on it again, he'd only commented on the aroma in his kitchen.

The lamb back-straps are marinating in the fridge. The salad is prepared and only needs to be tossed with the dressing just before serving, and the potatoes are roasting in the oven. The frozen ice-cream tiramisu cake, which I made last night, and which also doubles as his birthday cake, is hopefully setting in the freezer nicely.

Ryan is out at a fancy-dress birthday barbeque. He left this morning whilst I was at the gym, so I've managed to pull most of it off without him even being aware. He is due back at the apartment around five and so the cover is set; it should work out nicely. I quickly finish cleaning the kitchen, walk into the living room and turn the music up loud before I rush to the shower to get myself ready, in case our guests arrive a little early.

As I'm applying mascara to the last few lashes, I hear the front door open and close. Perplexed, because it's only four o'clock, I walk out and through the kitchen to see Ryan walk through the lounge, an annoyed expression on his face. Recognising his costume as Peter Vincent, the vampire slayer from *Fright Night*, I draw in my breath. The tight, black leather pants hug his backside and legs and make him look enormously tall. His bare torso, complete with fake tattoos, is only partially covered by the long black coat with a single button drawing it together. His bare chest and firm stomach, peeking out the top and bottom of the coat respectively, draw my eye, making my breathing spasmodic. There is a residual tan from his time in Australia. He still dons the long black wig, the fake jewellery and facial hair, and his eyes are heavily lined with black Kohl pencil. If it wasn't for the look of thunder on his face, I would gladly throw him against a wall and take him then and there.

The moment he enters the kitchen, he starts ranting, ripping off the fake facial hair and wig and depositing them on the island bench as he travels past it, not even noticing the licentious look I am passing over him. He bellows, "Un-fucking-believable! The side door to the stairwell is blocked by a delivery van so I just had to walk through the fucking downstairs bar dressed like this! Can you imagine the looks I got? Deirdre was on the bar and she wolf-whistled… she fucking *wolf-whistled*! Anyone who hadna seen my mad dash before that certainly turned to look then. How bloody embarrassing! I wanted to scream at her to shut the fuck up. Stupid idiot!"

He looks at me and takes in my expression and his eyes dart to my chest, spying the rapid rise and fall as I struggle to control my breathing. "What's the matter?"

I can't find my voice. I almost pant out my answer. I only manage to croak out, "Peter Vincent."

His eyebrows dart together, then up and land somewhere near his hair line. "You recognise the character? Took me an age this morning to put it all together and then I had to explain to everyone at the party who I was; like they've all been living under a rock since 2011. I went in search of you first thing this morning to help me with the tattoos and makeup, but you were at the gym, I think. I managed to get them all on but this one on my neck is a little askew. I hope you don't mind but I borrowed your black eyeliner."

My breathing is ragged as I murmur, "Ryan… come over here."

"What? Why?"

"…because I want to look at you."

"What?"

I'm whispering now because I don't trust myself to speak, "Come here."

Ryan slowly walks over and stands before me. He looks a little worried. "Are you all right? You're talking like you're having a turn or something." He looks behind him and into the living room to see if anything is amiss. His eyes return to me and his brow is furrowed. "Is everything all right?"

"Kiss me."

"What?" His eyebrows rise.

"Just kiss me!"

He blinks at me, probably wondering what the hell has gotten into me. The effect he has on me is consuming!

"Kiss you?"

Jesus, is he deaf? Yes, kiss me you dolt!

"Yes!" I hiss as I reach up and grab at the lapels of the jacket and pull him in, so he is pressed up against me. I whisper, "Kiss me" again up at him. I think a penny drops because his expression changes, but instead of kissing me, the idiot throws his head back and laughs. I feel stung and foolish. Embarrassed and angry, I let go of his jacket lapels lightning fast and growl, "Don't make fun of me!"

Ryan's expression flits between confusion and mirth until he realises that I wasn't joking, I really do want him to kiss me.

As if zapped by electricity, he throws me hard up against the fridge and kisses me thoroughly. He almost knocks the breath out of me, which only adds to the fire between my thighs. I'm back here again, in a fog of uncontrollable lust and I'm frantically unlacing the leather pants while he busies his hands on my shirt, recklessly all but tearing it from me, popping buttons all over the kitchen in his haste to reach my breasts restrained within.

Yanking down his pants, and freeing his erection, I fumble in my jeans' pocket for the condom I put there for just such a spontaneous emergency. My fingers close around it and I slam it on the bench in victory. I am tearing at the wrapping while he continues to kiss and undress me. Sliding the latex sheath over him, I bend down to yank my own pants down. I'm almost in a frenzy as I finally get the damn things down and kick them off. I shimmy out of my knickers and throw them over my head as he picks me up and unceremoniously dumps me onto the island bench, sliding a tea towel under my backside before I land.

He thrusts into me and I see he's surprised to find me already accommodating. Green Day's 'Jesus of Suburbia' is pumping out of the stereo, making for an excellent rhythm. He is thrusting into me over and over and it feels insane. I am getting close to climax when he stops suddenly mid-thrust and asks if I'm comfortable. What? What the hell? Why are we stopping? Exasperated, I bark at him, "Don't stop, for God's sake, don't stop now."

His mouth drops open in shock. He grabs my thighs and yanks me towards him as he thrusts himself in. The tea towel allows me to slide across the bench to meet his thrusts, forcing him deep inside. It feels so good that I want to scream but I'm too scared to open my mouth because I don't know what is going to come out of it. He thrusts again, and it is my undoing. I'm already there. I lift my head to look at him see his face reflect his climax. He pulls me firmly against him as he thrusts one last time, effecting a primal cry to tear from my throat as I topple into sensory oblivion. Unable to contain himself, he moans loudly, then collapses from the waist up on top of me, struggling for breath.

After our hearts stop hammering and our breathing calms, he rises up and pulls me up with him. "What was that?"

He probably thinks I'm a sex-craved lunatic – my behaviour of late certainly suggests so. "I can't work out if it was the black leather pants or the eyeliner but, holy God, I've never wanted anything as much as I wanted you, right then and there."

He smiles at me. "You're a surprise, Phoebe." He disentangles himself and darts to the bathroom to clean up whilst I go in search of my underwear and move about the kitchen collecting my shirt buttons. He returns with just his trunks on to find me still naked except for my bra, on my hands and knees searching frantically in the kitchen.

"What's up?"

"I can't find my knickers. I threw them over my head; did you see where they went?"

"Um, no. I wasn't watching where you threw those. I was somewhat... distracted."

I look at my watch. "Shit, Ryan, they'll be here soon. Go have your shower."

Racing from the room, Ryan runs off to shower while I race to my room to find another pair of knickers and slip back into my jeans. I reapply my lipstick and try to comb out the tangles in my hair. About ten minutes later, Ryan re-enters the kitchen dressed in jeans and a tee, finger combing his hair. "Hey, Pheebs, can you help me take the last of this eyeliner off? I look like a drag queen in denial."

He called me Pheebs. Leaning over him, my face inches from his while trying to remove the remainder of his eyeliner, there is a knock at the door. Ryan calls out, "Come in." Panic rises up because I know its Ryan's family, so I try to step back from Ryan, knowing the people are not who Ryan thinks are coming to dinner, but Ryan pulls me back and asks me to finish removing the eyeliner. Without looking up, he yells out to our guests, "Phoebe's just removing the last of this eyeliner, so you don't give me shit about wearing eyeliner... because real men don't wear eyeliner, right?"

"Well, why would ye be wearin' eyeliner, you great ponce?" Upon hearing his sister's voice, Ryan sits bolt upright, almost impaling his eyeball on the cotton bud.

"Beth, what are you doing here? I left you at the party."

"Weel, the woman tendin' to ye has organised a family dinner for yer birthday. Hellooooo, Phoebe, nice to meet ye finally." Beth walks towards me and embraces me fondly. Ryan cannot mask his surprise as he looks at us embracing above him.

Another knock at the door and Ryan's brother, Karl, plus Logan and Bella and Ryan's father, Donald, enter. Beth has explained my presence to them so there is no awkwardness, just the warmth of his family as they animatedly greet me. Logan and Bella tear into the room and command our attention, as only children can do, and Logan wraps his arms around my leg. I squat down and give them both a cuddle in greeting. I'm pleased they are happy to see me. I turn to Ryan and frown at him. "Close your mouth, Ryan, or you'll swallow a fly."

Donald wheezes out a laugh and slaps me on the back like an old friend. "You and I are going to get along just fine, young lady, just fine." Logan leaps onto Ryan's lap with total abandon and almost succeeds in making him scream. The hard heel of his shoe has rammed into Ryan's jewels, making him groan and squirm in his seat. Bella admonishes her brother for hurting Daddy, and Logan's bottom lip juts out and starts to quiver, but Ryan holds up a hand and tries to calm Bella, hugging Logan tight as he tries to put himself back together, beads of sweat appearing on his forehead from the agony of his aching balls. I don't know where to look so I glance at Ryan's brother and greet him for a distraction from this awkwardness.

Karl doesn't hide his expression as he looks me up and down with what appears to be appreciation. I am regretting my tight blue tee. I'm uncomfortable under his gaze, so I walk off into the kitchen in search of drinks. I look back over my shoulder and I can see Karl watching my arse. I'm a little weirded out by his impenitent stare.

He's a good-looking man, quite pretty for a gent, but I am currently rather attracted to his brother.

Whilst Ryan busies himself opening gifts and reading cards, having already provided drinks, I ladle the heated minestrone into bowls, which I cart to the dining table. I announce loudly, "Soup is served" to the entire room in general and place a small bowl of freshly grated parmesan and a sliced, warm, crusty loaf in the centre of the table. Everybody stands and makes their way over, politely thanking me for going to the trouble. Flapping a hand dismissively, I am embarrassed by the attention. "It was nothing, I make this all the time at home. The kids and I love it."

"No husband, Phoebe?" Karl asks. Jesus, don't beat around the bush.

"Karl, you don't ask that!" Beth reprimands.

"Oh, that's okay. No, we broke up not long ago… but we're still good friends. It's only been a few months so I'm still finding my feet, so to speak. That's why I'm here. My manager felt I could do with a little time out from it all when the position came up to help Ryan with the transition. I jumped at the chance."

Ryan busies himself with his napkin, not sure where to look, and I see colour rise up his neck. He still has a little residual eyeliner near his eyelashes and he looks sexy as hell. Only minutes ago, he was between my thighs on the bench top, thrusting and grinding. My own cheeks flush. Fancy having thoughts like that at a table surrounded by his family. I look across at Ryan to see him watching me; he knows exactly what I'm thinking. I blush again before turning to my soup. Karl looks like he's watching a tennis match as he glances between Ryan and me, frowning at our unspoken conversation.

Finishing quickly, I return to the kitchen to check the potatoes. Ryan wanders in behind me with the empty bowls in his hands. "I'll just light the barbeque," I announce as I search the drawer for tongs. I see Ryan focus on something on the other side of the kitchen and I follow his gaze to see something dark poking out from under the fridge. It's my missing underwear! Conscious of his family sitting at the table in full view of the open-plan kitchen, Ryan steps forward and stomps his foot over the knickers. I wasn't expecting this, so I jump and look askance at him. "Got it," he announces. I see my knickers poking out from under his shoe.

"What was it," Beth calls out. Without breaking eye contact with me, Ryan replies with a wicked grin, "Just a cockroach."

I narrow my eyes at him and hiss, "Cockroach is it?" I bend down and scoop up the knickers and shove them into the pocket of my jeans.

"Sorry," he whispers, "I panicked!"

"Yes, well, we all know how you perform in a crisis, Ryan. Helga and the turkey-stuffing incident taught us that much."

Ryan guffaws, so I give him a withering look, which only makes him laugh harder.

"I'll go cook the lamb." With an eye roll I leave the kitchen with Ryan still chuckling in my wake.

Outside on the balcony I heat the plate under the barbeque hood and turn to look into the living room at Ryan's family while I wait. Ryan and Karl stand talking in the living room on the other side of the glass door, facing me. I watch Karl's mouth and try to read his lips. It looks like he asks Ryan, "Have you tapped that yet?" Judging by Ryan's surprised reaction, I am correct. I smile winningly at them both and wave, giving them a false sense of security as they discuss me. Karl shrugs his shoulders and adds, "She looks fuckable, why not? Are ye getting fussy, Ryan?"

Ryan turns abruptly and barks something undecipherable at Karl.

Karl appears to be unapologetic, "Yeah, but this one's living in yer hoose. Ye're both single, surely you've thought about tapping that? If ye're not going to, do ye mind if I have a go?" Oh my God, this guy is ridiculous.

Ryan glares at his brother then shakes his head before turning and walking away into the kitchen.

I turn away from the scene and place the marinated meat onto the searing hotplate. The smell is mouth-watering. The sliding door opens behind me and Ryan appears with a glass of chilled chardonnay. He closes the door behind him before handing me the glass. I can see Karl watching us both from the other side.

"So, Karl's pretty concerned that you haven't 'tapped this.'" I giggle as I point to my crotch.

Ryan is incredulous, "You could hear that?"

"No, but you're both pretty easy to lip read. If he only knew the tapping that has been going on here."

Ryan's shoulders sag a little. "He does all right with the girls. He's got the prettier face and the biceps that make all the girls swoon. If the two of us are in a room, the girls always migrate towards him."

I turn the lamb on the hotplate, then return my attention to Ryan and waggle my eyebrows. "Well, the two of you were just standing side by side in that room and I was looking at you, imagining myself kissing you everywhere."

Ryan's mouth drops open. Smiling up at him, conscious that Karl is watching his brother's back but cannot see me as I stand directly in front of him, I run my tongue along the bottom edge of my top teeth then slide my tongue along my bottom lip, "Mmm, you sure taste good, MacGillivray." I give him a mischievous smile before I turn to remove the lamb from the hotplate. Turning off the burners, I ask slyly, "So, what are you going to do with that?" gesturing towards his crotch.

"I'm going to stay out here and clean up this hotplate while I deflate enough to walk back into that room."

I move around him and, with a plate of meat in one hand and my glass of wine in the other, I'm forced to open the sliding door with my foot. Karl leaps forward to help. "Thanks, Karl." I smile winningly at him.

Karl remembers his manners and takes the plate of meat from me, following me into the kitchen. Loosely covering the meat while it rests, I dish the potatoes into a large bowl and toss the salad with the dressing. Lastly, I slice the succulent meat and layer it on a small platter. Happy with the presentation, I take everything into the dining area and place the food in the centre of the table, calling everyone back to the table to eat. Karl taps on the glass of the sliding door and gestures for Ryan to come back inside, pointing at the dining table. Whilst everybody busies themselves dishing up, I replenish the drinks before sitting down and helping Logan and Bella.

Afterwards, Ryan and I remain in the kitchen cleaning up and stacking the dishwasher with the dishes Beth and Karl have brought in. It was decided that we all need a little break before we sing happy birthday and cut the cake, to make room for the rich dessert and coffee. Ryan swirls his tea towel and whips it at my backside. "Piss off MacGillivray!" I warn.

Ryan grins at me and says, "Challenge accepted," before he repeats the manoeuvre. I choose not to participate and walk out of the kitchen and into the dining room in search of any dishes that have been left behind. Ryan, annoyingly, follows me and thwacks my backside with the tea towel again. That's it! I forget momentarily that we have an audience and turn on him, "Ryan, you are like an annoying little brother, bugger off!"

The silence of our guests brings me back, so I turn to Ryan's family and announce, "We should have cake," and almost run into the kitchen and set the kettle to boil.

By the time they all leave, and the kitchen is clean and I am exhausted. Ryan closes the front door and walks into the living room to meet me.

"Thank you so much for organising that. It was great to see my kids on my off weekend and having my family all together was great. Nobody's ever done anything like that for me before."

"You're kidding! Really? It was my pleasure." I have to stand on tiptoes to loop my arms around his neck, pulling him in to meet my lips. I'm calm and happy and I enjoy the feel of him pressed up against me, taking our time with this kiss; it's nice to feel aroused without the blazing fire. We kiss for a long time, then retire to my room to perform a beautiful slow dance that is gentle and satiating and completely devoid of urgency.

29

Unwrapping The Girl

Phoebe

I wake to an empty apartment. Ryan has an early morning meeting, but I'm not required until midday. I stretch lazily and curl back up in the doona. Today is his birthday. What can I give him for a gift? I've only known him for a couple of months, but I've been swapping bodily fluids for a good part of that. I remember, with a pang, that we only have another few weeks before I have to return home. I force the thought out of my mind. If I dwell on that I'll get all maudlin and it will ruin what is left of our time together.

I lay in this cocoon of comfort for a good fifteen minutes, thinking of possible gifts he might like, when an idea forms in my mind.

I catch the train to the shopping mall, locate and visit the large department stores, the smaller stores, the boutiques and a thrift shop, but all to no avail. In desperation for the one little item that I can't secure, I leave the mall and locate a sex shop, hidden down an ally in a seedy-looking group of shops. My skin crawls as I walk into the store and past a creepy-looking middle-aged man, who is reading the back of a DVD cover, his hand moving inside his pants pocket. How perverted! As I walk further into the store, the girl behind the counter yells across the store at me, "If you're looking for the dildos, they're down the back on the left."

I want to run out of the store like the hounds of hell are snapping at my ankles. I'm mortified and my face burns so red that it almost sets my hair on fire. I smother my embarrassment and look across at the owner of the nasal voice and see she has jet-black, brilliant-red and fluorescent-green spiked hair, and I'm reminded of the punk hairstyles from the 1980s. I swallow my pride and decide that if I ask, I might actually get what I want sooner so I can get the hell out of this disgusting place.

"No, actually, I was looking for the lingerie section." I sound hopeful and it makes me cringe.

"Like knickers and stuff? Just past the dildos but before the blow-up toys."

"Thanks," I mumble. Shit! Briskly walking towards the back of the store, I can't help but notice the vast array of sex toys on display. Surprise is an understatement and there is a creepy thread of conversation that I'll be having with Chelsea when I next speak with her. There are toys I am passing that I have no idea how they should be implemented. Others are self-explanatory. Clearly, I have lived a sheltered life. I finally spy the lingerie and other clothing, mostly sexy outfits – leather and crotch-less underwear – displayed with an array of whips and other paraphernalia.

As I flip through the racks of superhero lingerie and naughty maid outfits, I spy what I've been searching for and hurriedly make my selection, return to the counter and make the purchase, practically running out of the store. I shudder, stow my purchase in my handbag and continue on to the office; anywhere but here. I am a prude.

*****

Leaving the office at the end of the day, I decide to go via the gym, so I can shower and dress for Ryan. When I return to the apartment it is almost six, but the apartment is dark and unlit. Thinking that I've returned before Ryan, I head straight to my bedroom and dump my work things on the bed. I take out the small gift box and make my way towards the kitchen, veering into the living room to put on some soft music first. Just as I enter the kitchen, Ryan's voice startles me in the dark. "Whacha doin'?"

I scream in fright and almost clear my own height as I vault off the floor. I spin around, my hand on my rapidly beating heart, and see in the gloom the shape of Ryan sitting on a single dining chair, propped up against the wall beside the kitchen counter. My eyes have adjusted, and I can see him now. He is sipping a tumbler of whisky that tinkles with the chime of ice cubes floating in the amber.

I find my voice, "Why are you sitting here in the dark?" Ryan looks sad and I have a tremendous desire to walk over and hug him, but I manage to stifle the motherly response. "Is everything okay?"

His voice holds notes of regret and sadness as he sighs, *"I'm fine." Dismissive... he doesn't want to talk about it.*

Is he thinking about his ruined marriage and the lack of his children to celebrate his birthday today? Then, as I move a little closer, he asks, "Did you wear that to the office? I'm trying to remember what ye were wearing." *Subtle enquiry.*

"No, I just changed." *Masked surprise, I'm astonished he noticed my attire.*

"Are you going out?" *Notes of misery creeping into his voice.*

"No, I changed for you." *I want to make you feel special.*

"Why?" *Suspicious... another surprise?*

"Well, I didn't know what to get you for your birthday, so I thought I'd just give you this." *Hopeful.*

I hand him the small gift box. Ryan takes his time opening it and masks his horror when he discovers the most repulsive tie nestled in the box. Cobalt-blue with bright-purple and florescent-green paisley swirls; it is the quintessence of hideously garish. He looks up at me, not sure how to react. I smile at him; this is a joke, Ryan. Taking the tie from him and looping it around his neck, his breath hot on my neck beneath my ear makes everything south of my bellybutton clench.

"I thought you could be the hot boss and I could be your slutty secretary. You can unwrap me and I'll do whatever you want… I really want that pay rise." I run my tongue seductively over my top lip and caress my own breasts in mock B-grade pornography. Ryan is silent and looking at me with a completely blank expression. I don't know what to do. He is just staring at me and I feel suddenly unsure. Perhaps he does not want this. A hot wave of humiliation at the narcissistic and over-confident measure of my proposed gift washes over me, and swiftly, I change gears to hide my embarrassment, "Or I could change into some jeans and take you out for a drink at a bar? Maybe we could celebrate that way." I am disappointed to feel tears prickle at my eyes.

His voice is hoarse as he whispers, "No, I want to unwrap you."

*

Ryan

My misery vanishes instantly, and I am looking at this beautiful woman who stands before me; taking in the effort she has put into wrapping herself up. The black dress with the detailed neckline hugs her body from her breasts all the way to where it ends, mid-thigh. A zip travels the whole length of the dress in the centre. She has on sheer black pantihose and black patent leather heels. She is walking towards me and it feels like all the breath has been sucked from my lungs. She reaches behind her head and removes a single hairclip, which has her hair falling in shiny waves about her face and shoulders and I feel an insane thump in my chest. I don't want to break the spell, so I whisper, "Come here and sit down."

She stands before me and seductively announces, "I can't sit down; my dress is too tight. You'll have to unzip me." I don't want to take my eyes off hers as I reach up and pull the zipper, but my eyes are orbs of betrayal and I see before me her beauty unfold as the zipper moves down slowly, revealing the swell of her magnificent breasts snugly secured in a lacy bra. As the zipper travels south, her lacy briefs are revealed and then the black suspender belt and lacy tops of her stockings.

My breath catches in my throat at the sight of her. "God help me; you're wearing suspenders."

She's whispering in the dark, and there is lust caught up in her voice, "Yeah, there's a story behind those." The zipper reaches its end and the dress springs apart.

I'm giddy with desire, probably blood loss as the big stallion dick she thinks I have is primed. I almost snort and make myself hoot out a laugh but she is looking at me with those eyes full of desire and it's all I can do to slow my pace.

I run my hands up the length of her thighs to her hips and pull her forward to stand astride me. Our eyes are locked, and my breathing is laboured as I continue exploring her and brush my hands over the lace of her bra, my thumbs stroking the exposed tops of her breasts. I want to tear her clothes off and plunge in but I'm sure she wants me to take it slow.

Running my hands back down the length of her and hooking my thumbs under the lacy top of her knickers, I try to gently ease them down, but something is stopping them. I look at her knickers in front of me and it's too dark to see why the removal is hindered. Phoebe places a finger under my chin and raises my gaze back up to meet hers and whispers, "You have to unfasten the suspenders first." Slowly turning around, she demonstrates by deftly unfastening the back of one of the lace fasteners holding the stockings in place. She uses her other hand to unhook the second fastener. As she slowly turns back to face me, I slide from the chair to kneel between her thighs, focusing on the task at hand.

My fingers don't fail me as I dexterously free the first, then the second fastener. I look back up at her from between her thighs and she is biting her bottom lip. Pressing my lips against the top of her thigh, I kiss my way to her groin as she sways and groans. I'm still looking up at her as my mouth finds the juncture of her thighs. Softly, I kiss the edge of her lacy underwear and she runs her fingers through my hair in encouragement.

I brush my lips across the satin front of her briefs before I move to the other thigh, kissing my way back up to her groin. She is groaning audibly as I kiss her through her underwear, applying more pressure, and it is so hot to watch her face contort. Her fingers are still caught in my hair and they tighten as she increases the pressure, forcing me harder against her, and I don't know how much more of this I can take before my own release. I have to close my eyes because I want to feel myself thrust deep inside her, the warmth of her all around me, and if I continue watching I'm not going to make it through the next few minutes.

❦

Phoebe
The delicious sensation of the thin satin material separating his mouth and my bare flesh is surreal. I'm climbing and immediately release the pressure on his head and pull away, to prolong the joy. He pulls my underwear all the way down and, as I step out of them, for a single moment he kisses my bare flesh. A gasp escapes me; his mouth and his tongue are warm against my naked flesh and it's becoming increasingly difficult to control my breathing. My voice is barely audible as I beg him to rise.

He stands and dips his head to kiss me zealously. I groan into his mouth and involuntarily push my pelvis against him.

"You're so responsive," he breathes, pulling away to look into my eyes. "I want to be inside you."

I am trying to keep the easy pace as I unbutton his suit pants and let them fall in a puddle on the floor. Turning my attention to his shirt,

I slowly unbutton him all the way to the top then slip inside his open shirt to run my hands up the smooth, hard surface of his chest, under his arms and around to his back. I am pressing kisses to his chest and I'm climbing again; I need to have him right now. I reach into my bra to retrieve the condom and promptly slide it over his erection. He sits down, never once breaking eye contact, and pulls me with him. Straddling him, I slide down over him and breathe in sharply as I feel him deep inside. Moving in small circles, it is only minutes before I feel the beginning of my orgasm. I have to stop and abruptly hiss at him, "Ryan stop, don't move."

"What's wrong?" he looks worried as he searches my face. I see his face relax and he starts to slowly move again. I momentarily panic… this is his gift and I don't want to ruin it with my premature climax. "No stop, if you move, I'm going to…" I am trying to get off him, trying to slow it down a pace for him.

Ryan jerks me back down and pulls me hard against him and his voice has a gravelly quality to it as he grates, "It's my birthday, and I *want* you to."

Keeping a firm grip on my hips, he starts thrusting and circling and, as I look apologetically into his eyes, he whispers, "Look at me, don't close your eyes." I want to call out and I want to cry, and I never want it to end. I wonder if I'm becoming unhinged as I start to drift but Ryan jerks me back. "Look at me," he whispers.

Looking into his eyes, it is a conscious struggle to keep them open. I want to close them and let them roll back into my head, but he won't let me, and the result is an intensity that is pure lunacy. Ryan's eyes start to glaze and for a moment he looks lost. As I look into his eyes, flitting between pleasure and pain, his mouth slackens, and I know he is there with me. His fingers clench and dig into my thighs and he grips me hard during the last wave and it feels exhilarating.

When he finishes, he presses his forehead just above my collar bone in the curve of my neck. I lift his head and gently drop a soft kiss on his mouth. "Happy birthday." He wraps his arms around me, hugging me hard as I run my nails up and down his back lightly.

"Stay with me tonight, in my bed," he whispers. "I want to wake up with you at least once before you go."

* * * * *

His bed smells of him and I am utterly sated as I sink into his embrace. I hand him another small gift. "There's more?"

"It's just something small but don't feel you have to like it. If you don't like it, just say so and I can easily change it. I promise I won't be offended."

Ryan rolls onto his back and fusses with the wrapping. I look at him and see he is pleasantly surprised to see the 'Tardis' cufflinks nestled in the box. Reaching over me, he puts the box on the bedside table beside me, kissing the tip of my nose as he does so, and wraps himself around me again.

"Tell me the story about the suspenders," he murmurs into my hair.

A chuckle bubbles out of me at the memory of the sex shop.

When I've finished, I look up to see Ryan's face scrunch up in distaste.

"I had actually planned on gifting myself to you, but somehow it all ended up the other way around. Don't get me wrong, I'm not complaining, but it's not my birthday."

"It was the most amazing birthday present I've ever unwrapped. Very sexy, you earned your pay rise."

This makes me smile. I don't want to ruin our beautiful mood, but I have to know why he looked so sad. "Hey, why were you sitting alone in the dark when I arrived?"

He heaves a sigh and confirms my suspicions. "I was thinking how much I miss my kids and how I didn't do anything wrong, but it feels like I'm being punished. Then you walked in and made me feel very, very happy."

I look up to see him smiling and I wish we could stay like this forever. Snuggling into him, I wrap my arms around his neck and nuzzle, enjoying the way I fit into him and wondering how the hell I'm going to cope when it all ends in a few weeks.

30

Across The Miles

Phoebe

"Hello, beautiful!" Chelsea yells enthusiastically.

"Hello, gorgeous girl. How are you?" It's wonderful to hear her voice. I've missed her and everything 'home' for weeks.

"I'm absolutely fabulous, thank you for asking." She smiles coquettishly at me, stalling.

"Oh, piss off, cut to the chase and tell me how your love life has been."

Chelsea rolls her eyes and smiles dreamily.

"Really? That good, eh? It's about bloody time. Apart from that…?" I am delighted by her joy.

"What do you mean apart from that? That is *everything*! Do you know how long it has been since I had a man take me there… multiple times?"

"Yeah, I do… during the Jurassic period if I recall correctly."

"Bugger off!"

"Okay, so you've been doing other stuff, surely, other than riding him like a champion stallion."

"Sure, we go out for dinner, then we come here and shag. We go to see a movie, then we go to his house and shag. I'm walking like John Wayne here!"

Argh! Classic Chelsea overshare. "I get the picture. What are you up to tonight?"

"It's still tonight and I just got home from shagging him at his house… look at your watch woman! Tomorrow night I'm going over to his house and he's going to cook for me, and he's asked me to bring a change of clothes, so I'll be shagging him then sleeping beside him all night. I'm so excited to wake up with him." Chelsea almost squeaks in excitement.

"Oops, sorry, it is morning here and I forgot we're in different hemispheres. So, sleepovers… reality starts now. You never know what he's going to be like to sleep next to. He could snore like a buzz-saw or gasp like an octogenarian on death row or, worse, fart like a camel."

"As long as he doesn't shit the bed, I'll be fine. If he's a farter, I'll curl up in his lap and blow his tackle around. I can play the bugle as well as any man."

"Oh, Chels, you're all class."

"Always. Sooooo… how is the Scot? More to the point, what's the wife like? Do you feel like a third wheel?"

"Actually, she's not on the scene. They broke up in Australia and she came back here with his kids, so he had to move back over here to see them. Cold and selfish bitch, I hear. I've not had the pleasure of meeting her yet, but I've heard her talk about me and it wasn't nice. She's trying to get back with him but he's having none of it. I'm not even sure why they broke up.. none of my business."

Chelsea starts to interrupt with a question, but I shut her down. I'm not going into it with her because it's still a little raw. Howard is a turd… an insignificant turd, and Catherine is a bitch.

"It's a long story, happened not long after I got here. I'll explain it all in detail when I get home."

Resigned to not getting an answer, Chelsea moves on. "So, if the wife's not in the picture, surely he's lonely and starved of sex. Are you banging him?"

I leap up and close the door. "Jesus, don't beat around the bush, Chels."

"Phoebe, it's me. When have you known me to be delicate or

prance around a subject? Feet first, always. Tell me you're not 'making love' to the guy, for God's sake."

My voice is emphatic as I answer, "Of course not, I'm riding him roughshod all over the apartment."

Chelsea belts out a laugh "Aaand? Gimme more!"

"Fine, he's fucking awesome. My loins contract just thinking about him."

"Really? Better than John?"

"Oh, I knew you would ask that."

"Let me answer that for you. Of course he is better than John. John likes dick – this guy likes pussy. Aaaaand?"

"And what?"

"Details, keep up."

My face flames. As I lower my voice to a whisper and put my face close to the monitor, I hiss, "He's in the next room. I'd die if he heard me banging on about banging him."

Chelsea rolls her eyes skyward, exasperated. After a pause, I answer the question left hanging, "Suffice to say he's ticking all my boxes, sometimes more than once in a single session."

"I *knew* it. You've got that 'I'm getting some and it's grand' glow about you."

"I don't have a glow." I flap a hand dismissively at the monitor, secretly hugging myself at the very thought of his prowess in the boudoir.

"Actually, I'm going on a mini trip with him and his family to Scotland on Friday. It's a decent drive so we're taking a train and then hiring a minibus at Inverness because there will be us, his kids, his dad, his brother and his sister. His father owns a cottage in Dunkeld, wherever the hell that is, somewhere in Scotland, and we're going there. I'm so excited to be going to Scotland I could scream."

Chelsea's interest is aroused. "Does his family know you're banging the brother, slash, son?"

I frown at her. "Shit no! Nobody knows. It's just sex. I've got to come home in a few weeks. I won't be telling John and the kids about it either, even when I get back. You have to keep this to yourself. All those years of just John... this is thrilling and exhilarating and I'm loving every second of it, but I can't allow myself to become emotionally involved. I live on the other side of the world."

Chelsea looks concerned. "Aw, hon, you sound like you already are emotionally involved."

I don't want to think about the inevitable. "I'm sad to be leaving. I don't want to think about it. I'm having the time of my life and he makes me feel beautiful and desirable and he knows exactly what to do with his... um, rather large member. He's very pretty to look at."

"Oh my God! Did you just call his dick a member? Why are you being so coy? Tell me straight up!"

"Okay, he's got a great wand and he's not afraid to make magic with it."

Chelsea guffaws in an unladylike manner.

I lean closer to the monitor like an excited teen. "Last night was his birthday so I surprised him with some lingerie. I have got to tell you about the sex shop..."

"What? You went to a sex shop? Little Miss 'Oh I can't own a dildo' went to a sex shop? What did you get?"

"Nothing kinky, just some suspenders, but while I was there some old guy was rubbing himself. There we so many shelves of stuff, you should have seen some of it! Some dildos I'm sure were petrol powered and required a kick start. I couldn't get out of there fast enough. Disgusting. But I have to tell you, the education on all things pervert was worth it because last night was amazing."

Chelsea is laughing at my dildo reference, so I continue whispering, "The sex is so different to John. I don't know if it's just the different personality that he has or if it's because he's not hiding in a closet like John was, pretending to feel it, trying with all his might to be what a husband should be but failing miserably. That sounds harsh but it's the truth. Now that I look back at our lives together, it was always me who was instigating the sex and it just didn't feel like this does. We were more like friends than lovers and our sex was robotic. It had its peaks, but it was nothing like this. I had nothing to compare it to, so I thought it was normal, and most of the time I was like 'what's all the fuss about', you know? I've been so busy pointing the finger at him and calling him out for lying by omission, but I haven't stopped to think how hard it must have been for him. The guilt he must have felt for not feeling how a heterosexual man should have. I can't imagine being the way I am and being expected to behave and perform in a different way. It would be the equivalent to you and I being heterosexual and being expected to act like a homosexual. Could you imagine that?"

"Ew! Never, ever, *ever* would I munch on a munchero. I don't want some chick's tits in my face either. Ew!"

I'm surprised by how vehement her response is. "You sound almost homophobic."

"No, I'm not, just the thought of having sex with another woman is a little repulsive so I'm kind of agreeing with you. You've really done some soul searching over there. Have you spoken to John lately?"

"Not yet, he's on the list. I'll be calling him and the kids next… they don't go to bed at senior's hour. I miss my kids something fierce but I'm damned if I'm going to wish the next couple of weeks away. Ryan is only recently single, too, as I said, so we're going at it like rabbits, but neither of us expects it to go anywhere."

"Senior's hour? Gimme a break. I've got to get up early tomorrow for an appointment with the specialist. Enjoy the sex while you can. I'd better sign off and go to bed. I want a full report about the trip to Scottsville. I can't wait for you to get back. I want so badly for you to meet Gavin… and I want to hear more about Ryan's giant dick."

"I want to meet Gavin too. Wait, what are you seeing the specialist about?"

"I just want to ask if it's a possibility for me to get DBS. I know it's still experimental and there's a whole stack of criteria that needs to be met for me to be a candidate, but I just want some information from someone who knows their shit, so I can make an informed decision as to whether I actually want to go down that path, let alone if I qualify. There's no guarantee it will work either."

"DBS? What the hell is it?"

"Deep brain stimulation."

Horrified, I almost yelp, "Seriously, Chels? Why now? This guy is fine with your Tourette's."

"Because I just want to know if I'm a good candidate and if I can improve with it. I don't know enough about it and I'm not saying I really want to go ahead with it… I'm just trying to be normal, you know?"

"Aw honey, you are normal. Doesn't Gavin make you feel normal?"

"He does but it's embarrassing. I nearly kicked him in the face the other day."

I have to stifle a giggle. The image in my head is hilarious but the embarrassment is very real to Chelsea.

"Okay. Send me an email about the appointment when you're done. And don't make any decisions without me, okay?"

After ending the Skype call with Chelsea, I take a moment to gather myself before I call John, Seth and Mercedes. As I stand and stretch, I decide I might go in search of coffee so I wander into the kitchen. It is early morning, but I need to finish up and get to the office.

Ryan looks up as I enter the room. He is sitting at the table with his glasses perched on the end of his nose, reading the paper.

"Hi, all done with the family?"

I look sheepish. "Actually, I haven't called them yet. I've been speaking with my bestie. I'm just getting a quick coffee and I'll Skype them then we'll go. Is that all right? How long have I got?"

"We really need to be gone in about half an hour. Can ye wind it up in that time?"

"Absolutely, I'll be quick. I just need to hear their voices. I'll be out in about twenty-five minutes. I'm already dressed and ready to go and, of course, if we're a couple of minutes late, I'll make up the time."

Ryan looks affronted. "Dinna be ridiculous. I'm not a prick! I just need to be in a meeting at nine thirty and have to prepare for it."

"I didn't mean to suggest…"

Ryan holds up a hand. "Go and make the call, O'Brien, for fuck's sake." I see the grin stretch his lips and I prance back to the study to call my babies, without my coffee.

John answers straightaway. "Phoebe, hello. How are you faring?"

It feels strange to hold a polite conversation with a man I've been married to for over half my life.

"Hi, John. I'm really well. How is it going over there?"

"Oh, it's going really well. Before I call the kids, I just wanted to let you know that Seth is doing really well and finally healing. I think he still has the odd bad day, but when he does, he comes to me and together we talk about Brandon and how he's coping. He's been back and forth to see the counsellor a lot, but he says he doesn't think he needs to go anymore. He's happy just to talk with me, and of course he writes. He knows the opportunity to seek counselling is open to him should the need arise but for now he's just happy to move forward at his own pace."

A hand goes involuntarily to my chest in relief. "Oh, John, that's so good to hear. I'm so relieved to know that. What about Mercy? Has she been giving you grief?"

"Actually, Mercy is the biggest surprise of all. We've turned a corner and we're getting along just fine now. I think that you going overseas has been a blessing in disguise for her. She can't hide behind her veil of indignant adolescent fury anymore. We've had some talks and she's in a better place. I think you'll see that yourself when you talk with her. She's had a little trouble with the girls at school but she's in a good place now."

"Is she still dating Josh or was he a flash in the pan?"

John smiles warmly. "She's still with him. He's a very thoughtful and considerate young man. I really like him, and I think he's good for Mercy. He'll come over for dinner for her birthday next week."

"Yeah, I'm going to miss her birthday. John, before you get the kids, I just wanted to say to you that I'm sorry for my reaction when your sexuality all came to light."

John shakes his head dismissively, no doubt wanting to avoid the conversation about how his sexuality came to light, but I need to get this out and absolve him of the guilt. "I was upset and angry and I was so busy feeling my own pain that I didn't stop to think about you and yours. Since I've been over here and away from the situation, I can see clearly that nothing is black and white and what you've managed to maintain all these years must have been hard. I want you to start moving forward. I don't need to ask you to be discreet because I know you wouldn't put yourself in a situation where the children might see something untoward happening… I mean, how well did we manage to have sex for over twenty years without being caught?"

"Phoebe, you forget that the first time we ever had sex your father caught us."

I *had* forgotten. "Oh yes, that was mortifying!"

John chuckles at the memory. "I really did love you, Phoebe, I love you still, but not the way a man should love a woman."

"Yeah, I know."

"Right," John interrupts, "I'll go and get Mercy."

As he moves away from the screen, I reflect on his words. I am touched by his thoughtfulness and another pang of guilt rocks me. Mercedes comes bounding into the room, excited to see me and looking every bit the girl I raised as opposed to the surly teenager she recently transformed into.

"Oh my God, Mum, I miss you so much."

As she gushes, I struggle not to cry, but my voice betrays me as I respond, "Hello, beautiful. How are you?"

"Aw, Mum, don't *you* cry because then *I'll* cry, and it will just be one giant sob fest!"

I laugh through the tears. "So, how are you, baby girl?"

"I'm good. School sucks, I'm just about to do the mid-year exams. I'm studying like crazy, but I just hope it's all going in."

"You'll be fine, sweetheart. How's Josh?"

"Oh my God! He is just awesome. He is doing the SACs like Seth and the poor guy is just so exhausted from studying. I've only seen him once this week and it was only for half an hour so I'm missing him like crazy. How are you going over there?"

I tell her I'm enjoying myself, and that the weather has been mild by Australian standards, but nice by English standards. I tell her about the horse riding, about my impending trip to Scotland and how grateful I am to my host for showing me around London and letting me stay here. I tell her everything except what's been going on personally and it sort of feels like I'm lying. Maybe one day I'll tell her about my amazing affair, but not now. For now, I just want to hear her voice and enjoy her bubble of joy.

"Sweetheart, I'm going to be in Scotland for your birthday, so I won't be able to Skype you, but I will try to call you."

She waves a hand at me and says we'll celebrate when I return. I make a mental note to buy her something in Scotland for her gift. Before she signs off, Mercedes leans in close to the monitor and whispers, "Make sure you ask Seth about Mio – those two are getting quite cosy."

"Wait, ask about who…?" but within seconds Seth is before me.

"Hi, Mum, I just heard Mercy whisper about Mio, so I'll just come out and say… I met a girl, she's really cute and we haven't even been out on a date yet, but we will after this round of SACs. Now that we have *that* out of the way, how is good old London town?"

He's not getting out of it that easily. "Hello, darling, I look forward to meeting Mio. What nationality is she? I've not heard that name before."

"She's Japanese. Her name means 'beautiful cherry blossom', which is beautiful."

"Nice, I'll bet she's cute."

He dimples as he whispers, "Actually, she's pretty damn cute and *really* nice."

We touch on the subject of Brandon and I find that John is correct. He really is healing, and I feel safe talking about it. Seth explains that he's had some nightmares but is doing okay. Relief floods me and I see that my family is coping just fine without me. He apologises as he says he needs to study for tomorrow's test and, reluctantly, I say farewell.

* * * * *

As I wander back to the kitchen, Ryan has gone, and I panic as I look at my watch. I only spent fifteen minutes on the Skype calls so I'm right on time. As I make my way to my bedroom to retrieve my bag and jacket, Ryan meets me halfway and presses me up against the wall, kissing me breathless. "Riding me roughshod all over the apartment, hmm?"

"Aw, man, you heard that?" My face heats up.

"Yep, and something about contracting loins…"

Oh, how embarrassing. He knots his fingers in my hair and kisses me again. "I was so fucking relieved to hear you weren't talking to your family like that. C'mon, we've got to go."

I find my voice and sigh, "Okay."

31

Scotland Or Bust

Phoebe

We're all packed up for the fun-filled trip to Dunkeld. I'm a mixture of excitement for the trip and concern about travel sickness. Ryan returns from a quick visit to the convenience store, where he ducked in to fetch me some travel pills. I am sitting on his kitchen bench as he reads the back of the pack, advising that I take two tablets half an hour before we leave. We're about to go downstairs to load up the two black cabs that will take us to Kings Cross Station where we'll board our train. Ryan pops a couple of pills out of the foil packaging and hands me a glass of water to wash them down with.

"Who's driving from Inverness to Dunkeld?" I ask.

Ryan pulls my knees apart and steps between them, leaning in for a deep kiss. His mouth is warm, soft and already familiar. I know his scent and I know how he tastes; I wonder if we'll be able to snatch moments like this during the trip and wish for a fleeting moment that we were going away alone. Finally, he pulls away and answers. "Karl is driving. Beth will ride gunshot and backseat drive his ear off for the entire two-hour trip. I think you should sit behind Beth, close to the front of the minibus, in case you feel ill. I'll sit beside you, and Dad will sit on the single seat across from us. Bella and Logan will more than likely sleep intermittently for half of the train trip and Logan will definitely nap in the minibus, but we have an in-car video system packed so they can watch movies in the van. On the train trip we'll have one stop for about fifteen minutes in Waverly, Edinburgh, and then go on to Inverness."

"Okay. Do I need my passport for when we get to the Scottish border?"

Ryan looks at me like I've grown a second head. I patiently look at him, waiting for his answer. Finally, he smiles. "No, you won't need a passport to get into Scotland because there are no border controls between England and Scotland."

The prick grins like I *am* the village idiot and adds, "Scotland is part of the United Kingdom."

Shit, I forgot that. I feel stupid, but he leans forward and kisses the tip of my nose, so I drop it. Instead, I smile up at him and pull him in for another kiss. The door opens to admit Beth, Karl, Donald and the children and we spring apart like we've been doing something naughty.

Karl announces, "All the luggage is in the cabs. In about two minutes, Dad and the kids will be too so… we're just waiting for the last two adults." He waggles his eyebrows at us.

Ryan stiffens his spine and tells me to grab my bag while he locks up.

As we all clamber into the black cabs, I'm starting to feel excited.

*****

Forty minutes into the train trip, the travel sickness tablets kick in and I'm drowsy. The constant sway of the train as it travels along through the outskirts of London is lost in my delirium and I struggle to keep myself upright. My lids are heavy, and I cannot appreciate anything because it feel like I've been kicked in the head by a horse.

"How are you feeling, are you tired?" Ryan asks, and it takes an eon for the words to travel through my ears, unjumble in my brain and slowly create the sentence before I can elicit any kind of response. I try to assemble my thoughts to form an answer, but my lips are glued shut and the muscles in my mouth will not part my lips to emit the words. All that comes out is, "mfeelngtard."

I can't even move my head to look at Ryan, but as I stare listlessly at the seat back in front of me, his face pops into view and he looks into my eyes, frowning at me.

To my horror, I can no longer hold myself upright and I tilt forward until my head smashes into his forehead. He yanks his head back and my head continues its momentum to hit the seat before me. A moment of panic has me screaming "Arrggghhh, help me I'm going to fall!" but all that slowly leaks out of my mouth with a mouthful of drool is "Mnah." I slowly slide from the seat, powerless to stop the trajectory of my body, and drop like a sack of potatoes onto the floor. My head lands hard on the footrest and my knees make twin 'bonk' noises as they hit the floor; I'm aware that my bum is stuck up in the air and I look idiotic but I'm powerless to help myself. Ryan's strong arms somehow pull me upright from this awkward position without snapping my neck and I wonder how he is doing this because I may as well be dead for all the help I'm offering.

I can hear both Beth and Karl's voice quietly asking Ryan what's going on. Ryan answers in a whisper, "I think it's the travel pills, they've knocked her out. Either way, she's out for the count. I hope she wakes up before we get to Inverness because she weighs as much as a dead Shetland pony." Karl snorts and I yell at him to stop being a dick, but only manage to emit a noise like a camel growling.

I'm cradled by Ryan before he switches positions and rests my head on his lap and the rest of my body on the other seat. There is nothingness until I wake to the sensation of the train slowing and, momentarily, I don't know where I am. I raise my head and the first thing I see is Ryan's face. What? He is smirking at me and I'm trying to work out where the hell I am when the memory of the travel pills comes back, and I am mortified. I look down and see I have drooled all over Ryan's crotch and he looks like he's had a mini accident. He looks down at himself and utters "Shit" under his breath.

I smirk back at him. "Sucks to be you, better than trying to carry a dead Shetland pony though, I guess."

Ryan's face goes beet-red, "You heard that? Sorry, I thought you were unconscious."

I smile at him, light hearted, and bloody grateful to have woken up. "I'd neigh at you if I could be bothered but I'm still a little punch-drunk." I feel the lump on my forehead and it's like a giant egg.

I look at Ryan and he winks as he whispers, "Joseph Merrick has nothing on you." He dimples as he says it and my stomach flutters. I look out of the window as we pull into Waverly Station and I experience a pang of regret that we cannot stop for a look around. I've wanted so badly to come to Scotland at some point in my life and wish I had weeks to spend here. I hope Ryan is true to his word and we get to see some of England for another mini break before I leave.

As we step off the train, Logan points at Ryan's wet crotch and innocently asks, "Daddy, did you do wees in your pants?" Ryan's face turns an unhealthy shade of dark red.

I save him the embarrassment of trying to find an answer that will quell the snickering of Ryan's siblings and answer for him, "No, I had some tablets that made me go to sleep and I used your daddy's legs as my pillow. Unfortunately, I dribbled a little bit, oops."

Bella looks at me with eyes wide in surprise. "Really? I saw mummy sleeping on top of Daddy once, but I think she was having a bad dream because she was making noises and squirming around like I do when I have a bad dream."

Karl can't help himself and guffaws. Ryan's face is so red it looks ready to explode off of his shoulders, Donald is chuckling to himself quietly and Beth has her back to us, but I can see her shoulders shaking as she tries to contain her mirth. I don't know what to say to make it better for Ryan, or to add to Bella's confession, but I can't just leave it all hanging in the air, so I actually make it worse by saying, "Well, your daddy is very comfortable to sleep on top of." The moment the words are out of my mouth I'm dying inside with regret.

Ryan is exasperated, "Jesus!"

Karl is snorting, Donald is openly laughing, and Beth is giggling with her face hidden in her hands. I am too frightened to open my mouth for fear of never being able to get out of the hole I'm digging. Bella comes to the rescue. "Yes, once Logan and I slept on the couch with Daddy and he *is* very comfortable."

We're called to reboard the train and the stopover of a short fifteen minutes is over. The next three and a half hours or so goes by with Ryan pointing out places of interest along the way. By the time we pull into Inverness Station, it's almost five in the afternoon. I'm unsettled because all we have eaten are snacks and I need a proper meal to set me straight.

As Ryan, Donald, Beth and I retrieve the luggage and herd the children from the train, Karl collects the seven-seater minibus and meets us all outside the station.

It takes me a stupid amount of time to strap Logan into his seat because I am completely out of practice and useless with simple instructions. I look over to see Ryan struggling with Bella's seat and feel a little relief, although Ryan's job is made harder by an insistent Miss Bella who professes that she is quite capable of doing up her own seatbelt. After much fuss, Ryan has to clip the holster-style belt system together himself, much to Bella's disappointment. Beth has set up the in-car DVD system.

As expected, Karl is the designated driver and Beth calls gunshot. I sit near the window and Ryan straps himself in beside me; Donald looks sleepy on the seat opposite us. Ryan retrieves a small hip flask of whisky from his travel bag and pours Donald and both of us a shot to distract us. Donald almost moans in pleasure as he sips the single malt. Shortly after finishing the glass, he bunches his coat on the window and drifts off to sleep. I can hear Buzz Lightyear berating Woody behind us while Karl and Beth talk quietly in the front seat. Ryan leans over under the pretence of pointing out sights along the way, but his arm snakes around my waist and the firmness of his chest as he leans against me. His breath is warm on my ear and he whispers, "I have an insane urge to kiss you, right here, right now."

I am aware that Karl can see us in his rear-view mirror at any time, so I go along with his pretence and look out the window, pointing at nothing as I whisper back, "It's not kissing I'm imagining." Ryan takes a deep breath and crosses his legs.

When he finally speaks, his voice sounds weirdly high and I know it is because he is trying to contain his arousal. "I'm sneaking into your room tonight."

"Mmm," is all I can manage as I cross my legs, too.

Beth speaks loudly from the front seat and I try to pay attention, but I'm conscious of the heat radiating from Ryan as he presses himself harder against me.

"That's the River Tay." She is pointing out of her window. "It's the longest river in Scotland and one of the five big Scottish salmon rivers." Beth is enthusiastically giving me a history lesson on the river and it provides a reason for Ryan's proximity, so I listen and take in her knowledge, and hope Ryan and I manage to snatch a few moments alone at some point over this break before we both explode with desire.

"The river actually starts quite small, in Ben Lui I think, and changes its name a few times before it passes through Lock Tay. It's almost two miles wide at the end. Did ye know that, Ryan?"

Ryan finds his voice and unfolds himself to sit upright as he answers, "No I didna. I love the part of the river that goes through Dunkeld. It's a lovely spot in late summer, looks so picturesque with those old larch trees."

"Aye," says Beth, "Quite romantic, it is."

Beth and Karl share a look of conspiracy, and Ryan's eyes slide to mine. They know something is going on but I'm not sure how much or if I'm being paranoid. We've been mindful to be discrete.

It's dark by the time we make it to the cottage. We lug the bags inside and set the children up with the television to keep them occupied. As Beth and I start to make up the beds and set the table for dinner, Donald lights a cheery fire and Ryan and Karl nip into the Dunkeld Fish Bar to collect our order of fish and chips. My stomach grumbles loudly, which makes Beth laugh. Ryan has had the forethought to keep the beer, wine and soft drinks in a cooler bag with ice blocks the entire trip and they are refreshingly cool.

Donald has retreated to his room to unpack. Bella and Logan are animatedly rediscovering the toys in their cottage room so Beth and I settle on the couch for a chat while we wait for dinner to arrive. We talk about my family in Australia and Seth and Mercedes. She enquires how long John and I have been estranged and I honestly tell her it's not been a long time. She doesn't ask intrusive questions but I find the conversation comfortable so I offer more than I otherwise would.

"We don't actually hate each other, we had to split because my husband kept something very important a secret for many years and I accidentally found out. We couldn't continue the way we were because, well, because the lie he's been living with is a deal breaker. I was angry and upset with him when it first came to light but being away from the situation has given me some perspective, and I realise how hard it must've been for him to be living this lie for all these years."

Beth does not mince words, so when she says matter-of-factly, "So he is gay?" I don't feel shocked or horrified, I actually feel a little relieved that I can speak about it with her.

"Yes. So you can imagine the problem that created?"

Her accent is strong and her query sounds particularly Scottish, "How did ye find oot?"

"I came home sick from work to find him having sex with another man in our bed."

"Christ! That's terrible but I understand how ye feel. My first husband was bisexual, so I kind of know where ye are, but we were only together a couple of years."

I want to cry with joy that somebody else shares my predicament and knows what I am going through. I have so many questions I want to ask but I don't want to appear rude so I try to make my questions as non-invasive as I can.

"Did you already know?"

"Aye, I knew he was bisexual. He fell in love with another man. The other man happened to be Pete, my cousin, so…"

"Oh! Are you still on speaking terms with him… or your cousin for that matter?"

"I am but I wasna for a good six months. Not only because he cheated with another person, irrespective of the gender, but because he kept from me that he was more into men than women. His father was quite homophobic and Thad was scared of his father, so he married me knowing full well that I was not really going to be able to make him happy. He said that he found me quite masculine. What a prick! Thankfully, he told me that after I'd already married Michael. When I told Michael what Thad had said, Michael said my ex-husband was an idiot and wouldn't know his arse from his head, and didna have an eye for beauty.

"Uncle Geordie, Pete's father, was also homophobic so they had to keep their love a secret for years. He was a hard man. Most of us feared him. He was my mother's brother, he was the eldest and he ruled his family with an iron fist. He actually slapped my Aunty Jean, his wife, across the face for daring to talk back to him. The next day he came home from work to an empty house – she'd taken the kids and all the furniture and fled. She didn't even leave a note, just up and left. Stick that in your pipe and smoke it, Geordie!"

Beth chuckles to herself before continuing, "I loved Thad. I felt angry and disappointed and hurt, and I couldna understand how he could love me and be attracted to someone else. It's hard to understand something if you're not of the same mind. He's married to my cousin now, you know? Got married last year in Edinburgh and they're going to adopt a child from South Africa, if all goes well. Thad sees his mother and siblings but not his father and, as for Uncle

Geordie, nobody sees him anymore, but I do see Thad and Pete everywhere. I canna escape him even if I want to.

"Then I met Michael. Of course, I held him at arm's length for a very long time. I had trouble with trust after Thad, but it was actually Ryan, my baby brother, who sat me down and told me in no uncertain terms that I cannot punish Michael for how Thad wronged me, nor could I tar all men with the same brush. He told me that I could vera well miss out on the love of my life because I was behaving like a thick-headed mule. Of course, I told him to fuck off."

I laugh at the image of her stern brow as she advised her brother to butt out. "This was all before his whore of a wife slept around. Poor Ryan, walking in and finding the stupid bitch sucking the neighbour's cock. Then she ups and leaves the country, taking their kids, and he has to follow her back and gets every second weekend with them like *he's* done something wrong. If I ever see her crossing the road, so help me I will stomp on the accelerator pedal and run the useless sack of pig shit doon."

I am shocked at Beth's vehemence and saddened for Ryan, and I wish there was some way I could ask him about it without sounding like I'm trying to syphon gossip out of him. Beth is shaking her head in anger and a little ray of sunshine filters through me because he has her in his corner. Beth's brow smooths and she continues like there was no mention of Catherine, "…and then Michael got sick and I nursed him through cancer. That brings about a lot of forgiveness in its wake, so I just didn't have room inside me for resentment. Thad was the first man I'd been with so I didn't know any better I guess, but when I met Michael, oh, he was so different. He made me feel beautiful and not at all masculine. Sex with Thad was all wrong, but I didn't know until I fell in love with Michael and we made magic together."

It is at this point that I wish I could interject with my own revelation concerning sex but, of course, the guy that is causing all the fuss is her brother and I'm sure Ryan does not want me throwing it about, so I keep quiet.

Beth sighs. "I loved Michael with every part of me… I'll never love another like I loved him. He died in my arms, ye ken?"

She looks up at me and her lashes are glistening with unshed tears. My heart is squeezing at the thought of what she has endured. "I'm sorry you lost him, Beth. How long were you married?"

"Fifteen magical years. He was my rock… my world. As they say, it is better to have loved and lost than to have never loved at all… but I feel so incomplete without him." She pauses and draws a deep breath before continuing, staring down at her fingers as they fidget with the edge of her cardigan. "I couldna give him children. Not through lack of trying, though. After two miscarriages and a stillborn, the last one nearly broke us, we gave up on babies in the end. We were content with each other, really happy, and we got a cat. Murray was cute and near the end spent most of his days curled up against Michael. It's like he knew. Then after Michael passed away, Murray would wander the hoose looking for him, meowing in the middle of the room and it sounded so mournful. Then he would curl up with me and give me love while I sobbed. I think animals ken things. My regret of not having his children was very strong after he slipped away from me, and I had nought to remember him by, day in and day oot, that we had made together with wee traits of him somewhere in them.

"Sometimes I think back on the night that he passed. It was a clear night and the sky was full of stars. I felt like it should have been a miserable night with lashing winds and rain beating on the windows to match the storm inside my heart. After I called the morgue, I was left alone with nothing but memories and I felt bitter and angry at the injustice of it all. He was a beautiful man and I felt like I'd been wronged by the universe; that the one person in the world who made me whole was taken awa' from me too young, when there is so much evil out there allowed to walk amongst us. I questioned everything, especially my belief in the almighty, and I've struggled to come back from that even today. Michael was my everything. It has been two years but it feels like only yesterday. I loved him, I love him still." The last part she says in just a whisper.

She stares wistfully into the fire and I think she might actually be about to sob when the door opens to admit Ryan and Karl, and the delicious scent of fish and chips swirls in with them and makes my mouth water in anticipation.

Beth collects herself and dabs at an errant tear before putting on her 'older sister' face and walks off to fetch the children for dinner while I trundle off in search of Donald.

* * * * *

After the kitchen is clean and we're all settled in, Karl asks everyone what they'd like to do tomorrow. I've never been to this grand part of the world and I'm up for anything. Ryan checks his phone and announces tomorrow's weather to be mild and sunny, with little to no wind. We decide a sightseeing day is in order. We will visit Dunkeld Bridge, the cathedral and pop in to visit the cathedral museum. Then Ryan proposes a picnic lunch on the River Tay, where the children can feed the ducks and play at the playground. We'll have an early dinner in town before returning to the cottage. They're assuming I'll be exhausted. I am here as a guest so I am actually out of line when I ask, "Is it far to the Culloden fields? I'm fascinated with the Jacobite rising."

Donald almost pops a hip out of joint when he bolts upright and announces that we will visit Culloden on Sunday. I am beyond excited and have to physically stop myself from bouncing in my seat. "Our clan fought in the Battle of Culloden. I'm fierce proud of 'em," he says.

Beth rolls her eyes and advises she'll take the children for the day, perhaps out for ice-cream, and Karl announces he'll take advantage of the opportunity to visit some friends who live nearby. I look at Ryan and advise that he doesn't have to come if he'd rather not, but he says he'd love to come. Donald almost deflates with relief and I remember Ryan saying that he doesn't really drive anymore because his eyesight is not what it used to be.

I can barely contain my excitement for Sunday's adventure but will try to show an interest in the history of Dunkeld tomorrow, too, for Donald's sake.

Long after the children and Donald have retired, we are sitting around the fire. The warmth is making me drowsy, and when I can no longer stifle my yawn, I announce that I am going to bed.

I pay little attention to myself in my nightly ritual, taking a quick shower to wash off the day and hoping it doesn't invigorate me, then brushing my teeth before finally falling into bed. I fall into a deep and exhausted sleep. I rise to the surface sometime in the small hours when the bed dips beside me. In my sleep-fuzzy brain, I brush off the intrusion as John retiring. At some point, I remember that John and I are estranged and I am in Scotland with Ryan and his family.

My eyes fly open and my body reacts with alarm until I smell him and it makes me smile in the dark. I smell whisky on his breath as he scoots over to me and I'm elated to find him aroused and ready for me. I turn and press myself up against him and bury my face into his chest, inhaling deeply. I remember that I've been asleep and probably have death-breath so I leap out of bed and hurriedly brush my teeth. When I climb back in, the moonlight gleams off Ryan's teeth because he is grinning like an idiot and it makes me smile.

He rolls on top of me and kisses me thoroughly. Our coupling tonight is slow, sensuous and thoroughly satisfying. Afterwards, we snuggle and Ryan sets his alarm for 5am to ensure he's out of my bed and in his own before anyone else in the house is any wiser.

I awaken from a pleasant dream by the gentle squeak of my bedroom door opening. I raise myself up on my elbows to see Bella tiptoe into my room. I turn abruptly to Ryan and hiss at him that Bella is in the room and he needs to go. I can see the whites of his eyes glowing in his panic. Bella creeps up to my face and whispers, "Can I sleep with you tonight?" As I nod my consent, I nudge Ryan with my foot; he has slipped under the covers. He slips away from me and hear the gentle thump as he rolls off the bed and lands quietly on the floor on the other side. As I scoot over to allow Bella room, I stroke her hair to distract her so that Ryan can make his escape.

"What's up, sweetheart?" I ask in the dark.

"Nothing, I had a bad dream and I went into Daddy's room but he's not there. I don't know where Daddy is."

"Maybe he's popped to the loo?"

"Maybe," she sighs and I actually hear her drift into sleep with the abandonment only a child can produce.

Ryan

Bloody hell, that was close. I cannot believe I was reduced to crawling out of the room on my hands and knees, in the nuddy, with my jocks balled in my fist! I was wondering why Bella chose to come into Phoebe's room before I heard her say that she'd gone to my room first and couldn't find me.

I gently close the door and slip my jocks back on, then tiptoe back to my room. I see something out of the corner of my eye and spy Beth lurking in the dark with a glass of water in hand. She has stilled and probably thinks she has evaded detection. I pretend not to have seen her. I don't want to explain anything to her and I hope to God she doesn't bring it up. I don't want to have that conversation and I want to enjoy Phoebe guiltlessly for the few weeks I have left with her.

I'm trying really hard to enjoy the sex without getting emotionally involved, but that is becoming increasingly difficult, given that she smells amazing and feels even better. I find that I'm looking at her and it's not just desire that keeps me excited, but the thought of spending time with her, kissing her, wrapping her in my arms, smelling her. Even to my own thoughts that sounds creepy... but she does smell good. I don't know if it's her perfume or deodorant or shampoo – I mean, women use a ridiculous amount of stuff just in the shower alone. I don't want to think about her leaving in a few short weeks.

As I crawl into my cold bed, I reflect on tonight's brief encounter. It hasn't been such a long time since we started this thing, but it has quickly become a familiar tango between the sheets. I like her, I like the taste of her and I *really* like the feel of her. As I drift off, I remember that I have left my phone in her room. Fuck! I have to get back up and creep back into the room to retrieve it.

As I sneak into the room, I can hear Bella's breathing because it's quicker than Phoebe's, but I can hear Phoebe's too. I look at her relaxed face and, as I gently reach for my phone, I have to stifle a yelp when her eyes pop open and stare openly at me. She mouths, "What the fuck are you doing?" I pick up my phone and point to it. There is an almost imperceptible nod as she acknowledges the reason for my return. I sneak from the room like a thief in the night, leaving her door ajar, and slide between the cold sheets of my own bed again. Sleep finally comes, and it is pleasant until my alarm goes off at 5am because I forgot to turn the fucking thing off! I am not gentle when I hit the 'fuck off" button and drift back to sleep.

✦-✦

Phoebe
The day dawns bright and I'm excited to get up and discover Dunkeld. I gently shake Bella awake and she makes a girlish little groan as she stretches. In front of her, Logan sits up with a halo of sleep-fuzzy blonde hair. I neither heard nor felt his appearance in the bed during the night. "Where did you spring from?"

His voice is quiet when he says, "I woke up and Bella wathn't there, so I went into Daddy's room, but he was snoring very loud and Bella would not like to hear that. Then I came in your room and here she is!" He shoots his chubby little arms into the air in joyous celebration of his discovery last night; eyebrows raised and a huge grin on his chubby face.

Bella giggles and says, "Oh you!" and tickles him into fits of giggles. These kids are freakin' adorable!

I make a quick call to Mercedes to wish her a happy birthday before I get up. They have just wound up dinner at John's and she is chirping at me, "Josh bought me a silver charm bracelet for my gift, and he told Dad and so Dad and Seth both bought me a charm each. It's so beautiful, Mum! Oh, and I got some gift vouchers and a couple of books from Dad." At least now I know what I can get her as a gift.

I wander into the kitchen to discover that Beth woke early and has nipped to the supermarket. On her return she makes us a cooked breakfast of eggs, bacon, sausages, stuffed tomatoes and enough toast to feed an army. We are full to bursting as we leave the cottage and make our way to the bridge. As we wander into the town centre, Donald proudly relays some history of the town. "Ye know, the town of Dunkeld was destroyed in 1689 with most of the houses being burnt to the ground."

My interest is piqued. "Really? How?"

"Well, on 21st August 1689, Dunkeld was attacked by aboot four thousand Jacobites. The battle raged for sixteen hours or so and by eleven that night, they were on the verge of defeat when the Jacobites withdrew. Only three houses in the village were left standing. Battle of Dunkeld, it was. There's still musket ball holes in the walls of the cathedral."

While I'm fascinated, the MacGillivray siblings are groaning and eye rolling. I am assuming they've all heard this before. I turn to Ryan. "Any chance you could pop into a café and grab us a coffee… perhaps meet us at the cathedral bridge?" Of course, Ryan jumps at the chance to escape the lesson. Both Beth and Karl leap into action too, so just Donald and I enjoy our stroll to the bridge with a history lesson of his home town an enjoyable exchange between us.

At the bridge I ask him when it was built.

"Oh, that's not as old as ye would think. 1809, I believe."

"Really? Why wait so long? Surely people needed to cross the river."

"Och, I think they'd tried to build a bridge before then, but the river had vera strong currents and is prone to flooding, so before the bridge I think they used a ferry. This is all from memory, my grade-school teacher drummed this stuff into us. Most of my fellow pupils were bored senseless but I was fascinated, actually considered becoming a historian at one point until it became evident that my parents couldna afford to pay for me to have a higher education, so in 1962 I moved to West Bromwich, near Birmingham, and got a job making car bodies at Jensen Motors.

"I let a room in a house near the factory and that's when I met my Alice. She was Scottish too. My mother *did* say I should never bring an English girl home. Alice lived three doors doon from where I was boarding. She was the most beautiful woman I ever clapped eyes on. For some reason that I will never ken, she fell for me. We married, and we had babies and we lived in the tiniest house you could imagine. I hated it there and I longed to return back here. I stayed there until Jensen's ceased trading in 1976. After that, I came back home, and I brought my wife and children back with me. Alice loved Dunkeld and felt she was finally home."

Donald's eyes sparkle when he speaks of his wife. I want to know what happened to her but don't want to push him. so instead I ask, "Is there a meaning behind Dunkeld's name?"

"Yes. Dunkeld means 'The Fort of the Celts'. We had that drummed into us from when we were little bairns."

Up ahead I spy Ryan, Beth and Karl. Donald tactfully stops the history lesson. When the children grow bored with the bridge and cathedral, we move to the park to enjoy our picnic lunch. Ryan is absent, so I ask Beth of his whereabouts. She says he's returned to the car to collect the lunch, drinks and the corn he pilfered from the cottage for the children to feed to the ducks. Casually, Ryan returns, and the children bounce around him, eager to run to the lake's edge to feed the ducks.

Beth, Donald and Karl walk with Bella and Logan to the ducks while I spread the blanket over the grass and unpack the basket. Ryan looks up at their retreating backs and leans in to plant a kiss on my mouth. As soon as he draws away, I look up to see Karl walking back to us. I'm not sure if he saw anything but Ryan silently shrugs so I let it go. He pours us both some wine and we sip in companionable silence.

When Karl arrives at the side of the blanket, he reaches into his coat pocket, which he had discarded earlier, and retrieves his phone. He holds it up. "Forgot my phone… it's for pictures," and then he grins at us. Ryan grins back. Karl turns on his heel to go back the way he came. As I look back at Ryan, he winks at me and holds up his glass in a silent toast. I hope he slips into my room again tonight.

Ryan

I want to have her to myself for a few hours, but we're surrounded by family and Karl is being a dick. I don't know why we keep up the pretence of a platonic relationship when Beth and Karl clearly know something is going on. As Phoebe makes busy spreading out the picnic, she sets aside two plates and starts dishing up a small feast for my children.

I can hear Logan and Bella squealing and I decide I should join them. I clearly hear the word 'babies' and know there is a mother herding her ducklings along the water's edge. Phoebe places plates over the children's dishes to fend off an assault by the crawling locals and stands to join me at the lake with my kids. I instinctively reach for her hand but drop it when I realise what I've done. She is grinning at me with her mouth stretched wide, her white teeth showing, and it makes my ears roar with the sound of thunder as blood is pumped into my nether regions.

As we approach, Bella squeals with delight and runs to grab my hand, pulling at me to hurry up before the little ducklings disappear. Her excitement is contagious, and I find I'm forced to jog to keep up with her as she bounds away in glee. The tiny ducklings are running to keep pace with their waddling mother. She is guarded and looks about nervously. Bella stops a good distance away and watches the procession as they make their way to the water. Effortlessly, the mother glides into the lake and, one by one, the babies jump in after her. I try to remember the name of a group of ducks. Beside me Phoebe says, "They make a cute little raft on the water." I am staring at her… because she read my mind.

She looks pointedly at me and says, "What?"

I shake my head. "Nothing," but it is something. She winks at me and a swarm of butterflies take flight in my stomach and I'm suddenly light headed. I am so affected by her. I decide that I will make it my business to sneak into her room tonight and lock the bloody door behind me.

32

It's A Braw, Bricht Moonlit Nicht The Nicht

Ryan

After dinner, Dad announces he's exhausted and excuses himself to retire early… one down. Beth, who has bathed and dressed Logan and Bella, returns from reading a bedtime story and says she's also done in and retires… two down. Karl looks like he's got enough energy to run a fucking marathon, so I don't know how to get rid of him. I'm glaring at the back of his head, trying to make it explode, but he is oblivious to me, so I ask Phoebe if she'd like to take a stroll to see Dunkeld by moonlight.

Karl's head whips up and he looks like he is going to ask if he can come along, but I give him a look that should make his spleen dissolve, and he visibly pulls his head in, returning to his newspaper. Although it's not a cold night, I tell Phoebe to bring along her jacket because it can get a little chilly if the wind picks up.

As we close the door behind us, I hold out a hand and she slides hers inside mine. I like the way it feels; small, delicate and snug in my clumsy giant paw. She smiles up at me, so I raise her hand to my mouth and brush my lips over her knuckles. They're warm and smell faintly of her perfume. As we step off the porch, I see the lights extinguished in the living room and the curtains move.

I pull Phoebe to me and whisper, "Look at the edge of the window, put your face close." Karl's face peeks around the curtain and both Phoebe and I jump up and scare him. We hear him yelp inside the house and we're giggling like teenagers. Beth's light comes on and so does Dad's, so we sprint away guiltily. Stupid twat, what's he playing at, spying on us?

We walk hand in hand, in companionable silence until we reach the end of the street. Under the old-world street lamp, I pull her in and kiss her heartily. Her mouth is soft and warm and tastes of the wine she had with dinner, and I don't want it to end but she pulls away and she's breathless. Her eyes crimp and I know by her breathing that she's feeling it, so to douse the flames I drag her along with me and we walk it off.

As we make our way along Brae Street, we can hear, even from this distance, the Athol Arms pumping with what sounds like a live band. I am nowhere near to sleep so I ask Phoebe if she'd like a drink and some live music. Once inside, it is crowded and teaming with people drinking and singing along to the songs the band is covering. I find a relatively quiet corner and plonk Phoebe in it while I go in search of drinks. To my horror I see Sally Murdoch at the bar, a friend of Catherine's. She always makes my stomach lurch, which had Catherine in fits of giggles. She liked to see me squirm because she's a little twisted. There's something lecherous about Sally and I suddenly regret my decision to come here. What the fuck is she doing here in Dunkeld anyway? She shamelessly makes a move on me.

"Hello, handsome, fancy seeing you here!" She is all fluttering eyelashes, her fake fingernails clicking on the bar and with what she thinks is a seductive smile plastered on her face, but she actually makes my skin crawl. She turns her cheek for a peck, so I feel obligated to politely kiss her cheek but just as I get close, she quickly turns and puts her wet, collagen plumped lips on mine. Argh! I reel back in disgust and have to take care to arrange my features, so I don't look as repulsed as I feel. I want to scrub at my lips with salt to get rid of the wet, fat feel of hers. I try to suppress a shudder. Pressing herself up against me, she breathes out, "What's a nice boy like you doing in a bar like this?"

Argh, she is drunk and slovenly and slurring her words, and I want to run out of here like my arse is on fire. I manage to extract myself from the talons clasping my arm. I dart around the bar in the hopes of losing her gaze before I run to the corner and quickly usher Phoebe out of the bar and back onto the street. She asks what's wrong and all I can do is shudder. I give her a brief description of the woman slithering along the bar and I can see she is shocked by my reaction.

"I'm sorry, Phoebe, there is something so sleazy about her. She makes my skin crawl. I don't want her to run back to Catherine and report us… you heard first hand how possessive *Catherine* is." She shakes her head at me and smiles. She's happy to walk away. We're back on Brae Street and I feel like I can breathe again. I extract my hand from Phoebe's and wipe it on my jeans. "Sorry, I've got the sweats."

We're a good distance away from the bar now so I bring her knuckles back up to my lips but they're cold. "Hey, you're cold. You want to just go back to the cottage? We can have another glass of wine and hope the hell Karl has gone to bed. Jesus, I need a neon 'fuck off' sign. The guy just doesn't get the hint! Maybe I'll sneak into your room again, if you're okay with that?"

She has the oddest expression on her face and I'm trying to fathom what's amiss until she whispers, "Kiss me." I look at her for a few seconds, at her soft pretty mouth and warm amber eyes with the dark flecks dancing around the pupils, and I want her *now*. I'm not gentle when I pull her in and kiss her hard and I press myself up against her because I want to feel her, all of her. I want her naked and supine under me. She finally pulls away. She's as breathless as I am.

We walk briskly back to the cottage and I'm delighted to find the lights out; the cottage is shrouded in darkness. After I deadlock the door, I sneak a peek at the children to see that they're sleeping soundly with their little cherub faces peeking out of the sheets. Phoebe is undressing in her room, so I enter to find her naked. Shedding my clothes on the way to the bed, we are fierce and frenzied and both of us reach our climax fast.

I forget to set the alarm and drop into a deep sleep with Phoebe cradled in my arms. I wake in the small hours to discover that my arm has gone numb while she's sleeping on it. She stirs when I try to extract it, so I wait for her to settle and end up falling into another deep sleep.

When we finally wake it is full daylight and my arm is a dead weight. Phoebe leaps out of bed and panics that we've over slept, and there is no way to go into the kitchen without alerting the rest of the family where I've slept. She is standing in the middle of the room in her tee, socks and knickers and she looks absolutely adorable. Her panic is comical, and it takes all my fortitude not to laugh at her expense. Quickly dressing, I manage to button my pants just as the door opens to admit Bella. She looks quizzically at me and I tell a bald lie to my daughter, telling her I came to wake Phoebe, grateful that I am standing and have my pants and socks on.

She grins at me and yells, "Aunty Beth is making pancakes. You better be quick, or we'll eat them all!" and she darts out of the door. A flurry of dust motes floats about the room in her wake and Phoebe winks at me.

33

The Measure Of A Man

John

Roberta's brow is furrowed, and she looks worried. "Are you sure it's the right time, John? Could you perhaps venture into it slowly?"

"No, I have to do this. It's not going to be pretty, but I need to do it, its part of 'moving on' for me."

"Okay, well you need to remember that there is nothing wrong with you. It is not unhealthy, it is not abnormal, and it is not 'sick' to be attracted to the same sex." She says the word 'sick' like it's a filthy word; my heart warms a little. She continues, "It does not make you a heathen, a sinner or the spawn of the devil either. I know you're feeling a little nervous but try to remain calm and not anxious. He will pick up on that and it will convey to him that you're feeling guilty. Don't do that, John, you've got nothing to feel guilty about. You've come a long way since you started your journey of truth. I wish you luck, John"

"Okay, I think I'll do it today… like ripping off a Band-Aid." I look up from my wringing hands and she's smiling at me. I think she's proud of my progress. I'm pretty glad I've had Roberta in my corner, making me feel normal and giving me the guts to do what I have to do.

She nods at me then changes the subject. "How's Mercy coping with her pregnancy?"

"She's coping really well and I'm really proud of her. Her boyfriend is supportive and helpful. He's a nice boy, Josh. His parents are not hiding their disappointment, but they've finally moved past the line of thinking that this is a form of entrapment by Mercy. She's not calculating, they're both just young and… naïve, I guess."

"And how are the two of *you* getting along?"

"Me and Mercy? Oh, we're in a great place. I don't know how long it would have taken to mend our fractured relationship if this hadn't happened. Don't get me wrong, I'm not pleased with the situation, but its like… when bad things happen, that the universe throws little curve balls into the mix. She's really handling herself well and I'm proud of her." Fractured? Next thing I'll be skipping around in gold hotpants at the LGBT Pride Mardi Gras in Sydney… something inside me whispers, "Would that be so bad?"

Roberta interrupts the conversation in my head. "Have you spoken with Phoebe lately?"

"I have, just the other day. She actually apologised for her reaction to the whole coming-out thing. She said she can't imagine how hard it must have been for me to carry on day to day living this lie. I have to say, I almost cried. It's such a big thing to hear that. I feel like we could actually be friends after all this. I mean, I do love her, always will, but I love her as a friend and I guess she knows that. Time apart has really helped her move forward. She has always been the kind of person who burns white-hot when upset or angry, and then it burns out and she moves on. She doesn't hold a grudge or stop talking, she just throws her tantrum and then sits in the corner to lick her wounds. A little time and she's a different person. She said you can't love someone for twenty-odd years and then turn it off like a switch. There are a lot of people who would not have handled it as well as she has. She seems happy over there."

Roberta nods at me and I realise I've been rambling, but there's nothing more to say on the subject. As the silence grows between us, I get fidgety. I don't want to have the next conversation with her, I don't want to see her face fall when I tell her I can't see her anymore because money is tight… but I can't keep coming to see her if it means I stress out afterwards because I'm out of dosh. I squeeze my hands tight and start to wriggle in my seat. Of course, she picks up on it straightaway, that's what she does. "John, is everything alright?"

I almost stutter because I don't want to see her disappointment. "Um, okay." I take a deep breath and continue, "Roberta, I can't afford to come anymore." I sit forward because I want her to know how much I appreciate her help and it's only the money that is the issue. "Don't get me wrong, I'm so grateful for all you've done. It's just that I have both the kids living with me and there are additional expenses for Mercedes since she got pregnant, and with the kind of work I do, I get paid in stages and it's a few weeks until the next lot of money comes in…" I trail off because she has put her hands up to silence me, probably because I'm rambling.

Her expression is warm, and she says, "That's fine, John. You don't have to explain to me, I get it. However, I was wondering if we could have just one more chat, no fees, this one's on the house, to discuss what happens when you tell your parents. Maybe we could chat in a café over a coffee, not here at the rooms. I would like to talk about how it went and go through how it made you feel. I just want to make sure you're all right after it."

I am flabbergasted by her offer. I would love to be able to sit with her in a café and chat like friends. Annoyingly, tears prick at my eyes. She covers my awkwardness with brisk conversation. "Of course, should the need to see me professionally arise again and you're still in this financial situation, still call me and I'm sure we can work something out… maybe a payment plan or something?"

I stand to leave, and I feel weird. We've been having these weekly sessions for so long that it feels like I've been talking to a friend. My first instinct is to embrace her but that would overstep the bounds of client and therapist. She reads my body language and thrusts out a hand to end my inner turmoil. I shake her hand; it's warm.

As I leave, I almost skip down the steps before I remember that

I have to have a shitty conversation with my parents today, and after that I'll probably never see them again.

* * * * *

As the door swings open, Mum's face breaks into a huge smile. She is pleasantly surprised to see me. I haven't seen them since the shit hit the fan, which has been months. They're a good hour-and-a-half's drive away so they don't expect us to pop over all the time, but they're also reluctant to step outside of their comfort zone to make the trek themselves.

They don't like driving at night, they're up with the birds and they go to bed with them too. Dad is always busy fixing stuff and pottering about the garden, now that he's retired, and Mum is always making cups of tea or washing cups for the next one. Then there's church and the church people they associate with who live in their local community. These people are very proper, and they don't drink alcohol or eat takeout or swear or use the Lord's name in vain. They don't break *any* of the rules and they stick by the ten commandments. It's like they're stuck in the 1950s and have fought with every ounce of their being to resist change and conformity.

We walk inside the house and Mum heads straight into the kitchen to put the kettle on. In her world, everything needs to be discussed over a cup of tea with a bickie on the saucer beside the cup. My heart bounces around inside my chest and my stomach is flip-flopping because I know this is going to be hard. She asks after Phoebe and the kids while she fusses with the tea, and I smile at her and say they're all well. I will tell them that we're no longer together and living at different addresses, but I will use the topic to segue into my sexuality. Then I'll be dead to them. I sit at the kitchen table feeling like a queer lamb about to be led to the slaughter.

Mum opens the kitchen window and calls to Dad to come inside for a cup of tea. He saunters in a couple of minutes later and his face lights up when he sees me. This makes me feel worse inside and I'm trying to keep my internal turmoil from showing on my face. He shakes my hand vigorously and slaps me on the back, familiarly. We sit down, and I sip at my hot, sweet tea. I don't actually take sugar, I haven't had sugar in my hot beverages for many years now, but I don't tell mum because she thinks she knows me, and I wouldn't hurt her for the world; it's just easier to drink it the way she makes it. I'm going to miss her the most.

"It's great to see you, John. How have you been?" Dad asks.

"I'm well, thank you," I say politely. I'm acutely aware that it sounds like I'm holding a conversation with someone else's parents because we're polite like acquaintances and not at all like family. I swallow hard.

They ask about the kids and Phoebe and I tell them the kids are fine and Phoebe is in London working for a few weeks. They have loads of questions about that and I'm grateful she's over there for work so it's not such a stretch, but Dad is onto my discomfort because I can't hide it. I am squirming like I'm in the principal's office and he's narrowing his eyes at me because I look like a sinner.

"Is anything amiss, John?"

I take a deep, steadying breath because now I start my slow and inevitable descent into the fiery pits of hell. My voice sounds quiet and calm and doesn't quaver like I expect it to. "Yeah, there are a couple of things I need to tell you."

Mum is all concern. "What is it, love?"

"Okay, there's no easy way to say this so I'll just… say it." Dad is glaring at me sternly, he doesn't do cloak and dagger well, and Mum looks worried that it's something really bad. "Phoebe and I have separated."

Mum's hand flutters to her mouth and Dad appears to look a little relieved, which is really confusing. Mum sounds like she's seconds away from tears and her voice is oddly high as she asks, "Oh, love, what's happened? Is there another… man?"

There it is... the worst possible thing that can happen in a marriage, in my mother's eyes. It must be another man; what other reason could there possibly be that couldn't be fixed with a prayer and a cup of tea? Her eyes look moist and full of concern for me and my heart breaks. I look at Dad, Oh God, he looks sorry for me... and I just blasphemed in my head, shit.

His eyes are soft. "I'm sorry to hear that, son, real sorry." He leans forward and pats my shoulder in a caring, fatherly manner. Now I want to run back home and leave it there. I don't want to do this. I want them to look at me with the love they feel in their hearts right now, at this moment. I don't want them to go to church on Sunday and pray for my dark soul to be released from Satan's steely grasp. Here goes.

"It's my fault, really."

Mum sits back in her chair and gives me an admonishing shake of her head. "Oh, John, you didn't? Tell me you didn't lie with another woman."

And we're back to infidelity. Of course not, but I *did* lie with another man... is that the same? I don't want to disappoint them, but I have to. I need to do this so I can move forward and be free of these shackles that have bound me to these lies for so many years. I want to be... free. I shake my head and keep looking at my lap. "No, I have, um, I have..."

Mum reaches for my hand and gives me a reassuring squeeze, and there are actually tears in her eyes. Oh, holy crap, she thinks I'm going to tell her I have cancer or something life threatening. Her face is crumpled with concern and it's making the whole thing too much. This is so much more fucked up than it should be. What kind of a bitch would Phoebe be if she left me for cancer? They're gonna wish that I only had cancer – not this disease that I have *chosen*.

"I'm gay." There, I've said it.

Mum looks confused. "What do you mean?"

I resist the urge to roll my eyes. My face feels hot and clammy and I'm actually shaking a little. "Mum, I mean that I am gay. I am attracted to men, not women. This is why Phoebe and I broke up."

She still looks confounded. "I don't understand. When did all this happen?"

What the hell? It didn't happen. I didn't just wake up one day and decide to try a different gender. Dad is frighteningly quiet, and his mouth is moving like he's chewing something. "It didn't *happen*, mum. I was born this way. I have always felt this way but for all these years I have pretended to be something else because religion made me think that there's something wrong with me. So, I pretended to be heterosexual and although I really did, and still do, love Phoebe, I'm not in love with her. I don't feel the way I should."

Dad finally finds his voice and it is low and menacing, "When did you allow Satan in, son?"

I'm still his son at this point but here it comes. "Dad, I haven't allowed anyone in."

His voice is almost a growl when he says, "It's not normal and you know it! It's disgusting, and the Bible says——"

I round on him because I have finally found my pride. "Oh, to hell with the Bible, Dad! It's not disgusting, it's who I am. There is nothing wrong with me."

His arse actually jumps out of his seat "I can't believe that *my son* would lie with another man. It's beastly and it's *not normal*! I've never felt more ashamed!"

I want to cry and scream that I *am* normal and that I love them both, but there is no point. There is no room to negotiate. I knew we would end up here because he is unapologetically disgusted in me, so I just stand and quietly say, "I'm still me, I'm still your son."

Mum has her face buried in her apron and she's sobbing into it.

Dad hisses, "You are *not* my son, you are the spawn of the Satan and I want you out of my house."

I take one more look around at this home I grew up in, trying to commit it to memory. I look at the tired wallpaper and the neat, old-fashioned furniture, and I see how set in their ways they are. I can hear Mum's sobs echoing around the kitchen and it is breaking my heart. Dad is breathing hard, like a steam train, and I can't tell if it's anger or an effort to stop from crying himself. I turn at the front door and whisper, "I love you," and then close the door on them forever.

I have parked three houses up the street because I knew it would end like this, and I knew I would need a couple of minutes to pull myself together before driving. I walk down their front path to the edge of the lawn and turn back to see Mum's face in the window, tears streaming down her cheeks, and it's all red and scrunched up in anguish. I wave and blow her a kiss, like I did when I was small, and I wait for her to raise her hand and catch it like she used to, but Dad storms up behind her and pushes the drapes closed. I slip the note, with a long apology and my new address on it that I wrote at home before I came, into the letterbox. I'll never stop hoping.

I sit in my car and look at my dashboard. I have a heavy feeling, like something is weighing me down, and a tightness in my chest. I thought I would feel free but I am bereft of any emotion whatsoever. I start the car and head home. It hits me on the freeway and I cannot stop, obviously, so I cry while I'm driving at one hundred kilometres an hour. I have a few moments of panic when the streaming tears momentarily blind me, so I pull over to the emergency stopping lane and sob my heart out.

By the time I make it home I feel like I am a hundred years old and my eyes are swollen; my face is red and blotchy. I quietly open the front door and try to sneak down the hall and into my bedroom, but Seth sees me and asks if I'm okay. I want so badly to be a strong parent right now, but I feel like a weak child and my face falls as I shake my head, no. Seth, my deep and troubled child, who carries the weight of the world on his shoulders, hugs me and asks if I want to talk about it. I'm not sure if I want to talk about it but I have to tell him what happened so that he and Mercy understand why they won't be seeing Grandma and Grandpa anymore.

We sit together in the lounge and I tell him of my visit. "I'm not sure that you and Mercedes will see them again. I mean, I'd love for you two to visit them every now and again, without me, but they don't want to see me anymore." Then I have another thought; how are they going to handle the news of Mercy and the baby? Poor Mum, I'm sad for her.

Seth

I leave Dad to have a nap to get over the emotionally draining day he's endured, and set off to meet Mio for a coffee. On the way, as I'm walking through the neighbourhood, I find that I am thinking about Dad's quandary, and I'm disappointed in his olds. What an arse Grandpa can be. He is so unbending and stiff… and poor Grandma, sobbing at the table like that. Bloody religion is ruining the world. All the wars and the violence and the beheadings… surely God is not pleased with his plan?

I reach the café and recognise Mio by her shiny dark locks. She has a little makeup on and it complements her natural beauty. Her skin is alabaster and her cheeks are pink with the chill. She smiles warmly at me as I walk in and plonk down beside her. "Hello there, stranger. What'll it be?"

She smiles at me. "Hot chocolate, please."

I mumble something stupid like "cool" to her because I am nervous. After I place our orders; hot chocolate for Mio and a soy chai latte for me. Our drinks arrive shortly after. She frowns at mine and asks what I'm having. I tell her and she says, "Tosser" at me. I like this chick a lot.

Mio tells me how she is going with her preparation for the next round of tests. Year twelve is brutal and it's make or break time because whatever happens this year goes towards our end-of-year score, and decides if we get into our chosen courses at the universities of our choice. Every one of these tests counts and it's scary. I ask Mio what career she's working towards.

"I'm hoping to get into midwifery. I want to complete my bachelor of nursing first, that will take three years, and then I'll complete a master of midwifery after that. I can do a bachelor of midwifery straight up but I want to keep my options open. I may actually enjoy nursing on its own but if I want to go into neonatal, which is where I think I'll be heading, I have to take this path. My parents would prefer I become a doctor but I like the idea of nursing. What about you?"

"Paramedics. I've wanted to be an ambo since I can remember."

"My parents would love you. I've got one brother studying to be a GP, and one who's a qualified neurosurgeon; he is getting head hunted. I'll never measure up."

"My parents couldn't give a shit what I do. It's up to me. Although I think they draw the line at bumming around, smoking weed and playing video games all day. I do have to work and make it count.

Outside in the courtyard of the café where we are sitting alone, because it's cold, we talk comfortably for a good hour, then she looks at her watch and tells me she has to go. She works at a newsagency in the shopping strip a little further along and her shift starts in fifteen minutes. I ask if I can walk her there and she beams at me. She almost makes my heart stop. I've got a yearning to run home and write down all the things that are flying through my head. She makes poetry fly about my headspace and I feel giddy with it.

We leave our empty coffee cups on the table and head to the back gate of the courtyard, which will lead us to a small lane behind the coffee shop. I close the gate behind us and, as the latch clicks home, I turn to find her standing close to me, like 'inside my personal space' close. The wind picks up and the leaves swirl a tiny whirlwind about our feet. Her hair is blown away from her face behind her and her mouth looks full and soft with the light shine of residual lip-gloss. I can't help myself, I lean down and kiss her. She doesn't slap my face, she doesn't push me away and she doesn't recoil in horror.

She moves closer and slips her arms around my neck and we're making music with our mouths. I'm aware that her small breasts are pressed against me and trying really hard not to disgrace myself, so I take a micro step back, which doesn't translate to her. She pulls away; her face is flushed and the taste of strawberry lingers on my mouth.

Reluctantly, we turn to walk towards the shopping strip and she slides her hand in mine like it belongs there. We're silent, we don't require words and we're neither embarrassed nor apologetic. The crunch of the dried leaves and twigs sounds loud and foreign in our steps. When we get to the newsagency, I tell her I'll see her on Monday and she nods her pretty head and turns to go inside, then thinks better of it and turns back to me, offering a chaste peck on the mouth. She disappears inside the door without a backwards glance.

I float all the way home. The house is quiet and I hear Dad's soft snores in his room, so I lock myself away in mine and write poetically about Mio… my heart is alive and flying.

34

Where Fierce Men Fall

Phoebe

It is almost three hours in the minibus to the Culloden Battlefields. Ryan is driving, and I am riding gunshot because, annoyingly, I suffer travel sickness. But I don't take a pill today that will render me senseless and ruin the trip. We are quiet in the van with the low and steady hum of the engine and a clear, sunny day shining down on us. I'm drowsy, and my eyelids are heavy when Donald surprises me from the companionable silence. "What fascinates ye about the Culloden Battlefields, Phoebe?"

I'm embarrassed to tell him that my fascination started with a historical love story by my favourite author that involves time travel, the Loch Ness monster and witches, but I can't think of any lies that will immediately take me safely there. "To be honest, it started with a series of books that I fell in love with about twenty years ago and I found myself fascinated by all things Scottish after that."

He surprises me with, "Jamie and Claire, ye mean?" I nearly give myself whiplash and I turn to look at him in the seat behind us. He winks at me. I love the guy. I can't stop the grin that splits my face.

I wonder about the tartan that belongs to the MacGillivray clan and imagine Ryan in a kilt. I sneak a look at Ryan and he's concentrating on the road, so I ask Donald, who is a wealth of knowledge, "Following the Culloden Battle, was it really against the law for a Scot to wear a kilt?"

"Och, aye," says Donald. "It was illegal for a Scot to wear any Highland dress, including a kilt, plaid or tartan after the battle in 1746. The battle was in April and the Dress Act came out in August of the same year." He turns to face me. "After the Jacobite Rising, Cumberland ordered all survivors to be hunted down and killed. Many innocent people in surrounding regions were killed. The Dress Act was repealed in 1782, but the damage had already been done… Scotland had changed forever." Donald looks out the window again. He is gloomy about the whole historical debacle. I think I'll change the subject.

"Do you have a MacGillivray kilt?"

Donald turns and smiles at me and he's all teeth; false and neatly lined up like a picket fence. "Aye, I do and so do both of my boys." I slide a look to Ryan and he reddens before quirking an eyebrow in my direction. My imagination runs rampant until Donald pulls me back to the now. "I've got it with me at the cottage if you'd like to see the colours when we return."

I stifle a squeak of excitement, but Donald hears it. He grins at me because he likes my girlish enthusiasm, despite me being middle aged.

"Our clan motto is 'Touch Not This Cat.'"

What? What the bloody hell does that mean? I don't want to ask because I might sound disrespectful, so I don't say anything. What a weird motto. Did they scream those words when they ran across the fields with their swords raised and their faces contorted with fear and bravery?

We've arrived. Ryan parks the van and we climb out and walk towards Leanach Cottage, a single-storey, thatched building. It is quaint and beautiful, and I can't help but run my hand over the stones that form the outer walls and wonder how many in history have done the same. As I turn and look out over the fields, an acute sense of reverence washes over me. I am awed by the history that took place here, of the massive hand-to-hand battle that wiped out hundreds of men and saw the end of the clans afterwards. Donald continues, and Ryan doesn't seem bothered by the telling. "Back then, our clan chief was Alexander MacGillivray. He was killed leading his men on this very field at the Battle of Culloden. There's a graveyard in Dunlichit that commemorates those who fell, but here at Culloden there's a stone that mentions us and others."

I bounce on the balls of my feet, stupidly excited to see it. Ryan is all dimples as he and Donald get caught up in my enthusiasm. We walk quietly to a mossy stone that states: '*CLANS MACGILLIVRAY MACLEAN AND MACLAGHLAN ATHOL HIGHLANDERS*'.

We follow Donald along the path to another spot in the fields and find a stone inscribed with 'WELL OF THE DEAD WHERE THE CHIEF OF THE MACGILLIVRAYS FELL'. I watch Donald as he puts a hand on his heart and closes his eyes in silent respect for his ancestors. Ryan reaches for my hand and gently kisses my knuckles. It's hard not to be affected by this place. The wind whips up around us across the naked field and I swear I hear voices carried on the wind. I know it's just my imagination but when I feel Ryan shudder beside me, I wonder if we're all going a little bit mad.

Slowly, because I don't want to break the spell, I turn, and we make our way to the visitor centre. Here we learn factually, without the romance of the book series, about the events leading up to the Battle of Culloden and a staggering figure of over 1,200 men, dead in just one hour. As fascinating as the exhibitions are, the experience leaves me weary. Donald looks done in too, so I ask if we should perhaps leave for home.

Our van ride away from the fields is quiet. We call into Newtonmore on the way back for a light lunch and a restorative cup of tea. Donald is quiet, and I don't probe him for any further information on his clan or the history of their demise. Twenty minutes into the trip home, Donald is dozing with his head against the window. Ryan's left hand is on his thigh, so I pick it up and put mine in it. He risks a glance in my direction and I smile up at him and mouth that Donald is asleep. I wish we were alone, and I could snuggle up against him but we're in a minibus and we're still over an hour from the cottage. "Do you really have a kilt?"

Ryan grins at me. "I do but it's been packed away for years. Catherine was not a fan of a 'man in a skirt'. I had to wear one for a cousin's wedding once and she couldn't look at me without scrunching up her nose. The minute we got home she told me in no uncertain terms to 'take that garish garb off'."

"Was that Pete and Thad's wedding?"

Ryan looks incredulous. "How… Beth?"

"Yes, we had a chat the other night. We've got some stuff in common."

The look of incredulity is back. "And what exactly would that be?"

"The man I've been married to for many years is, in fact, gay." Ryan yanks his hands out of mine to control the car as he oversteers around a pothole and it shakes Donald awake. I put a calming hand on Donald's arm and soothe, "Sorry, Donald, we nearly hit a rabbit." Donald nods tiredly and allows the motion of the moving van to lull his heavy lids closed.

I can see that Ryan doesn't know what to say or how to broach the subject so he gingerly wades in. "Did he just come out and say it? How could you not know he was gay?" His voice is low, but I can hear Donald's gentle snores and know he's dead to the world in the seat behind us.

"He was the only man I'd ever been with so sex with him was all I'd ever experienced. It was okay, but it wasn't like sex with you." His face tightens, and I can see he is pleased with the news. "I came home from work one day to find him in bed with another man."

"Shit!" Ryan blurts out and covers his mouth. "Sorry."

"It was quite a shock. I had no idea, not a clue, so you can imagine my surprise. I didn't know what to do so I left the house and went to stay with a friend, Chelsea, overnight until I could face him. Stupidly, we tried counselling but it wasn't working for me, so he continued on his own. We told the kids, he moved into an apartment and then this opportunity came up and I came here to clear my head."

"Why the hell would you try counselling?"

"I don't know, it was just such a shocking mess that I guess we needed to try something. If nothing else, I became inexorably alerted to the fact that he is what he is and that I'm not what he wants or needs."

"I'm sorry, Phoebe, I really am."

I shrug at him because there's nothing else to say.

※

Ryan

Her ex is gay? I can't believe it. I'd never have guessed. No wonder she wants to go at it like rabbits all the time. I wouldn't have been more shocked and surprised if she'd told me she was a hermaphrodite... although I'm pretty sure I'd have noticed. My mind wanders... I try to think of a word that would describe both genitals. Perhaps a penina... or a vagenis? Oh, yes, vagenis. I'm grinning at the word when Phoebe asks loudly, "What are you grinning at?"

"What? I'm not grinning." Oh shit, I *am* grinning... at the word vagenis because I am like a child. She just told me about her gay husband and I'm sitting here grinning. What the hell is wrong with me?

"Sorry, I was thinking about something and um... not about your situation, I'm sorry. I was just... sorry." My God, she must think I am a twat! My face feels hot and I know it's red. Quick MacGillivray, think of something to say that's not about her gay husband. My brain spits out something stupid, "So he moved out?" Of course he moved out, she just said he moved out. What the hell is wrong with you, idiot schmuck? "Well, of course, you did say he moved out. Sorry, sorry, there are no words coming into my head... right now... at this moment." My face is boiling hot and I'm just speaking crap. I look at her and I'm sure I look like a rabbit caught in the headlights because she bursts out laughing.

"What?"

"You're panicking. Why are you panicking?"

"I'm not panicking. What makes you think I'm panicking?" I am fucking panicking because the only shit that is coming out of my mouth is senseless words because I was thinking about vagenises and she's just told me her whole world imploded a few weeks ago.

"Because you're speaking the way you behave when you panic."

"No, I'm not." Yes, I am. Why am I denying it? There is just silence in the car broken only by Dad's snoring behind me and the hum of the engine. I can see in my peripheral vision that she's still looking at me. A bead of sweat breaks away from my forehead and trickles down my temple to drop off my chin. There it is, panic in a drop of fluid. I risk a look at her and she's still looking at me quizzically, her mouth stretched really wide in a face-splitting smile. Her enjoyment of my discomfort is not lost on me. "You okay?" I venture.

"Sure," she replies. "What about you?"

"I'm... I'm doing okay. I'm good."

"Wanna tell me what you were thinking when you went to your special place?"

No, I do not. I don't want to say it out loud, but my mouth decides against my iron will, and just blurts, "Vagenises!" I glance sideways at her to see she is a mask of both alarm and confusion. How the bloody hell am I going to explain this?

"What's are vagenises?" She's grinning again so I calmly advise that it's a word I came up with joining the words penis and vagina… like there is absolutely nothing weird about my thought processes.

She starts to laugh. "You know what? I don't even want to know why you went there! I'm not touching that one."

I smirk. "Yeah, that's probably a good idea."

"Are we all going out for dinner tonight? I'd like to shout everyone dinner if we are."

"Beth was thinking of making a pork roast at the cottage while we've been out, in her words, 'gallivanting about the killing fields'. She makes a mean roast, our Beth." The conversation moves on to Beth's prowess in the kitchen. She asks if Catherine was a good cook.

"She wasna too fussed with cooking, didna enjoy it. It was mostly me who did the cooking. What about your husband, er… ex-husband? Can he cook?"

"John is a great cook. We both cook and although I'm a good cook, John's cooking is great. There's a difference… and he makes dessert afterwards. Don't get me wrong, I enjoy cooking, but I never get adventurous like he does. He has a go at different cuisines; he's really good at cooking Thai food."

My mouth starts to water because it's been hours since we ate in Newtonmore. I'm glad we're nearly at the cottage. Dad abruptly stops snoring and sits up in his seat. He sees we're almost at the cottage and starts to look restless. I'm looking forward to stretching too, my legs and arse feel stiff and a little numb.

As soon as we're inside the cottage, our senses are assailed by the delicious scent of roasting meat. Bella and Logan come tearing around the corner and leap at me. I pick Logan up and balance him on my arm while I squat down and hug little Bella. She holds up a picture she's drawn and my heart falls. Bella has drawn a family picture of us with our names above our heads. We're all holding hands and smiling. Above the fourth figure, which she's drawn with a triangular skirt, stick legs and arms and enormous balloons for feet, she has written in her scrawly hand, 'feby'.

35

A Womb With A View

Mercedes

Sipping my third cup of water, I'm trying to fill my bladder for this ultrasound so the technician can see the images of Lentil. So not only do I have to endure this embarrassing internal examination, I have to endure it all with a screaming bladder. I'm a little nervous about seeing little Lentil for the first time, no matter how small or seahorse-like he or she is.

I wish they'd hurry up and call me because I'm busting to pee and I'm not sure how much longer I can hold it all. I'm almost dancing in my seat. Dad leans over and asks if I'm okay. I tell him I'm busting so he walks over to the girl behind the clinic reception desk and tells them quietly. The stupid bitch looks over at me and yells across the waiting room, "You can go and let a little bit of urine out but don't empty your bladder." My face goes red because everybody in the room is looking at me. Josh squeezes my hand and I'm sweating as my bladder threatens to burst, so I briskly walk to the bathroom.

I break a nail all the way down to the tip of my finger trying to unbutton my jeans before I wet myself, and I have to stifle my moan as I finally get to let go. Then alarm bells start ringing in my head because I can't stop. I can't stem the flow! I finally manage to shut the floodgates, but I think I've emptied it all out now. Shit, shit, SHIT!

I almost run out of the bathroom to the water filter and fill another cup, which I gulp down, hoping to replace the fluid I just expelled but knowing it takes ages for it to make its way down. I turn to find Dad and Josh looking at me from a doorway… and a chick in a white nurse's uniform is standing with them holding a clipboard in her hand. We follow her into the room. She hands me a gown and I have to get naked and come out in the gown. I ask Dad and Josh to wait outside because I don't want them to see her put something inside me. Gross.

The ultrasound technician introduces herself as Elizabeth. She wastes no time with niceties as she inserts the wand, which she calls a vaginal probe, inside me. It hurts like a bitch. I'm clenching on the probe and she apologises for the discomfort but there's nothing I can say. I apologise for almost emptying my bladder, but she says it's fine; she's distracted by something on the screen.

Oh God, please don't let there be anything wrong with little Lentil. She removes the wand and throws the sheet over my crotch. Squirting warm blue gel from a tube all over my stomach, its hard not to flinch. She moves what looks like an odd-shaped microphone over my stomach. She frowns at the screen. "How far along do you think you are, Mercedes?"

"About eight or nine weeks I think Doctor Hanson said."

She shakes her head and says, "I think you're more like twelve or thirteen weeks along." I'm surprised. She says, "I'm going to get another technician in here. Would you like me to call your dad and brother in?" Ew! He's my boyfriend. What kind messed-up family has the brother turn up to the ultrasound? I tell her he's my boyfriend out there with my dad, the father of the child, and tell her to bring them in.

She leaves, and I half sit up as I pull the sheet up to make sure my pubes are all covered before the others come in. She re-enters the room with another, older woman; Dad and Josh trail behind them looking awkward. She tells them to sit while the two technicians talk shop to each other. She pushes the sheet down, uncovering my pubes again. Ugh! She squirts more gel onto my stomach and starts zooming the microphone thingy around again. The older woman confirms that our baby is actually over three months in size, around twelve to thirteen weeks.

She turns a dial and a weird but fast 'Darth Vader' sound echoes around the room. She looks at me and smiles, "That's your baby's heart beating." Josh smiles at me. She tells us that everything looks good and healthy, and points to the microphone thing and calls it a transducer. She counts out loud the ten fingers and ten toes and, without even asking, refers to Lentil as 'he'. I look at her and say, "So we're having a boy? You can see his… penis already?"

She smiles at me and says, "You can sort of guess the sex at this stage. It looks like a boy, but I can't confirm it." The older woman frowns at her and I wonder whether she's in deep shit for not asking if we wanted to know the sex of the baby. The one holding the transducer continues; she doesn't feel the glare of the older woman on the back of her head.

Angry woman speaks loudly, "We're not always correct so we usually reserve telling the parents until twenty weeks when the genitals are formed, and we know for sure, and only if they ask to know."

Josh grabs my hand and kisses the inside of my palm and my fingers. He is excited about little Lentil. We're having a little boy. I wish Mum was here, I wish I could be telling her our exciting news. I don't think about him tearing me apart when he comes out, I don't think about how we will cope. I just know I won't be able to give him up because I love him already. He's ours and he's not a mistake; he's a surprise.

❦

John

I watching my baby girl look at Josh with the excitement of impending parenthood and it's all wrong. They're both excited about their baby. I wish Phoebe were here. I really need to discuss this with her. I wish she would hurry up and come back. She's going to be very upset when she finds out.

I can't believe Mercy's a third of the way through this pregnancy. She's about to go into her second trimester, according to the technician. She obviously screwed up her cycle dates because she's almost a month further along than we thought. They're just kids, how can they bring up a baby? I can see Phoebe and I raising this child while they finish school. What about university? What about this poor little boy?

We're quiet all the way home. I wait in the car while Josh and Mercy race in to change into their school uniforms and grab their bags. It dawns on me that I'm going to be a grandfather. I'm not old enough to be a grandfather! I'm going to be a grandfather and I'm going to be raising my grandson. Oh God, there's warring emotions inside me; excitement and fear.

The whole situation is made so much worse when I drop them at school. They look so young and vulnerable as they walk off. They're too young to screw up their lives. I'll wait for Phoebe to return so we can discuss how to tell them that giving this little boy up for adoption is the best thing they could do for themselves and the child. But if we were pregnant in high school, Phoebe and I would have kept it for sure. This is such a shitstorm.

36

Love Has No Boundaries

John

My face is so close to the monitor that my breath fogs up the screen. I really have to make an appointment with an optometrist; these old glasses from my youth have served me well in the past but my eyesight is bad. I complete the final check on the plans before I print them on the new 3D printer.

I've had a house full of technicians for the last two days setting up the new printer and syncing it with the Wi-Fi and my PC. I don't understand their technical jargon and felt like I was in the way so in the end I gave up and stayed in the kitchen baking, until they'd finished and left. I hope it works for me now like it did when they were here.

Mercy and Seth are still at school, so I've been going great guns this afternoon; I'm really in the zone. The doorbell chimes and scares the crap out of me. I hope it's not Desiree in unit two. She keeps making excuses to come over here on the pretence of borrowing sugar or an egg. I'm stifle my impatience because I want to finish this project before the kids come home. I adjust my face, so I don't look as interrupted as I feel and yank the door open… it's not Desiree.

Mum is standing on my doorstep. I don't know what this means. She smiles at me and asks, "Can I come inside, John, or would you rather I didn't?" I remember my manners and step back, inviting her in. Closing the door behind her, I walk past her and I can see that she is nervous and wringing her hands. I feel a little mean as I walk past because I don't give her any comforting words or a reassuring hug.

I'm not sure what I'm in for so I don't say anything. I hope she doesn't start preaching… or asking me to change because I *really* don't fancy that conversation. She follows me meekly up the hall and into the sunny kitchen, where I pull out a chair for her at the round table.

Lucky for her I've got an array of sweet biscuits freshly baked, which I arrange on a plate. I put the kettle on for tea and take the teapot down. After I pour the tea and we're both sitting quietly in the silence, she looks down at her hands, which are clasped tightly on the table in front of her. Why can't she look at me? Is she so ashamed?

Her breathing is weird, like she's struggling for air and I'm unsure if I should ask her if she's okay or just let her find her words. A fat tear plops onto her shaking, clasped hands and I feel like a heel. She's upset. I reach across the table and put my hand over hers. They're oddly cold.

She starts to sob, and she kisses the back of my hand that covers hers. Her hot tears are cascading over my hand; I don't know what to do. She looks so wretched. I wait. Finally, she calms and gulps big air. She raises her head and her eyes find mine. They're puffy and red rimmed and it hurts that I am unwittingly causing this much hurt for her.

I have to take the high road; she's my mum and she's come all this way. "Mum?" She shakes her head at me. I don't know what that means. I try again, "Mum? Are you okay?" She shakes her head again. She tries to speak but her mouth is gummy with saliva. I give her time to collect herself and pour the tea. After a moment, she swallows hard and has another go.

"John. I'm so sorry I hurt you. I know you can't help the way you are, but I won't pretend to understand. I don't understand what you are but you're my son. I can't stop loving you because you're… different."

I have to ask. "Does Dad know you're here?"

She nods. It can't have been easy for her to come so I ask her why she changed her mind and went against Dad's wishes. "I've been so conflicted, John. I didn't know what to do so I asked the Lord for guidance." I suppress an eye roll. "I went into the living room and took my old Bible down from the bookcase and it fell from my hands. When I bent to pick it up, I saw that it had fallen open at Isaiah. So, I read Isaiah 66:13 and saw: 'As one who his mother comforteth, so will I comfort you,' which roughly translates into: 'A mother's love is a reflection of God's love'. It's like He sent me a sign, John. It's like the Lord was giving me direction… and permission."

I suppress a sigh. I don't agree with her opinions on religion, but this is her world.

She continues, "So I told your father what happened. He, of course, went on to preach about how an idle mind is the devil's workshop and anything could be misinterpreted, but I was having none of it. I asked him if he believes that his word is louder than the Lord's? He pulled his head in after that. We have reached… an agreement. I told him I cannot stop loving my son because of the way he was born. I also reminded him that the Lord tells us we must learn to accept the faults of others, just as God has learned to accept our own faults."

I'm not going to mention that my homosexuality is not a fault. What *is* a fault is that I misled my wife and best friend because I was raised to believe homosexuality is sinful… and a choice! She releases my hand, wraps hers around her tea cup and takes a sip. Closing her eyes, she savours the tea. When she opens her eyes, she smiles at me. Her face is no longer blotchy, her delicate skin has been restored to its natural state and she looks relieved; almost at peace with herself.

For the next forty minutes we talk about anything but the elephant in the room. She mentions the weather, asks if I have a garden at all here. I tell her I have a small courtyard and she asks for a tour. We're polite and amicable and she walks slowly around the small garden, admiring its simplicity. When we get back inside, Mercedes wanders into the kitchen. She stops in her tracks and looks wary, looking to me for some indication that bedlam has not just befallen all of us. I give her a nod followed by a shake indicating that Grandma and I are okay but that she doesn't know you're up the duff.

I see Mum's gaze travel to Mercy's bust. "Wow, you've really grown into quite a woman, haven't you?" It is all I can do not to burst out laughing. Moments later Seth enters the room and, seeing how relaxed we all are, he embraces Mum warmly. I look behind him to see an extraordinarily beautiful girl standing awkwardly in the hall. She smiles shyly at me, so I walk over and introduce myself. Her hand is warm, her fingers are long, and she looks altogether very delicate. She is exquisite.

Seth remembers himself, "Oh, guys, this is Mio. Mio, this is my family. My dad, John, who you just met, and I'm sure you've seen Mercy around school? This is my Grandma. Grandma, this is Mio."

Mum embarrassingly blurts, "Ooh, aren't you an exotic one." I see Seth flinch and Mercy's eye widen in alarm; my face lights up like a monkey's arse in heat.

Mio takes it in her stride and smiles warmly at Mum. Today, of all days, Seth had to bring her home when my mother is here. I offer Mum more tea and, thank goodness, she says she has to leave. I'm emotionally exhausted but grateful she has found it in her heart love me for who I am. At the door, she turns to embrace me and it's warm and familiar.

"I love you, John. Always remember that. A mother's love knows no boundaries."

37

Towards The Light

Mercedes

I snuggle closer to Josh on the couch. I love him so much. He puts his arm around me, which is what I was hoping for. As much as I like the thrill of scary movies, I hate the unpredictability that keeps me poised on the edge of my seat. Every time I jump, I wonder what it's like for Lentil, hearing my heart pounding. The music is building so I know another jump scare is imminent. I try to bury my face in Josh's armpit. He giggles like a kid and pulls away; I forgot how ticklish he is.

A sharp pain hits my stomach and I feel like I've been stabbed. An "Ouch!" involuntarily escapes me. The stab is followed by an ache, deep in my belly. Trying to remember what I've eaten today, I wondering if something has disagreed with me. Wriggling uncomfortably, I decide to wait for another sign from my bowels before I visit the loo.

A few minutes later, the cramps start up again and decide not to mess with fate. I do not want Josh to see me shit my pants. He looks up at me, concern scribbled all over his handsome, chiselled face. "You okay, babe?"

"Yeah, I've just got some cramps and I think I might have an upset stomach. I'm just going to pop to the loo, just in case." Another cramp clutches at my lower abdomen and a sharp pain shoots through me so I'm momentarily halted. This is going to be noisy so I think maybe I should use Dad's loo, so Josh doesn't hear me. Another sharp pain; this one is a little stronger and feels more like a throb.

Josh lowers his eyes to my stomach where my arms are wrapped protectively over Lentil. Suddenly he yells, pointing to my crotch. "Mercy, you're bleeding! Should you be bleeding?"

I look down at the spreading stain on my jeans and run for the bathroom. Josh follows close behind. As I pull down my pants, there's blood everywhere. Oh God, what's happening to me? I say a silent prayer to protect little Lentil. I yell to Josh on the other side of the door, "Something's wrong. Can you get Dad please?"

I hear Josh's feet thudding up the hall as he runs, yelling out to Dad, then Dad's feet thudding at the other end of the hall running towards me. Dad sounds panicked as he asks Josh, "What's happening?"

"Mercedes is bleeding. I think we need to take her to hospital."

Dad takes the few steps to the bathroom door and knocks loudly. "Mercy, you okay in there, honey?"

Sobbing, I have this terrible feeling of dread, "Dad, I think I need to go to hospital. My stomach hurts really badly and there's blood, a lot of blood."

"I'll get the car, honey. Josh, you get some towels and tell Seth where we're going. Then bring Mercy out and we'll go."

* * * * *

I'm alone in the room with the doctor after he has completed his examination, the stethoscope still clasped between his forefinger and thumb as he straightens. I don't want to hear what he has to say because his face is screaming my worst fears. I fidget with a thread on the sheet covering my lower body, I silently pray for a miracle.

The doctor sits in the chair beside me and looks at me with a solemn expression. Oh God, he's going to say it. "I'm Doctor Phillips, Miss O'Brien. May I call you Mercedes?"

"Sure." Just say what you have to say… oh no, please don't say it.

"Unfortunately, Mercedes, you're having a miscarriage. Do you know how far along you are?"

Another sharp pain hits me but this one is in my heart. I've finally come to terms with my pregnancy and I've been looking forward to meeting little Lentil. I don't want our journey to end this way, however unfortunate our circumstances were. I fight really hard to contain my grief as I speak. "I was almost fourteen weeks... so the baby is gone?" My voice sounds like it belongs to a little girl.

"Well, you're still in the process of the miscarriage. Did you actually pass anything amongst all the blood?" I shake my head, no. "Chances are that you've perhaps passed it, but we still have the placenta to be expelled. We will help that along for you with an injection. We need to be sure it has all come away cleanly and left nothing behind. I recommend a dilation and curettage, known as a D&C. It is a surgical procedure often performed after a first-trimester miscarriage. It is how we ensure we have removed all remnants of your pregnancy to make certain your uterus returns to normal function afterwards. You're very young and it's best to do the procedure whilst you're under anaesthetic to ensure you don't feel too much discomfort. There is bound to be some further cramping tonight until you pass the placenta. I'll go outside and speak with your father and explain that we will need to keep you here overnight. We will perform the D&C procedure in the morning after you've rested. We will keep you comfortable and can give you some medication to take away the discomfort you're experiencing from the miscarriage. I will send your father in after I've spoken with him. Would that be okay?"

I nod mutely at him. I'm so desperately sad that I will never meet my baby. My voice sounds childish as I ask, "Why did I lose the baby? What did I do wrong?"

Doctor Phillips takes one of my hands in his. "Mercedes, miscarriages are not uncommon. You haven't done anything wrong. It usually happens by chance and is the cause of at least half of miscarriages. This doesn't necessarily mean you will have problems conceiving or staying pregnant later on. You're very young. Was your pregnancy planned?"

"No, it was a… surprise, but I had come to terms with it and was preparing to be a parent. I don't know how to feel other than sad."

Doctor Phillips is warm, and he has a nice manner. "Mercedes, there is no correct way to feel. If you're sad or upset, you need to allow yourself time to grieve your loss. If you feel it necessary, some counselling may help you to come to terms with your miscarriage." He departs the room, leaving me alone with my aching heart.

A tear rolls down my cheek and dangles momentarily before it drips from my chin. I look at the tear stain spread on the white sheet. There are little specs of black mascara in the drop, which mars the perfect grey of the tear on the white of the sheet. The edges of the teardrop are wavy; I expected the drop to be perfectly circular. While I'm sitting here looking at this, something slides out of me. I think it must be a giant blood clot or the placenta and I'm almost too scared to lift the sheet to look.

When I pull back the sheet, it takes me a moment to realise what I am looking at. Little Lentil is lying on the sheet between my legs in a little burst bubble, a red meaty mass near him. He is a perfect tiny human, lying in a pool of blood and muck and the broken bubble. I reach down and pick him up gently. I hold his tiny delicate body in my hand. His legs are curled up around his tummy and the umbilical cord is wrapped around one of them, the chord disappears into the mass still on the sheet. I can't help it; a howl escapes me and I sob over my hand and my dead baby.

Immediately, Dad is on the other side of the door asking if I'm okay. I can't stop sobbing so Dad pokes his head in and I think he sees what is in my hand. He tentatively walks over to me and puts an arm around my shoulder. Dad is crying too. This would have been his grandson. I look up at Dad and sob "Don't let them throw him away."

Poor Dad is struggling to control his emotions. He stands and says, "I'll go get the doctor now, honey, and I'll send Josh in." Josh quietly comes into the room and sits beside me. He asks if he can see. Poor Josh, this is his baby too. He leans over and looks at his tiny child… who didn't get to take a breath or blink his eyes. Josh is trying to be manly but there are tears on his lashes. He stares at Lentil.

The doctor precedes Dad into the room and leans over me as I cradle my dead child. Gently, he asks if I'd like for him to wrap him up.

John
As the doctor turns to find something to wrap him in, I surreptitiously snap a photo of the scene. Mercy kisses it and whispers goodbye. My heart is breaking for poor Mercedes and Josh as they huddle together around the tiny little form.

Finally, the doctor produces a small cloth the size of a large handkerchief. He gently takes the tiny thing from Mercedes and wraps it with the gentleness and care that makes my heart ache. He has done this before.

I'm sure that someday in the not so distant future I will feel relief for the rectification of this erroneous pregnancy, but I can't help feeling a little sad that the child could not have lived. Perhaps Phoebe and I could have helped raise the child for them. I leave Mercedes and Josh alone with their deceased infant and quietly slip out of the room.

* * * * *

I gently nudge the door open and poke my head inside. Mercy lies propped up on pillows. She looks so small and helpless, surrounded by drips and other paraphernalia. She turns her head, perhaps because she felt the air become disturbed by the door's movement, I'm not sure. Her face crumples and she sobs, "Oh Dad, the baby is gone."

I rush to her side and cradle her in my arms. "I know, darling," I murmur into her hair. She sobs into my tee shirt and we stay like this until her sobs subside.

When she calms a little, I whisper, "You mustn't blame yourself. These things happen all the time for a whole host of reasons. It just… happens, that's all. Can you promise me you'll never blame yourself?"

She nods and pulls away to look up at my face. She looks so young and vulnerable. Her eyelashes are clumped in wet spikes and the whites of her eyes are stained red from her grief. I notice the skin on her lips is peeling; they look a little sore.

"They have to keep me here overnight because I have to have some procedure to make sure everything came away properly. I know I was too young, and I know it's probably the best scenario, but I think I'd really started to come to terms with it, with being a mum. He was only little, but I'd started imagining him growing inside me and I was looking forward to feeling him kick. And then I was wondering who he would look like… me or Josh. I can't believe that after fourteen weeks he's just… gone."

"Aw, darling. Look, I think Josh is pacing the corridor outside the door. The nursing staff want you to rest so would it be okay if Josh came in to say goodbye? I'll take him home because the poor boy is trying to be brave for you, but I think he needs to fall apart a little."

Mercedes reluctantly smiles. "Of course, poor Josh."

I open the door and beckon Josh back into the room. He stands at the bed looking at Mercedes and wringing his hands. He's unsure what to say or do so he plonks himself in the seat I vacated earlier and takes her hand in his. "Are you okay, babe?" Mercy advises that she has to stay overnight.

Josh *almost* makes me laugh. "Yeah, I heard him telling your dad. You've got to have a D&M or something."

Mercedes actually does laugh and it's a pretty tinkle in the dark and foreboding quiet of this room. "It's a D&C and it's just a little procedure to make sure everything has come away properly. A D&M is a 'deep and meaningful' conversation."

Josh reddens, but he smiles briefly before concern robs his face. "Are you really okay?"

"I really am, Josh. I'm just sad that the baby died."

"Aw, babe, of course you're sad. You were just getting used to the idea of being a mum. I'm sad too, but I think I was still gobsmacked from the whole 'you're going to be a dad' thing and it hadn't quite sunk in yet for me. The nurses told us we have to be quick because you need your rest, so I'll say goodbye to you now and I'll see you tomorrow. You can text me if you want later… if you're allowed."

"I'm allowed. I'll let you know how I'm feeling a little later on."

"Okay. I love you, babe."

"I love you too."

He plants a kiss on Mercy's peeling lips and exits. I say a brief goodbye, which is hastened by the entry of the frowning nurse who wants me gone. I kiss the top of her head and give her a reassuring hug.

"Seth is grabbing an overnight bag with a toothbrush and a change of clothes for tomorrow, and maybe a book for you to read if you're up to it. I'll drop Josh home and get dinner, so Seth will drop the bag off to you himself. He'll be on the tram by now, so he won't be long. There's a TV on the wall over there too; the remote's in the draw, apparently." I whisper the next bit, so the glaring sentry don't hear. "I've already told him he has to be quick, so the nurses don't growl at him. I'll see you tomorrow, sweetheart. Rest up."

In the car on the way home, Josh is looking out the window with his whole body turned away from me. The poor boy. As we pull into his driveway, I turn the engine off and put a hand on his shoulder. "Are you okay, Josh?" He turns to me and his eyes are red from crying the whole trip home. I slide my arm around his young shoulders and give him a hug.

"I just wish I could take the pain away from her and just have it myself. She's so upset. I wish I could say something to make her feel better, but I don't know what to say. I… I just don't know what to do."

I tell him that there's nothing anyone can do, and she'll feel sad and upset for a while, and its okay for him to feel sad too. "Do you want me to come inside and explain to your parents what's happened?"

He shakes his head. "No, I'll tell them. Thank you, Mr O'Brien."

"Josh, it's John. Call me John, okay?" He nods, and then he's gone.

Telling Seth was difficult, and when he returns from dropping the overnight bag off at the hospital, it's apparent that he's still reeling from the news. He didn't stay at the hospital long because, he said, the nurses were positively *glaring* at him. "She looked weary too, so I made my visit brief." Bless him, ever the thoughtful one. Seth took flowers in for her to cheer her room. When we sit down, he's inquisitive about what his little nephew looked like at just fourteen weeks. I don't want to show him the picture, so I tell him he just looked like a tiny little human.

Seth breathes, "Poor Mercy."

* * * * *

When I go into the hospital the next day, I'm alone because I've convinced Josh to go to school. It's not long until his end-of-semester exams and he needs to make every minute of this last year count. Mercedes has recovered from the procedure earlier this morning, and she has devoured a large healthy breakfast. I'm delighted that her appetite has returned. She has another small display of flowers arranged in a small box on her side table and I enquire who sent them.

"My friend Genevieve sent them. They're bright and sunny"

It's a relief to see her smiling. "I like Genevieve, I think she's a keeper."

I tell her I need to go settle everything before we can go home and she bites her lip. I stand to take my leave, but she tugs at my hand and pulls me back down.

"Dad, I'm really sorry about how I've behaved since we discovered you're… um… you know, gay. I was confused and angry and childish and…"

I try for an understanding gesture, not a patronising one, as I pat her hand. "It's okay, darling. It was a shock to everybody in the family and I'm fighting my own guilt about that and how it has affected everyone. As hard as it is for you to understand, you have to know that I regret none of the lies. I loved your mum very much, and I still do, and if we hadn't been married then we wouldn't have had you and Seth, and you two are the light of my life. My sexuality is irrelevant when it comes to being a father. You and Seth are my priority, you always have been, and you always will be. Let's leave this conversation for another day, honey, today is for healing."

Mercedes suddenly sits up in alarm, wincing, "I just remembered, I was supposed to have a Skype call with Mum tonight. Can you tell her I got an invite to someone's house and forgot? I really don't want to tell her about this."

"That's thoughtful of you, Mercy. I'm so proud of you, you know that?"

"Even though I got up the duff at fifteen?"

"We all have errors in judgement, yours was just… colossal."

She looks a little playful, "Um, can you really say mine was colossal when yours lasted most of your adult life?"

"You've got me there."

Mercedes smiles at me as I stand and kiss her forehead. Let the healing begin.

38

A Slate Wiped Clean

Mercedes

The smoky aroma of barbequing meat makes for a salivating situation that is hard to talk around. It's a cloudless day with the sun sitting high in the cerulean sky; it's the perfect winter setting for a low-key gathering such as this. Even my thoughts are mature and poetic… Seth would be proud. Dad, Seth and I have perched ourselves on stools in a quiet corner of Simon & Maisy's back garden. Our plates show little evidence of our lunch, with only smudges of condiments smeared under the askew cutlery.

A jumping castle takes up most of the grassed area in the centre of the yard, and a long, winding queue snakes around the inflated attraction. The children are chatting excitedly amongst themselves as they wait for their turn; their excitement palpable.

As I close my eyes and lift my face to the gentle breeze that stirs my hair, I let out a sigh of contentment. The mirror this morning showed that the colour has returned to my cheeks and I'm feeling somewhat restored after the devastation of my miscarriage. The discomfort following the curette procedure only lasted a day or so, but Dad has been fussing over me like I'm as fragile as glass.

I've made peace with myself and have stopped the guilt for what had ultimately been a gift in disguise. Dad said I was too young to even contemplate the upheaval the pregnancy would have made to my young life, and also, the difficult decision that Josh and I would have encountered with regards to the future of our child and a lifetime of living with that decision.

He's a wise man, my father. Josh has been such a thoughtful, caring support during the days that followed the miscarriage. He's been battling assessment tests in most of his subjects at school and I'm trying not to be too much of a distraction for him, although he calls my visits a welcome ray of sunlight. Josh has the power to make me swoon.

Dad's hand squeezes mine; he's still worried. I smile reassuringly back. He has been such a doting father; working from home and only disappearing in short bursts to ensure he's available to me should I need homemade chicken noodle soup – his cure for all ails – or the comfort of his arms when I cry. We've grown so much closer since the pregnancy and miscarriage. I still feel like a shit for the way I treated him when he first came out to us.

Dad's best mate, Simon breaks free from a group of new arrivals and strolls over to join us, seizing a stool from another table on his way over. I'm so glad Dad has Simon in his corner.

"My God, there are so many kids here! I don't really know half of these people. Maisy sees them at mother's group, kindergarten and school. I feel like a guest in my own home. How are we all? Anyone need a drink?"

Dad answers before any of us can get a word out. "Nope, we're all good here. How are you, Simon?"

Simon lets out a huge sigh. "Can't complain." He turns his attention to me. "How are you, Mercy? Your dad said you've been a little ill. What's up?" Dad starts furiously shaking his head and flapping his hands at Simon and the poor guy goes bright red because he didn't know he wasn't supposed to ask.

I put Simon out of his misery instead. "Oh, just a little 'women's trouble', if you know what I mean."

Unbelievably, Simon's colour deepens as he holds up both hands defensively. "Say no more…" He reaches over and pats Dad's shoulder. "And with Phoebe away, you had to take over. Sucks to be you, man. How *is* Phoebe, have you heard from her lately?"

"Actually," Seth answers, "we speak with her every two to three days. We haven't mentioned that Mercy has been ill, she'll just worry and cut her trip short; you know what she's like."

Simon nods. "I do, she's a stress head. Is she having fun over there?"

Dad speaks to her the most so he knows how she *really* is "She is, Simon. The break has done wonders for her. She went over to Scotland for some sightseeing with this guy she's working with and his family."

Simon raises an inquisitive eyebrow… Dad shakes his head. "I don't think so, mate, but he is a good-looking bloke. I met him once when we were having a Skype conversation. I think I'd be happy if she was getting some kind of therapy, though, if you know what I mean."

Oh my God, did Dad just say that? Aarrgghh! How embarrassing. "Ew, Dad!" I give him my most stern face.

Annoyingly, Seth laughs hard. "Nothing like a parent to overshare the inappropriate," he gasps.

Dad gives us a conciliatory look, like he forgot we were here. "Sorry guys."

Maisy sidles up behind Simon and puts her hand on his shoulder. "Sorry to interrupt, guys, but my brother has just arrived." She looks at all of us. "He doesn't know anyone here as he's moved from interstate recently. Simon, would you mind introducing him to a few people?" Simon pales because he's just told us he doesn't know anyone either, but he stands and obediently follows Maisy into the house.

I take dad's hand and enfold it in both of mine. "Dad, Mum will be fine. You've made me realise how important you are to so many people. I'm sorry that Grandma and Grandpa made you feel less for how you were made, but I'm kinda glad you found out later because you're the most amazing dad. And Grandma has come full circle. It must have been hard to go against everything she believes in and to defy Grandpa. That was a huge step for her. I hope Grandpa comes around too. That would be wonderful."

"Here, here," agrees Seth.

John

I have to take a deep breath because my emotions are all over the place. I feel like sobbing in a most unmanly way in response to the beautiful words coming out of my daughter's mouth. They're like a salve to my wounds. Seth puts an arm around my shoulder and gives it a squeeze. A simple embrace can convey so much. My kids have made me feel validated and it goes a long way to paving the way to acceptance within myself. I think I needed their acceptance more than I'd allowed myself to believe.

Simon reappears in the doorway with a tall chap wearing jeans and a polo shirt; a jacket is draped over his arm. He looks a little uncomfortable, as you do when joining a gathering of people you don't know. They wander over to a group and Simon makes introductions. As I watch them, I appreciate the physique of this guy.

Then Simon turns and makes his way to our table, the good-looking guy following. "Hi guys, this is Maisy's brother, Matt. Matt, this is my best mate, John, and his kids, Mercedes and Seth."

Seth and I stand to shake Matt's hand while Mercedes gives him a welcoming wave. Simon continues, "Matt's just moved to Melbourne a month ago. Where is it you work?" He looks at Matt, who frowns back at him. "I'm a paramedic, Simon."

"Oh shit. Sorry, mate, thought you were a lawyer or something."

Matt exudes patience. "I was an accountant but found it to be… unstimulating. So I went back to school and became an ambo."

A light bulb goes off above Simon's head and he points an accusatory finger at Matt. "Oh yes, you were too." Matt endures his brother-in-law with great patience.

He turns his gaze on me and my stomach drops and flips over. Jesus, his eyes are a ridiculous shade of blue, like cornflower blue with a really dark circle around them, and he's got the longest eyelashes I've ever seen on a bloke. I'm glad I'm sitting down.

He must feel comfortable with us because he starts talking, like he's known us for ages. "I've only been on the job for six months or so and wasn't enjoying Sydney so I found a placement here in Melbourne and made my escape and… here I am." I sincerely hope my face is not relaying my thoughts.

A child retching noisily interrupts the conversation. The sound of splattering vomit on PVC summons a chorus of disgust from the queuing children. Another child spontaneously retches all over the newly planted azaleas in the garden bed. Parents from all directions start running towards the ailing children. Simon groans and sinks in his seat. "Fuck, just what I need. I told Maisy not to have the kids eat before jumping. Look at that mess." He jogs over to the jumping castle to assess the situation. Seth turns back to Matt, instantly intrigued.

"Wow, a paramedic. That's a huge career shift. I'm in year twelve at the moment and that's what I want to do so I hope I get into the universities I've applied to."

Matt looks at Seth then does a double take; narrowing his eyes at him. He opens his mouth to say something then closes it again. After a moment he says, "Cool! I wish I'd known what I wanted to do when I was in year twelve. I was wandering around with my head in a funk. I had no direction, no pull. Our dad was an accountant and he encouraged me to become one. I was good with maths, so I went in that direction. Two years into the course and I knew it was a mistake, but I'd invested so much time and effort already, it seemed the only course of action, so I completed the studies and became a CPA. I went to work in my dad's firm. It didn't take me long to realise I wasn't going to be happy as an accountant."

Mercedes looks at Matt and then back at me. Oh God, she's picking up on something. I try to douse the flames. "Seth's known for a long time, haven't you, mate?"

"I knew from about year eight that I wanted to be some kind of doctor. I thought about cardiology but it's such a specialised field and takes so many years before you get there. So, I settled on a paramedic."

I've got to get out of this guy's presence for a few minutes to recalibrate, so I stand and announce, "I'm off to the bar for another glass of red. Matt, can I get you a drink?"

"Actually, I'd love a glass of cola if I could. I've brought a small bottle of Scotch with me, knowing my sister wouldn't have any." He reaches under his jacket and produces a medium-sized bottle of blended Scotch, which he holds up to me. "Care to join?"

My heart almost stops. Stupidly, because I'm flustered, I utter, "Ahhh, a man after my own heart. I'd love one." And then I realise what I've just said. I spin on my heel and make my way to the kitchen to grab the glasses and cola. I'm horrified at the inappropriateness of that statement and wonder what the kids have made of it. Jesus, can you even say that to another man when you're gay? Well, Matt doesn't know I'm gay so…

I risk a peek through the glass sliding doors and note both of my children still engaged in conversation with him. I look down the length of Matt's back and find my eyes resting on his firm butt. Matt shifts his weight from one foot to the other and I watch the right gluteal muscle bulge and strain against the material of his jeans. Those jeans are so tight.

Mercedes suddenly looks at me and quirks an eyebrow. I'm stunned into silence and my cheeks flame because I've been caught perving. I turn and briskly walk from the window. As I return to the table, trying to avoid Mercy's gaze, I can feel it steady on me. I look straight into her eyes and the little shit winks cheekily at me as I deposit the glasses on the table. Mortified, I squeeze my eyes shut, and when I open them, mouth the words, "I'm sorry," to her.

Mercedes beams a smile at me and gives an almost imperceptible shake of the head to convey she is fine with it. I hand one of the glasses over to Matt and, as his finger touches mine, a jolt akin to lightning shoots though me. I have to work hard to look unaffected. I feel like a teenager with a crush. Matt sits himself down in the chair that Simon vacated and the four of us enjoy a relaxed conversation.

Matt talks about his work. "There's a seedy side to every city, but with Sydney, the drugs and the bad stuff are just a little too in your face. There's a culture there; the rich think they can do whatever they please, like the rules don't apply to them. The amount of drug overdoses I attended in my first six months as a paramedic was phenomenal, and most of them were very young people. Not just that, the ice problem has reached epidemic proportions, in Sydney and Melbourne."

Mercedes looks concerned, "how can you keep yourself safe? How are you going to know if someone is going to fly off the handle?"

"Well, you don't. You don't know if you're going to be treating a violent person until you actually get there. If the patient is overly aggressive, sometimes you have to call and wait for police back up before you can attend them, even if they're bleeding or with someone in dire need of our help. I'll admit, it's pretty scary."

Matt jiggles the ice at the bottom of his glass and tilts it towards me. "Do you feel like another?"

Bugger, I have to be a parent. "I'd better not, I'm driving these two home." I angle my head towards Seth and Mercedes.

Seth, my wonderful son, comes to the rescue. "Dad, I haven't had anything to drink. I'll drive us home if you want to have a couple more."

"Are you sure? I really don't mind, Seth. I thought you were going to have a beer today."

Seth curls his top lip a little. "Yeah, I'm not feeling it today, Dad, you go ahead."

Relief washes over me. I want to have a few drinks with this guy.

"Thanks mate, you're a gem. In that case, Matt, same again," and I hand him my glass.

Matt gives me a relaxed wink and everything inside my chest flutters.

Seth

As Matt is pouring himself and Dad another drink, I look past Dad and I swear I glimpse the familiar dark silken hair of Mio, disappearing through the glass doors into the kitchen. I'm still looking in that general direction, unaware that Dad is looking at me. "What is it, Seth?"

"Huh?" I look at Dad a moment and his question registers. "Oh, I thought I saw someone I know."

Then Mio pops her beautiful self back out of the doors and looks straight through me. Wow, I'm invisible now? I wave enthusiastically at her until she focuses on my face.

Her eyebrows shoot up in surprise. "Seth, hello! What are you doing here?"

My God, she's beautiful. That soft flowing shirt gently rests on her fine arse, which I swear she somehow poured into those jeans. They look painted on. I remember myself. "Hi, Mio, Simon is my Dad's best mate. What are you doing here?"

"I babysit these little munchkins." She points in the general direction of the jumping castle. "Have done for years now." It's like we're the only two people on the planet and my breath catches in my throat because she is gorgeous. I'm not sure if she gets this from all the guys, but the effect she has on me is profound. Already in my head I'm writing poetry about her hair and her beautiful face.

"Really? Fancy that. It's a small world." Mercedes clears her throat and I jerk back to the here and now. I turn to our group. "Dad,

Mercedes, you've met Mio… and this is Matt, Maisy's brother, he's a paramedic." I wish I could punch myself in the head for that. Why the hell am I telling her his occupation? Mio grins at me and the embarrassment dissolves. "Here, you take my seat, I'll go get another. Would you like something to drink?"

"I'd actually love a soft drink if they have any."

I go in search of a chair and drinks. I look everywhere for a stool and they're all occupied. I contemplate pulling one out from under a fat man's butt, just for shits and giggles, but I'm not that arsehole. I'm usually unflappable but, today, I'm flapping about like a thirteen year old. I finally find a stool way over on the other side of the deck and I look at Mio as I'm walking back. She has strikingly beautiful chestnut-coloured eyes and her hair is impossibly silken. Her figure is slight and willowy and I want to get her alone, just to kiss her again.

Maisy flies out of the door and ushers everyone inside to sing to the birthday boy. Excited children squeal with delight as they hastily make their way inside. Justin, the birthday boy, spies Mio and runs into her embrace. She gives him a familiar hug.

Her voice is like water cascading gently over rocks, "Hey, Jus, how's the birthday boy? You look taller… are you taller?"

Justin grins up at her. Aw, he has a crush on her. I know how you feel, little buddy. "I might be 'cause I'm five now!" He holds up an open hand to demonstrate his age. Mio bounces her hand off Justin's in a high-five.

She turns to the group. "I should go inside."

Dad announces, "We're all going inside to sing happy birthday to the birthday boy." As we stand around the table singing to Justin, Mio slips her hand inside mine. I can't breathe. I'm glad it's not me blowing out those candles.

☙❧

John

After the song, about three-quarters of the gathering makes their way home with their exhausted or screaming, sugar-high children. The conversation has gone from shouting to be heard over the din to a civilised noise level. Maisy takes her three children upstairs for a bath and to watch a movie to restore calm before bedtime. She returns shortly after and now that the children have vacated the jumping castle, the slightly inebriated adults take a turn. I am surprised to see Maisy and Simon holding hands and jumping like excited children; giggling like a teenage couple at the beginning of their relationship as opposed to a couple with a brood of offspring and twenty-odd years' marriage under their belts. It warms my heart.

"She really landed on her feet with Simon. They're so perfect together," Matt says as we watch them.

"I was just thinking that."

Seth confers with Mercedes and Mio and then stands, addressing me, "Dad, Mercy and I are going to go now and I'm going to drop Mio home as well. Are you ready to go yet?"

Aw shit, I don't want to go yet. I'm enjoying myself for the first time in a long time. After a moment's pause, I decide I'll stay so I advise Seth to go ahead and I'll catch a taxi home later.

"Have you got a key?"

I don't have a key, it's on my keyring with the car keys. Shit. "Actually no, if you're taking my car keys I won't be able to get in."

"How about I take the spare off the hook and hide it somewhere in the front yard? I'll text you where I've put it."

"That would be great! Don't forget though... and don't make it so hard for me to find I need a deerstalker cap and a magnifying glass to find it."

Seth and Mercedes look at each other then back at me, confused. Matt bursts into laughter beside me. Seth asks "What?"

"Seriously, Seth?"

"Yeah, I don't get it. You're gonna have to spell that one out for me."

I roll my eyes and open my mouth to answer but Matt gets there first, "Sherlock Holmes."

Seth mouths an "Oh" but he doesn't look impressed by my cryptic description. Matt, on the other hand, thinks I'm a comedian.

"It's in my best interest to remember to put the key out because it's going to be my window you're knocking on if I forget."

Seth's face dissolves into pure joy when Mio saunters over. Seth thrusts out a hand to Matt. "Great meeting you, Matt. Thanks for the insight into 'the life and times of an ambo', it was fascinating."

Matt stands and my eyes are drawn to his bum again. I wonder what he looks like in jocks. I wonder if he wears trunks or jocks. Mercedes yanks me out of that thought when she leans forward and plants an affectionate kiss on my cheek. She whispers in my ear, "Don't do anything I wouldn't do," then audaciously winks at me.

My cheeks flare up and I look down at the table before me, feigning great interest in the condensation clinging to my glass, watching it pool on the table, forming a sizeable ring. I have to take a recuperative breath before I look up at Matt. Matt is looking oddly at me.

"They're great kids. I've often found it hard to communicate with their age group but your two are well rounded. They're a testament to you and your wife. Is she here?"

Fuck, awkward! "No, she's overseas at the moment. We've recently separated, but we're still good friends. She's actually overseas, um… sorting herself out."

"I'm sorry to hear that, John. Sorting herself out? Was the parting amicable or no?"

"Something like that." I'm aware that I sound sheepish and I'm awkward. Matt's interest seems to be piqued by my awkwardness and he smiles at me.

"What do you do for a living, John?"

"I'm an architect. Boring, huh?"

"Not at all, as long as you're happy. To be honest, I'm glad I was an accountant first. It was the only way I could afford to go back to school to get the second set of skills. Quarterly BAS and end of financial year paid for my tuition and kept me off the streets during the entire length of my second schooling. I still do the small ones and my family's tax returns, but I was happy to walk out of the accountancy practice. What about you? Are you happy with your choice of profession?"

"I am. Sometimes it's boring and mainstream but you get the odd client who wants something different. That's when my creative side kicks in and when I really start to have fun. Curved roof lines, houses without straight edges and, more recently, an innovative, multi-storey dwelling on an incredibly narrow block. I had to be seriously resourceful and think outside the square. The couple were really alternative and wanted ultra-modern fittings and fixtures, and they had the most amazing bathroom I've ever designed with a hammock-like bathtub. It was one of my most rewarding projects and it's been featured in a couple of magazines. I loved it. When I've sorted all my shit out with Phoebe, I'll design my own quirky house on my own little patch of paradise. It's a dream I've had forever."

"What's your home like now?"

"I'm currently renting a three-bedroom unit. While Phoebe is away the kids are staying with me. The house we shared as a family was very mainstream. Phoebe is incredibly… vanilla. She's conventional and hates off-the-wall design. When she gets back we'll put the house on the market and just go our separate ways until we can divorce."

"So there's no chance of a reconciliation?"

"No, we've parted for a different reason." Wanting to steer the conversation away from my failed marriage, I ask, "Are you happy here in Melbourne?"

Matt draws a long breath. "I'm still finding my feet but I had to get away from Sydney. I have an ex there and he wasn't taking 'no' for an answer. He's jealous and incredibly insecure and started stalking me; sending me angry and then apologetic text messages and emails telling me where he'd seen me and asking who this person or that person was. I found that I was actually getting a little worried and considered getting a restraining order against him. It's hard to completely get over someone when they're constantly in your face, so I came down here."

"Oh, you're, um…"

"Yeah, but Maisy doesn't know and neither do my parents. I haven't come out to them, and although I know I should because they're family but why should I have to come out? Heterosexuals don't come out and say, 'Hey, I'm hetero' so… why is it anyone's business?"

A huge sense of relief washes over me. "Well, it's not anybody's business. Would your family be accepting of your sexuality?"

"I'm pretty sure they would. I know Maisy would and my Mum has been saying to me since I can remember, 'when you meet your future partner, whether they're male or female', so I'm pretty sure she'd be fine with it."

"Mate, if your mum is saying that, it sounds like she already knows and is waiting for you to either work it out… or find the balls to tell her. She's letting you know it won't make a difference to her. How about your dad, will he be okay with it?"

"Sure, I don't think he could give a shit, to tell the truth. He loves me for me, not for my sexuality. Yeah, maybe Mum does know. What about you, is that what broke your marriage up?"

I'm astounded and momentarily bereft of speech. "Jesus, is it written on my forehead? Oh, did Simon tell you?"

"No, my 'gaydar' was pinging when I met you but the kids were a confusion. When did you know you were gay?"

I take a moment, "I guess I've known forever but my parents are very religious and it's well known in my house that it's unacceptable and a *choice*, so I thought there was something wrong with me and tried to push it from my mind. Don't get me wrong, I really do love Phoebe but it just didn't feel right. Then about three years ago I met a guy from Queensland who was holidaying in Melbourne and I found him attractive and... we had sex. It felt right. I didn't want to hurt Phoebe and I thought maybe it was a one off, I mean, it was just sex. But I found that I really am attracted to the male physique and I started to realise that my dad was wrong, it isn't a choice. The guilt was slowly killing me but it started to happen more and more often.

"Our relationship was changing; Phoebe and I were not having as much sex. With two teenagers in the house staying up to all hours or home during the day, the opportunity just wasn't arising as often, and we were going to bed at different times. Your libido slips and it becomes the norm to go from four times a week to once or twice a week. Then before you know it you're only doing it about once or twice a month, and it was starting to feel like a chore for me. I wasn't getting aroused easily with her and, God I can't believe I'm telling you this, started looking at gay porn to get me in the mood. Then I was picturing it in my head to actually perform the deed and making myself sick with guilt afterwards."

"Oh, man. That's really bad. So how did you finally tell her?"

Aw shit, I don't want to divulge this bit. "She came home from work one day and caught me having sex with another man... in our bed."

Matt runs his fingers through his hair, his expression incredulous. "In your own bed? Mate, what the fuck were you thinking?"

"Yeah, I know. First and only time, it was that first guy again, visiting from Queensland. He sent me a text that he was in Melbourne for a couple of days and asked if I'd like to catch up. My brain said 'yeah!' and then I wasn't thinking straight. Poor Phoebe came home from work ill and walked in on us. She was devastated, as you can imagine."

"So how is it amicable? Isn't she pissed off with you for cheating and living a lie?"

I feel that familiar pang of guilt all over again. "She was but she has been amazingly accepting after the initial shock. Telling the kids was bloody hard! Seth was mature about it. Mercedes, on the other hand, flew off the handle and wanted nothing to do with me. Something big happened to Mercedes recently and we've since made our peace. The counsellor was actually really helpful to me and my situation. I've moved on and she's given me her personal number if I need her, but I feel really good. I'm in a good place."

"Are you? Do you have any regrets?"

"Being gay is hard. It shouldn't be, but it is. There is so much judgement, but the only regret I have is hurting my family, especially Phoebe. Part of my therapy was to come out to my parents."

Matt makes a 'sheesh' face. "How did that go?"

"Not so well." I wave a hand in dismissal. "It doesn't matter, telling them was cathartic and a huge weight lifted from my shoulders. Mum came over a few days ago and had a cup of tea with me. She said she can't let me go because I'm her son. I'm grateful about that."

Matt suddenly startles and all the hairs on my arms stand up. "What is it?"

"I've just remembered where I've seen Seth before. Did your son recently lose a mate to suicide?"

Now all my hackles are up. "Yes, his best mate killed himself. Seth was downstairs at his house at the time,"

"In the bath? Did he slit his wrists?"

I wince at the blunt words. Matt leans in and puts his hand on mine in apology, "Sorry, that was callous. Did his friend take his own life in the bath?"

"Yeah he did, why?"

"I attended the scene. Seth was attempting CPR and we had to pull him off his mate. The boy's mum was hysterical, as expected. That was only my fifth call out after arriving in Melbourne – it hit me hard. I had to get half-pissed that night to get it out of my head. Usually, you can compartmentalise but there are times when the images keep flashing in your head. It wasn't so much the boy, although it makes me very sad when young people feel that there are no other options, it's the broken people left behind. His mum trying to pick her son up and screaming, 'My boy, my baby boy,' like he was three and Seth screaming out his mate's name, begging him to take a breath. That just fucked with my head."

"Yeah, Brandon was a really good kid but he was in a bad place."

Matt picks up his empty glass and asks me if I'd like another.

"One more then I'd better go home."

Matt refills the glasses then raises his in a toast. "Up your arse," he says on a laugh.

I almost spray the contents of my mouthful across the table. "Up yours too, mate."

After a moment's contemplation, Matt asks, "No pressure but do you want to catch up for a drink one night?"

"Like a date?"

He nods. "Yeah, like a date."

I don't even hesitate. "I'd love to. I'll give you my number."

Matt puts my number into his phone then sends me a quick text so I've got his. I look down at it: *I'll count the hours in between. M.* I can't breathe. This is how I'm supposed to feel, all tingly and fluttery. I've never felt like this before and I want to cry at the wonder of it all.

"I'll wait for the new roster to come out on Wednesday and then I'll text you a couple of dates to choose from."

I nod. "I'd like that."

Maisy and Simon join us. I look around and note that everybody else has gone. Shit, when did that happen? Probably when I was gazing into Matt's impossibly blue eyes. Just the four of us are sitting at the table; Maisy and Simon's children are already tucked into bed. Maisy sniffs Matt's glass and narrows her eyes at him.

"Is that Scotch I can smell?"

"It sure is, want one?"

"Absolutely!" Maisy leaps up to retrieve glasses from the kitchen.

Simon sips his beer and lets out a huge sigh. Poor bastard, he looks exhausted. I pat his back. "All over, mate, until the next one."

Simon shakes his head and takes another swig of beer. "Nope, we only have one party every year so the kids have to wait three years between parties. We have a family do for each of them every year, but the party thing we can only handle one of them a year. This year's was particularly exhausting. I still have puke to hose off the garden."

Maisy returns with her glass and sighs as she sags on her stool and sips her drink. Simon puts an arm around her shoulder and pulls her in for a kiss. They look at each other like they're the only two in the room. I never had that with Phoebe. We didn't get lost in each other's gaze like these two; we didn't have whole conversations with just our eyes. If this is normal, I've been missing it all my adult life.

Both Maisy and Simon look exhausted so I stand up and advise that I'm going to call a cab and go on home. Matt asks if he can share the cab, and I have my first conversation with no words, just my eyes. I could get lost in those pools of cornflower. Simon and Maisy look stupidly grateful.

In the cab we decide to drop Matt home first. As he exits the taxi, he turns to me and waves. I wave back and the cab starts to pull away. Matt turns and I see that fine arse of his as he makes his way up his driveway. It's now or never. "Actually, can you pull over and wait a minute? I think he's got something of mine… I'll be back in a minute."

I run back up the street after Matt and catch him as he's closing the front door. Throwing caution to the wind, heart hammering in my chest, I knock on the closing door and startle Matt, who swings the door wide in surprise. I lean in and plant a kiss on his mouth. I'm not sure how he'll react so I wait a beat before I take my leave. Matt blinks at me for a moment and then laces his arms around my neck, pulling me in for a deeper kiss.

I can barely keep my breathing regular. I lean against him, pressing against him and I can feel his arousal against mine as he kisses my face off. My tongue strokes against Matt's and my heart feels like it's going to explode out of my chest. The heat between us feels like it could singe our clothes. As we draw apart, both of our chests heaving, I whisper, "I'll wait to hear from you."

"Okay," Matt breathes. I turn and jog down the path to the taxi. I feel insanely giddy with excitement. I remind the driver of my address then sit back and try to pull myself together. I put a hand on my thumping heart, close my eyes and slow my breathing, waiting for the taxi to take me home where I can lie in bed and relive the kiss over and over, without the guilt that usually follows.

Mercedes
The familiar smell of the school assails my senses. It's my first day back since the miscarriage. As I approach the locker bay, I notice Monique making a beeline for me. My pulse quickens; I am not in any mood for a confrontation so Monique had better be ready for a shit fight. I'm finally at the end of my tether and if she thinks I'm going to take it lying down anymore, she's in for a huge fucking surprise. I can hear Monique calling my name, "Mercy? *Mercedes!*"

I stop walking and turn to glare at her. I hope you've brought your fight face, bitch. Monique's expression is missing the usual snarl I have come to expect. "Mercedes, hello. How are you?"

Fuck off. You're a bitch now, remember? I'm cautious and draw myself up tall and answer politely, no longer feeling the inclination for either a confrontation or an apology. I just want to be left alone. "I'm fine thanks."

Monique looks down at her feet. If it's going to be an apology, I'm not going to make easy for her. After a moment, she looks earnestly into my face. "Mercy, I'm sorry to hear about the baby. I didn't know…" She trails off, apparently uncertain whether or not she should continue on this thread or leave it alone.

I want her to piss off and I want to scream at her, "Surprise! I didn't die in childbirth!" but I stay quiet. My mouth is a tight line and I'm not in the mood for her shit so I continue to glare at her.

"Mercy, I miss you. I'm sorry for… for everything. I don't know what happened to me. I got jealous. I was jealous that you had a boyfriend, even if he is my brother. I haven't even kissed a boy yet, I lied about that, and I was pissed off with Josh for stealing you away."

I've held myself together for so long but it all just leaves me in an instant and now I'm boiling mad. "Are you a bloody child, Monique? Nobody stole me away. You knew I liked Josh and I was so excited when he asked me out. I wanted to share my excitement with you. You were my best friend. But you turned into a horrible, jealous bitch. You don't treat friends like that. You don't even treat enemies like that."

Monique has the decency to look embarrassed... but I'm not done. "And slut-shaming me? What the hell is wrong with you? It's not like I was standing on the corner throwing my pussy at any guy who walked past. I had sex with Josh – not the whole football team, but thank you for spreading vicious rumours about me, that was nice. You took our predicament and blabbed it to the whole fucking school! You slut-shamed me to anyone who would listen! How would you feel if I did that to you? But I wouldn't do that to you... because I'm not an *arsehole*!"

Monique is looking at her toes again and I don't give a damn. She has made my life a living hell for months and I'm damned if I'm just going to drop it all because she's finally found a conscience. I've lost my cool but I'm not sorry. She deserves the rebuke.

Rubbing at an invisible mark on the ground with her toe, Monique speaks without making eye contact because she's legitimately sorry. "Like I said, I just wanted to say sorry, that's all." And just like that, it's all gone. All the tension, the hurt, the anger, the fear, the humiliation, it all just falls away and I'm left feeling drained. I'm too young for this shit.

"Apology accepted." Then I turn and leave. I just walk away from her and the bullying and the constant ugly slut-shaming confrontation that has been my every day. I can feel Monique's eyes boring into my back as I gather my books and make my way to class. I hold my head up high and walk with purpose.

As I round the corner, I see her make her way to her locker. She should be feeling lucky. She escaped with only a small dent to her pride, but she should now be brutally aware that she's ruined our friendship. I don't have room in my life for her. I need to surround myself with people who are worthy. Monique is not worthy of me. Monique can have her little posse all to herself because I don't need any of them.

As I take my seat, Genevieve plonks herself down beside me and I smile at her. Genevieve is worthy. "You okay?" she ventures.

I nod at her – I am. "Thank you for the flowers, they were beautiful."

Dad's right, she's a keeper.

39

Return To Aus

Phoebe

The rain is pelting against the window. I'm grateful to be snuggled up in bed, cocooned in his duvet. The wind picks up and hurls sheets of rain against the glass and it's impossible to doze back into slumber with the unmelodious racket of Mother Nature's tantrum. My brain completely surfaces and, with a sinking feeling, it dawns on me that I have to go home to Melbourne in a couple of days. A heavy sadness descends and blankets me in fog.

Ryan slides an arm around my waist and draws me further into him so we're touching everywhere. I can feel his arousal pressed up against me and I wonder if he wants me… or needs to pee. I have an unreasonable urge to cry because I don't want to go and I don't want this romance to end. Lucky Ryan, he has slipped back into sleep and softly purrs near my ear.

I somehow wheedle out of his embrace and make my way to the bathroom. The feeling of sorrow will not leave me so I try to silently sob in the shower so Ryan can't hear. It doesn't work because he opens the door and steps inside, joining me under the jets. He doesn't ask what's wrong; he just takes me in his arms and holds me so I sob into his chest. He tells me he has taken today off, and since I've finished my temporary post, we can just spend the last few days together, absorbing as much of each other as we can before I have to go.

He makes me a ridiculous breakfast of eggs, bacon, sausages, tomatoes and hash browns, and although I'm not hungry I force as much down as I can because he went to all this trouble. Our eyes meet across the table and he reaches for my hand, pulling it to him to kiss my knuckles. My tears well again and he can see them so he suggests we get out of the apartment. Mother Nature seems to have found her lithium and the pelting rain stops momentarily so we dress and leave.

Ryan drives us out of the city to the county of Kent. The scenery is gorgeous and the sun has peeped out from behind the clouds to brighten both the scene and my mood; the suffocating fog lifts and starts to dissipate. We sip lattes in a small café and consume scones with fresh whipped cream and luscious strawberry jam. I think of the heart attack I have consumed today and, for a fleeting moment, wonder if I will be returning many kilos heavier than I left. I haven't weighed myself since I got here… perhaps that's a good thing. I don't want to think about returning to Aus sad, lonely *and* fat. It makes the fog creep in again.

Ryan drives us to an orchard owned by his cousin, Paul. He called ahead to tell Paul we're going to walk through the orchard, probably so he doesn't tear out of the house and point a shotgun at us, then we will pop to his house for a brief visit. I don't want to be with other people, I just want Ryan all to myself, but I pull myself together and stop behaving like a selfish teen; Ryan has found a way to lift the drear.

We have been treated to a spectacular display of floral beauty as the orchard is still in full bloom. The perfume in the air is a magical mix of apple and pear blossom, but it's delicate, not strong and heady. The fragile flowers are glistening with raindrops and make for a kaleidoscope of reflective colour. He holds my hand as we walk between the walls of white and pink and my mood soars. There is constant low hum around us and I know the bees are busily pollinating the flowers. Ryan talks about holidays spent here as a child and the belly ache endured one summer after eating unripened apples, a foolish decision that had awful consequences for him and Beth.

"We thought we were going to die! We couldna tell Aunty Mavis or Uncle Stanley. We were told not to eat the apples, so we'd stolen the fruit in the first place. The tart sourness was the attraction, but was also the problem."

"Gas?"

"Och aye, and an awful pain in the gut! Aunty Mavis found us groaning and clutching at our bellies by the packing shed and dragged us inside. She knew straightaway what we'd done but we were in too much pain to even look contrite. She called us stupid little fiends and gave us some fennel to crunch on. We didna feel much like eating anything let alone this weird liquorice-flavoured plant, but she was fierce mad with us, so we did as we were told. She made us an awful potion from fennel seeds, too, which Beth and I thought would finish us off. I must say, it worked a treat. Beth and I spent the night tooting in our beds and giggling our heads off. Never have I done that again."

I laugh out loud, "Did you say tooting?"

Ryan looks at me; his eyes crimped. "Aye, all that gas had to come oot, so we were farting like little engines all night long. The smell was ripe too, sulphuric like the fiery pits of hell. It's a wonder we didn't levitate in the fog!"

We walk through the orchard for a couple of hours and he talks of his childhood and teenage years and I share about mine. We laugh about the ugliness of the eighties and the hideous clothing we thought was so cool but now, on reflection, is cringe-worthy. It's a safe topic and we purposely steer away from my impending departure.

The sun disappears again, and the sky becomes darker and ominous. At the halfway mark of our trip through the orchard, the dark clouds come rolling in. Thunder rumbles around us and I'm torn between the thrill of a thunderstorm and the daunting knowledge that we're going to get soaked. I realise belatedly that the bees have disappeared.

Ryan stops suddenly and pulls me to him. He kisses me enthusiastically; his hands in my hair and I don't want it to stop, even though I can't breathe. Overhead, the heavens open up and, without warning, torrential rain teems down on us. I wish we could take this to another level, be naked in this orchard and free to make love right here and now. Finally, we draw apart, breathless. The drenching rain has our hair and clothes plastered to us but we are oblivious to it.

We continue walking in the pouring rain until we reach the end of the row of trees. A shed up ahead, provides shelter so we enter, dripping wet, and take a seat on a rusted old tractor that looks as if it hasn't moved in decades, watching the spectacular thunderstorm move across the orchard. Finally, the rain eases and we leave the shed and make our way towards the house at the far end of the rows.

Paul's wife, Natasha, hands us each a fluffy towel to dry off with, all the while shaking her head and tsk-tsking at the idiocy of city folk. Shivering, steam rises from both of us as we dry by the open fire; my hair frizzing into a hideous halo around my head. Ryan points at my hair and laughs.

Natasha makes us a lunch of fresh crusty baguettes stuffed with delicious homemade pickles and ham, cured by her Italian neighbour from her own pig. Even though I've eaten a hearty breakfast and scones for morning tea, I'm ravenous from the hours of walking and the cool weather, so I devour the baguette, which we wash down with beer. Paul talks about the recent perfect weather, albeit a late arrival, which has led to the beautiful blossom display and, hopefully, a bumper crop this year.

I notice Natasha's rounded belly under a maternity top and ask when her child is due. Silence descends on the table and Ryan's eyes bulge. Apparently isn't pregnant. Shit! The throbbing silence is broken by the cries of a newborn infant and I become almost flaccid with relief. I try to cover my embarrassment, "Oh, when did you have *your* baby?"

Ryan's face is dark with embarrassment and Natasha is defensive. "We thought you came to see the baby."

Paul is grinning at me and Ryan starts babbling beside me, "Well I wanted to surprise Phoebe, she loves babies, don't you, Phoebe?"

What? Shut the hell up, Ryan, what are you saying? Now I have to join in this thread of conversation because Ryan just threw me under a fucking bus.

"Oh, I do love babies, mine are all grown up. I'd love to meet your baby."

Natasha sniffs and I see two lactating circles spread on her top. I'm too scared to open my mouth. Paul is on the other side of the table enjoying my discomfort. She pops back with a tiny little bundle swathed in a pink blanket. Despite myself, I am immediately drawn to the squirming bundle. Natasha sees my interest and hands me her baby. I'm going to risk asking the question again, "Oh, she's beautiful, when did you have her?"

Natasha softens. "She's only two weeks old."

"Oh, she's just gorgeous, what's her name?"

Paul answers, "We called her Mavis, after my mum." I hold the precious bundle in my arms and I feel the joy that new life brings.

I feel the need to reassure Natasha so while Ryan and Paul talk apples and pears, I smile at Natasha, "Don't worry, your tummy will completely go down soon. It takes about six to eight weeks for everything to return to normal size. Mine took about two months to completely go down, a bit longer with the second. I'm sorry if I embarrassed you, that wasn't my intention. I just saw the maternity top and made an assumption."

"That's okay, I just feel fat. I know the hormones are making me a little teary and I'm feeling fat and ungainly... except for my boobs, they're just huge! Paul likes my boobs too but they're so tender with the milk."

Mavis screws up her tiny face and wails. I hand her to Natasha who unbuttons her top and pops out a giant boob sporting a substantial nipple and Mavis immediately latches onto it and starts drinking hungrily. I think nothing of it, it's a natural thing, but the tips of Ryan's ears go pink and I can tell he's a little embarrassed and purposely not looking.

Conversation resumes, and I chat with Natasha about little Mavis, and she over-shares about the details of birth because she is desperate for conversation with someone who has been through it and understands. Ryan's ears go pink again and I think I need to get us out of here before his head spontaneously combusts. After what feels like an eternity, the conversation ends, and I take my plate and glass to the kitchen and turn back to Ryan.

"Ryan, we should really think about going. It's going to get dark soon and we've got a long drive back."

Ryan makes a great pretence of looking at his watch then exclaims, "Shit, is that the time? Yes, we should go." Ryan should *never* become an actor because he's really crap at it.

We thank them for their hospitality and we're grateful to make it back to the car before it starts raining again. By the time we get into Kent it's bucketing down again. Ryan pulls into a bed and breakfast and runs inside to organise a room. He pops out and asks me to follow. There is a break in the rain, so I take advantage of it and dart inside.

Ryan comes in after me and he has a small bag with him. He holds it up. "I hope you don't mind, but I went into your room and grabbed a change of clothes for a couple of days' stay." Ryan has thought of everything, he even produces a new toothbrush, so he didn't have to rifle through my bathroom for necessities.

There is a large clawfoot bathtub in our ensuite, which we fill with steaming water. The complimentary bubbles project a floral bouquet throughout the room. There is a knock at the door and Ryan admits the owner, who carries an ice bucket bearing chilled wine and two glasses. After he leaves, we undress and submerge in the fragrant bath and indulge in an hour of each other's uninterrupted company. Water sloshes out of the bath onto the tiled floor as I sit astride him, and we make love in a slow rhythmic waltz.

Despite the stormy afternoon, the night is cool and fresh, so we walk to a restaurant to enjoy a quiet dinner in the back corner near an open fire. I've eaten enough food to fell a horse today so I choose a salad, but Ryan enjoys a hearty meal of steak and vegetables because he has hollow legs and a fast metabolism. I say no to dessert but Ryan wades in up to his elbows with a chocolate saucy pudding that makes me feel fat just looking at it.

I sleep spooned by Ryan and wrapped in his arms. I overheat and have to break away twice during the night because Ryan could roast a pig with his body heat, but I scoot back into his embrace after I cool off because there will not be many more opportunities for us to enjoy each other like this.

We wake late and indulge in croissants and coffee in our room before visiting a modern art gallery. We enjoy a late lunch of wafer-thin slices of prosciutto, ham, salami and an assortment of cheeses and breads. We're stuffed full when we visit the mediaeval town of Canterbury and take in the beautiful cathedral. We retire early to our room and cuddle up on the couch to watch a movie on the small television, neither of us able to eat another meal before bed.

On the Sunday morning we check out of the B&B and luxuriate in pastries and fresh coffee in a nearby café. I think I'm going to have to pay for extra luggage for the trip back to Melbourne just for my arse alone. Afterwards, we stroll hand in hand through a farmers' market and stumble on a little craft stall within where I buy small gifts for Mercedes, Seth, John and Chelsea. I find a little jewellery stall and buy a silver Tinkerbell charm for Mercedes' charm bracelet for her birthday.

The weather is mild on the drive back to London and we arrive back at the apartment late in the afternoon. I cannot push it away anymore because I'm leaving tomorrow and so I have to pack. The heavy leaden weight of sadness envelop me again and I can't escape it. Ryan helps me pack my cases because he doesn't know what else to do, and there are no words to take away the sadness we feel at leaving each other.

We enjoy each other twice tonight and both times he takes me there. Afterwards I sob into his chest because I don't want to go and we're probably never going to see each other again. He runs his hands up and down my back in a comforting gesture until my sobs subside. When I finally pull away from him and sit up, his eyes are wet and he begs, "Please don't go. I don't want you to go."

"I have to go, Ryan, my family is there."

And then he says it, he actually bloody says it, "But I've fallen in love with you."

Great, now I'm sobbing again and he's sobbing and it's just awful. He begs me again, "Phoebe, please don't go."

My words sound high pitched and whiny because I'm trying to talk and cry at the same time and conscious that my face is probably red, screwed-up and ugly... but I can't help it, this hurts.

"Ryan, I have to go. My family is in Melbourne and your family is here in London. There is no way we can make this work. I don't want to go; I feel the same way towards you."

"You feel the same way? Why can't you say the words then?"

"Because if I say them out loud then it's real. I have to go, you know I have to go."

Ryan concedes because there *is* no way to make this work, so he stops begging and making this harder than it already is. I wash my face and crawl back into his bed to be spooned and cocooned by him for the last time. I breathe in his scent and I keep touching and kissing his arms and neck and chest... trying to commit him to memory. I finally fall asleep three hours before I have to rise again.

We take a shower together. He kisses me for a long time; I'm reminded of our kiss in the rain in the orchard. Then he kisses me all over and does things to me that take me higher than I've ever been before. When we finally have sex, we don't make love... it is fierce and hard up against the tiled wall of the shower, and when we climax, we are loud. Moments later we are entwined in a messy tangle on the shower floor with the cascading water pouring over us, sluicing away our tears. Ryan sobs in my arms. I have to get ready to go.

When I finally emerge from my room, rolling my case down the hallway and clutching my stuffed unicorn, I see Theresa and Jonathan in the entrance. I look askance at Ryan but he shakes his head. Theresa breaks the silence. "We're taking you to the airport. Ryan called us this morning and asked if we could do him this one favour."

I look at Ryan and he looks tortured. "You're not coming?"

He doesn't trust himself to speak. He doesn't even look at me as he shakes his head no.

Jonathan looks awkward so I put him out of his misery. "Okay then, we'd better go."

I'm not going without a goodbye hug so I walk over to Ryan, who is sitting on the arm of the couch with his shoulders hunched low; his head down. He doesn't look up but I put my arms around him awkwardly and whisper goodbye near his ear. A sob breaks from Ryan's chest and he puts his hands on my waist and pulls me fiercely to him, sobbing into my t-shirt. Tears roll down my face once more as I look over his shoulder at Theresa and Jonathan, who are wide-eyed in surprise at the door. Knotting my fingers in his hair I force his head up and peer into his face.

I whisper, "Thank you for everything... I love you too." Then I gently kiss my lover's lips for the last time.

The car ride to the airport is quiet and uncomfortable. Nobody knows what to say so nobody says anything. At the airport, Jonathan gives me a self-conscious hug; he's still shell-shocked by Ryan's grief. Theresa embraces me and murmurs in my ear, "We didn't know you two had become... um... that involved. I'm sorry you have to go, I wish you could stay."

I pull away and smile tiredly at her. Emotions are exhausting. "We didn't mean for it to happen, it just... happened. I don't think either of us wanted to fall in love but we did. It's a shitty situation but there's no way around it so... this is it." Theresa's eyebrows are up; she didn't expect me to use the 'L' word.

I make it through customs and order a glass of wine at one of the bars, distracting myself with the newspaper before we're allowed to board the plane. My phone beeps a message from Ryan: Hi Phoebe, I'm sorry I couldn't take you to the airport. I'm a mess. I just wanted to wish you a safe flight home and I wish you every happiness in your future in Australia.

Wow, that sounded final.

Hi Ryan. That's okay, I understand. I'll let you know when I get safely back home and we'll talk then.

I want him to know that I need to talk to him again. I don't want this morning to be the last time I ever speak to him. Our flight is called and I board the plane that will take me home to my babies and my life in Australia. I don't want to think about never seeing Ryan again. Forever is too long.

40

The Shards In My Heart

Mercedes

The airport is loud and busy. We're waiting with a huge group of other people for Mum to emerge. I cannot wait to see her. I've missed her so much. I have so much to tell her but, of course, I can't blurt it out as soon as I see her. There are loads of people walking through the gates, but where the hell is Mum? I'm trying not to panic that she's somehow missed her flight or we've got the details wrong. I look at Dad and he looks a little worried too. I've been counting down the hours and minutes until her flight lands and I'm anxious.

Finally, she walks through. She looks tired and worn out. When she spies us waving madly at her, her face bursts into a huge smile and she runs towards us, her arms out. She wraps me up in a hug; I hug her back just as tightly. She lets me go and does the same to Seth, only he's so much taller than her so she has to reach up.

My God, it's good to see her face. She hugs Dad like their marriage didn't turn to shit. The break has obviously done wonders for her because she looks great. There is sadness underneath her beaming smile though, and I wonder why. Perhaps she's just tired from a million hours in the sky.

We wait an eternity for her case to come around on the conveyer belt. She has fifty thousand locks all over it on every zip because she's paranoid about people sneaking shit into her case. Her paranoia makes me want to laugh out loud, but I've missed her so much I just can't give her any crap… yet. There's plenty of time for that.

On the journey home, she regales us with tales about the London office and some of the characters there. She is divulging something about some arsehole who was rude to her and got fired for being a douche bag, and then she is all weird and awkward about the next bit. I ask her straight up what happened, and she looks really uncomfortable. "What? Why can't you tell us?"

She rolls her eyes like a teenager and says, "Fiiiiine!" before launching in. Wait, that's *my* exasperated face, not hers. She's supposed to be all patience and calm, not tetchy teenager. What the shit happened to her in London? Then she gets to the point and I understand why she's uncomfortable with the telling of it. "So, we walk in and there is the housekeeper and her girlfriend doing really graphic stuff on his floor."

Seth is incredulous, "What? Are you serious? What did you do?"

And then, dear God, she says an acronym out loud, "LOL, we hid in the coat closet."

I can't help myself, "Did you just say LOL?"

She looks embarrassed for about a nanosecond and then her mouth is smirking. "Yes, and I know it doesn't mean 'lots of love', dork face."

Dork face? Oh, *hell* no! Seth and Dad are laughing so hard, I have to say something for my own self-respect, "I'm not a dork face, *you're* a dork face."

"What are you, five?" Mum is, like, fifteen. Oh my God, she went away for a couple of months and came back a teen. Groan!

※

Seth

Mum is amazing. I can't believe it has been so long. I've missed her so much and I can't wait to introduce her to Mio. She is really pushing Mercy's buttons in a sweet way. I love this new woman. It's like she went over there and actually found herself again. Dad's joining in the banter too and it's hilarious. This is the happiest our family has been in a long time.

So much has happened since she's been gone. She asks me how my tests have been going and how I'm coping after Brandon. I tell her I'm in a good place and she doesn't ask any more questions on the subject; she's happy with my answer. I wonder how she will take the news that Dad has been on a date. I hope she's okay with it because Dad is really happy and we've been watching him come alive; he is a different person.

He was a ball of nerves when they went out for dinner, but when he came home, he was almost skipping and dancing on air. Both Mercy and I were grinning at each other; it's actually cute that he's dating Matt. Everybody deserves that kind of happiness in their lives. I hope Mum finds someone else, now that she's sorted herself out. At some point, Mercy will have to tell her about the baby. That was such a heartrending thing to go through. I assume Mercy will tell Mum when she's ready though. I'm just so glad to have her home.

Phoebe

I'm so happy to be home. It is the last days of winter and I miss the mild weather of summer in London, but ours is coming. It seems that everyone in the household has moved on to happier times since I left. They've all mended in my absence. I sent Ryan an email this morning further to the one I sent when we returned from the airport… and a text. He hasn't responded to either, which upsets me. I sent him another email this evening and another text, which would be morning over there, but he hasn't responded to those either. I forward both messages to his work email, thinking maybe he didn't see them. Clutching at straws, I think, but I don't understand how you can just drop someone like a hot potato. I called him last night and left a voice message.

I've started looking for a unit nearby because in a few months our house will go on the market and we will all move on. It's too big for me and the kids will be drifting between my unit and John's. I've looked at two units but the first one was too small and the second one was in a block of many, with a view of a brick wall out the windows. Nope! I spoke with my realtor about possibly finding a townhouse with a small garden. I need a garden to potter in, and I'd prefer not to be in a body corporate so I've lined up some appointments for viewings tomorrow.

John told me this morning that he's met someone and has another date planned with him. He was so nervous telling me but I'm happy for him. He was teary when I told him as much and he said my blessings were cathartic. He also told me his mum has come around, which is a pleasant surprise. His dad is stubborn and is still behaving like a dick. I think even he will come around eventually because he loves his grandchildren and John is his son. It's still going to be stiff and uncomfortable, especially if he ever meets John's boyfriend… I'd love to be a fly on the wall when that happens.

I need to tell him about Ryan but I'm not ready to share that yet, and I'm waiting for Ryan to respond to my emails before I do. An email pings in my inbox but it's confirmation of my appointments from the realtor. Disappointment darkens my mood. My head is all over the place with jetlag and I feel drowsy.

Mercy gently knocks on the door. I beckon her in and she sits on my bed, taking both of my hands in hers. I'm alarmed but I'm trying to qualm my fears because I can't imagine what she's going to tell me. She looks into my eyes earnestly and says, "I need to talk to you about something." Oh shit, my stomach is full of rocks and I'm suddenly nervous.

Mercedes

Mum is nervous so I'd better cut to the chase. "While you were gone, I accidentally got pregnant." Her giant gasp tells me this was not what she was expecting. Involuntarily, she looks down to my stomach. I'd better put her out of her misery. "I lost it. I was thirteen weeks, almost fourteen weeks along."

Mum looks like she's ready to cry. "Nobody told me anything!"

"I know because I asked them not to. Would you believe that it was the very first time I had sex that I got pregnant?"

"Mercedes, you're only sixteen years old. You shouldn't be having sex, you're too young."

Good one, Mum. "It's a little late for the pep talk, Mum. I know it was too soon but it was my idea and I pushed Josh."

Mum looks like she doesn't believe me. "I thought Josh was better than that. How old is he? And haven't either of you idiots heard of a condom?"

Great, she's thinking statutory rape. I don't want her to blame Josh. "Mum, he's seventeen. He didn't rape me and we didn't break the law. Like I said, it's my fault because I insisted and my period was due so I didn't think I could get pregnant that close to my cycle. I just wanted to let you know that it happened and I didn't want you to find out some other way. Monique spread it around the whole school so everyone knew——"

"Everyone except me, that is." Mum butts in because she's shitty. This is not going how I wanted it to go. Bloody hell.

"Mum, let me start again, okay? In all that time we only had sex twice. We didn't set out to fall pregnant because we're not idiots. Josh didn't want to because we didn't have a condom but I talked him into it because I thought we couldn't get pregnant. Anyway, we went to have an internal ultrasound and that's when they told us we were a month further along. So I was actually pregnant before you left."

Mum shakes her head and turns the blame on herself; she's really great at doing that. "This is my fault. I was walking around with my head in the clouds all wrapped up in my own nightmare, completely self-absorbed. I should have seen this coming. Why didn't I see this coming?"

Oh my God, the woman is exasperating. "Mum, this is nobody's fault. It just happened." I look at my hands, which I'm clasping in my lap. "I held him in my hand. He was a tiny little human with fingers and toes and everything."

An anguished cry escapes her and I'm suddenly in her arms. "Oh, you poor girl, you poor, poor girl. I'm so sorry you had to endure that on your own."

I shake my head at her. "Dad, Seth and Josh were there. Dad told me he took a photo. It took me a while to be able to look at it. Do you want to see what he looked like?"

For a moment Mum looks horrified, but she's curious so she leans in and I show her. She covers her mouth and tears roll down her cheeks. I am at peace with this now. We have a small engraved stone in Dad's courtyard that marks his existence.

She asks what happened to him and I tell her we thought a funeral for a miscarried foetus was a little over the top but the hospital said they could cremate him for us. "We have a small stone that we engraved, which we keep in Dad's garden. I needed to have something to remember Lentil by."

Mum frowns. "You called him Lentil? Like the legume?"

"Exactly like the legume. I'd been calling him that because when we first found out I was pregnant, Josh asked how big he was and he would have been the size of a lentil. I was a whole month out so he was bigger than that but… anyway, the name stuck."

Mum smiles. "You're a beautiful girl, you know that?"

I smirk. "Yeah, Josh tells me all the time."

❦

Phoebe

I'm at the study nook desk, still reeling from Mercy's news. I can't believe my baby got pregnant and then endured a miscarriage, and *held it in her hands!* I had coffee with Chelsea early this morning and told her. She was so shocked and surprised that she had a Tourette's fit. She's still floating about with her new beau. I'm happy for her.

She asked if I'd heard from Ryan yet but I shook my head. She knew we were falling in love so she knows how sad I am. I can't fathom why Ryan won't respond to my messages and calls. I called him again last night and sent him another email after speaking with Mercy, pouring my heart out about the miscarriage and how I miss him and wish I could be with him, but he's sent me nothing. No acknowledgement, no response. It feels cruel how he's ignoring me.

I type an email to Theresa and ask if Ryan has been around and that I haven't heard from him. She responds straightaway with:

"Hi Phoebe, actually, I was in his office working late with him last night when your last email came through. He is getting your emails. I'm sure he'll get back to you."

I am dumbfounded, staring at my PC screen. What the fuck? I quickly type a response.

"Hello Theresa. Why doesn't he respond? I really miss him. We shared a beautiful thing and I want to stay friends. Can you please tell him that I want to stay in touch with him and I'd love to hear from him?"

She writes back:

"Sure, I'll let him know."

I look at my blank screen with a hopeful heart, silently begging him to call me or message me or something.

My phone vibrates on the desk beside me with an incoming message. My phone was on silent so I didn't hear it ring. It's a voice message and it's from Ryan. My breath catches in my throat, oh thank

God. I'm so filled with electric excitement that I run from the room to the couch because I want to be sitting when I hear his beautiful voice. My hands are shaking as I press 'play' on the message. It's been so long and I've missed him so very much. I wait for him to apologise and say he misses me too. My heart thuds in my chest as I hear him take a breath… then he speaks but his words are confusing me. "Phoebe, it's Ryan. I'm sending you an email explaining but… look, I need you to stop calling and emailing please. I can't… I can't do this anymore so… so goodbye. I'm sorry."

The room is closing in on me. I feel the weight of it settle on my shoulders, then I hear the distant ping of an incoming email. I drag myself to my desk. My hands are shaking and my breathing is erratic. Ryan usually has this effect on me but today it's because he is letting me go. I don't want to read the email but hope he'll explain why he is doing this, so I move my cursor over the closed yellow envelope and click it open.

"Hi Phoebe, Theresa has just sent me a text saying that you emailed her, asking after me. Please stop contacting me. I am trying to move on and your emails and calls are not allowing me to. I apologise for not making myself clear. I should have answered your first email and let you know that I need to stop correspondence between us. I thought my silence would convey that much but you keep calling and emailing and it appears I wasn't clear at all. As you said on that last day, there's no way we can make this work. It's in the past now and we have to look to the future. Let me get over you. I wish you every happiness, Phoebe, I really do, but I have to let you go. Ryan."

And just like that I'm broken again. How absolutely fucking brutal can a man be? My face is hot and I'm dumbstruck with shock. This is cold and callous and not like Ryan at all. I feel like a fool. He just completely shut me down. White-hot rage whooshes through me and I want to punch something. I feel humiliated and hurt and I start to sob without tears. I don't know what the hell is going on with me. I hiccup a sob but my eyes are dry.

My hands clench and unclench and I don't know what to do. I type several vitriolic responses because I'm angry and hurt, but in the back of my mind I know I'm not going to send them. I delete both drafts and shut down my computer. I run myself a bath and pour a large glass of wine; I'm back where I began in April and my heart is breaking all over again, only this time it's worse; I allowed myself to fall completely and utterly in love. Now my heart is shattered into millions of pieces and I'll never be able to put it back together again. I'm going to have to go walking around with pieces missing inside of me. My grief is absolute.

❧–❧

Ryan
I type the cold hard words into the email and my finger hovers for several beats. I close my eyes, stoic in my resolve, and hit send. God help me, I cut her off. I know what she has been through with her husband and I know she wants to keep me alive in her heart as a friend, but I can't do it. A grown man should not be crying day in and day out like I have been. I can't keep pasting a smile on my face when my heart is shattered like someone took a hammer to a piece of glass. I don't think I will ever allow myself to fall so deeply again. I'm not sure I'll ever fully recover from this one. She was perfect in every way except location. We can never make it work across the continents… so I have to let her go.

The weight of Beth's hand is heavy on my shoulder. She knows I loved her but she doesn't understand why I need to let her go. "Ryan, you've got to speak to her. Call her or email her, anything…" she stiffens beside me, she has read the 'sent' email on my screen.

"Ryan, I love ye, but for an intelligent man, yer a bloody thick-headed idiot. Ye've just cut her off."

I nod into my hands, which are full of my tears. I have never felt so heartbroken as I have since Phoebe left. Not when I saw Catherine sucking Robert's dick; that was rage. Not when she up and left with my children… that just pissed me off and upended my life because I had to chase her across the globe. And not when I served the bitch with divorce papers a couple of weeks ago, which she has refused to sign because she still thinks she can change my mind… which means it will end in court.

What Phoebe and I had, as short as our time together was… was love. I recover enough to string a few words together, "I had to let her go, Beth. I can't live without my heart and the only way to get it back is to let her go."

She shakes her head at me. "Listen to ye. Ye sound like a bloody Mills & Boon novel. Ye just shot doon yer only chance at happiness because ye're afraid of a little work. Like I said, I love ye, but you're a thick-headed fool sometimes."

Beth is breathing beside me like a steam train because she can't believe I'm such a dickhead. I wonder how Phoebe is across the miles. I wonder if it's raining there in her winter like it is here in the winter of my heart. Shit, I do sound like a Mills & Boon novel – my poetic bullshit is making me sick to my own stomach. What have I done?

I move to the living room and sink into the couch. The rain is pelting against the windows outside on the small deck and bouncing off the barbeque. I watch it run in rivulets down the glass and it matches the storm inside me.

Beth lets herself out of the apartment and leaves me alone in my grief, wondering if I'll ever be able to gather all the scattered shards of my heart.

41

Severed Ties

Phoebe

I've just endured another open house for inspection. There's been great interest and I'm hoping for a sunny day for our auction, which will take place next month in late spring. My garden is coming along and full of buds, which promises to make a spectacular display at the auction, too. I'm a little sick of all the constant tidying but John has been helpful and always on hand to help wherever he can.

It turns out that freshly brewed coffee and the smell of baked bread actually does work wonders in a kitchen when people are viewing. The realtor is confident we will get our asking price because our location is prime and a lot of people want to move into the area. I'm sad to leave this house though. Our children were born here and we've made many memories here. We also fell apart in this house and sometimes a change is good for new beginnings.

It's been over two full months since Ryan cut me off and it has taken all that time to get to the point where I don't want to howl all night long. The ache is still there, made all the more painful by his brutal amputation of all contact. I finally told John that Ryan and I had a fling and that both of us had actually fallen in love. He has been a comforting shoulder... scathing of Ryan for my benefit, but a great friend who understands me and gets my quandary.

I've also told the kids. They could see there was something sad underneath my façade and I hadn't been fooling them. Mercedes called me on it and asked what was amiss because she doesn't muck around; she gets to the point and says it as it is. I told both of them separately and both of them had different reactions. Mercedes called him an unintelligent git because… how else could he let someone as wonderful as me slip through his fingers. Seth, on the other hand, is quiet and sorry for me and always ready with a hug. He doesn't lose his shit very often. Mercedes loses hers enough for all of us.

Matt has moved in with John and they are beautiful together. Mercedes and Seth really like Matt, and every time Mercy speaks of John and Matt, she squeaks and says, "Oh, they're so cute together!" I've never seen John as happy as he is now. I'm not jealous of Matt, but I'm envious of what they have. I had that for a short time with Ryan, but it's gone now and there is just a void.

Every day I go through the motions but I'm hollow. It doesn't help that I'm surrounded by people in love. It makes my loneliness throb like a blind pimple. Seth and Mio, Mercy and Josh, John and Matt and Chelsea and Gavin… everyone has someone except me. I still can't believe he let me go, just severed all ties and let me drift away without even looking back to see what happened to me. I think that cold dismissal of me and what we had hurts the most.

When I fessed-up to the kids, told them about Ryan and me, I didn't go into the brutal email that ended us. I just told them that it would be impossible to conduct a relationship across two continents because his family is there and mine is here, so we've just left it and walked away. My children have been supportive but I can tell they're all walking around on eggshells. Seth has been trying to think of ways that we can make it work but he doesn't understand… Ryan let me go; he doesn't want me. No matter how many times I tell him the facts, I see the cogs turning inside his head, like he's trying to find a way for me to be with Ryan.

Theresa has been in contact but neither of us mentions Ryan. We talk about her cousin's horses, or about the office. She mentioned Howard's replacement, apparently a golden Greek god and he has all the girls falling all over themselves to help him. Someone in finance is pregnant, someone in IT got engaged… these are all safe topics. I'd love to know how he is going but I want him to tell me, not second-hand gossip from a friend. So I leave it alone and stop picking at the scab. The less I pick at the scab, I console myself, the smaller the scar.

※

Ryan

I'm stalking her on social media every day because I can't go a day without seeing her beautiful face. I copied her profile picture to my phone and sometimes I look at it two or three times during the day, just to get me through. I'm worried I will see another man with his arm around her on her profile page, but I asked for this so I have no recourse but to suck it up and deal with it if it happens.

She only posts pictures of herself and the family. I see her house is on the market. I wonder where she will live after it sells. Her garden looks pretty and the weather looks sunny and warm. I miss her so much and I know I'm not doing myself any favours by stalking her, but I need a fix, I need to see her before I go to work every day.

It took a long time for Bella and Logan to stop asking after her. She had a significant effect on them. Pretending we're still friends for their sake is hard because when I say her name, I have to stop for a second to clear the lump in my throat before I continue.

Apparently Catherine has a new man. I don't give a shit. Maybe she'll sign the papers and I can finally be free of her. If he ever yells at my kids I'm going to educate the prick with a clenched fist, but if he's nice to them, he's welcome to Catherine. A positive to come out of that is that I get to see my kids more often because she wants time alone with her boyfriend so they can screw each other's brains out. Whatever.

Theresa looks at me sometimes when she thinks I can't see her; she knows I'm a mess but she doesn't mention Phoebe. My new assistant, Phoebe's replacement, is petite and extremely efficient but she doesn't laugh and she doesn't joke; she is strictly business. She is polite and she does her job well then she goes home to her husband until the sun comes up again and she has to make her way back to the office to do her job again. I miss the banter Phoebe and I had here and I'm sure Theresa does too.

Phoebe probably hates me for the final email, which is what I was aiming for. I am an arsehole and deserve the sharp barbs my mind pokes at me.

Beth and I have a standing Tuesday dinner together every week, but she tactfully avoids any conversation about Phoebe. She hates Catherine with a passion so her name never comes up either. We choose safe subjects like Logan and Bella or the office. Sometimes Dad and Karl join us at Beth's house for dinner, like they have tonight. Karl can be a dick sometimes and he doesn't get it so he asks about Phoebe and is rewarded with a kick to the shins from Beth and a brow beating from Dad. He angrily yells, "Hey, what was that for?" because, well, he's a dick.

Beth tells him straight, "Because yer a dick, Karl." Took the words right out of my mouth. I just answer honestly that I haven't heard how she is but I assume she's well. Maybe that will get him off my back.

The silence at the table is deafening so Karl feels the need to fill it with words and tells me he has a great chick lined up if I want to double date. I hope she isn't anything like the last 'chick' he set me up with. I tell Karl that I'm fine and don't need a date. "Come on, man, you can't mope around forever. She's gone! It's been months and it's time to move on. This girl is great for a laugh and up for just about anything." I want Karl to piss off and stop throwing women at me like a quick roll in the hay will magically fix me.

"No thanks, mate, I'm not good company at the moment."

Karl is exasperated and chooses not to edit his ire at my 'moping', "For fuck's sake, mate. Get over it. It was a fling that lasted weeks. I you could just screw someone else you'll be able to put her behind you."

I'm fed up. I don't want him to diminish what Phoebe and I had down to a mere screw. I open my mouth to empty both barrels at him but Dad beats me to it, "Karl, that's enough! He doesn't want to be set up with someone and he's not like you. He doesn't want meaningless sex with just anyone and he has a right to be as mopey as he bloody well likes! Get off his case."

Karl is taken aback by Dad's outburst, as am I. I suddenly feel exhausted so I stand and take my leave. Dad hugs me longer than usual because he understands my pain, but he doesn't know I was an arse to Phoebe and deserve my loneliness.

Back at my apartment I open up her page again like a creep. There are pictures of her and her friend Chelsea drinking bubbles with huge smiles on their faces. I can almost hear the echo of her laughter. I shut down the computer and retire to the couch. It feels like I'm never going to smile again, but the red wine numbs the stinging edge of it. Lucifer leaps onto my lap and massages my thighs with his paws and little claws but he doesn't look like he's ready to settle and sleep there, he is looking at me like he knows I'm a tumultuous mess and he wants to fix me.

He stands onto his back legs and puts his paws on my shoulder, industriously rubbing his face on my chin, giving me a feline hug of support. I bury my face in his fur and stroke his silky coat, accepting his affection before scratching his face and making him rattle like a motor with his noisy purr.

It's raining again because we are marching towards winter. I'm sick of the rain and the grey days and I want it to bugger off. "London is as green as fuck so stop already!" I yell. Lucifer is startled and jumps off my lap in protest at my outburst. It takes a full ten minutes to coax him back because I need him tonight, but when he finally curls in my lap he is facing away from me and giving me his butt… apology accepted but he thinks I'm a dick!

There is a knock at the door and I wonder who it is. Nobody buzzed from downstairs so it has to be someone in the complex or someone I know. Lucifer is none too pleased that his comfort has been disrupted again and darts down the hall all hoity, with his tail flicking angrily, to Phoebe's bed. He's done with my shit tonight. I open the door and Beth is standing there. I wonder if I've left something behind but she wraps her arms around me and, to my horror, my bottom lip quivers and I tear up on her shoulder. When I finally get my shit together, I take her coat and dripping brolly and invite her in for a glass of wine.

"Talk to me, sweetheart. Ye're in a very bad place and ye canna lock it all up inside."

I'm tired of holding it all in so it pours out of me like somebody opened a floodgate. "Aw, Beth, I fell in love with her. In the short time we were together I loved her more than I have ever loved anyone before her. I was so completely and utterly happy… and then she had to go away. I begged her to stay but she couldn't. I understand why, she lives there and I live here but it really hurts, Beth, it hurts."

She doesn't yell at me to grow a set and toughen up. She takes my hand in hers and says, "Ye've got to contact her, Ryan. I know ye told her to stop with the emails and although I think that was a shitty thing to do, I understand why ye did it. But ye've got to send her something… an email or a letter, and you need to tell her how you feel."

I shake my head at her. "I can't do that, Beth. That's awful and unfair. I cut her off months ago. Maybe she's started to move on now, and me sending her an email or letter or anything… it's just going to open that whole wound right back up again. I'm not that much of a prick."

Beth sighs and sits in silence for a while, sipping her wine. Finally, she says, "Weel, you've got to do something because you're miserable and I don't know how much longer Dad and I can sit by impotently and watch you deteriorate. Ye're still very much in love with her, we can see that. Ye have to think of something." As an afterthought she adds, "Don't be pissed at Karl, he's just trying to help in the only way he knows how. He comes off sounding like a knob but he doesna know what to do and he's as worried about ye as we are."

"I'm not angry at Karl… but God help me, don't let him set me up with another blind date. The last one was horrible. If I meet someone, it has to be by chance. I can't go looking and I don't want to be set up. It has to just happen… like Phoebe did. She was perfect and nobody set us up. We accidentally met through circumstances and we fell in love. I want that again."

Beth grabs my hand in a tight grip. "There's someone out there for you, hon, I know it in my heart. It's just that you told her to piss off when you emailed her that last time."

Jesus… NOT HELPFUL, BETH!

42

The Soft Down Of Nascent Wings

Phoebe

It is a magical mid-summer morning and I'm standing in my garden, disturbing clouds of insects as I water before the hot forecast day bakes it dry. Mother Nature is quietly casting a glowing spell over our beautiful city with a flick of her wrist and the sweep of her wand. My garden has popped with a plentiful array of colours and scents; my senses sing along with me and I don't give a thought to the neighbours who must endure my joyous yodelling. Sunday mornings abundant with birdsong and the gift of blooms make me smile.

The house sold in early December for an amazing A$250,000 more than we were expecting, and I am so overjoyed I could skip like a nymph amongst the plants and insects. I found a fantastic three-bedroom townhouse with a small manicured garden only five blocks from this house. I put a deposit on it last week and it will be mine in eight short weeks when we settle on this house. Everything is falling into place and I finally feel settled and happy within myself. My smile is ready and the storm within is quiet.

We all had Christmas together here as a farewell to our time in this house. John and I put on a fabulous feast, cooking side by side in the kitchen in amicable companionship. We served baked ham and roasted pork with oodles of vegetables, and cold seafood as well.

The day dawned beautiful and clear, and a comfortable twenty-eight degrees made for a magical farewell.

We opened the bifold doors and all windows to let the breeze in. The fans spun lazily, and conversation was relaxed and happy. Mio's family returned to Japan to visit family, so she joined us for the feast as well. We ate too much, and all of us lay around for the afternoon getting over the feast and dozing in and out of a food coma.

We saw in the New Year at John and Matt's unit and sat in the small courtyard to watch the fireworks above from the park at the corner of the street. We all got tipsy; we even allowed Mercedes a glass of bubbles to celebrate the year that was. Josh joined us for the evening and, having turned eighteen years old, he was allowed to drink also. My thoughts turned to Ryan at midnight, but I forced him from my mind lest I ruin my own celebration. I am pulled back to the now by cicadas as they start to sing and throb in the morning heat; I find them familiar and soothing.

Mercedes breaks the spell and yells like a fishwife from the window in the second floor living space, disturbing my reverie. I glare at her because even the birds have been startled into silence by her caterwauling. "There's someone at the door."

"Answer it, then!" I bellow from the garden. I cannot hide my exasperation.

She makes eyes at me and nods her head and I wonder what the hell is wrong with the stupid girl. "Can you come inside, please?"

For fuck's sake! Can't she handle the simplest task? How did they survive when I wasn't here? Stomping over to the tap, I turn it off angrily but leave the hose snaked around the garden path and between the plants because after I give her a talking to, I intend to return to it and hopefully my joyous mood.

Still stomping, I walk up the steps and onto the deck before I yank the door open. The thunderous expression on my face falls away when I see Ryan standing at my kitchen bench, his face bereft of anything; a closed book staring back at me. My heart falters and shock shoots through me from top to bottom, leaving my toes tingling and my nerves on end. He looks so very tall standing in my kitchen, his angular face looking warily back at me, his chest heaving.

For months now I've imagined how wonderful it would be to see his face again, but not now. Now that I've finally moved on, I am not happy that he has turned up on my doorstep to make the thunder boom and the lightning strike and the storm inside start up all over again. I'm fuming and my mouth purses into a tight angry buttonhole; my glower is glacial. His eyebrows shoot north, and his Adams apple bobs as he swallows hard. I startle both Mercy and Seth with my ire. "What the hell are *you* doing here?" I yell.

This is not what he was expecting, and he suddenly stammers. His voice is soft, and he sounds very unsure of himself. "Hi, Phoebe, I was just wondering if perhaps we could talk for a moment?"

Oh, hell no! Four months have gone by with not a single fucking word and I am not pleased to be graced by his presence. "Oh, now you want to talk? You cut me off... you actually sent me an email asking me to stop contacting you, and you didn't even have the decency to let me down gently. I was in love with you and you broke my bloody heart!" My chest heaves with tumultuous emotion.

He winces at my words and has the grace to look chagrined. He looks down at his hands and not at my eyes. When his eyes finally meet mine, they are stormy and laden with regret. "I know, and I'm sorry..."

I am so upset and angry that I don't let him finish. The storm is raging within and it's channelling this hurricane of angry words, which I spit at him with a vehemence even I'm surprised by, "It's too fucking late!" my voice booms through the open space. "Why are you here? I finally let you go and now you're back like a vigorous strain of the clap! Why are you here?"

He is shocked by my outburst and he looks very unsure. His bottom lashes are wet, and I see a tear break free and travel down his cheek. His voice breaks with emotion, "I thought if I could just block you oot… not hear from you, that I could move on and get over you… but I couldna and I canna… I just had to see you."

His distressed state is affecting me, but my wounds are still gaping and ugly, so I give him nothing. "What do you want from me?"

The room is silent except for the ticking of the clock on the wall above the kitchen sink. Mercy and Seth are like statues and I must look hideous; my face scrunched in anger. I don't care. No one moves; we're all frozen in this moment. Ryan breaks the silence with a whisper, "I love you."

Incredulous, I yell at him, "What?"

He says it again, louder. "I love you. I canna just turn it off. Time and distance hasna made a jot of difference. I love you… so I had to try one last time."

His phone bleeps a message… still nobody moves. Why after all this time is he here in my kitchen telling me this? I don't want to hear these words now… after months of mourning him and finally putting him and us in my back pocket. It's too much and I want to run away. I need to get out. I want to be anywhere but here in this room with him because my heart just can't take it again.

❦

Ryan

I'm too late. The door has closed, and I missed my chance. It feels like a cold iron fist has reached inside my chest and is squeezing my heart. I am aware that her children are here in this room with us, but I don't care, they can watch me beg. "Please, Phoebe, please…"

She shakes her head at me and says "no" over and over, slowly walking backwards away from me. Her voice is thick with emotion and she sobs, her breathing wretched. Her hands are up and all defensive and she shakes her head sobbing, "No, no! Don't you dare, don't you bloody dare." I take a step towards her, if I can only hold her in my arms just one last time, but her head is shaking vigorously, and she walks away from me faster. She says again, "No."

My phone bleeps another message and the loud ping is startling in the silence of the room. Her kids are wide eyed and watching it all unfold like a nightmare in this sunny room lit up with the brilliance of the blue sky and warm sun. It's now or never because if she gets out of the door, to chase her is to terrorise her. I make a run for it and manage to grab one of her delicate hands. I plant kisses on her palm and her fingertips, and I repeat, "I love you." It's a cruel move, but I'm desperate. "Please, Phoebe," I beg, "…please."

Tears course down her face and I see her resolve falter. I pull her closer to me, gently; I don't want to scare her. I kiss the inside of her elbow and taste her perfume. Her eyes are glassy with the tears and her mascara has stained her tears dark. Taking her other hand, I kiss those fingers too and I know I've won. She doesn't fight me, and she stops pulling away. I inch closer to her until she's only centimetres away, her mouth swollen from her emotion, her lips slightly parted.

I lean in and she allows me to touch her lips with mine. I release her arms and cradle her face in my hands, my thumbs gently wiping away her tears. I kiss her again and she lets me. Her eyes are hopeful and teary, and she looks so vulnerable. I let out the breath I'm holding and close the gap between us. On a sob, she throws her arms around my neck and I finally feel her warmth through my clothes. My arms surround her, and she fits so perfectly there. My frigging phone bleeps again and disturbs our beautiful moment.

"Answer that bloody text, will you?" She makes me laugh because her exasperation brings forgiveness and chance.

I smile into her face. "It's Jonathan and Theresa, they're waiting in the car outside – waiting to see if you turned me away or…"

She cuts me off. "They're here? Well what are you waiting for, tell them to come inside." She slides her arms around my neck again and my heart thumps against my rib cage and, like a pubescent teenager, every part of me throbs with excitement. I send a quick reply.

She breaks from my embrace as Jonathan runs up the stairs and inside the house, wraps his arms around her, swinging her around in a huge hug. Theresa is teary and Phoebe's children are watching it all unfold in open-mouthed awe.

Phoebe

The six of us lean back against our chairs in the warm evening breeze. The mosquito coil is keeping the blood-thirsty insects at bay. Mercy and Seth are relaxed and enjoying the chatter around the table and have clicked easily with Theresa, Jonathan and Ryan. The remnants of our barbequed meal attract crawling insects but everybody at the table is oblivious, so I grant them pass.

I sneak a peek at Ryan; he sits quietly beside me. He looks back at me and rewards me with a wink that makes my heart flutter and my stomach flip-flop. I'm a mixture of nerves and excitement to get Ryan alone. I still don't know how this is going to work because we're still separated by oceans and many miles, but he is here, and he says he loves me so I will wait.

We move inside, where the house is still warm but not hot or muggy. Ryan joins me in the kitchen to help stack the dishwasher and secure leftovers in the fridge. "You sold your house I see." It's a bit hard to miss the giant sign outside with the massive 'sold' sticker brightly slashed across its face.

"We did. Were you surprised to see the 'sold' sign?"

He smiles at me then floors me with his next comment, "Not really, I knew the auction was in December and that it sold. I've been stalking you on social media for many months."

My mouth opens and closes like a fish. Ryan pulls me to him and kisses my breath away and it all comes back to me, wave after spectacular wave. I breathe in his scent deeply because I've missed it and him; my lips still tingling from his kiss. It feels good to be home.

* * * * *

I close the front door following the departure of the jetlagged Theresa and Jonathan. Seth and Mercedes have decided to stay at John's house to give us space. As soon as the door mechanism snicks into place, Ryan spins me to face him and presses me up against the wall. He kisses me hard and long with a familiarity I have missed. Breathless, desire pools in my groin but we have things to discuss so I take his hand and drag him down the hallway and back into the living space. We sit facing each other on the lounge suite and I ask the question that has been on the tip of my tongue since I stopped swearing and yelling at him.

"How are we not in the same place, Ryan? How has four and a half months made a difference to our situation? You're still over there and I'm still here." I feel trepidation because I don't know what he could possibly say that will change things.

"I called the Melbourne office and told them I may be moving back here, and, if I did would there be a position, any position, open for me. Would ye believe Nick Hartley resigned two weeks ago and they've been going through the process of interviewing replacements with an employment agency?"

I'm perplexed. No matter how many times I turn that name over in my mind I can't conjure a face to match. "Who's Nick Hartley?"

"Nick was my replacement, remember?"

"Oh shit, really? What happened with Nick?"

"Apparently, he wasna too fond of my assistant, Evelyn. Do ye remember Evelyn that ye met in the café with me?" I nod, of course I remember her. "He mentioned to one of the sales reps that they had a hot assistant at his last placement and he wasna enjoying the 'view'. I wasna sure if you would turn me around and send me on my way with a boot in the arse, so I said it was a little up in the air. But the job is mine if I want it."

"What about Bella and Logan, Ryan. You can't not see your babies… it will be unbearable."

He smiles. "I've spoken with Catherine, who has a new beau by the way, and told her I'm pretty sure I need to go back to Australia. She didna ask why and I didna offer any explanations. She's so caught up in her own self-importance that I'm sure she doesna really care. Anyway, we've devised a tentative arrangement that we've passed through our lawyers and written it up to post with the courts if my 'transfer' goes through. I get to Skype them every Friday night and Beth will have them on my weekends. Beth will always put them first and she'll make sure when she has them that they see Dad and Karl too."

He takes a deep breath before he continues, "Every six months, I will have them for three to four weeks, depending on kindergarten, school and work commitments. In the middle of the year, I will travel to the UK, and at the end of the year, in the Australian summer, they will travel here and stay for Christmas, at least this year, with me… with us. Catherine has said she'll more than likely want the children with her every second year, of course, and they'll arrive after Christmas on those years. Beth said she and Karl might visit and bring the babies with them if they do. It will be hard at first, but I want us to work, if you will have me?"

I can't believe what I'm hearing. He has literally moved heaven and earth so we can be together. Before I realise I've physically moved, I launch myself across the expanse of couch between us and straddle him, finally giving my heart permission to love again. I don't know if we can pull this off, if he can bear to be without his children for so long, but I guess we will cross that bridge when we get to it. He pulls away and sheepishly adds, "But I'm a package deal… Lucifer comes too."

The soft down of nascent wings, of new love, stretches out and ruffles in the breeze that gently filters through the screened door.

About the Author

Donna Newlands lives in Melbourne, Australia with her husband and two children. One night, she woke in the dark possessed by the story of a dysfunctional family navigating the dangerous edge between truth and lies, betrayal and redemption. Eighteen pages of notes later, she fell asleep knowing this was a book she had to write.

Her memoir, 'Shit Happens', under the pen name of Doona Moolands, was published in 2014. With many short stories behind her, available as blogs on her website www.doonamoolands.com, 'Threads' is Donna's debut novel.

www.ingramcontent.com/pod-product-compliance
Lightning Source LLC
Chambersburg PA
CBHW031938080426
42735CB00007B/181